# Bridging East-West Psychology and Counselling

# Lifetime Achievement Award
## in Multicultural Psychology

*presented to*

## Dr. Pittu Laungani

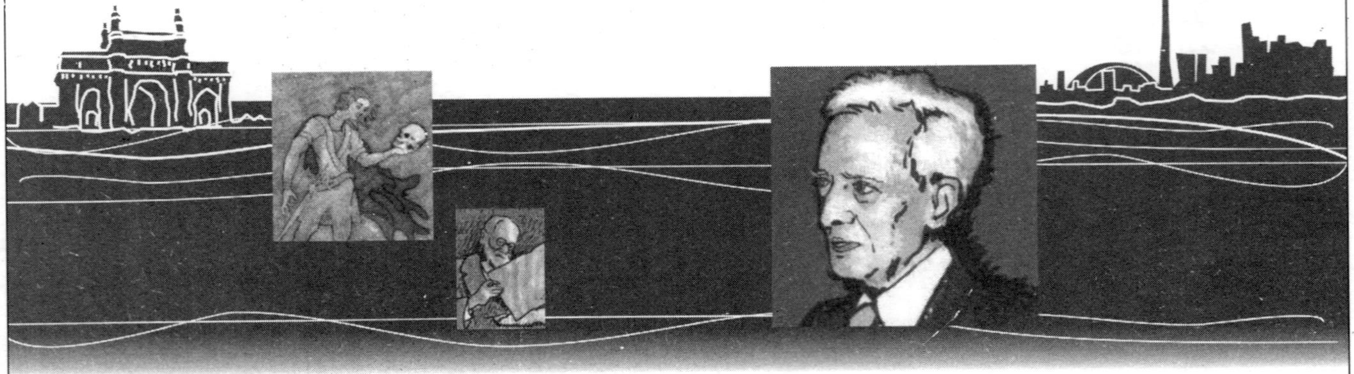

Department of Adult Education and Counselling Psychology
Ontario Institute for Studies in Education
University of Toronto

Dr. Jane Gaskell
Dean

Dr. Lana Stermac
Chair

June 28th, 2005

OISE UT

# Bridging East-West Psychology and Counselling

EXPLORING THE WORK OF PITTU LAUNGANI

*Edited by*

**Roy Moodley**
**Aanchal Rai**
**Waseem Alladin**

SAGE www.sagepublications.com
Los Angeles • London • New Delhi • Singapore • Washington DC

*First published in 2010 by*

**SAGE Publications India Pvt Ltd**
B1/I-1, Mohan Cooperative Industrial Area
Mathura Road, New Delhi 110 044, India
www.sagepub.in

**SAGE Publications Inc**
2455 Teller Road
Thousand Oaks, California 91320, USA

**SAGE Publications Ltd**
1 Oliver's Yard, 55 City Road
London EC1Y 1SP, United Kingdom

**SAGE Publications Asia-Pacific Pte Ltd**
33 Pekin Street
#02-01 Far East Square
Singapore 048763

Published by Vivek Mehra for SAGE Publications India Pvt Ltd, typeset in 10/12pt Minion by Star Compugraphics Private Limited, Delhi and printed at Chaman Enterprises, New Delhi.

**Library of Congress Cataloging-in-Publication Data**

Bridging East-West psychology and counselling: exploring the work of Pittu Laungani/ edited by Roy Moodley, Aanchal Rai and Waseem Alladin.
p. cm.
Includes index.
1. Psychotherapy—Cross-cultural studies. 2. Cross-cultural counselling. 3. Psychiatry, Transcultural. 4. Ethnopsychology. 5. Laungani, Pittu. I. Laungani, Pittu. II. Moodley, Roy. III. Rai, Aanchal, 1982– IV. Alladin, Waseem.

RC455.4.E8B75 616.89'14—dc22 2010 2010009919

**ISBN:** 978-81-321-0445-2 (HB)

**The SAGE Team:** Elina Majumdar, Meena Chakravorty, Sanjeev Kumar Sharma and Trinankur Banerjee

*Cover design by Elke Goebel.*

# Contents

# Acknowledgements

We offer our sincere thanks to all the contributors in this book. Almost all of them knew Pittu Laungani personally and professionally. Their contribution is a celebration as well as a critique of Laungani's work. We would like to thank our many colleagues and friends in Canada, Britain, the United States of America and India who have in many different ways contributed directly and indirectly to the book. In particular, we wish to thank Ann Laungani for her support and encouragement throughout the process of the book's development. Appreciation and thanks to Anissa Talahite, William (Bill) Hall, Shukla Dhingra, Stephen Palmer, William West, Charles Spielberger, Dr (Bro.) Mathew Panathanath and Rev. (Bro.) George Padikara.

Our thanks and appreciation also to the late Mr Tejeshwar Singh and Dr Sugata Ghosh of SAGE India.

The editors and publishers warmly acknowledge the kind permission to reproduce papers from *Counselling Psychology Quarterly* and the generous support from Taylor and Francis/Routledge in waiving copyright fees and Michelle Whittaker for facilitating this tribute to the late Dr Pittu Laungani.

**Chapter 1:** This chapter was previously published in *Counselling Psychology Quarterly*, 18(4), 247–259, (2005). © Taylor and Francis/Routledge.

**Chapter 4:** A version of this chapter was previously published in *Counselling Psychology Quarterly*, 18(4), 261–276, (2005) as 'In the Therapist's Chair: Professor Lana Stermac in conversation with Dr Pittu Laungani'. © Taylor and Francis/Routledge.

**Chapter 5:** This chapter was previously published in *Counselling Psychology Quarterly*, 15(4), 385–397, (2002). © Taylor and Francis/Routledge.

**Chapter 6:** This chapter was previously published in *Counselling Psychology Quarterly*, 7(1), 107–123. (2004). © Taylor and Francis/Routledge.

**Chapter 11:** This chapter was previously published in *Counselling Psychology Quarterly*, 18(1), 61–71. (2005). © Taylor and Francis/Routledge.

**Chapter 15:** This chapter was previously published in *Counselling Psychology Quarterly*, 17(2), 195–207, (2004). © Taylor and Francis/Routledge.

The editors and publishers would also like to thank Professor Stephen Palmer, editor of the *International Journal of Health Promotion and Education*, the journal of the Institute of Health Promotion and Education for allowing us to reproduce previously published work of Dr Pittu Laungani.

**Chapter 20:** This chapter was previously published in *International Journal of Health Promotion and Education*, 44(1), 17–13, (2006). © Institute of Health Promotion and Education.

# Foreword

I first met Dr Pittu Laungani in 2005 when I had the opportunity to bestow upon him the OISE/University of Toronto Lifetime Achievement Award for Cross-Cultural Counselling and Multicultural Psychology. This engaging human being did not come across as the usual academic you meet; he was engaging and friendly, connecting and objective, and above all, he was 'frank talking'. Professor Laungani not only confronted the challenges faced by those defined as 'ethnic minorities' but was, above all, able to use this experience to produce one of the most thought-provoking and influential critiques of ethno-centricity in the field of counselling. The depth and significance of his ideas became clear to me when I committed myself to be acquainted with his writing on a wide range of topics, such as cultural diversity, recovering from life threatening illness, death bereavement, stress and psychotherapy. It is indeed a great pleasure and an honour to contribute the foreword to this important collection of essays on Dr Laungani's scholarly work. This book, *Bridging East-West Psychology and Counselling*, is an important endeavour done in the field of counselling with a particular relevance to our multicultural society at large. It comes at an important time when our society is seeking to better understand its own diversity.

Thanks to the editors, meticulous and rigorous selection and organization of chapters written by scholars and counselling researchers, this comprehensive, well-informed and analytical critical perspective on Dr Laungani's work is now available to future generations. This book is a bold attempt to capture the essence of Laungani's work in cross-cultural psychotherapy from a variety of angles and place it in the context of contemporary interrogations about race, ethnicity and mental health. Beginning with a section on 'Building Multicultural Bridges' and ending with personal reflections by his colleagues, this book offers a clear and coherent analysis of his work. The text is reader-friendly, rigorous, and well-researched. Moreover, many of the chapters also present new ideas and current research being undertaken in the field of counselling and psychotherapy. This book is valuable for not only academics but also policy makers whose work is to translate ideas into policies and legislations so that we can have a society not only preoccupied with ensuring law and order, but a more humanistic and democratic society that is sensitive to the needs of its people.

Profiled in the book is the subliminal life of Pittu Laungani, an exceptional life dominated by humanism and a dedication to learning. Pittu once spoke to me about being from a family that believed that money, not education, was the way to assess a person. Rather than allow Pittu to go to university, his father sent him to work in a department store in Hong Kong. However, after a year, Pittu decided to attend the University of Bombay, where he eventually stayed on as a lecturer. At the university, his head of department told him that he stood little chance of becoming a professor as he was not a Brahmin. His desire for an academic career—and his need to complete his PhD—led him in 1966 to embark on what he called his 'passage to England'. London eventually became his home, and he stayed there for the rest of his life.

Dr Laungani also spoke to me about the various barriers he faced throughout his academic career, first by being told he would never achieve academic success in India, and then later when confronted by racism as a Black person in Britain. I identified with Dr Laungani's journey, myself being one of the first Black members of the provincial parliament in Canada, and the first Black Speaker of the Ontario Provincial Parliament, in a province that prides itself of its diversity and multiculturalism. I am sure that Dr Laungani's ideas as presented in this book will also speak to many people from many communities that have experienced similar struggles, as well as to anyone who wants to understand the complex and diverse world we live in.

One of Laungani's main critiques of Western counselling is about its over reliance on an unquestioned rationality and its lack of understanding of the ways in which beliefs and differing moralities and world views can affect self-perception and perception of others. Immersed in both Western rationality/materialism and Eastern faiths/spiritualism, he was able to see the strengths and flaws in both with the objectivity of also being distanced from both. This unique vantage point allowed him to make an immense contribution to cross-cultural psychology and add a profound human understanding to the role of cultures and their influence on individuals. As he once wrote: 'Faith without reason is blind, and reason without faith is dangerous.' Never despairing of the human condition, he did much to enlighten our understanding of it.

Laungani's work, I understand, caused controversy among his colleagues. Laungani did not favour the term 'multiculturalism', comparing it to post-modernism, 'a philosophy of despair'. This was particularly reflected in his books *Asian Perspectives in Counselling and Psychotherapy* (2004) and *Understanding Cross-Cultural Psychology* (2007), where he discusses the impact of cultural differences upon cross-cultural relationships. I am sure that this collection of critical essays on his work will throw more light on some of the complexities of Laungani's ideas and stimulate the academic debate about multicultural counselling. As the editors in the introduction state: 'Pittu Laungani was a multiculturalist in the true sense of the word in that he not only wrote about cross-cultural and multicultural issues in psychology, counselling and therapy but also lived his personal life to reflect his ideas about plurality, in particular he was attached to ancient and contemporary Indian philosophy and culture,

Chinese culture, ancient Greek philosophy, while at the same time connected to contemporary English culture and Victorian English culture in a profound way.' What this collection gives us is a vast perspective on what it means to work with the diversity and complexity of the human psyche and gives us an understanding that one model does not work for everyone.

Dr Laungani's ideas are critical for the understanding we have of our society and make me hope for more collaboration between parliament and scholarly work in the future. Issues to do with counselling and mental health are complex and can have negative societal impact and permanent psychological damage to individuals. Academics have a task as professionals to follow this dialogue through by getting together with the policy makers and the politicians to continue to inform, continue to explain their studies and research. This dialogue is important because, without it, academic research can have little impact. Similarly, as legislators, we can feel rather lost at times, trying to debate these issues and not being privy to most academic studies or just understanding them in a rather general form. One of the reasons for my enthusiastic support for this book is the possibilities it opens for understanding our society regardless of what country we are from and regardless of what discipline we are in. I am certain this book will prove a valuable resource that, on the long term, could inform policy making and legislation for a more equal society.

Finally, this book is more than a useful resource for academics and practitioners in the field of counselling and multiculturalism. It is above all a tribute to Pittu Laungani who sadly left us too soon, a year after I had the opportunity of meeting him. I feel that I have had the distinguished pleasure to have met a man, an individual who reflects the finer qualities of what we are all about. Pittu Laungani expressed to me his love for life; he exhumed a demeanor that revealed his particular connection and his dynamic engagement with reality. When we look at his academic achievements, we somehow feel that he is far removed from us. Yet, Dr Pittu Laungani was a warm, engaging and forthcoming individual whom I felt very comfortable with because of the immense sense of humanity in both his world view and his personality. This edited collection of critical essays on his work attests to the huge cannon of work that he has given us. It will, in years, continue to bear much fruit and prepare students, researchers and scholars to engage with ideas well into the 21st century. Yet, it is not only an important intellectual contribution to the field of multicultural counselling: it is a book that engages us all in the debate about human dignity.

**Dr Alvin Curling**
Senior Fellow
Centre for International Governance Innovation (CIGI)
Ontario, Canada
Former Speaker of the Ontario Provincial Parliament
Former Canadian Ambassador to the Dominican Republic

# Introduction

> If one were to construct a solid counselling bridge across Eastern and Western cultures, it would be necessary to examine not only the cultural factors but also the epistemologies, which guide the professional work of counsellors and therapists. (Laungani, 2005: 254)

**Pittu Laungani** argued for the inclusion of Eastern cultural practices and epistemologies into Western counselling psychology and psychotherapy. In doing this, he drew attention to the problematics of Euro-American counselling and psychotherapy theories and practices. In his voluminous writings, Pittu Laungani has asked many critical questions relating to culture, psychology, science, ethics, death and bereavement. For counsellors the question that seems important to highlight is: Can counselling psychology and psychotherapy support the process of helping individuals and groups transcend the cultural, physical and psychological boundaries so that people can live in peace, mutual trust and harmony? 'But as long as counsellors, therapists, academics remain entrenched within their own cultural boundaries such a dream is unlikely to be realised' (Laungani, 2004: 206). He also argued that such a transcendence will not 'lead to a corrosion of one's traditional values, one's cultural identity' and reassuring his readers that 'despite economic prosperity (or economic deprivation) people do not jettison their own cultural identity. Human beings, like chameleons, have the distinct ability to adapt and incorporate the changes within their cultural identity, without wrecking their ancient structure' (Laungani, 2004: 202). This understanding of culture allowed him to freely enter into textual spaces of Western counselling psychology tradition without anxiety about his own cultural loss and supported him in his robust critique of many aspects of Western counselling and psychotherapy approaches. He also critiqued the Eastern philosophies and world views that were against the basic tenets of human rights, such as the widespread abuse of the caste system. Indeed, the *Bhagavad Gita* does not recognize the caste system as a way of discrimination or deprivation of Human Rights; and Krishna states categorically that before 'God' there is no caste, and King Yudistira offers his seat to a 'low' caste person.

Pittu Laungani has written extensively in many areas of psychology, counselling and psychotherapy. His writings cover a wide range of topics, themes and practices, many of which were written from personal and private experiences to empirical research on various aspects of psychology and medicine. For example, in his book, '*It shouldn't happen to a patient: A survivor's guide to fighting life-threatening illness*', Laungani (1992) has written candidly about his own life-threatening illness (he was diagnosed as having polymyositis—a condition that affected his body, his muscles, movements, as well as his immune system. His awareness of his illness and its effects on his inner world led him to share lessons learnt in 'Therapeutic strategies for coping with a life-threatening illness: A personal testament' (Laungani, 2003). Besides writing about philosophical, psychological and medical topics, he also wrote a number of plays for the theatre.

Pittu Laungani was a multiculturalist in the true sense of the word in that he not only wrote about cross-cultural and multicultural issues in psychology, counselling and therapy but also lived his personal life to reflect his ideas about plurality. In particular he was attached to ancient and contemporary Indian philosophy and culture, Chinese culture, ancient Greek philosophy, while at the same time he connected to contemporary English culture and Victorian English culture in a profound way. His interest in these various cultures was more than just academic; he adored them as well as was repulsed by them, as is seen in his critique of them in many of his works. His most virulent criticism was of course on the Eurocentric and ethnocentric focus of counselling psychology and psychotherapy, positioning the Rogerian approach or the client-centred method as the most imperialistic (Laungani, 1997).

Pittu Laungani was educated by the Jesuits at St Xaviers College, Bombay or Mumbai as it is now; spent his teenage years in Hong Kong before starting his academic career at the University of Bombay; he came to England in 1966, lived most of his life in England; taught at an English university, married an English person; and, wrote plays for the English theatre. Yet, he did not lose touch with his Indian roots. As he says: 'Although I have lived in England for more years of my life than I have lived in India, there is within me an Indian-ness…for surrender would mean the loss of my birthright and with it my moral integrity' (Laungani, 2007: 49). This is seen throughout his research and writings, some of which are republished in this book.

The idea for this book was conceived in June 2005. Pittu Laungani received the Lifetime Achievement Award from the Centre for Diversity in Counselling and Psychotherapy (CDCP), at the Ontario Institute for Studies in Education (OISE), at the University of Toronto on 28 June 2005.

The award was offered in recognition of his outstanding scholarship, research and practice and to celebrate a lifetime of distinguished professional contribution to the theory, research and practice of psychology, particularly in multicultural counselling psychology. The CDCP, OISE/UT award is offered every two years, at the university's biannual Critical Multicultural Counselling and Psychotherapy Conference. At this conference, leading scholars and researchers in the field of multicultural counselling and psychotherapy reflect and critically examine the scholarship and research of the awardee to celebrate the pioneering work as well as identify the future potential of the awardee's work. An important part of this process is to record the history of multicultural and diversity counselling, psychology and psychotherapy through the work of the pioneers in this field. The conference that was held to honour Pittu Laungani generated a high level of scholarship and critical debate eventually resulting in two special edition journals. A special issue on 'Death and Bereavement across Cultures' was published by the Institute of Health Promotion and Education in their journal, *The International Journal of Health Promotion and Education*, Volume 44, No. 1, 2006. This special issue considered the work of Pittu Laungani in relation to death and bereavement. The *Counselling Psychology Quarterly* journal published, in Volume 18, No. 4, December 2005, papers on Pittu Laungani's keynote from this conference and his 'In the Therapist's Chair' interview (these are reproduced in this book as Chapter 1 and Chapter 4). Many other presentations from this conference are brought together in this book by some of the most celebrated and highly respected scholars and researchers in the world of cross-cultural counselling and psychotherapy, and multicultural psychology; others wrote especially for this volume.

## HOW THE BOOK IS ORGANIZED

We begin the book with a general introduction that discusses the central issues that Dr Laungani had been concerned with during his career, his ideas and practices that led on to the multicultural aspect of Psychology. The book is then divided into five parts:

### Part One: Building Multiple Cultural Bridges

In this part we begin with a key paper by Pittu Laungani. In Chapter 1, *Building Multicultural Counselling Bridges: The Holy Grail or a Poisoned Chalice*, Pittu Laungani discusses, in much detail, his ideas concerning multiculturalism, individualism, communalism and Popper's three worlds of epistemology. In his discussions, he attempts to answer the question: 'Can we healers and menders of fractured psyches, bruised souls, promote the idea that in collective goodness lies individual goodness and work towards creating a harmonious multicultural society?' This discussion is followed by Amrita Narayanan in Chapter 2: *The Reciprocal Gaze: Pittu Laungani's Musings about Culture and Stress*, in which she discusses Pittu Laungani's writings on culture and stress. Laungani believed that the particular set of values and demographic trends that characterize Indian culture call for an Indian model of stress that is distinct from Western models. She also explores Laungani's commentary on the preponderance of Western stress models and his model of cultural differences between India and England which acts as a bridge between traditional Indian and Western models of stress and coping. In Chapter 3: *Traditional Healing and Spirituality: Pittu Laungani Building Bridges in Counselling*, Roy Moodley discusses Pittu Laungani's call for the integration of Hindu spirituality and the various South Asian traditional healing methods. He explores Laungani's critique of Western counselling psychology which, in turn, sets the scene and a rationale for the integration of traditional methods. The chapter offers a number of suggestions to counselling psychologists for the integration of traditional healing methods into their practice. In Chapter 4: *Dancing with the Master: An Interview with Pittu Laungani*, Lana Stermac interviews Laungani about his life and work. She engages Pittu Laungani in a discussion of his interest in the field of cross-cultural psychology and how it intersected with his life along with his insight into his theories and current interests.

## Part Two: Playing Amongst the Pillars of East-West Psychology

In this section, we begin once again with Pittu Laungani addressing critical issues related to cross-cultural counselling and Western psychology. This is offered in Chapter 5: *Cross-cultural Psychology: A Handmaiden to Mainstream Western Psychology*. Laungani continues in Chapter 6, *Unresolved Issues in Philosophy and Psychology: Implications for Therapy*. In Chapter 7: *Playing Amidst the Pillars: Pittu Laungani and Yogic Psychology*, Amrita Narayanan critiques Western psychology and explores Laungani's work in relation to individual psychic anxiety, individual experience and alleviation of suffering, and offers a framework for understanding psychic anxiety that actively includes self-definition, culture and values in its thinking through a presentation and discussion of fundamental concepts of cultural yoga psychology. In Chapter 8: *South Asian Traditional Healing in Counselling: Laungani's Search for a Transcultural Approach*, Aanchal Rai and Roy Moodley, discuss Pittu Laungani's critique of Western counselling; his attempts to highlight the growing gap between South Asian mental health needs and the Western mental health services; his efforts to find a transcultural approach that will work in the diaspora; and his ideas for including South Asian traditional healing practices in counselling psychology and psychotherapy. Roy Moodley follows this discussion in Chapter 9: *East-West Journey in*

*Counselling Psychology: An Interview with Pittu Laungani*, a personal interview in which Pittu Laungani shares his personal and private moments in his life.

## Part Three: Towards Wisdom in the Practice of Counselling and Therapy

In Chapter 10: *Transcending the Boundaries of Counselling: Pittu Laungani as Master Counsellor*, Juris G. Draguns explores the four major themes that are discernible in Pittu Laungani's work: identifying the implicit assumptions underlying Eastern and Western counselling; integrating his own personal experience in making counselling more perceptive and effective; elevating death and dying to a central concern of psychology, both basic and applied; and linking the objectives and operations of counselling to the fundamental concerns of epistemology and philosophy of science. In the process of grappling with these concerns, Pittu Laungani advanced counselling as the art and science of helping human beings help themselves, not only in adjusting to the vicissitudes of life, but in acquiring wisdom. This discussion is followed by Pittu Laungani in Chapter 11: *Caste, Class and Culture: A Case Study* in which he explores all these issues. In Chapter 12: *Pittu Laungani, a Bicultural Psychologist: Commentary on 'Caste, Class and Culture'*, Alan Roland offers a commentary on Pittu Laungani's chapter. He says: 'Rarely does one see a psychotherapist who can really write, who introduces tension and drama in a lively way in his case study. His stance as a psychotherapist is overtly Western, a kind of cognitive therapist who guides himself by Karl Popper's rational ideas of problem-solving. He also places a high value on maintaining a patient's autonomy; and is also enormously sensitive to and knowledgeable of Indian cultural/psychological issues, which permeate his understanding of the patient: marital arrangements and social change; bicultural self of immigrants; Indian father–son relationship; clashes between Indian and English sensibilities and values, all deeply internalized'. In Chapter 13: *Solitude of Unbearable Shame: An Analysis of Two Case Studies by Pittu Laungani*, Sabar Rustomjee explores the meaning of shame, especially unbearable shame, which 'rises when one feels emotionally overwhelming humiliation, accompanied by the conviction that one's credibility, honour and very sense of self-worth has been totally destroyed forever'. She assesses two case studies by Pittu Laungani through the lens of unbearable shame and highlights the importance of this aspect in therapy. In Chapter 14: *Becoming a Cultural Chameleon: Pittu Laungani, Western Counsellors and Multicultural Clients*, William West draws his work from two interviews that he conducted with Pittu Laungani, as well as other meetings and e-mail contacts that he has had with Pittu Laungani regarding Western counsellors and non-Western clients. The chapter first considers Pittu's critique of Western counselling, of its avoidance of religious issues, of the cultural ignorance of many counsellors and their lack of knowledge of non-English languages. William then explores the potential application of Pittu's work in India relating his ideas to some Indian writers on counselling. Finally, he examines Pittu's notion of counsellors becoming chameleon-like as a possible way forward for working with clients from diverse cultural backgrounds.

## Part Four: Multicultural Transitions and Therapeutic Relationships

Part Four begins with Chapter 15, Pittu Laungani's ideas on *Counselling and Therapy in a Multicultural Setting*. In this chapter he explores a number of critical issues, which are pertinent to the transformation of counselling in a multicultural context. This chapter is followed by Ruth M. Litjmaer's Chapter 16: *Migration, Cultural Values and the Medical Model: Pittu Laungani and Psychotherapy* in which she critically discusses the experience of culture shock when people migrate and the use of a second language; the differences and similarities between Eastern and Western cultural values in psychotherapy and the use of medication and psychological treatment based on the medical model. In Chapter 17: *Tortoises and Turtles: Pittu Laungani, Cultural Transitions and Therapeutic Relationships*, Fevronia Christodoulidi and Colin Lago discuss the challenges involved in assisting culturally different clients manage their attempt to integrate mainstream culture; what factors are responsible for resilience and maintaining congruence of self as clients move between cultures. These issues are explored in relation to Pittu Laungani's work. The crucial importance of therapists acquiring sensitivity when assisting clients who face the effects of cross-cultural transitions is highlighted, emphasizing the need for discovering a mutual ground among contrasting cultural values and achieving both acknowledgement of dynamics of culture and transcendence of cultural barriers, as it may appear possible within a fruitful therapeutic relationship. Chapter 18: *Transcending East/West Boundaries: Pittu Laungani and Cross-cultural Counselling* by Maya Hammer and Waseem Alladin, examines Pittu Laungani's perspective on whether culture and cultural values can be transcended in the field of counselling and psychotherapy. Drawing on Pittu Laungani's work in cross-cultural psychology, they provide an outline of the different cultural values known to Eastern and Western cultures and how these values are represented in therapeutic relationships. Maya and Waseem then provide suggestions that have been mentioned by Laungani, by the means of which, culture and beliefs can become a part of counselling and psychotherapy, instead of being sidelined or ignored. Sandra E.S. Neil in Chapter 19: *Pittu Laungani, Multicultural Humanism and Eclectic Psychotherapy* explores Pittu Laungani's work in relation to cultural values, models, traditions and norms of both patients and psychologists into the therapeutic setting. The chapter discusses the 'Multicultural Family Chessboard' method which has reference to multigenerational as well as multicultural realities in psychotherapy. Finally, to conclude Part Four we offer one of Pittu Laungani's critical papers as Chapter 20:

*Religious Rites and Rituals in Death and Bereavement: An Indian Experience,* which reflects on his research and scholarship in this field, with particular reference to South Asian understanding of this process.

## Part Five: Personal Reflections of Friends and Colleagues

This section comprises warm reminiscences that reveal the kind of person Pittu Laungani was, and what he stood for to his friends and peers. It begins with Antoinette D. Thomas' reminiscence in which she poignantly reveals how Dr Laungani, who was terminally ill with paralysis, polymyositis and pulmonary fibrosis, simply refused to be paralyzed and continued with his work, setting a brilliant example of 'mind-over-matter' as a means of survival. Pittu Laungani's wife Ann R. Laungani writes about her life and time with Pittu Laungani; his ideas and writings; and his illness. This is followed by short pieces of remembrances and celebratory reflections by Pittu Laungani's colleagues. Stephen Palmer describes Pittu Laungani's role as his Ph.D. advisor and illustrates Pittu Laungani's excellence that is evident in his work, especially his work on death and bereavement; the last volume on this subject was eventually completed by Stephen Palmer after Pittu Laungani's death. Waseem Alladin reflects on Pittu Laungani, the person behind the professional, and the long relationship that they shared over the years academically and personally. As editor of the *Counselling Psychology Quarterly*, Waseem Alladin had the opportunity of publishing many ground-breaking articles by Pittu Laungani. Waseem Alladin also comments on Pittu Laungani's humorous personality. Uwe P. Gielen reflects on their first and subsequent meetings and the critical role that Pittu Laungani played in the international psychology scene. Richard de Zoysa writes about their initial meetings; interactions with Pittu Laungani starting from Cricket to discussing the works of Burtrand Russell and Socrates. He describes Pittu Laungani's life and the various events that make him an inspirational person. Finally, Nicolò Pipitone, who writes about Pittu Laungani's illness. He describes Pittu Laungani's attitude towards his illness as 'Dr Laungani never attempted to belittle or deny the devastating consequences that myositis had had on his life; at the same time, he took up right from the start the challenge posed by his condition with extreme determination and courage'.

## REFERENCES

Laungani, P. (1992). *It shouldn't happen to a patient.* London: Whiting & Birch.

———. (1997). Replacing client-centered counselling with cultural-centered counselling. *Counselling Psychology Quarterly, 10*(4), 343–351.

Laungani, P. (2003). Therapeutic strategies for coping with a life-threatening illness: A personal testament. *Illness, Crisis & Loss, 11*(2), 162–182.

———. (2004). Counselling and therapy in a multi-cultural setting. *Counselling Psychology Quarterly, 17*(2), 195–207.

———. (2005). Building multicultural counselling bridges: The holygrail or a poisoned chalice. *Counselling Psychology Quarterly, 18*(4), 247–259.

———. (2007). *Understanding cross-cultural psychology*. New Delhi: Sage Publications.

## PART ONE

# Building Multiple Cultural Bridges

# 1

# Building Multicultural Counselling Bridges: The Holy Grail or a Poisoned Chalice

*Pittu Laungani*

## INTRODUCTION

**Rudyard Kipling**, the Nobel Laureate, in *The Ballad of East and West*, wrote, '*Oh, East is East, and West is West, and never the twain shall meet*'. Mark Twain made a similar statement with reference to himself and his wife, the Twains, who for one reason or other, despite their prior arrangements, kept missing each other. I shall, however, argue that it is possible for the East and the West to meet on terms of friendship and equality and with a genuine desire to learn from each other and respect each other's differences and worldviews. But before I start I should like to clarify two points:

1. The blueprint of the bridge that I propose to present you with is *one of many such bridges* that other academics from different cultures might wish to construct.
2. Whether our attempts to construct such a bridge result in our finding the Holy Grail or a poisoned chalice, we shall discuss toward the end of the paper.

I should also like to make it clear that the ideas I put forward are not in any way unique or original. I am indebted to the great thinkers of the past centuries. All I can hope to do is to display some of their ideas and place them before you for your consideration. But I must not overlook the possibility that each of you may interpret those ideas differently. As Cicero in *Julius Caesar* remarks:

*But men may construe things after their fashion*
*Clean from the purpose of the things themselves*

*Julius Caesar (Act 1, iii.)*

It is this subjectivity of our perceptions and interpretations that strikes at the very root of all counselling theories. There are some who would disagree. They would argue that their perceptions and interpretations are guided by reason and logic and are thus objective. But, as Kant argued in his *Critique of Pure Reason*, 'reason leads us into self-contradiction and impasse, for reality does not correspond to reason, *therefore it cannot be possible even in principle for us to understand reality by the use of reason alone*' (cited in Magee, 2002: 178). Kant struck a fatal blow at the formulations of the rationalist philosophers insofar as their claims to understanding the nature of reality were concerned. However, I do not wish to decry the value of rationality in human affairs. As Cicero, the great Roman philosopher, pointed out several centuries ago, 'the whole foundation of humanity consists in the links between person and person, whether foreigner or member of one's family, and that these links are "kindness, goodness, generosity and justice"' (Grayling, 2003). Cicero justified this philosophy by assuming that there is in all men [and women] a divine spark of reason. The possession of reason conferred on human beings a duty to develop themselves to the full as civilized and educated individuals (Grayling, 2003). In any counselling situation *our observations and interpretations are guided by rationality and logic. But what needs to be made clear is that they do not necessarily form the basis of arriving at truth!* We shall return to this very important theme later. But before we turn to the construction of multicultural counselling bridges let us briefly consider the nature of multiculturalism itself.

## MULTICULTURALISM

It is a term that defies a precise definition. It is best seen as an umbrella term, which incorporates within it a variety of shades of meanings, attitudes, beliefs and values. The major elements of multiculturalism are summarized as follows:

### Major Elements of Multiculturalism

- All human beings are products of their own culture.
- Multiculturalism is not a political credo.
- Each culture has its own uniquely acquired ways of construing its own world(s), which give meaning to their lives.
- Within each culture there exists a plurality of values and traditions.

- The 'plasticity' of human behaviour enables persons to transcend (within certain limitations) their own culturally embedded boundaries.
- Each culture is in some ways flawed because no culture has all the answers to the Socratic question of what constitutes the good life *and how it should be lived* (Parekh, 2000).
- Each culture has something of value to offer to another culture and, equally important, has something of value to learn and imbibe from another culture.
- A mixture of cultures is more likely to lead to an enrichment of one's intellectual, emotional, artistic, spiritual, humanitarian and moral visions.

## The Multicultural Movement

The multiculturalism movement—or rather crusade—started in the 1970s, first in Canada and Australia, and then in America, followed by other European countries including the UK, Sweden, Denmark and Germany. In the last three decades there has been a steady flow of people from the EU countries, Eastern Europe, the new Commonwealth countries, Africa, Hong Kong, Korea, Thailand, China, New Zealand, Japan and countries in South East Asia and South America. Hosting countries are mainly Australia, Britain, Canada, America and several European countries. Persons coming to the West have included a vast assortment of political refugees, asylum seekers, highly educated professionals, tourists and other types of 'settlers'. The question that has been raised is how will the respective governments of each Western country deal with the new arrivals? There are serious issues related to individual rights, duties, equities, equal opportunities, freedom of speech and worship, health and medical care, childcare, the care of the elderly, the infirm, the handicapped, mentally ill, problems of language, prejudice, learning, education, housing, gender differences, sexuality, to name but a few. There are other questions too: the freedom to live in accordance with their own value systems, without fear of discrimination, persecution and rejection? How will all these vital issues be dealt with in a satisfactory manner?

One of the major characteristics of humanitarian societies is their concern for the minorities, the underprivileged, *living not only within their own societies but also the immigrants.* But not all Western nations are united in such humanitarian concerns. Opinions are divided. At one end of the political continuum are those who see themselves as *their brothers' keepers* and at the other end those who view immigrants at best as potential resources for 'cheap labour' and at worst as 'spongers' and 'exploiters' of the system. Such conflicting and antithetical views are not surprising. Past history points out that human beings are perhaps the only species that finds it difficult to live, not only with themselves, but also with one another. Human beings to a large extent are the only species that kills for fun, pleasure and profit. Human beings are perhaps the only species that imprisons, incarcerates, tortures and executes people who hold beliefs that are different from those of their captors.

Among many politicians too, there is an often-voiced opinion that for multiculturalism to 'work'—whatever that might mean—it is up to the migrants to abide by the norms and values of the host country. This would speed up the process of assimilation and integration within the mainstream society. Occasionally, politicians go to absurd lengths in their attempts to create a unified multicultural society. Here is a recent example from Britain. The recently 'deposed' Home Secretary (or Minister) suggested that all immigrants, recent and old, needed to learn the British National Anthem, as a test of their loyalty. This was a bizarre suggestion, to say the least. One wonders how many indigenous native-born white British know the words of the National Anthem. Besides, one could train a parrot to recite the National Anthem! Luckily, the idea was aborted in its embryonic stage.

When persons leave their own culture and emigrate to another, they do not leave their cultural norms and values behind or jettison them at the frontiers of their chosen country. They bring with them their culturally acquired psyche as well as their familial, social and communal norms and values, their hopes, aspirations and their fears, their dreams and their nightmares, their art, music, literature, and everything that was an integral part of their culture. Without invoking a Darwinian formulation—'the survival of the fittest'—most people have the ability to adapt and incorporate changes within their cultural identities. Over time, most people succeed in acquiring a fairly fluid bicultural persona, which allows them to switch from one cultural persona to the other as demanded by a given situation. Alan Roland (1988) in his excellent thought-provoking book, *Cultural Pluralism and Psychoanalysis,* introduces the term bicultural personality. He refers to a 'bicultural person' as 'walking a tightrope', albeit an existential tightrope. I can testify to Roland's observations. At a personal level, I have lived in England for more years than I have in India. But within me, there resides an indefinable 'Indianness'—the turtle shell. I can neither discard it nor, for that matter would I like to! As the Nobel laureate, Naipaul (2003) points out, no intelligent person, however individual his/her vision, can be separated from his society and his culture. My inability and my refusal to transform myself into a compliant English 'clone' is at times construed as a form of wilful aggression. Needless to say it often gets me into hot water. But I would rather accept the defiance than the surrender. For surrender would mean the loss of my 'birthright' and with it my moral and existential integrity.

In keeping with Roland's formulations, I would agree that it is difficult if not impossible to relinquish one's identity that one has developed over the years and pull out a completely new one—with the speed of a magician pulling a rabbit out of a hat or the great Skinner pulling a habit out of a rat! I have learned to play the '*game*'—with its own, idiosyncratic rules—of living in two cultures or two worlds without consciously tilting the balance either into one or the other, though the switch is not always easy, and at times even painful. Juggling with two personas can lead to a variety of existential dilemmas. Luckily, in my own case I see my own bicultural personality differently. Like a chameleon, I am able to switch my persona from being 'Indian–Indian' to 'Indian–English' and when in India, to 'English–Indian' or (recycled) 'Indian–Indian'. It is only after reading Alan Roland's book that I 'discovered' why I had chosen to call my novel *The Chameleon.* I thought it was a good title for a novel. But the full impact of the title dawned on me when I brooded over Roland's concept of a bicultural person. Over the years I have come to see a bicultural persona as a beautiful summer garden with lush green lawns, tropical ferns and flowers blooming side by side, along with a few winters of discontent. Perhaps my Jesuit education, which involved imbibing a mixture of religions, languages, friends, nationalities, gradually instilled in me a set of qualities, which have made it possible for me to live in two worlds with less discomfort than I might otherwise have experienced.

But whether one achieves a total metamorphosis—Kafkaesque or Elysian—is debatable. One carries one's culture like a turtle in its shell. The shell offers safety and protection. When danger—physical, psychological, existential—threatens, one withdraws into one's shell, as a mauled animal might into its lair. The shell is solid and robust. But, destroy the shell and you destroy the turtle.

## Building a Multicultural Counselling Bridge

The bridge which I envision will rest on eight pillars, four Western and four Eastern. The material for the bridge has been gleaned from respective philosophies, ideologies, value systems, religious texts, etc. I humbly acknowledge my indebtedness to the great ancient world religions and contemporary Western thinkers. The pillars supporting the bridge are:

| *Western cultures* | *Eastern cultures* |
| --- | --- |
| I. Individualism | I. Communalism |
| II. Cognition | II. Emotionality |
| III. Free Will | III. Determinism |
| IV. Materialism | IV. Spiritualism |

A few points need to be clarified. Each set of two pillars should be seen not in dichotomous terms, rather as a dimension, ranging from one end to the other. A dichotomous approach tends to classify people in 'either-or' terms. Such an approach is limited in its usefulness. People seldom fit into neat theoretically formulated and/or empirically derived categories. The sheer complexity and variability of human behaviours and responses, within and between groups or a given culture, precludes serious attempts at such categorical classifications. A dimensional approach on the other hand takes account of human variability. It has the advantage of allowing us to measure salient attitudes and behaviours at any given point in time and over time. It also enables us to hypothesize expected theoretical and empirical differences and changes in positions along the continuum both within and between cultural groups.

The theoretical and the empirical bases of these factors have been described at length elsewhere (Laungani, 1993, 1995, 1997, 1999, 2000, 2001, 2004, 2005; Sachdev, 1992; Sookhoo, 1995). All four dimensions in each culture coalesce together and allow us to form two divergent—but not necessarily incongruent—worldviews of the people of Eastern and Western cultures. A comprehensive analysis of each of the four dimensions—the beliefs, attitudes and values they subsume and the behaviours arising therefrom—has been described elsewhere (Laungani, 2004). The major relative differences between Eastern and Western cultures can be summarized as follows:

| *Individualism* | *Communalism* |
|---|---|
| Emphasis is on personal responsibility, self-reliance and self-achievement. | Emphasis is on collective responsibility and collective achievement. |
| Individual needs may override the needs of the family. | Individual needs are subordinated to the needs of the family. |
| Identity development is achieved through critical stages, such as those postulated by Freud, or Erikson. | Identity ascribed, even imposed on the individual. It is generally caste/class or subgroup-related. |
| The acquisition of identity is seen as a critical and traumatic process. | Since identity tends to be 'imposed' upon the individual, there is little room for 'experimentation'. |
| Family life and relationships operate on a *horizontal* model. | Family life runs on a *hierarchical* model; elders are deferred to. |
| Emphasis on nuclear (or one-parent) families. | Emphasis on extended families. |
| Social behaviours tend to be 'class-related'. | Social behaviours tend to be caste- and religion-related. |
| Pollution and purification are seen in terms of hygiene. | Pollution and purification are seen in spiritual and caste-related terms. |
| Religion tends to be less important; secularism important. | Religion plays a dominant role in everyday life. |
| Rituals, if any, tend to be secular. | Religious rituals play a dominant role in day-to-day behaviours. |

| *Cognitivism* | *Emotionalism* |
|---|---|
| Emphasis on rationality and logic. | Emphasis on feelings and intuition. |
| Feelings and emotions tend to be kept in check. | Feelings and emotions tend to be expressed freely. |
| Emphasis on work-and-activity. | Emphasis on establishing relationships. |
| Relationships are often a by-product of work. | Work is often a by-product of relationships. |
| Relations are based on shared interests and commonalities. | Relations are generally based on caste, extended family networks and religion. |
| The concept of time plays an extremely important role in the lives of Westerners. | Easterners have a 'flexible' and 'loose' attitude towards time. Things will get done when they get done. |

| *Free will* | *Determinism* |
|---|---|
| Emphasis on freedom of choice. One can, within limitations, set goals and attempt to achieve them. | Freedom of choice limited. Restriction imposed on an individual by one's caste and family orientations. |
| Proactive: Where there is a will, there is a way. | Reactive: Whatever happens is destined to happen. |
| Success or failure due largely to individual effort. | Although effort is important, success or failure is related to one's *karma*. |
| Self-blame or guilt is a residual consequence of failure. | No guilt is attached to failure. |
| Failure may lead to victim-blaming. | No blame is attached to victim. |
| Luke-warm beliefs in rebirth and after-life. | Very strong beliefs in the cycle of birth, rebirth and after-life. |

| *Materialism* | *Spiritualism* |
|---|---|
| The world is 'real', solid, physical, objective. | The empirical world is illusory and transient. |
| Rejection of contradictory explanations of phenomena. If *a* is *a* it cannot be *not-a*. | Co-existence of contradictory explanations of phenomena: *a* can be *a* and also *not-a*. |
| Reality is external to the individual. | Reality is internal to the individual. |
| A strong belief that reality can be perceived only through scientific enterprise. | Reality can be perceived through contemplation and inner reflection and through transcendental meditation. |

The question which now arises is this: Would it be possible for counsellors from Western and Eastern cultures to meet and work together as equal partners?

Can one envisage a situation where counsellors, regardless of their own cultural origins and backgrounds, will counsel clients from a different social, cultural and ethnic backgrounds with the same ease as they would clients from their own culture? It is clear that the differences between Western and Eastern cultures present two distinct worldviews or differential theoretical perspectives. The differences also reflect differences in their epistemologies. Is it possible for the two worlds to meet?

There are three major problems that require our attention.

1. Proliferation of counselling theories in the West
2. Subjectivist epistemologies
3. Ethical considerations

Let us discuss them briefly.

## *Proliferation of Counselling Theories in the West*

Recent years have witnessed an unprecedented growth in counselling theories. Let me present you with a few eye-catching 'theories' gleaned from Howard's book, *Challenges to counselling and psychotherapy* (1996).

### ***Some Contemporary 'Theories' of Counselling***

- Vita-erg therapy
- Zaraleya psychoenerget technique
- Elavil sleep therapy
- Psychedelic therapy
- C1C2 Project psychotherapy
- Bio Scream psychotherapy
- Logotherapy
- Soap opera therapy
- Neurotone therapy
- Mandala therapy
- Senoi dream group therapy
- Anti expectation psychotherapy

Most of these theories are embarrassingly naïve and so ill-conceived, that to refer to them as 'theories' is to insult the divine origin of the term theory. Sadly, all such theories:

- lack clearly formulated conceptual frameworks;
- lack any dominant unified paradigm(s);

- are seldom subjected to any severe critical tests;
- are in a state of *epistemological anarchy*—where '*anything goes*';
- promote conflicting views concerning the nature and purpose of counselling;
- betray inadequate training in counselling;
- offer subjective evaluations and assessments by their practitioners

The question is what does one do with such theories? David Hume, the 18th century Scottish philosopher, in his book *Inquiry,* offers a dazzling solution:

**David Hume's Solution** If we take in our hand a volume—of divinity or school metaphysics for instance—let us ask: Does it contain any abstract reasoning concerning quantity or number? No. Does it contain any experimental reasoning concerning matter of fact and existence? No. Commit it then to the flames, for it can contain nothing more than sophistry and illusion (Schacht, 1984). In keeping with David Hume's advice, let us commit most of the contemporary 'theories' to the flame. What we are left with are a few theories: the psychoanalytical (with its variants), the person-centred (with its variants), and cognitive-behavioural (with its variants). To these three, one might add the current intensive efforts by clinical psychologists and psychiatrists to explain every aspect of human behaviour in neurophysiological and neurophilosophical terms, thus dispensing—supposedly—at one stroke with the age-old Cartesian mind–body dualism (Churchland, 1986). The Freudian and neo-Freudian theories, as we know, explain human actions and behaviours by invoking unconscious processes at work within the individual's psyche, which should come under the control of the ego or self. The person-centred theories, on the other hand, assume that human beings have the capacity to think and behave rationally. With subtle and indirect guidance (non-didactic) from the counsellor, they are able to resolve their problems, empower themselves and become 'masters' of their destiny. The cognitive-behavioural theories combine mental processes with human actions, which are reinforced when the client 'performs' the 'desired' behaviour or abstains from performing the undesired behaviour. These are the current tried, trusted and reliable theories. I use the words tried, trusted and reliable, but intentionally left out the word valid.

*I believe it is important to remind oneself again and again and again that neither the popularity of a theory nor a high degree of consensus among its practitioners guarantees its value or validity.* As Imre Lakatos (1978), the eminent epistemologist has explained, a theory may be valuable even if no one believes in it and it may be without any value even if everyone believes in it. In other words, the value of a theory is independent of its popularity and its reliability. A universal belief in the geocentric theory of the universe, lasting over a thousand years was destroyed by Copernicus and later by Galileo when they expounded the heliocentric theory. *Thus, what is important is the quest for objective knowledge, not subjective knowledge.*

## Subjective Epistemologies

No counsellor, therapist, psychoanalyst, psychologist, in fact, no scientist works in a social vacuum. Our ideas, approaches, techniques, values, methodologies are to a very large extent influenced by our culture and the dominant epistemology (or epistemologies) to which we subscribe. Even the problems we investigate and the methods we use are culture-related. It would be a rare Western counsellor or psychotherapist who would attribute a client's distress to the mysterious workings of evil, malevolent spirits that had invaded the client's body and soul. But such explanations play a fairly dominant role in many countries, including some parts of the West Indies, such as Haiti, Grenada, and parts of South America, Africa, in England among the African communities, in India, Pakistan, Malaysia, Indonesia, the South Pacific Islands, and elsewhere (Moodley and West, 2005). This is not to say that myths and mysteries, rites and rituals, divine interventions and God's will have no role to play in theory construction. They do. In fact they serve as excellent starting points. One has only to consider the growth of scientific thinking in ancient Greece to realize the important role played by myths, fables, mysteries and supernatural explanations that served as a stepping stone for formulating bold ideas and conjectures to explain the universe in *natural* terms instead of in terms of divine interventions. These were then subjected to critical tests and examinations to establish their value (Popper, 1963, 1972). In fact as Popper and several other philosophers of science have pointed out, all science initially starts with myths and mysteries, which provide a rich source for ideas, conjectures and theories.

If one were to construct a solid counselling bridge across Eastern and Western cultures, it would be necessary to examine not only the cultural factors but also the epistemologies, which guide the professional work of counsellors and therapists.

### Popper's Three Worlds of Epistemology

One of the great exponents of epistemologies is the late Sir Karl Popper. In his book *Objective knowledge: An evolutionary approach* (1972), Popper expressed his thesis on *'three worlds of epistemology'. Karl Popper's three worlds of empistemology:*

#### World 1 (The Physical World)

- World of material objects: inorganic, organic
- Earth, rivers, mountains, trees, minerals
- Aeroplanes, rockets, cars, computers, houses, etc.
- Factories, mills, all other material objects

**World 2 (The Mental World)**

- World of mental states
- World of feelings, emotions, beliefs, attitudes, values
- Subjective assessments and evaluations
- Subjective knowledge, intuitions, viz., 'I know'

**World 3 (The Objective World)**

- World of ideas in the objective sense, critical arguments
- Theoretical systems, scientific propositions
- Problems and problem situations
- Objective contents of thought

**World 1 (The Physical World)** The existence of a solid, material, physical world is an indisputable fact, despite what a few 'idealist' philosophers might construe.

**World 2 (The Mental World)** The mental world is subjective, private and internal. It consists of our feeling states, emotions, attitudes and all our subjective assessments and evaluations. Popper argues that, 'traditional epistemology has studied knowledge or thought, in a subjective sense; in the ordinary usage of the words "I know" or "I am thinking"' (Popper, 1972: 108). To transpose these ideas into counselling terminology, a counsellor might state that '*my client seems to be in a state of anxiety. I know, because I have seen him in such a state before and have also seen many other clients in such a state before*'. These evaluations arise out of the counsellor's work experiences, feelings, intuitions, observations and his/her own subjective interpretations of the client's mental and emotional states.

However, many counsellors are often unwilling to recognize that the interpretations offered by one counsellor may be in sharp contrast to those offered by another. One wonders whether many counsellors are aware that even a congruence of interpretations can be explained by offering different sets of hypotheses. One might argue that the practice of Indian forms of meditation 'lead to' beneficial consequences; lowering of one's blood pressure, slow-down of one's heart rate, feelings of well-being and tranquillity. However, similar responses can also be obtained by biofeedback techniques and other equally plausible explanations. Popper points out that *subjective epistemologies have little or no relevance in promoting objective knowledge*. Knowledge acquired through such subjective claims is temporary and evanescent. Theories formulated on such subjective considerations come and go. They fade and disappear.

**World 3 (The Objective World)** The idea of World 3 is not as unique or original as it sounds. Plato was one of the earliest philosophers to present this formulation when he proposed his world of Forms, or Ideas, a world of *higher realities, which are unchanging, timeless and incorruptible.* (Those familiar with Indian philosophy will note the striking similarity between Plato's world of Forms and the concept of *brahman* expressed by Shankara in the Advaita Vedanta.) Popper points out that Plato's world was an objective, autonomous third world, which existed in addition to the physical world and the world of the mind.

World 3 epistemology is a world of ideas, scientific propositions, theories, critical arguments, logical and rational criticisms; tomes in libraries, pure thought. *It is the world of objective knowledge.* Although created by the human mind, and although arising in World 2, it comes to enjoy an independent existence of its own. As an example, let us take prime numbers. All prime numbers, as we know, are odd numbers. We also know that a prime number is indivisible by any number other than by itself. But when we consider number 2, we know that, (*a*) it is an even number, and (*b*) it too is indivisible by any number other than by itself. This mathematical finding *with* its anomaly—though discovered by the human mind—is irrefutable and incontrovertible. Whether the discovery of prime numbers can be traced to the Egyptians or to Pythagoras the great pre-Socrates philosopher in the 6th century BC, or to someone else is not the point. The point is that mathematical formulations, scientific propositions, tried and tested theories exist in a world of their own and are uninfluenced by subjective epistemologies. Now the question is this: which of Popper's three worlds do contemporary theories of counselling inhabit? *Without a doubt, World 2!* In fact, most, if not all of our attempts to understand the mental processes of the client (and even our own) start in World 2, and that is where most of them remain.

In my humble opinion I feel that it is essential that the current major theories of counselling, which are 'rooted' in World 2 epistemology are modified or reformulated so that they can be subjected to rigorous critical tests. Those that fail to meet with rigorous testing should, like malignant lesions, be excised. It is only then that theories of increasing objectivity and increasing truth content can be generated, and become 'permanent residents' in Popper's World 3 epistemology. Otherwise there is the danger that the field of counselling may compromise its professional integrity and degenerate into quackery.

## Ethical Considerations

It would be naïve to deny the moral and the ethical basis of any counselling encounter. One expects the counsellor and/or the therapist to operate from the highest moral and ethical standards. But since the entire field of ethics is riddled with disagreements and dissensions it is difficult to arrive at the best course of action even in a relatively innocuous situation. There are two issues of concern.

1. Ethical universalism
2. Ethical relativism

Let us deal with each separately.

***Ethical Universalism***

Is there one universal code of ethics to which people all over the world from time immemorial subscribe, viz., Ethical Universalism or Ethical Absolutism? Three thousand years ago, Socrates raised a fundamental question: how shall we live our lives? Socrates believed that *virtue* was closely related to the most important characteristic in our attempts to lead a good life. Virtue was closely related to knowledge. No man, Socrates argued, sins wittingly. If people acquired knowledge they would become virtuous. Knowledge to Socrates was founded on the premise of rationality and was acquired by the dialectical method, which Plato incorporated in all his plays. Knowledge thus enabled a person to know the good from the bad. *And to know the good was to do the good.* Wrongdoing occurred through ignorance or lack of knowledge. Socrates, of course, was referring not only to individual good lives—yours and mine—but also to collective good lives. In proposing a relationship between knowledge and goodness, he was also proposing not only a rationalistic moral philosophy, but also a philosophy of Ethical Universalism or Ethical Absolutism. His proposal would suggest that ethical 'laws' are permanent, timeless, ageless, and are applicable to the entire world from time immemorial. Although there is undeniable merit in such a proposal, it runs into at least three difficulties:

1. Does having rational knowledge necessarily induce us to lead a good and virtuous life? Were that the case, it would follow that regardless of differences in culture, gender, age, race, religion, caste, colour, learning, education, poverty, prosperity, health, illness, etc., we would all be able to live with one another in peace and harmony. But that clearly is not the case. We do not all live with one another in peace and harmony.
2. There is no guarantee of a one-to-one correspondence between intentions and actions. Knowledge of differences between right and wrong does not always lead to appropriate actions. One might know what *is right* and what one *ought* to do, *but one may not do what one ought to do.* The relationship between 'is' and 'ought' is tenuous and the 'distances' between the two, often unbridgeable.
3. Popper (1963, 1972) points out that even the most well-intended human actions do not always lead to their intended consequences. *They may also lead to unintended consequences*, which may turn out to be the opposite of what one might have desired or intended. This is because it is quite difficult to predict the short- and long-term consequences of our actions.

It is reasonable to assume that all counsellors, therapists, clinical psychologists, psychiatrists, in the course of their work encounter several such moral ethical dilemmas when dealing with their clients, be they from the same or different cultural backgrounds. A few counsellors might possess the dubious 'virtue' of shutting off the moral considerations, and operate in a sanitized, antiseptic environment. But no sensitive counsellor is likely to ignore the moral considerations, which form an integral part of a counsellor's therapeutic process.

### *Ethical or Moral Relativism*

Are ethical and moral judgements relative to one's upbringing, intelligence, personality, and above all the culture, which one is born and socialized into? Our conceptions of ethics and morality, which are a product of our enculturation, may vary from those of others (Hospers, 1990; Levy, 2002; Russell, 1955; Williams, 1985). And who is to say that one set of conceptions is more moral than others? Are there objective ways by which one moral principle can be tested against another? Is it 'better' to execute a convicted murderer by a lethal injection or by stoning the person to death? Or not to execute the murderer at all! This raises the vexing problem of *moral and ethical relativism*, a problem to which no universally acceptable solutions have thus far been offered. What happens, or should happen when counsellors' conceptions of morality are at variance with those of their clients? What ought a counsellor to do in such a situation? Should the counsellor accept the client's moral position at the cost of foregoing his/her own? Should the counsellor arrive at a compromise of moral values? Are such compromises possible? Or, should the counsellor stick with his/her own moral principles despite their being at variance with those of the client? Difficult though these issues are, one cannot—indeed *ought not*—(notice the moral imperative) disregard these issues.

## CONCLUSION

We have travelled a long way and I feel that we are left with far more questions than we are with answers. Although the questions may seem rhetorical and even unanswerable, I believe it is important to ask them. Not to ask questions is an admission of despair. Is it conceivable that people from different communities and cultures who speak different languages, worship different gods, engage in different cultural practices, eat different foods, hold different beliefs and values, construct their individual, social and collective worlds differently—is it really conceivable that they can come together and live together in peace and harmony? Can we learn to merge, mix and melt, accept, assimilate and accommodate our differences and diversities and create a genuine multicultural society, where each member is equal to the other, equal before the law, and respect for the law of the country, freedom from alienation, discrimination, persecution, rejection and victimization? Can we as healers and menders of fractured psyches, bruised souls, promote the idea that in collective goodness lies individual goodness and work towards creating a harmonious multicultural society? Is such a utopian society within the bounds of possibility? Are our attempts likely to succeed? Will we finally discover the Holy Grail? Or are our efforts doomed?

It is now time to raise the final question, which I have kept until the last: the question of the Holy Grail or the poisoned chalice. I should like to stay clear of the mystical and the mythological connotations attached to the term Holy Grail. Nor do I wish to see it as an explicitly Christian symbol, where it is described as the cup of the Last Supper and the chalice in which Christ's blood is caught (Morgan, 2005). To me its appeal resides in its use as a metaphor, which stands for relentless Promethean struggle, unending quest, a desire for ultimate achievement and the transformation of one's dreams and desires into reality.

The pursuit of the idea—regardless of its logistics—of constructing counselling bridges across cultures is not unlike the quest for the Holy Grail. But given that no one so far has succeeded in finding the Holy Grail, it might well turn out to be a futile quest, which may lead to a poisoned chalice. One cannot rule out the possibility that our quest to construct counselling bridges may founder. Ah, but what nobility in such a grand failure! It is also possible as the ancient Greeks, including Xenophanes, Heraclitus and Democritis pointed out, that we may be in possession of the Holy Grail and not realize that it is the Holy Grail. The Greeks were aware that our knowledge concerning reality and the world in which we live is *conjectural*. To quote *Xenophanes*:

*But as for certain truth, no man has known it,*
*Nor will he know it; neither of the gods,*
*Nor yet of all the things I speak.*
*And even if by chance he were to utter*
*The final truth, he would himself not know it:*
*For all is but a woven web of guesses.*

With the best will in the world even our concerted attempts may fail. As the Player King in *Hamlet* remarks:

*Our wills and fates do so contrary run*
*That our devices still are overthrown,*
*Our thoughts are ours, their ends none of our own.*

But the romantic in me believes that it is better to have tried and lost than never to have tried at all. I know not what the answer is, or what it might be. Luckily, I am sustained by hope—blind, reckless hope. The last thing, if you recall, that came tumbling out of Pandora's box was 'hope'. Life without delusional hope is like a body without a soul.

## REFERENCES

Churchland, P. M. (1986). *Neurophilosophy*. Cambridge, MA: MIT Press.
Grayling, A. C. (2003). Preface in *Cicero—A Good Life*, trans. Michael Grant. London: The Folio Society.
Hospers, J. (1990). *An introduction to philosophical analysis*. London: Routledge.
Howard, A. (1996). *Challenges to counselling and psychotherapy*. London: Macmillan.
Lakatos, I., Worral, J. and Currie, G. (Eds) (1978). Falsification and the methodology of scientific research programmes. The methodology of scientific research programmes, Imre Lakatos, philosophical papers Cambridge University Press 1. Cambridge: Cambridge University Press.
Laungani, P. (1993). Cultural differences in stress and its management. *Stress Medicine, 9*, 37–43.
———. (1995). Patterns of bereavement in Indian and English societies. *Bereavement Care, 14*, 5–7.
———. (1997). Replacing client-centred counselling with culture-centred counselling. *Counselling Psychology Quarterly, 10*, 343–351.
———. (1999). Death among Hindus in India and England. *International Journal of Group Tensions, 28*, 85–114.
———. (2000). The changing patterns of Hindu funerals in Britain: Cultural and psychological implications. *Asian Journal of Psychology and Education, 33*, 2–14.
———. (2001). Hindu deaths in India. *International Journal of Health Promotion and Education, 39*, 114–120.
———. (2004). *Asian perspectives in counselling and psychotherapy*. London: Brunner-Routledge.
Laungani, P. and Gielen, R. U. (Eds) (2005). Family life in India. *Families in global perspective*. Boston, MA: Allyn & Bacon.
Levy, N. (2002). *Moral relativism: A short introduction*. Oxford: One World Publications.
Magee, B. (2002). *Confessions of a philosopher: A journey through western philosophy*. London: Phoenix Paperbacks.
Moodley, R. and West, W. (Eds) (2005). *Integrating traditional healing practices into counselling and psychotherapy*. Thousand Oaks, CA: Sage Publications.
Morgan, G. (2005). *The holy grail*. England, Harpenden: Pocket Essentials.
Naipaul, V. S. (2003). *Literary occasions: Essays*. Oxford: Picador.
Parekh, B. (2000). *Rethinking multiculturalism: Cultural diversity and political theory*. New York: Palgrave.
Popper, K. (1963). *Conjectures and refutations*. London: Routledge & Kegan Paul.
———. (1972). *Objective knowledge: An evolutionary approach*. Oxford: The Clarendon Press.
Roland, A. (1988). *Cultural pluralism and psychoanalysis*. New York: Routledge.
Russell, B. (1955). *Human society in ethics and politics*. London: Allen & Unwin.
Sachdev, D. (1992). *Effects of psycho-cultural factors on the socialisation of British born Indian children and indigenous British children living in England*. Unpublished doctoral dissertation, South Bank University, London.
Schacht, R. (1984). *Classical modern philosophers*. London: Routledge & Kegan Paul.
Sookhoo, D. (1995). *A comparative study of the health beliefs and health practices of British whites and Asian adults with and without myocardial infarction*. Paper read at the 53rd Annual Convention of the International Council of Psychologists, Taipei, Taiwan.
Williams, B. (1985). *Ethics and the limits of philosophy*. Cambridge: Harvard University Press.

# 2

# The Reciprocal Gaze: Pittu Laungani's Musings about Culture and Stress

*Amrita Narayanan*

## INTRODUCTION

**Despite** the gradual proliferation of multicultural models of stress, many non-Western countries, notably India, continue to rely exclusively on Western models of stress and stress-related psychometric instruments (Laungani, 1996). In an effort to address the dominance of Western stress models in India, Laungani has written extensively on the limitations of Western methodologies and theoretical models of stress in the Indian context (Laungani, 1996, 2001, 2002). His continuum of value-based cultural differences applied to stress research offers a way of accounting for cultural variations in stress, particularly differences between the cultures of India and England.

Culture is a somewhat recently woven thread in the fabric of stress research (Chun et al., 2006). The 30-year-old field of stress and coping, has, in the last decade, begun to attend to the role of culture and cultural meaning-making in the shaping of the human stress response (Wong and Wong, 2006). The possibility that stress can be emic—a culture-specific concept—has been difficult to digest because stress is also etic—culturally invariant in terms of many aspects of its biology. Biopsychosocial definitions of stress have gradually begun to integrate culture into the discourse of stress research, but the field is starved for theories—general principles that explain and account for variation as well as invariation in human behaviour across cultures vis-à-vis stress (Wong and Wong, 2006).

Wong's Resource–Congruence model (1993) was the first important theoretical model acknowledging the relationship between stress, appraisal and culture, suggesting that what is stressful is defined by culture, as are choices of coping mechanisms (Chun et al., 2006). More recently, a model depicted an ongoing transactions between the environmental system and a culture-based personal system that together exert a joint influence on transitory life events, cognitive appraisals, coping skills and the health and well-being of an individual (Chun et al., 2006).

Having made the link between culture and stress, researchers sought to identify specific cultural pillars that impacted stress appraisals and coping in different cultural contexts. Hofstede's (1980) (as reviewed in Oyserman et al., 2002) constructs of individualism and collectivism are examples of a well-studied set of cultural pillars that generally differentiate cultures (Oyserman et al., 2002). The constructs were originally thought of as bipolar with individualism applying more to Western, and collectivism to non-Western cultures. Over time, the model was conceptualized as more of a continuum, with individuals in Western and non-Western cultures holding some combination of individualist and collectivist values.

Laungani built on Hofstede's original two constructs and added three more pillars to suggest a four-factor conceptual model of cultural differences between India and England. The four factors are opposing cultural value-dyads: individualism–communalism, cognitivism–emotionalism, free will–determinism and materialism–spiritualism. For each end of the continuum, Laungani explains how a strict adherence to that value has its own particular source of stress and its own expectable coping mechanisms (Laungani, 2002). Placing the four factors on a continuum and applying the model to stress, allows a framework for what might be considered more stressful for an Indian versus a British individual and suggests ways in which individuals from the respective culture groups would be likely to cope differently with the stress (Laungani, 2002).

Laungani has generalized the four-factor model to Eastern (represented by Indian) and Western (represented by British) cultures. However, the specifics of his original conceptualization (India and England) are relevant for their historical and cultural ramifications.

In this chapter, I will develop Laungani's vision of a non-Western model of stress for India using primarily a psychodynamic definition of stress as an agent of inner tension or conflict that has biological correlates and that may or may not be symptomatic (Menninger, 1954). Using the metaphor of eyes and vision as a framework, I will (*a*) trace possible reasons for the preponderance of Western models of stress in India, (*b*) critique Laungani's model within the context of India's history, evidence from other research and current demographics and (*c*) suggest a role Laungani's model may have in the modernization of traditional Indian models of stress.

## A HISTORY OF DISLOCATED EYES

Laungani attributes the lack of a uniquely Indian vision of stress to India's steady gaze towards the West instead of towards herself. In his words:

> A mentality bordering on the slavish has led to their [Indians'] unquestioning and uncritical acceptance of Western—in particular American—perspectives in their work on stress. The West in a metaphorical sense has been the star to which they have hitched their wagons. It has been their guiding light.... Definitions of stress articulated by Western psychologists, methodological strategies fashioned by Western psychologists, batteries of psychometric instruments constructed and used by Western psychologists—they have all been taken on board. Lock stock and barrel. (Laungani, 2002: 40)

Scholars who assign reasons for the predominance of Western thought in India tend to cite the demoralization of the national intellectual psyche and the anglicization of Indian academic institutions that took place during the British colonial epoch of India's history (Viswanathan, 1990). If eyes are the metaphor for self versus other regard, the century-long active British colonial endeavour in India was a veritable ocular transplant (Viswanathan, 1990). Certainly from the perspective of policy, colonialism was designed to turn the gaze of the natives towards England (Viswanathan, 1990). In the words of colonialist Thomas Macaulay, the British goal was 'to form a class who may be interpreters between us and the millions whom we govern, a class of people Indian in blood and color, but English in taste, in opinions, in morals, and in intellect' (Clive and Pinney, 1972: 91). The project of anglicizing the Indian intellect was undertaken at a number of levels, but a few events stand out in this regard. First, the English Education Act passed in 1835 instituted English as the medium of higher education in Indian schools from sixth grade onwards rather than as a foreign language course as had previously been the policy (Joshi, 2002). Second, English prose fiction, a hitherto unknown genre of literature was introduced and quickly absorbed by literate Indians, both in English and in translation, an act which scholar Priya Joshi describes as 'the single most significant incursion into the Indian cultural landscape' (Joshi, 2002: 99).

I believe that the primacy of English over Indian thought was asserted not only in the verbiage of British policy but also in the unconscious association between victory and Englishness that developed in the Indian mind. To be educated in India past the mid-1800s meant to learn that everything English and Western was more worthwhile than everything Indian, writes historian William Dalrymple. He illustrates the association between Englishness and superiority by citing the words of the Mughal poet Azad: 'The important thing is that the glory of the winners' ascendant fortune gives everything of theirs—even their dress, their gait, their conversation—a radiance that makes them desirable. And people do not merely adopt them they are proud to adopt them' (Dalrymple, 2007: 478). Dalrymple is one among a few scholars who have noted the conscious or unconscious allure of things English that deeply saturated the cultural values of educated Indians from 1800 onwards (Joshi, 2002).

I would argue that for an educated Indian, Englishness feels uncannily like home. It is therefore perhaps not entirely incongrous that Laungani notes a minimal articulation of 'Indian' thought and theory among Indian stress researchers. The narrow scope of theoretical exploration and the Western methodology of English-educated stress researchers in India are, I believe, by-products of an education system created for the task of assisting the British colonial venture by '... enriching the vernacular with terms of science borrowed from the Western nomenclature' (Clive and Pinney, 1972: 191).

Indian theories of stress are not so much absent as washed out in the torrent of Western education. Given that the nature of Western scientific research is increasingly based on physicalism and reductionism, finding Indian ways within it is a challenging proposition at best (Cornelissen, 2003). To assert a different kind of reality and ontology as is true of Indian science means that researchers who have been taught to evaluate themselves through Western eyes have to journey beyond their inner-psychic Western audience. This is an especially difficult task during a time period where funding and public accolade depends on fitting research to the Western paradigm. As such, even research on traditional Indian therapies, such as yoga and Ayurveda has focused on deriving empirical proof that substantiates its veracity rather than assuming some basic ontological truth and building on theories within the discipline (Narayanan, 2007).

I am not arguing that Western science be purged from the Indian academic ethic, rather I believe that Indian researchers can benefit from claiming their inner-psychic Western selves. This means recognizing those parts of themselves that are truly Western and integrating these parts into themselves rather than splitting off these parts as an 'other', and then trying to legitimize themselves to this other. As this psychic task of integration proceeds, rather than creating research for a Western audience (the 'colonizer' with whom the Indian has a vertical relationship) researchers will be more likely to use their English education as tools sans servility in a more horizontal relationship with the West. As Pittu Laungani puts it:

> It is only when cultures meet—on equal terms and as equal partners both as research scientists and as clinicians—and express a genuine willingness to share and learn from each other that [*sic*] we might find tentative answers to the questions which concern us all. (Laungani, 2001: 151)

Acknowledging the tools of a Western education, paradoxical as it may sound, can help make the shift from using Western science as an instrument of colonization and help us, as Indian researchers, take back our eyes.

## RECLAIMING VISION IN MODERN URBAN INDIA

As penetrating as the colonial experience was, I believe that an important part of the decolonization process means acknowledging India's push-back, in other words exploring the complexity of the colonialism as an encounter rather than as pillage. While India's sense of anger and victimization is understandable and is justifiable as portrayed by scholars such as Viswanathan (1990) who see the colonizer–colonized experience as vertical and simplistic, I believe the effect of colonialism on psychic conflict and stress can be better understood via the perspective of scholars like Joshi (2002) who see Indians and British in the colonial encounter as each 'illuminating the other in multiple and irrefutable ways'. Such a perspective begs the question of whether Indian and British values can realistically be placed in opposing dyads as they have on Laungani's continuum. Despite the evidence offered by Laungani in the form of Sachdev's research on English schoolchildren, critics such as Roland (2005) and researchers such as Sinha et al. (2002) offer evidence that Indians may not fit very neatly into the 'Indian' values. This section of the chapter will describe Laungani's 'Indian' and 'British' factors and how they apply to conceptualizations of stress, discuss the research that supports a more complex spread of these factors and suggest some mediating factors that may predict an Indian's level of proximity to one or another end of the continuum.

In a culture-based formulation of stress, Laungani's model offers some ideas about how individuals from Indian and British cultural value-sets might differentially experience and cope with stress. Indian culture is characterized in Laungani's model by communalism, emotionalism, determinism and spiritualism (Laungani, 1996). In the 'Indian' cultural reality group, expectations are a guiding force and dangers to the group as well as deviations from group norms, whether perceived in self or others, are among the biggest stressors (communalism). Free expression of feelings is important for psychological comfort and emotionally restrictive settings are experienced as stressful (emotionalism). Relationships are the primary source of self-esteem (emotionalism). Belief in predestination by a higher power is experienced as comforting and self determination may be experienced as stressful (determinism). Internal rather than external reality is considered to be of highest credibility, and life events are coped with by inner reflection (spiritualism). In the 'Indian' cultural reality, an emphasis on material and outer achievement may be experienced as stressful (spiritualism) and empirical science's emphasis on externally valid proof and facts would be considered an over-investment in what it is at best an illusory reality (Laungani, 1996).

Laungani attributes the values of individualism, cognitivism, free will and materialism to British culture. These values represent 'British' correlates of the 'Indian' values described above (Laungani, 1996). In the 'British' cultural reality described by Laungani, self-reliance is emphasized and events resulting in a diminished sense of agency may be felt as threatening (free will). Life stressors are expectably controlled using logic (cognitivism) and individual effort is thought to be the biggest component in success or failure (free will). Self-esteem may be threatened by impingements on work and time which are significant stressors (cognitivism). Culture is founded in an external reality whose existence can be empirically verified (materialism) and phenomena that cannot be physically seen or empirically proven are thought to be threatening (Laungani, 1996).

While the eight pillars that make up the four-factor model do address some significant and real differences between the cultures, in reality the picture appears to be more complex (Roland, 2005). Researchers who studied the individualism–collectivism/communalism dyad originally found Indians to be towards the collectivist or communalist end of the continuum (Triandis, 1995), but over time further studies have suggested that Indians are both collectivist and individualist at the same time, in a way that Hofsteade's bipolar model cannot explain (Sinha et al., 2002). Using a few case examples, Roland has elaborated on the individualism–communalism dyad to suggest that Indians tend to be just as if not more individualistic than Euro-Americans. However, the expression of this individualism tends to be very different from that of Euro-Americans and in particular very much more discrete, thereby not only supporting inner individualist values but also supporting outer collectivist behaviour (Roland, 2005).

Roland's (2005) distinction between Laungani's four 'values' and the behaviour that he and his colleagues observed among Indians offers some food for thought that is also explored in Sinha et al.'s (2002) empirical study that looks at individualist versus collectivist values among over 500 college-educated Indian subjects. Sinha's study separated values from behaviour, exploring both individualist/collectivist intentions and behaviour. Participants were asked to describe how they believed people with their similar background would respond to 20 different situations that called for prioritization of individual or family/collective needs, wishes or desires. While the researchers found that a clearly individualist pattern of intention and behaviour is rare, they determined that even among Indians, adherence to individualistic versus collectivist values vary under different sets of circumstances (Sinha et. al., 2002). Moreover, the responses suggested that Indians often try to realize their individual desires through generating collectivist behaviour that still supports individualist intentions. In other words, being Indian does not mean being less individualistic so much as it necessitates combining individualist and collectivist behaviours and intentions in complex ways depending on the situation and the meaning that is ascribed to the situation (Sinha et al., 2002).

When Laungani's model is considered in light of Sinha et al.'s (2002) and Roland's (2005) comments about the potential complexity of the values held by Indians, the question of limitations to the four-factor approach arises. At first glance, usage of Laungani's eight pillars as an explanation of variance in stress offers some preliminary ideas on types of internal conflicts that might be most stress producing in Indian and British individuals. Yet, the previously mentioned research suggests that there are at least three mediating factors that stand out, in whose presence the eight-pillar model demands more complex development. These are urbanization, education and immigration, the former two culled from Sinha et al.'s research and the latter from Roland's case studies.

Sinha et al.'s (2002) study, posits a relationship between increased prioritization of individualistic values and urbanized environments. Though they did not study Laungani's model directly, by parsing out intentions/desires from behaviour, Sinha et al.'s study uncovered individualist values among Indians that tend towards the 'British' end of Laungani's continuum. The researchers concluded that the changing socio-economic scenario in India has induced a shift towards cultivating individualist intentions (Sinha et al., 2002). Despite this shift, Indians still try to fulfil these individualist intentions in a way that also takes into account communal needs (Sinha et al., 2002). Roland's (2005) subject pool was among Indians who were living abroad, who also seemed to have a complex application of the so-called Indian and British values. Finally, my own observations on the Indian education system in the previous section suggest that an over-valuation of the 'British' values might be present in the psyche of educated Indians with a resultant complex set of inner-psychic conflicts and stress.

If education, urbanization and immigration are factors, which create shifts along Laungani's continuum for Indians, then the intersection of these three mediators with the eight pillars/four factors may be helpful in further developing Laungani's model. In a country that is still predominantly rural, these three groups—the educated, the urbanized and those living in Western countries—are differentially exposed not only to Laungani's 'British' values but also potentially to a worldview that upholds these values as ultimately universal (Laungani, 2002). Sachdev's study (Laungani, 1996) which suggests that the more polarized differences in value systems persist till today among Indians who have been raised in Britain is limited by its failure to systematically separate intentions from behaviours as did Sinha et al. (2002). This leaves the subjects' response style open to the question of whether they were responding in terms of their inner wishes and intentions or the outer behaviours that they would be most likely to pursue. In addition, demographic information about the families of the children who participated in Sachdev's study is not available making it difficult to situate them clearly vis-à-vis the three mediators described thereby making the study inadequate evidence for the existence of purely 'Indian' values among his subject pool.

Both Sachdev and Sinha's studies raise the topic of a fourth mediating factor that I will briefly mention here but not develop extensively because such a discussion merits its own investigation that falls outside the scope of this paper.

This fourth factor is the idealization of some of the 'Indian' factors particularly collectivism and spiritualism in Indian religious texts and social discourse. I believe that immigrants such as those evaluated in Sachdev's study may be especially vulnerable to some of the idealized Indian cultural values because their adherence to these values also serve as crucial anchors of cultural identity to a Diaspora afloat. They may be likewise especially vulnerable to the stressors and inner-psychic conflicts that go along with idealizations that are to approximate in the context of their surroundings. Studies that parse out intention from behaviour like Sinha's are well poised to capture discrepancies between idealized behaviour and actual behaviour and therefore form an invaluable part of the sound development of Laungani's four factors.

Should the above hypotheses about mediating factors hold some weight, then in fact Indians who have been educated, urbanized or who live in Western countries merit further study as a group in and of themselves, whose complex set of values suggest a distinct set of internal conflicts and stressors. For at least this group of people, both Western and Indian approaches to stress may be relevant. In contrast, rural populations in India may fit quite neatly on the 'Indian' end of Laungani's continuum, or more likely have their own set of mediating factors related to different ways of perceiving and solving problems and meriting further research. Difference in culture and values of the urban-educated Indian researchers and their rural subjects may necessitate as much an anthropological as a scientific perspective in their study methodology.

Laungani's continuum can serve as a meaningful way for Indians to identify culture-based stressful conflicts while taking into account traditional values, colonialism and the global present. By acknowledging that Indians educated in English have a shared cultural heritage with Britain that has impacted their value system, a shift is created in the post-colonial psyche through an integration, rather than a rejection of India's colonial past. Such a shift reduces the sense of the Western 'other' by integrating the other within the self. A space is thereby created for a more egalitarian relationship making room for research on stress from a traditional Indian perspective without giving up the objectivity that is gained from an outsider's vantage point.

## VIEWING TRADITIONAL INDIAN STRESS THEORIES THROUGH A LAUNGANIC LENS

Laungani's vision of cultures on equal footing as well as his model itself have a role to play in the process of claiming a Western-influenced, yet essentially Indian perspective on stress. This section of the chapter will discuss how Indian researchers have gone about the modernization of traditional models with an eye to a Western audience, borrow from the previous section to suggest how change in the psyche of the researcher will result in changes in the nature of the researcher and finally use an example to point out how Laungani's model might serve a bridge between 'Indian,' and 'British' in this process.

India has birthed and nurtured an ancient biopsychosocial model of stress that is accompanied by its own cognitive-behavioural model of stress reduction in the form of yogic psychology, physiology, anatomy and practices (Feuerstein, 1998; Le Page, 2002; Narayanan, 2007). Yet, to an English-educated Indian who has been schooled in Western rather than Eastern thought as is the practice in Indian psychology departments, traditional models of stress may be unfamiliar. Indian psychologists have been conspicuously absent from the work of re-interpreting traditional texts to a modern audience, rather this has been the preserve of Western Indophiles (Le Page, 2002).

India's academic psychology community has approached the process of researching traditional psychology from a strictly Western perspective in that their efforts have been directed towards the empirical verification of Indian 'therapies' (Narayanan, 2007). The latter approach has unfortunately largely reduced the psychological and psycho-spiritual theories that comprise India's yogic psychology to a group of techniques and exercises that no longer are clearly held together by unifying theories (Narayanan, 2007). The many empirical studies on the efficacy of yoga and meditation for stress-related conditions, for example, point to the strong desire among Indian researchers to revive Indic models that had disappeared under the British education (Raghuraj and Telles, 2004). However, many of the studies are fraught with the after-taste of Macaulay's injunction because in their attempts to present as scientific a perspective as possible, they strip down and reduce the very pieces of yogic theory and details of yoga practice that make them scientific and meaningful (Narayanan, 2007). In Launganic terms, these studies, which could topically serve well as a foundation for an Indic model of stress, instead attempt to evaluate the traditional healing practices of one culture using the tools and methodology of another. More specifically, yogic psychology arose in a socio-cultural time and place in India's history that was self-reportedly more spiritualist and less materialist and yet, the tools being used to evaluate it are those that have been developed in Western culture that fall squarely on the materialist side.

I am not denying that a flexible balance between materialist and spiritualist approaches is crucial in culling an Indian model of stress, in fact this is probably very necessary because of the diversity on the materialism–spiritualism spectrum that is present in India. However, in seeking a value-balanced perspective while researching traditional concepts, researchers must rely equally on methodology arising out of both value systems, and the approach to traditional Indian medicine has thus far not been so. I believe that researching traditional techniques is a very particular type of scientific endeavour, one that includes revitalizing the unconscious knowledge and collective memory of traditional medicine that is present in the researchers themselves. There are several steps in such an endeavour. The first is to develop a deep intuitive and intellectual understanding of the socio-cultural time and place in which the traditional models were constructed. Second, somewhat akin to how archaeologists render an excavation presently meaningful through study and hypothetical story-building, researchers must make meaning of traditional models to make them a useful import from another time India to the present time India, and diversity of Indians. The renewed model to which meaning—including interpretations that make parallels to modern science—has been added can then be adapted for empirical testing. Having moved through this socio-historical process, Indian researchers may be more open to embracing a true spirit of empiricism born of a pure and genuine curiosity for an Indian science versus a motivation for legitimacy in the eyes of the Western world.

Left untouched, the traditional Indian models of stress fall so far to the 'Indian' side of Laungani's continuum in their theoretical content that they may be less applicable to many modern-day Indians who have been educated in English and significantly exposed to Western culture. Laungani's model is important here because it provides a lens for looking at traditional models and considering the value systems imbued therein. The concept of the five *kleshas* from Indian yogic psychology is a case in point. Translated as obstacles or perhaps loosely as 'stressors', the *kleshas* are based on the possibility of an ideal state of mind, the state of yoga (Laungani, 1996). This state of yoga is equated with complete relaxation and the absence of the stress response (Feuerstein, 1998). The five *kleshas* are: *avidya* or ignorance, *asmita* or sense of self as an individual, *raga* or desires, *dveshas* or aversions and fears and *abhinivesa* or fear of death (Desikachar, 1999; Le Page, 2002). As an example, I will further describe two of these *kleshas* showing how when viewed through the lens of Laungani's continuum they are distinctly rooted in the 'Indian' value system, suggesting that their psychological relevance may be broadened by a more integrated perspective as described earlier.

The stressor *avidya* or 'ignorance' is being triggered when an individual perceives himself as separate from the natural universe and from other human beings (Desikachar, 1999). A number of symptoms could result from this trigger, including what we know in the West as depression and anxiety (Le Page, 2002). In Laungani's model, the concept of *avidya* as a trigger could be considered the result of a collective/communal value orientation, but in fact, it is even further on the continuum than Laungani's communalism because it includes connection with not only the human community but the physical environment as well. Thus, in yogic psychology, a sense of separateness from others or from the earth itself is a form of stress. Another related stressor is *asmita*, the sense of 'I' as desire-fulfilling agent who controls its own destiny. Both these so-called stressors from India's yogic psychology are important cultural pillars in Western psychology.

*Avidya* and *asmita* have embedded in them a value system that is antithetical to Laungani's described 'British' value of individualism. Yet, to most English-educated Indians operating in modern urban India, while these concepts may be intuitively familiar, the self-awareness to detect the very existence of the individual self as stressful is unlikely while the conflict between the desires of the individual self and the desires of the communal body or group self can certainly be perceived as stress producing. Similarly, many urban Indians may be unlikely to identify the sense of 'I' as an agent of destiny as stressful but can probably point to culture-based rules about what the 'I' can and cannot do as stressful and agree that the gap between the idealized and actual behaviour of the individual self may be stress producing.

Without adaptation such as I have been describing, the *klesha*s do not stand so much as a model of stress as much as a set of scriptural aspirations or idealized psychic states that fall squarely on the 'Indian' end of Laungani's continuum in terms of value orientation. My suggestion is that Laungani's model be used in the process of adapting the *klesha*s so that each one describes the conflicts that an aspirant to the stress-free state may encounter in his/her path. A detailed adapted model of the *klesha*s would note how these conflicts differ among urban and rural Indian populations thus leveraging the lens of Laungani's model to build a model of stress reflective of the multiculturalism and complexity inherent in Indian culture from among concepts that are already strong in the Indian unconsciousness.

## CONCLUSION

Laungani's legacy to the field is two-fold, as his work and vision have enriched both the field of Indian and global multicultural psychology. In both cases, his contributions have been visionary, politically innovative and detailed in descriptions of pathways for future research where cultures are on equal footing.

For the field of Indian stress research, Laungani's vision is for a psychic and academic independence that promotes uniquely Indian theories of stress, research methodology and research topics. Politically, it is a cry for Indian researchers to claim a sense of agency for their work and desist from slavishness to the West. Writer Lenny Mendoza-Strobel has described two important psychological steps that help colonized peoples become agents of their own destiny and free of enslavement. These are (*a*) transforming consciousness, through the reclamation of ones cultural self and (*b*) the recovery and healing of traumatic memory (Strobel, 2001).

Laungani's vision and model together serve as a pathway in the reclamation of the Indian cultural self because they acknowledge diversity in the Indian cultural self vis-à-vis a greater or less impact of 'Indian' and 'British' values.

Set in context, the model creates an understanding that there are both within group differences in the experience of stress among Indians based on factors such as urbanization and education, as well as between group differences among India, England and the Diaspora. Laungani fosters the transformation of consciousness described by Strobel by raising awareness of 'British' values among Indian psychology researchers. Through an increased awareness, Indian researchers can be more thoughtful about the value-driven choices they make in their work. When cultures are placed on equal footing in a post-colonial context, a safe space arises where ancient archetypes and cultural meanings are recovered in the psyche of resident and Diaspora Indians. There is no longer the risk of losing the credibility associated with Western science because there is no longer the black and white choice of one or another culture when both lie on level ground. The traumatic memory of colonialism is thus healed and the colonial encounter is integrated.

From the perspective of multicultural psychology, Laungani's vision is for a meeting of cultures on equal footing. His perspective, in which culture, science and health are bedfellows, is an antithesis to the split that present-day Western empiricism makes in this regard. By suggesting that science, medicine and healing are culturally derived phenomena, Laungani opens up the political question of whether scientific progress in terms of Western empiricism is as much a cultural endeavour as any other. Highlighting the cultural relativism of science allows multicultural psychologists to perceive the delicacy of the pathway on which they tread when making assertions or choices in the name of science whether in research or in practice. When science is viewed as a cultural transmission, issues of cultural privilege and traumatic memories of previous cultural transmissions such as colonialism can be integrated into the development of research methodology. Researchers, clinicians and writers birthed into this climate, can partake of a science that integrates history and culture into its own particular empiricism.

## REFERENCES

Chun, C., Moos, R. and Cronkite, R. (2006). Culture: A fundamental context for the stress and coping paradigm. In P. Wong and L. Wong (Eds), *Handbook of multicultural perspectives on stress and coping* (pp. 29–53). USA: Springer.

Clive, J. and Pinney, T. (Eds) (1972). *Thomas Babington Macaulay: Selected writings.* Chicago: University of Chicago Press.

Cornelissen, M. (2003). The need for the Indian tradition. *Psychological Studies, 48*(3), 38–52.

Dalrymple, W. (2007). *The last mughal: The fall of a dynasty: Delhi 1857.* New York: Knopf.

Desikachar, T. K. V. (1999). *The heart of yoga: Developing a personal practice, revised edition.* USA: Inner Traditions International.

Feuerstein, G. (1998). *The yoga tradition: Its history, literature, philosophy and practice.* Arizona: Hohm Press.

Joshi, P. (2002). *Culture and consumption: Fiction, the reading public and the British novel in colonial India.* New York: Columbia University Press.

Laungani, P. (1996). Cross-cultural investigations of stress conceptual and methodological considerations. *International Journal of Stress Management, 3*(1), 25–35.

———. (2001). The influence of culture on stress: India and England. In L. L. Adler and U. P. Gielen (Eds), *Cross-cultural topics in psychology (2nd edn)* (pp. 149–169). Westport, CT, US: Praeger Publishers/Greenwood.

———. (2002). Stress, trauma and coping strategies: Cross cultural variations. *International Journal of Group Tensions, 31*(2), 127–154.

Le Page, J. (2002). *Yoga therapy.* Brazil: Integrative Yoga Therapy Press.

Menninger, K. A. (1954). Regulatory devices of the ego under major stress. *Journal of the American Psychoanalytic Association, 2*(2), 280–310.

Narayanan, A. (2007). What empirical evidence is available for the impact of a yoga practice on different aspects of the self? Can Brahman be operationalized? Psy.D. Dissertation, Pacific Graduate School of Psychology-Stanford University Psy.D. consortium, *Dissertation Abstracts International, B 68*, 07.

Oyserman, D., Coon, H. M. and Kemmelmeier, M. (2002). Rethinking individualism and collectivism: Evaluation of theoretical assumptions and meta-analyses. *Psychological Bulletin, 128*(1), 3–72.

Raghuraj, P. and Telles, S. (2004). Right uni-nostril yoga breathing influences ipsilateral components of middle latency auditory evoked potentials. *Neurological Sciences, 25*, 274–280.

Roland, A. (2005). Commentary on building multicultural counseling bridges. *Counselling Psychology Quarterly, 18*(4), 283–285.

Sinha J. B. P., Vohra N., Singhal S. and Sinha R. (2002). Normative predictions of collectivist-individualist intentions and behaviour of Indians. *International Journal of Psychology, 37*(5), 309–319.

Strobel, L. M. (2001). Coming full circle: The process of decolonization among post-1965 Filipino Americans. USA: Giraffe Books.

Triandis, H. C. (1995). *Individualism and collectivism.* San Francisco, CA: Westview Press.

Viswanathan, G. (1990). Currying favor: The politics of British educational and cultural policy in India, 1813–1854. In *Colonialism & other essays.* Oxford: OUP.

Wong, P. and Wong, L. (2006). *Handbook of multicultural perspectives on stress and coping.* USA: Springer.

# 3

# Traditional Healing and Spirituality: Pittu Laungani Building Bridges in Counselling

*Roy Moodley*

## INTRODUCTION

**In** *Building Multicultural Counselling Bridges*, Pittu Laungani argues that every counsellor, psychologist and psychotherapist is influenced by the culture and the dominant epistemologies around her or him. This creates a tension in multicultural societies where competing and sometimes contradictory healing practices, cultural values and epistemologies are engaged with. As Laungani says, 'If one were to construct a solid counselling bridge across Eastern and Western cultures, it would be necessary to examine not only the cultural factors but also the epistemologies, which guide the professional work of counsellors and therapists' (Laungani, 2005a: 254). In arguing for the inclusion of Eastern cultural practices and epistemologies, Laungani drew our attention to the Eurocentric ways in which counselling and psychotherapy theories and practices have developed. In an interview with Collard (2005), he expressed his doubts about the relevance and effectiveness of Western counselling approaches to South Asian clients, saying: 'I was discontented with cross-cultural psychology when I started to get absorbed in it. I found that as a discipline it was—and to a large extent—still is an American enterprise...many of their models do not make sense to me...to a large extent a 'force fit' on Eastern cultures' (Collard, 2005: 8). In particular, Pittu Laungani expressed his critical view of client-centred (person-centred) therapy arguing that it 'runs into serious problems' for ethnic minority clients as it does not focus on their particular cultural identities (Laungani, 1997). Many client-centred scholars, at least anecdotally, argue that his understanding, assumptions and critique of client-centred therapy is not an informed one. Indeed, many ethnic minority counsellors in the UK, for example, are themselves person-centred therapists which attest to the fact that this approach works for them. Clearly, as a critical multicultural psychologist, Pittu Laungani was not alone in voicing his dissatisfaction of the Eurocentric focus of counselling psychology (Lago, 2007; Moodley, 1999, 2000, 2007; Sue and Sue, 1990).

For Pittu Laungani, the integration of Hindu cultural and traditional healing methods was just the kind of change that psychology needed to develop appropriate methods in a multicultural society. He advocated the inclusion of religious and spiritual ideas to be part of therapy. In 'Hindu Spirituality and Healing Practices' (2005b), Laungani wrote: 'Hinduism does not separate the sacred from the secular' (Laungani, 2005b: 139), suggesting that concepts such as religion, spirituality and cultural healing are an integral part of the Hindu society. Throughout his work, Laungani constantly connected religion, spirituality and the divine (as a critical part of Hindu culture and society), strongly suggesting that they can make a significant contribution towards psychological health and well-being. While Pittu Laungani was not a religious person in the institutional sense of the word, he saw himself as spiritual (personal communication, June 2005). Laungani lived in England for most of his life, yet identified strongly with South Asian and Hindu culture. Since the sacred and the secular are inseparable in the Hindu culture; this made Pittu Laungani feel spiritual. While his cultural location connected him to the spiritual, his critique on institutional religion provided him with the tools to critically examine issues of spirituality, religion and traditional healing.

The process of attempting to integrate cultural and traditional healing practices into counselling psychology is a difficult one, and one that is riddled with numerous problems. Indigenous and traditional healing practices still remain in the shadows of the colonial and anthropological interpretations of the West. For example, the practice of Voodoo is regarded as 'evil' in the West, but to many Caribbean people it is a spiritual and traditional healing practice (Fernandez-Olmos, 2003). While many South Asian traditional healing practices, such as yoga, meditation, Ayurveda, and so on, are more acceptable in the West, they are still seen as exotic or practised outside the framework of the mainstream healthcare institutions.

This chapter attempts to 'throw' some light on the silhouettes of indigenous, traditional and cultural healing, first, by considering the reflexivity of counselling psychology, its potential openness to new ideas and the problematics of incorporating methods of the 'Other'. This discussion raises the question of cultural contexts within which psychological meanings are produced and reproduced. The chapter also explores the various South Asian traditional healing methods, such as Ayurveda, *unani*, *sahaja*, shamanism, *siddha*, *spiritism* and ancestor consultation. Finally, in this chapter, some suggestions are made for the integration of some traditional practices. Throughout these discussions, the chapter attempts to reflect on Pittu Laungani's ideas and commentary on these issues.

## REFLEXIVITY OF COUNSELLING PSYCHOLOGY: POTENTIAL FOR BRIDGE BUILDING

The discourse of psychotherapy and counselling is a reflexive one, and in its short history has undergone many changes; incorporating many new ideas from the numerous cultures of the West; indeed, as a result of this inclusion, psychotherapy has become much richer in its theory, research and practice. However, this openness to inclusion appears to have many limitations, some of which is generated by political ideologies and Western cultural hegemony. In the past, this position has led to the exclusion of philosophies and wellness practices of non-Western cultures. Even those that incorporated ideas from non-Western cultures often failed to appreciate or grasp the depth of the material they appropriated; in a number of cases they failed to acknowledge the cultural sources of their work. For example, Carl Jung 'borrowed' and incorporated many North American aboriginal cultural elements and Eastern religious and philosophical elements into psychology, namely, dream interpretations, suggestions through trance-like states, healing circles and others, but made no reference to this 'borrowing'. Indeed, it is only in the last decade that there has been a marginal shift in including wellness practices of non-Western cultures; for example, the inclusion of mindfulness meditation in therapy. Yet, many of these practitioners too are not being 'mindful' of the history and origin of these practices.

Clearly, no single culture, including the West, has exclusive rights to the development of counselling psychology and psychotherapy. Global cultures from their earliest beginnings have been engaged in some form of therapeutic and wellness process, as part of their evolutionary sustainability. Therefore, all cultures have much to offer in terms of understanding people's physical and mental health. It seems critical therefore that counselling and psychotherapy be open to integrating traditional healing methods of non-Western cultures. Indeed, the hegemonic cultural influences of European social thought (concepts of the self, the subject and its implications for healthcare) has run its course, and to some extent has failed to provide multiple ways of knowing, interpreting and deciphering the human predicament in a post-colonial, post-structuralist and post-modern world. The colonial knowledge base has led to much repetition and recycling of the same ideas and paradigms in physical and mental health, to the extent that treatments are now extremely generic. The network of meanings that constitute an individual's response to illness, distress and wellness tends to get lost among the research data. Since traditional healers and healing practices are constructed around the philosophy of addressing individual needs in a holistic way, many ethnic minority clients in the past tended to seek out those healers. The inclusion of the philosophies and psychologies of other cultures, particularly those of the former colonies can be a rich source of new and innovative ways of doing counselling psychology and psychotherapy.

The history of psychotherapy has shown that it is a reflexive one, changing in many different ways since its beginning with Freud, Jung, Klein and others. Though the discipline perhaps is open for change, are counselling psychologists and psychotherapists ready for this creative possibility? Pittu Laungani made numerous efforts to make such changes possible. In all his writings he was constantly striving to build bridges between counselling psychology and Hindu culture, often arguing that psychological representations, presentations and cure seeking can only be arrived at within a cultural context.

## CULTURAL CONTEXTS, PSYCHOLOGICAL MEANINGS AND CURE SEEKING

A constant theme in Pittu Laungani's writings was the comparison between the philosophies of the East and West, arguing that the West was basically material and the East generally spiritual. At times, this kind of analysis is meaningful and allows for a particular understanding of these two different worlds, but could easily fall prey to gross generalizations of world views that are constantly converging and diverging as a result of globalization, Western ideologies and Euro-American cultural hegemony. In making a case for the East/West binary and the two different cultural philosophies, Pittu Laungani illustrated his arguments using the *Law of Karma* and the concept of *maya*. Accordingly, Laungani suggested that South Asians in adopting a philosophy of *maya* saw the external world as illusionary; and, the purpose of human existence was to transcend this illusionary existence, renounce materialism and attain spiritual awareness 'and finally liberate oneself from the bondage of the cycle of birth and rebirth, thereby attaining *moksha*. It is then that one's soul (*atman*) merges with the ultimate *brahman*' (Laungani, 2007: 79). The *Law of Karma*, noted Pittu Laungani (2005b), is the most unique and significant feature of South Asian culture, particularly to the Hindus. This deterministic belief motivates and drives the world view of the Hindus, and accordingly they 'invoke the gods and seek their beneficial interventions...guidance is sought from priests, gurus, and other healers' (Laungani, 2005b: 144)...and 'since the different constructions of mental disorders reflect the distinct value orientation of each culture' (Laungani, 2005b: 146), it stands to reason that South Asian clients may desire or seek traditional healing solely or in conjunction with counselling psychology and psychotherapy for their health and mental health needs.

Clearly, Western European counselling and psychotherapy alone would not be sufficient as a course of treatment since illness is culturally constructed. According to Good and Good (1982: 148), 'the meaning of illness for an individual is grounded in...the network of meanings an illness has in a particular culture...and the care patterns that shape the experience of the illness and the social reactions to the sufferer'. Furthermore, Bhugra and Bhui (2006) argue that each society culturally determines states of distress and give rise to models of healing that are in keeping with that culture's understanding of distress, so that

> Possession states in India can help resolve local conflicts by involving the local community in the healing process; possession becomes a means of seeking help in that specific cultural context. Knowledge that spirits of the ancestors and gods are present on earth and can possess an individual's body is a prerequisite in a society which offers the possessed person culturally compatible healing. (Bhugra and Bhui, 2006: 47; Marsella and White, 1982; Perera et al., 1995)

According to Pittu Laungani:

> Illness, disease, and death are explained not only in medico-legal terms in large metropolitan cities, but also in religious and spiritual terms. These two sets of explanations—religious and scientific—reside side-by-side, impervious to logical contradictions. Thus, a disease may be construed in terms of sorcery, bewitchment and the malevolent influences of evil spirits, and yet would not averse to seeking allopathic, homeopathic, Ayurveda and herbal medication. (Laungani, 2007: 253)

The availability of different kinds of cure will then become part of the patient's theory of illness and cure which he or she would have built up over time using culture as the foundation. In other words, clients will be able to, if given the opportunity of receiving different cures (for example, talking therapy and traditional healing), systematically organize the expression of their problem into the discourse of the healer and healing methods, thus 'presenting their subjective distress to each therapist appropriately...competing and contradictory cures can be held alongside or in tandem with each other without necessarily creating conflict in the patient' (Moodley, 2000: 164). According to Gonzalez Chevez (2005) traditional healers and healing systems contribute and are reconstituted in the context of a cultural system that elaborates its cognitive strategies (Kleinman, 1980).

## INTEGRATING TRADITIONAL HEALING INTO PSYCHOTHERAPY

Pittu Laungani's search for a transcultural approach to counselling and psychotherapy led him, as discussed earlier, to the philosophical and religious texts of the Hindu culture. His ventures into the Vedas invariably pointed him in the direction of traditional healing, spirituality, meditation, Ayurveda and religious rites and rituals, all of which are written about, some more than others, throughout his career. Although Pittu Laungani did not directly call for the integration of South Asian traditional healing into counselling psychology and psychotherapy; he did however contribute a critical chapter on 'Hindu Spirituality and Healing Practices' in *Integrating Traditional Healing Practices into Counselling and Psychotherapy* (Moodley and West, 2005). Elsewhere, he made reference to the benefits of practices such as meditation. For example, he noted that 'the practice of Indian forms of meditation lead to beneficial consequences; lowering of one's blood pressure, slow down of one's heart rate, feelings of well-being and tranquility' (Laungani, 2005a: 255). Indeed, the practice of mindfulness meditation currently appears to be enjoying a privileged place not only in Cognitive Behaviour Therapy (CBT), but also in many other counselling approaches as well.

Clearly, there are many questions that need to be asked before counsellors can venture into the use of traditional healers and healing in psychology since much about the role that traditional healers and healing play is still not known in the West, particularly in counselling psychology and psychotherapy. Indeed, there is now a growing interest in this area (Moodley and West, 2005). Currently, a major project is being undertaken by a number of researchers at the University of Toronto to explore the role of African, South Asian and Caribbean traditional healers and healing practices in the greater Toronto area. Funded by the Canadian Social Science Humanities Research Council (SSHRC), the research is attempting to consider the role of the healers in counselling, health promotion and education. The author of this chapter is the principal investigator on this project. Aanchal Rai, one of the editors of this book and a key researcher on the project, has completed a study on South Asian healers in Toronto (Rai, 2008). Since this research is being conducted in the West, it is expected that the outcomes would be of benefit to the communities living in the West as well as add new knowledge(s) to the current practices of counselling psychology and psychotherapy. Accessing indigenous traditional healing practices for the further development of Eurocentric practices such as counselling and psychotherapy is always complicated by history, culture, power relationships and the inherent contradictions of different healing methods. Indeed, attempting to find some understanding of the complexity of South Asian traditional and cultural practices is problematic because of the way in which indigenous knowledge(s) are perceived and constructed in the West. The racist underpinnings of the colonial era and Western cultural hegemony concerning non-Western cultural and religious practices still seem to pervade some of the academic and clinical landscape in the West.

The rationale for integrating traditional healing practices into counselling and psychotherapy is based on a number of factors, for example, the current counselling psychology and psychotherapy discourse is embedded in Eurocentric theory; ethnic minority groups have introduced their approaches to health and well-being into Western culture through the processes of globalization and mass migrations. Many of the healing traditions of non-Western cultures, such as naturopathy, homoeopathy, acupuncture, yogic healing, psychic and faith healing and the new age therapies are being accessed by middle-class North Americans (Heber et al., 1989; Moodley and West, 2005; Poulin and West, 2005). Many clients engage therapists from different healing traditions as complementary cure seeking strategies. Indeed, for many clients from ethnic minority communities, there is no hesitation in seeking help from two or more healers, even for the most negligible of illnesses (Littlewood, 1990). This is undertaken because traditional healing practices appear to address some of the crucial health concerns that may not be adequately addressed by conventional (allopathic) medicine because of its philosophy of treating the whole person. Allopathic health care has been criticized for splitting the patients into body, mind and spirit, thus depersonalizing and objectifying the patient. On the other hand, traditional and alternative forms of healing are concerned with helping patients repair their emotional, mental and physical unity, to cope with disease, distress, disability and recovery and prepare them for pain and suffering, and even helping them prepare for death (Waldram, 2000). Tseng and McDermott, in reviewing traditional methods indicate that, 'it is becoming more and more clear that such simplistic notions regarding therapeutic approaches as considering one approach universally primary or superior are no longer tolerable and that many techniques seem to be effective with the same problem throughout the world' (Tseng and McDermott, 1975: 378).

Integrating cultural, spiritual and traditional healing practices into counselling psychology and psychotherapy raises many interesting and challenging questions. Not least among them are: Should integration be considered in the first place? Can traditional healing practices from one culture be transplanted in another culture? Can only certain aspects of cultural healing practices be translated? Is it authentic to practice a particular traditional healing method when only one half of it is available as a process? For example, can the West practice yoga without the spiritual aspect of this method? Is it beneficial to clients if it is practised in this way? What are the ethical questions related to appropriation of spiritual, cultural and traditional healing methods by the West? There are no easy or straightforward answers to all these questions. Indeed, not all traditional healing practices are appropriate or applicable outside the cultures they evolve in, even for members of the diaspora living in the West.

However, many South Asian immigrant communities still continue to seek the help of traditional healers for various reasons: for some, traditional healers are their 'first call of cure seeking' before they can even contemplate Western medicine or psychotherapy. For others, seeking a traditional healer is the result of encountering numerous barriers when seeking Western health care, for example, institutional racism, lack of cultural sensitivity from health care workers, low cross-cultural competencies by practitioners, language issues, religious and spiritual concerns, and so on. When traditional healing cannot be easily accessed in the West, individuals tend to go back to their 'home countries' to seek out particular types of healers. For example, a study among South Asians showed that mentally ill British Asians may travel to Asia for treatment. It also found that almost a quarter of those from one sample who had visited the subcontinent had visited an Asian healer while they were there (Ineichen, 1990). Moreover, Ineichen suggests that many British South Asian patients 'may side-step conventional medical services and prefer to approach Hakims or other alternative healers' (Ineichen, 1990: 1670). In an interview of South Asian psychiatric patients in Britain, all indicated that they used traditional healers for their mental illness in collaboration with Western medicine (Dein and Sembhi, 2001). This situation has been going on since the South Asians arrived in the West as immigrants. As Rao points out, in the 1980s 'traditional methods are experienced concurrently or followed by the modern methods of health care' (Rao, 1986: 292). Indeed, this practice appears to be growing at a fairly rapid rate where 'more and more people are seeking out the services of traditional healers alongside conventional treatments' (Moodley et al., 2008: 159; Moodley and West, 2005).

## HINDU SPIRITUALITY AND SOUTH ASIAN TRADITIONAL HEALING

In 'Hindu Spirituality and Healing Practices', Pittu Laungani (2005b) writes that the Vedas (literally means 'to know, to perceive, to understand', and so on...), being the holiest of the holy books of the Hindus, 'consist of hymns, verses, and poems, and are primarily concerned with Vedic ritual, prayers, sacrifices, the chanting of secret mantras' (Laungani, 2005b: 139). The Vedas constitute four books—*Rig Veda*, *Sama Veda*, *Yajur Veda* and the *Atharva Veda*—all of which form the basis of South Asian traditional healing practices. For example, the *Rig Veda* records the healing method of *Bhuta vidya*, a magico-religious procedure dating back to 500 BC. The *Bhuta vidya* is also recorded in India's philosophical and religious literature, the Puranas, Upanishads and the *Bhagavad Gita*. The *Atharva Veda* refers to devils and spirits as causes of illness and prescribes cures for them. The Vedas point to the general belief that the cause of mental maladies lay in the supernatural, thus reinforcing the need to seek remedies in religious and magical techniques. And since these conceptualizations are culturally embedded, they are best resolved through practices that are from the same culture because the network of meanings for a person's illness is deeply embedded in that culture. Indeed, this understanding goes back to the era of the Vedas when aspects of therapeutic science developed. The roots of many traditional healing practices can be found in the *Atharva Veda*, the oldest literary source of South Asian medicine. In the evolution of traditional medicine this nature-cure healing still remained as the basic foundation for all forms of treatment to the current age (Chakrabarti, 2001). The practice of Ayurveda today, for example, is based on the literature of *Atharva Veda*. Other forms of South Asian traditional healing are: *Unani*, *Sahaja*, *Shamanism*, *Siddha* and *Spiritism*.

***Unani*** (Islamic medicine) originated in Greece, and was brought to India by the Arabs and Persians. The golden age of Unani was from the 13th to the 17th centuries in India but suffered a setback during the British Colonial rule. However, it had a momentous development since the independence of India. Unani aims to restore equilibrium of various elements and faculties of the human body.

***Sahaja*** therapy signifies the 'innate nature' that a person is born with. Its characteristics are closer to humanistic psychology; emphasizing the social and environmental aspects of a person's well-being (Kumar et al., 2005).

***Shamanism***: Shamanic practitioners are known by different names. A Muslim healer is called a *Pir* or *Sayana*, and a Hindu healer a *Baba*, *Ojha* or *Tantric*. Shamans regard themselves as conduits between the supernatural and the patient, and through the processes of 'possession' and 'exorcism', healing is conducted (Kumar et al., 2005). In *Shamanic Performances: Healing Through Magic and the Supernatural*, Moodley (2005) suggests that the Shaman's interpretations of the patient's illness and the subsequent solution to the problem could well make the whole process appear magical and supernatural to the patient. The dances that accompany the Shamanic rituals are more like a psychodrama than the verbal group therapy in which patients express their feelings and experiences, in words.

***Siddha*** is a system of healing, dating back to 5000 BC, that originated in southern India. Like Ayurveda, the treatment is directed to restoring balance and equilibrium of the three cardinal humours (*vattam*, *pittam* and *kapham*). Treatment is individualized to meet each patient's needs (Kumar et al., 2005).

***Spiritism*** is based on a belief in reincarnation and the use of mediums who mediate healing through a process which stresses the concept of spiritual 'fluids', around the body (Hohmann et al., 1990). Historically, the mediums were known as *Deonra* (a magician cum witch doctor), 'who can study the symptoms of a disease and find out by sight whether it is a case of spirit intrusion, or the interference by witches or sorcerers or due to natural causes' (Majumdar, 1973: 428).

## WHAT CAN COUNSELLORS DO TO BE INVOLVED?

Counsellors and psychotherapists who desire to engage with traditional healers and their healing practices can do the following:

- Acknowledge that indigenous and traditional healing practices are acceptable and are a recognized form of intervention for a client who chooses such a process. By acknowledging that indigenous, cultural and traditional healing practices are age-old methods that have historically been used to alleviate their physical, mental and psychological problems, clients will be more receptive of counselling and psychotherapy even if they do not attend or need the services of a traditional healer. The therapeutic relations will be founded on mutual trust and the assurance that the process is culturally sensitive.
- Include some of the traditional healing practices as an integrated approach in her or his clinical practice.
- Acknowledge that the belief in empirically supported interventions has the potential to exclude traditional healing practices and may not be applicable to culturally diverse clients. Indeed, while little empirical research has been carried out to establish 'evidence' for the therapeutic benefits of indigenous healing practices, qualitative accounts suggest their critical role in restoring an individual's mental well-being and their ability to enhance Western counselling (Juntunen and Morin, 2004).
- Be open to discussing the role of traditional healers and their practices in the counselling sessions if clients bring up the topic. Counsellors can also make clients conscious of the current research in this area, especially 'good quality practices and practitioners', as well as the problematic areas of traditional healing practices, such as work of charlatans and bogus practitioners who may exploit unsuspecting and vulnerable clients, and the use of non-monitored medications that may contain levels of minerals and poisons that are unacceptable (Moodley and Sutherland, in press).
- Be informed about traditional, indigenous and cultural healers and their particular healing practices through the local community centres and religious places of worship; consequently, this will lead to professional partnerships within which referrals can be made by the counsellors as well as the traditional healers. This may eventually lead to the possibility of shared practice or consultation between the counsellor and the traditional healer.

## CONCLUSION

In his attempt to build bridges between counselling psychology and South Asian culture, Pittu Laungani drew on many theories both from South Asian religion, culture and philosophy, as well as the numerous theories of Western health and mental care practices. He critically examined the dominant cultural ideologies that encapsulate the theories and practices of counselling and psychotherapy in the modern diasporic age that currently prevents the full participation and inclusion of ethnic minorities in the therapeutic process. His arguments for the incorporation of the cultural elements into counselling psychology was made on the basis that ethnic minority clients construct the self as a sub-unit of the group, rather than as an individual and isolated self. Any therapy therefore with these clients will require a cultural-sensitive process. The inclusion of spiritual and traditional healing strategies into counselling psychology and psychotherapy appears to be significant if ethnic minority clients construct theories of illness representation and presentation models, and cure-seeking strategies that are themselves inclusive of religion, culture and the social conditions of the clients' geopolitical situation. Pittu Laungani argued for this paradigm shift to occur in counselling psychology, and health care in general. Moreover, throughout his work Pittu Laungani attempted to strive for a harmonious multicultural society. As he says:

> It is conceivable that people from different communities and cultures who speak different languages, worship different gods, engage in different cultural practices, ...can come together and live in peace and harmony...we can learn to merge, mix, and melt, accept, assimilate and accommodate our differences and diversities and create a genuine multicultural society...we can as healers and menders of fractured psyches, bruised souls, promote the idea that in collective goodness lies individual goodness and work towards creating a harmonious multicultural society. (Laungani, 2005a: 258)

## REFERENCES


Awanbar, D. (1982). The healing process in African psychotherapy. *American Journal of Psychotherapy, 36*, 206–213.

Bhugra, D. and Bhui, K. (1998). Psychotherapy across the cultural divide. In R. Moodley and S. Palmer (Eds), *Race, culture and psychotherapy* (pp. 46–57). London: Routledge.

Chakrabarti, D. N. (2001). Atharva Veda and the science of Indian medicine. *Journal of Asiatic Society*, XLIII (2), 24–26.

Collard, P. (2005). An interview with Dr Pittu Laungani. *Counselling Psychology Quarterly, 18*(1), 7–18.

Dein, S. and Sembhi, S. (2001). The use of traditional healing in South Asian psychiatric patients in the U.K.: Interactions between professional and folk psychiatries. *Transcultural Psychiatry, 38*(2), 243–257.

Fernandez-Olmos, M. (2003). *Creole religions of the Caribbean: An introduction from Vodu and Santeria to Obeah and Espiritismo*. New York: New York University Press.

Gonzalez Chevez, L. (2005). Latin American healers and healing: Healing as a redefinition process. In R. Moodley and W. West (Eds), *Integrating traditional healing practices into counselling and psychotherapy* (pp. 196–209). Thousand Oaks, CA: Sage Publications.

Good, B. J. and Good, M. J. D. (1982). Towards a meaning-centred analysis of popular illness categories: 'Fright-illness' and 'heat distress' in Iran. In A. J. Marsella and G. M. White (Eds), *Cultural conceptions of mental health and therapy* (pp. 141–166). Dordrecht: Reidel.

Heber, A.S., Fleisher, W.P., Ross, C.A. and Stanwick, R.S. (1989). Dissociation in alternative healers and traditional therapists: A comparative study. *American Journal of Psychotherapy, 43*(4), 562–574.

Hohmann, A. A., Richeport, M., Marriott, B. M., Canino, G. J., Rubio-Stipec, M. and Bird, H. (1990). Spiritism in Puerto Rico. Results of an island-wide community study. *British Journal of Psychiatry, 156*(3), 328–335.

Ineichen, B. (1990). The mental health of Asian in Britain: Little disease or underreporting? *British Medical Journal, 300*, 1669–1670.

Juntunen, C. L. and Morin, P. M. (2004). Treatment issues for Native Americans: An overview of individual, family, and group strategies. In D. R. Atkinson (Ed.), *Counseling American minorities* (6th ed.). New York, NY: McGraw-Hill.

Kleinman, A. (1980). *Patients and healers in the context of culture: An exploration of the borderland between anthropology, healing and psychiatry*. Berkeley: University of California Press.

Kumar, M., Bhugra, D. and Singh, J. (2005). South Asian (Indian) traditional healing: Ayurvedic, shamanic, and Sahaja therapy. In R. Moodley and W. West (Eds), *Integrating traditional healing practices into counselling and psychotherapy* (pp. 196–209). Thousand Oaks, CA: Sage Publications.

Lago, C. (2007). *Race, culture and counselling: The ongoing challenge* (2nd ed). Berkshire, UK: Open University Press.

Laungani, P. (1997). Replacing client-centred counselling with culture-centred counselling. *Counselling Psychology Quarterly, 10*, 343–351.

———. (2005a). Building multicultural counselling bridges: The holygrail or a poisoned chalice? *Counselling Psychology Quarterly, 18*(4), 247–259.

———. (2005b). Hindu spirituality and healing practices. In R. Moodley and W. West (Eds), *Integrating traditional healing practices into counselling and psychotherapy* (pp. 138–147). Thousand Oaks, CA: Sage Publications.

———. (2007). *Understanding cross-cultural psychology*. New Delhi: Sage Publications.

Littlewood, R. (1973). *Races and cultures of India*. London: Asia Publishing House.

———. (1990). From categories to contexts: A decade of the new cross-cultural psychiatry. *British Journal of Psychiatry, 156*, 308–327.

Majumdar, D. N. (1973). *Races and cultures of India*. London: Asia Publishing House.

Marsella, A. J. and White, G. (Eds) (1982). *Cultural conceptions of mental health and therapy*. Dordrecht: D. Reidel.

Moodley, R. (1999). Challenges and transformations: Counselling in a multicultural context. *International Journal for the Advancement of Counselling, 21*(2), 139–152.

———. (2000). Representation of subjective distress in black and ethnic minority patients: Constructing a research agenda. *Counselling Psychology Quarterly, 13*(2), 159–174.

———. (2005). Shamanic performance: Healing through magic and the supernatural. In R. Moodley and W. West (eds), *Integrating traditional healing practices into counselling and psychotherapy*, pp. 2–14. Thousand Oaks, CA: Sage Publications.

———. (2007). (Re)Placing multiculturalism in counselling and psychotherapy. *British Journal of Guidance and Counselling, 35*(1), 1–22.

Moodley, R. and Sutherland, P. (in press). Traditional and cultural healers and healing: Dual interventions in counseling and psychotherapy. *Counselling and Spirituality, 28*(1), 11–32.

Moodley, R., Sutherland, P. and Oulanova, O. (2008). Traditional healing, the body and mind in psychotherapy. *Counselling Psychology Quarterly, 21*(2), 153–165.

Moodley, R. and West, W. (Eds) (2005). *Integrating traditional healing practices into counselling and psychotherapy.* Thousand Oaks, CA: Sage Publications.

Perera, S., Bhui, K. and Dein, S. (1995). Making sense of possession states: Psychopathology and differential diagnosis. *British Journal of Hospital Medicine, 53*(11), 582.

Poulin, P. and West, W. (2005). Holistic healing, paradigm shift, and the new age. In R. Moodley and W. West (Eds), *Integrating traditional healing practices into counseling and psychotherapy* (pp. 257–268). Thousand Oaks, CA: Sage Publications.

Rai, A. (2008). *South Asian traditional healing practices in counselling.* Unpublished MA thesis, Counselling Psychology, University of Toronto.

Rao, V. A. (1986). Indian and Western psychiatry: A comparison. In J. L. Cox (Ed.), *Transcultural Psychiatry.* London: Croom Helm.

Sue, D. W. and Sue, D. (1990). *Counseling the culturally different: Theory and practice.* New York: John Wiley & Sons.

Tseng, W. S. and McDermott, J. F. (1975). Psychotherapy: Historical roots, universal elements, and cultural variations. *American Journal of Psychiatry, 132,* 378–384.

Waldram, J.B. (2000). The efficacy of traditional medicine: Current theoretical and methodological issues. *Medical Anthropology Quarterly, 14*(4), 603–625.

# 4

# Dancing with the Master: An Interview with Pittu Laungani

*Lana Stermac*

**How** does one describe Pittu Laungani? A scholar, a teacher, a visionary, a sage or perhaps a renaissance man? Unequivocally, one can say that Pittu Laungani was many of these things. His long and distinguished career resulted in 15 books, over 70 research papers, many book chapters and countless scholarly presentations. Pittu Laungani's productivity was impressive not only for its volume but for the lyrical and philosophical style he used, which emphasized erudition and breadth of knowledge in all the areas of psychology he wrote fervently about. First and foremost, Pittu Laungani loved language and words. His manner of expression and elegant loquaciousness were legendary. References to poetry, prose, the great literary masters and philosophers were eminently apparent in the abundance of writings he leaves us on cross-cultural counselling and psychotherapy and other areas.

Pittu Laungani had many passionate interests! He lived by his convictions and wrote about them in his voluminous work. Pittu Laungani emanated thoughtfulness in his professional work and his personal life. He was loved and respected by many and attained eminence and distinction in his field. Yet, Pittu Laungani was also a malcontent, a needle in the side of traditionalists and a rebel with a cause. What was his cause? Pittu Laungani posed a challenge to Western models of counselling and psychotherapy in general and critiqued person-centred approaches specifically as making assumptions about therapy that were not cross-culturally relevant. While he attempted to create an intellectual forum from which people could discuss and critically examine ideas related to different cultures and different ways of constructing the world, his critical analysis also created controversy and antipathy from a number of his critics.

The academic and scholarly work that Pittu Laungani leaves us is well-known. This volume and others no doubt, will describe and present much of this work in dedication to him. However, we also have words that Pittu Laungani himself speaks that go beyond his academic writing and present reflections on his life and work. I had the wonderful opportunity to interview Pittu Laungani in 2005 on the occasion of his receiving a *Lifetime Achievement Award* from the University of Toronto. The award recognized his outstanding scholarship, research and practice in the area of cross-cultural counselling and multicultural psychology. Pittu Laungani was exceptionally deserving of this award yet surprised to receive it! Used to the controversies and antagonism around his work, he was humbled and honoured by this recognition and focus on his work. As part of the honouring of Pittu Laungani, he kindly spoke with me in a candid and self-reflective manner. In the following interview he masterfully weaves a psychological exploration and journey through the 'tapestry of his life'. He states at the outset of the interview that he looks forward to examining and reflecting on his life because, and as stated in the Socratic dictum, 'an unexamined life is a life not worth living'. We have much to learn from our childhood experiences, he says, in understanding and carrying forward our ancestral past and culture. Ignoring the past can only be done at one's own peril!

Pittu Laungani begins by recounting some of his early childhood in Bombay through introducing history, philosophy and poetry. He recalls being overcome by emotion in seeing the flat in which he spent his early very happy days of childhood. This period of time, he states, remains a cherished memory of harmony and belonging and a time before he acknowledged feelings of 'outsideness'. Raised within a relatively orthodox Hindu family, Pittu Laungani nevertheless received a Jesuit education which he felt contributed to developing his cultural perspectives and to being a bicultural person from an early age. Despite the benefits of this early education, Pittu Laungani received little encouragement to attend university. He recounts a fascinating story of how a casual relationship with a customer in the family's business provided the impetus for his return to school and to the beginning of his university studies. This recollection leads to a sorrowful look at the strained father–son relationship that ensued.

Continuing in the interview, Pittu Laungani describes his university education and life in Bombay where some of the impenetrable barriers posed to Indian citizens of non-Brahmin castes became apparent. Precipitated by this experience of exclusion and, referring to Forster's *A Passage to India*, Pittu Laungani describes his 'passage to England'. Here new barriers were evident—those posed to the non-English in Britain. How did he manage? Pittu Laungani describes living within two worlds in England. While relationships with colleagues were at times difficult, as he felt that few of them ever had a real interest in other cultures, Pittu Laungani describes with substantial humour some of the communication difficulties he encountered throughout the years. Perhaps this made him assert his 'Indian-ness' with exaggerated ferocity, he asks. Despite this, he made lifelong and dear friends in England and it remained his home for the remainder of his life.

Pittu Laungani continues in the interview philosophically discussing the major differences between Eastern and Western cultures, the tension between faith and reason in Eastern and Western societies. Where does he stand with respect to faith? Does he believe in the 'Law of Karma'? Pittu Laungani discusses this and also describes the development of his interest in cross-cultural psychology as stemming from the multicultural and multi-faith experiences within India and not, surprisingly, within Britain. He describes the contradictions within India—a multicultural and diverse country yet with astonishing 'homogeneity in terms of beliefs, value-systems, child-rearing practices, and the extended family structures'. Pittu Laungani also discusses some current views on counselling and psychotherapy exploring notions of moral imperatives and moral relativism. He touches on the critiques of Western models of psychotherapy which he had written extensively on and emphasizes the mutual benefit that can be derived from learning from the 'other'.

There is much to say about Pittu Laungani but perhaps no one can say it better than he. I introduce you to Pittu Laungani, in his own words.

LS: Thank you very much for agreeing to participate in this interview.

PL: Thank you for inviting me.

LS: Roy Moodley had warned us about the critical state of your health and we were all very anxious about your trip to Canada. But I am so glad you have been able to make it.

PL: All I can say is that I am delighted to be here. It wasn't easy, mind you, but here I am.

LS: I sincerely hope you will have a safe journey back home.

PL: I hope so too.

LS: What I would like to do is to travel with you on a psychological journey into your life.

PL: What a terrifying prospect!

LS: Who knows, you might even enjoy it!

PL: One would need to be a masochist to enjoy the experience.

LS: In any case, you are free *not* to answer any question.

PL: Good, that's a relief.

LS: Let us go then, you and I……

PL: When the evening is spread out against the sky….

LS: Bravo! You too are an admirer of T.S. Eliot!

PL: Always have been.

LS: In your writings you have often extolled the virtues of the Socratic dictum that 'an unexamined life is a life not worth living'. Can you say a bit more on this?

PL: Certainly. This is what distinguishes us from animals. Animals have no powers of reflection. They live by their reflexes, their instincts, their emotions and by learning techniques of survival. But humans can reason, think, reflect, contemplate, reconstruct their past make sense of the present and even attempt to predict their future. Given these assets, it is to our advantage to reflect and examine the quality of our lives. We have no excuse not to examine our lives.

LS: I take your point. But do you actually believe that people sit down and examine their lives in the way in which Socrates has indicated.

PL: A few do. But as for the rest I have my doubts.

LS: So do I. Let us move away from this general philosophical problem—fascinating though it is—and turn to your personal life. Although I am not a Freudian in the strict sense of the word, I believe that one's childhood experiences have a major influence on one's life.

PL: I agree with you wholeheartedly. We carry our past, like a tortoise with its shell. But I would argue that we go beyond the tortoise's shell. We carry our ancestral past with us as well.

LS: By which you mean one's culture?

PL: Precisely!

LS: But how do we acquire this knowledge of our cultural ancestry?

PL: I guess it's partly through learning and experience, and partly through an evolutionary process of natural selection. It is possible that we inherit the templates of our progress over the centuries.

LS: It's sad that people do not understand the importance of the past in understanding the present—and even planning for the future.

PL: Interestingly enough the notion of the past leads to a paradox. In one sense we are all chained to our past by its history. In another sense, the very term—*past*—is an event, an experience, an episode that occurred and is now gone and will never be recaptured ever again—other than in one's imagination.

LS: I think that is why people tend to undervalue the importance of the past.

PL: Or overvalue it in certain cases.

LS: Like the Freudians?

PL: Perhaps.

LS: One often hears the phrase: *'Oh, its all in the past. It happened such a long time ago. What's the point in raking up the past?'* I strongly believe that trying to recapture the past is perhaps as dangerous as trying to ignore the past.

PL: You're right. One can only ignore the past at one's own peril. The past has valuable lessons to teach us. You might recall the famous words of Santayana the famous Spanish philosopher who said, *'Not to learn from our past mistakes will condemn us to repeating them in the future'*. As Winston Churchill pointed out *'the further backward you look the further forward you can see'*.

LS: Okay. Let us then move on to your past—your childhood—and see what lies concealed.

PL: Psychological skeletons in the musty cluttered attic of my psyche?

LS: We shall see. I am going to identify a number of themes that we can go into. It is possible that I may wish to steer you in one direction and you in another direction. One thing that I hope you will do is to let me know if I am going in a direction that you may not want to pursue.

PL: Ah, what a pity! Those might well turn out to be the juiciest parts.

LS: Best avoided. Could you tell us a bit about your family background?

PL: Permit me to go into my past in a roundabout way. A few years ago my wife and I went to Bombay, which is where I was born and grew up. One evening we were driving past the area where I had lived in a block of flats as a child. This was before we moved into the suburbs where my father had built a large two-storey family building. On an impulse I decided to show my wife the flat in which I had spent the craziest happiest carefree years of my childhood. All my happy memories of the eight years came flooding into my mind: my Indian and English friends, my Catholic and Muslim friends, my Parsi and Anglo-Indian friends with whom I played and quarrelled, the books and comics we exchanged, the school homework we all shared, the girls we teased and tried to fight over, the mischief we got into, etc. etc. So driven was I by the wild, uncontrollable impulse that I thought I would approach the present owners of the flat and buy it at whatever price they asked for. Had the owners been at home, I would, I must confess to my shame, made an offer to buy the flat—despite the fact I still have a flat of my own in our family building. Luckily for me, the owners were not at home and on our return to London, the impulse passed. I realized what an idiot I had been and sanity returned—but not unmixed with sweet nostalgia.

LS: Surely it was not the flat you wanted! The flat merely symbolized your desire to recapture your lost childhood.

PL: You're right. I realized that it is impossible and futile to try to recapture one's past.

LS: Would you have bought it if the opportunity had presented itself?

PL: Oh, without a doubt! There's no fool like an old fool. But I still dream of the flat and of the eight years I lived there. Once we moved away from the city centre into the suburbs, it wasn't the same. For a start I lost most of my friends, including the few English friends I had. They returned back home after Indian independence. Making new friends in the suburbs was difficult. We did not share common interests, and I pined for the happy life I had been robbed of by our move.

LS: Did you ever talk about your feelings with your parents, or with your brothers and sisters?

PL: Not at all. I was the youngest child in our family. My two brothers and my two sisters were much older than me by several years. I had no voice, if you see what I mean.

LS: In a sense therefore you were the only child.

PL: That's the reason why my friends mattered to me more than my family members. The fact that I came from a relatively orthodox Hindu background did not in anyway interfere with my Jesuit upbringing in school. (I am afraid I cannot boast of any stigmata.) At home, I participated in all the daily household prayers and rituals, including regular visits to temples, reading from the scriptures, and obedience and deference to one's elders at home and outside. The two lives, one at school and the one at home ran separately, and aroused no dissonance whatever. It was like living in two cultures simultaneously. I was what Alan Roland (1996) in his excellent thought-provoking book *Cultural pluralism and psychoanalysis*, refers to as a bicultural person.

My father was a very successful self-made businessman, with little formal education. And as is often the case with such persons, money was the measure of man. He was unwilling to send me to university, his argument being, that he had never been to university himself and yet had succeeded in becoming an extremely wealthy person. He was keen for me to join him in his business and not waste my time in getting a degree.

LS: So what did you do?

PL: I rebelled.

LS: The usual conflict, I guess—sulking, shouting, screaming, going off food—a conflict played out in thousands of families, in thousands of homes the world over. How was it resolved?

PL: He packed me off to Hong Kong to work as a salesman in a department store.

LS: Did you enjoy it?

PL: Yes and no. Although I missed them initially it was nice being away from the family. Hong Kong was a stunning city. Still is. There I had my first taste of freedom—and I can tell you *it was intoxicating*! I found the job very tedious and even soul-destroying. What also got me down was working with colleagues who were even less educated than I. They could barely speak English.

LS: And then?

PL: What changed my life was my friendship with a navigator who worked for Air India. He was a regular customer and came to Hong Kong twice a week. He once 'caught' me reading a book in the store, which we were not allowed to do and when he saw that I was reading Homer, he could hardly believe his eyes. He suggested that I should give up my job, return to India and do a degree or two—and not waste my life working in a department store.

I took his advice. I returned to India much to my father's annoyance. But working in Hong Kong for a year or so had 'distanced' me from my father and mother. By sending me away they had planted in me the roots of genuine independence in me. I was no longer frightened of them. He might even have thrown me out of the house but for the fact, that unbeknown to me, I had contracted intestinal tuberculosis during my stay in Hong Kong. A couple of operations later he relented; an uneasy truce prevailed between father and son. I joined the University of Bombay, completed my Bachelor's degree in psychology and then the Master's degree in which I was lucky enough to obtain a First. As a result, I was offered a job at the University of Bombay. That's how it all started.

LS: Why did you decide to come to England?

PL: For three reasons. I had started to work on a research degree in Bombay, but it wasn't going too well. It was an experimental study on the problems of sensory interaction. It was an interesting problem in psychophysics, concerning visual and auditory thresholds—revival of the old Weber-Fechner Laws of sensory perception. But as I had no basic grounding in physics, I abandoned the study. I was floundering. I felt I had fallen out of favour with my Professor, who was also the Head of the Department. Second, I was acutely aware that on a Lecturer's salary I would never be able to maintain the kind of lifestyle that I had become accustomed to, based on my father's wealth. I did not wish to remain beholden to my father and wanted to make my own way—materially and professionally—in my life.

LS: Was it a question of not wanting to remain beholden or was it a question of challenge—throwing down the gauntlet?

PL: Lana, you have the most wonderful talent for seeing through my rationalizations. You're right. It was perhaps, the latter.

LS: And what was the third reason?

PL: I learnt that as a non-Brahmin, I wouldn't stand much of a chance of being offered Chair. In those days, the academic profession was virtually the sole preserve of Brahmins.

LS: I imagine the situation has changed since then.

PL: The 'Mills of God....' My Professor suggested that I had five choices: I could go to Australia, Canada, America, or to England. The fifth choice was to stick around in Bombay and hope for the best.

LS: Why did you decide to come to England and not America or Canada?

PL: Perhaps it was the colonial mentality that I had unconsciously acquired. As a child I was educated in a Jesuit school. I was brought up virtually on the same books that were also prescribed to English children in England. I was also passionately fond of cricket, which I knew I would be able to play in England. At that stage in my academic career I was also fascinated by Professor Hans Eysenck's work in the field of personality, statistics and psychotherapy. I had read several of his books and I kept wondering if I would one day get to meet the great man himself and even do a Ph.D. under his supervision. London seemed a good choice. And that is where I came: A Passage to England.

LS: A reversal of Forster's *A Passage to India.*

PL: Yes.

LS: What got you interested in cross-cultural psychology? Was it before you came to England?

PL: India itself as you know, is a multi-cultural country. There are over 40 different languages and over a thousand dialects spoken in India. To this you must add different religious groups: Hindus, Muslims, Buddhists, Parsis, Sikhs, Ba'hais, Catholics, non-worshippers; and within each group are several denominations, several splinter groups. It is best therefore to refer to India as a multi-cultural, multi-faith country, rather than a country with a predominantly Hindu population—although statistically that is true. The variations in terms of food, eating habits, living conditions, climate, skin colour, levels of education and affluence, etc., point to an almost irreconcilable heterogeneity. Surprising as this may sound, one notices astonishing homogeneity in terms of beliefs, value-systems, child-rearing practices and the extended family structures. That is what brings India together.

It is best to see India as a bundle of contradictions—even conundrums. My initial 'training' so to speak in cultural diversity started in India. My professional interest in cultural differences, and diversity started as soon as I came to England.

LS: Could you tell us a little about what the immigration experience was like then and perhaps you could reflect on how this experience influenced your early thinking and your early work in the field of cross-cultural psychology?

PL: The main problem I experienced was trying to keep my identity intact. I imagine within me, there resides, an indefinable 'Indian-ness'—the turtle shell. I can neither discard it nor, for that matter would I like to! It is difficult if not impossible to relinquish one's identity that one has developed over the years and acquire a new one. One can chisel out a few cosmetic changes in one's psyche—just as it has become fashionable to do so with one's body. But one cannot re-forge an entirely different persona! One attempts to do that at one's own peril. But I have learned to play the '*game*'—with its own, idiosyncratic rules—of living in two cultures or two worlds without consciously tilting the balance either into one or the other, though the switch is not always easy, and at times even painful. Juggling with two personas can lead to variety of existential and dare I say, schizophrenic dilemmas. Luckily, in my own case the divergent strands within my own psyche have cohered which has enabled me to form an acceptable bicultural personality. Like a chameleon, I am able to switch my persona from being 'Indian-Indian' to 'Indian-English' and when in India, to English-Indian or (recycled) Indian-Indian. Perhaps my Jesuit education, combined with my Hindu upbringing, and the diverse cross-cultural inputs during my childhood have gradually instilled in me a set of qualities, which have made it possible for me to live in two worlds with less discomfort than I might otherwise have experienced.

LS: But surely, no one can be entirely free from such conflicts!

PL: You're right. One can but try.

LS: You have commented a number of times that it was a bit of a shock experience for you culturally in that many of your colleagues were never really interested in your culture, your values or your philosophy.

PL: That's right.

LS: Why do you think that was the case?

PL: I have thought about that a great deal. I can only speculate. (*a*) They may have found in me an awkward person to deal with because of my openness. (*b*) They may feel very secure within their own culture and among their own friends, sharing their own life style that the thought of trying to understand and befriend a person from another culture may not even occur to them. (*c*) There could be faint traces of an inherited imperialist past left over within their own psyche. (*d*) To understand persons from other cultures requires a genuine willingness to make the effort; also emotional sensitivity, empathy, and even a genuine desire to learn from them.

LS: When you came to England how did you retain your own cultural values and what aspects of traditional Eastern culture do you retain now? How did you cope?

PL: Initially I could not cope with the English way of life: their ability to communicate in understatements, their unwillingness or inability to express their feelings and emotions with the effortless ease with which we do. Without sounding unkind I referred to the English as being 'emotionally constipated'. They soon returned the compliment by referring to Indians as suffering from emotional diarrhoea. This initial inability to communicate openly made me assert my 'Indian-ness' with exaggerated ferocity. I coped by ignoring them and by building a wall of defence around me. But over the years I have acquired a few good, trusted, genuine friends. They matter.

LS: Let me now turn to the present. Many therapists normally begin a session by asking what it is that brings us here today. We are here today to honour you and the work that you have accomplished in a lifetime. So let me start by asking you what you think it is that brings you here today? What would you reflect on as the biggest contributions that you have made?

PL: I find this question difficult to answer. I do not believe that I have made any momentous contributions in the field of counselling, psychotherapy or cross-cultural psychology. In fact, when Dr Moodley suggested that your department was considering nominating me for the Lifetime Achievement Award, I couldn't believe it! Like a man pleading his innocence I kept asking myself 'Why me? God, what have I done to deserve this? I'm innocent!'

LS: Why did you feel that way?

PL: The truth is that I have never had any great faith in my own abilities. I have always wondered why anyone in his or her right senses would want to read what I write.

LS: Why do you say that?

PL: Perhaps you might be able to trace the reasons of my lack of confidence in my childhood experiences, which I have discussed with you in some detail. All I can say is that I enjoy writing and I get great kick out of seeing my writing in print. But that is all.

LS: Okay, let me push you a little further on that. You have a very large body of work and today you talked about the culmination of some of your ideas. Your talk today for instance combines many things that you have written about over the years. You have the art of constructing a tapestry into which are woven threads of philosophy, psychology, counselling, psychotherapy, not to mention epistemology and a generous sprinkling of humour. What would you reflect on as some of your major contributions?

PL: My main aim is to create an intellectual platform from which people can discuss and critically examine ideas related to different cultures and different ways of construing the world. I think privately we all have our own culturally embedded and idiosyncratic ways of understanding the world in which we live. Very few of us have the ability to step out of our own world and construe the world from another person's perspective. It is a miracle that we actually manage to understand another person—even when the person comes from our own culture, speaks the same language, and so on.

LS: Do you really believe that?

PL: I know it sounds cynical but I do. Let me give you an example. Ludwig Wittgenstein and Sir Karl Popper, as we all know are the most renowned philosophers of the 20th century. They both came from Austria; both came from highly educated and cultured families; both spoke the same language, ate similar kinds of foods, worshipped the same gods, and experienced the same fate of persecution at the hands of the Nazis, and so on.

The story goes something like this. In 1946, Popper was invited to give a lecture at the Cambridge Moral Science Club, to which several eminent philosophers, including Bertrand Russell and Wittgenstein were invited. At some point Wittgenstein got into an uncontrollable rage, picked up a poker and but for Bertrand Russell's swift intervention would have smashed it on Popper's head. The moral of the story is that if two geniuses are unable or unwilling to understand each other, what chance do we lesser mortals have at understanding one another?

LS: Would Wittgenstein have really hit Popper with the poker?

PL: Certainly! One could hardly call philosophy an ivory-tower armchair profession!

LS: Good God!

PL: But mind you, years later Popper got his own sweet revenge. He almost single-handedly demolished the philosophy of logical positivism and with it the famous Vienna Circle, which had as its members some of the world's greatest mathematicians, logicians, scientists and philosophers, including people such as Rudolf Carnap, Kurt Godel, A. J. Ayer, Alfred Tarski, Bertrand Russell and several others.

LS: From what you've just said I get the impression that we rarely understand people—not just from other cultures but from within our own cultural backgrounds as well. It seems we make up our minds and start looking for confirmations or disconfirmations of our pre-formed judgements.

PL: Which are thinly disguised stereotypes. The object is to transcend the stereotypes, suspend our judgements and acquire the patience and the humility to see the world from the other person's perspective.

LS: But is it possible to acquire that kind of understanding?

PL: If people are genuinely willing to try. Mind you, we may not achieve the sensitivity and the ability of Dostoevsky, or, Tolstoy or Shakespeare, or Sophocles, but we can certainly give it a damn good try. The need to understand *ought* to be our primary concern. What we decide to do with that understanding is a different matter altogether.

LS: I know you have already articulated the major differences between Western and Eastern cultures in your morning's paper. I would like to know if there is one significant factor, which you believe separates Eastern cultures from Western cultures.

PL: In my paper I discussed the four factors, which represent Eastern cultures and the contrasting four, which represent Western cultures. The ones that can be singled out are what I have referred to as 'spiritualism and materialism'. These to me are perhaps the most important distinguishing factors.

LS: Can you elaborate on that?

PL: The main conflict lies between faith and reason. I would submit that no man lives by reason alone. I would even go further and say that a large number of our beliefs that we live by are untested and unverified. If they were to be put to a critical test they would turn out to be non-rational, even irrational. But a belief in rationality is a comforting self-delusion that Westerners have turned into a fine art. Westerners appear to have put all their *faith* in reason. This is not to suggest that there are no other areas of conflict, but the one concerning their emphasis on rationality is significant to what I have been discussing.

LS: And Easterners?

PL: They appear to have relinquished reason to *faith*. I am not trying to decry the value of rationalism in human affairs. All the major philosophers in the world from the pre-Socratic right up to the present have extolled the virtues of human reason and rationalism. But there is a problem with rationalism... If rationalism is the dominant unifying philosophy in the Western world, it would be difficult—even impossible to explain behaviours such as violence, crime, murder, child abuse, suicide, mental illness, depression, alcoholism, drug addiction, obesity, sorrow, and several other ills which plague Western society. Surely rationality ought to be able to combat these destructive forces in their societies. Faith in rationality has become a meaningless *mantra*; its continued recitation is perhaps aimed at convincing Westerners themselves that their approach to life is far superior to those of people of non-Western cultures.

LS: So you think faith is more desirable than reason?

PL: No, I am not saying that. Faith and reason, like *dava* (medicine) and *dooa* (prayer) need to go together. Reason without faith can be potentially dangerous. And faith without reason can be blind. They are the two sides of the coin of life. There is great power in faith, just as there is in reason. Reason may solve problems but faith can move mountains. For instance the entire structure of Hindu belief systems is founded on the Law of Karma. And the Law of Karma is sustained by faith.

LS: You write about how important the role of karma and the caste system is in the lives of Indians and people of other Eastern cultures. Do you personally believe in the Law of Karma?

PL: My beliefs are neither here nor there. What needs to be borne in mind is this: it is a wonderfully formulated law. It offers an elegant and faultless and a complete explanation of the major concerns of humanity: life and death, birth and rebirth, sin and redemption, sickness and health, wealth and poverty, goodness and evil, and so on. It would be difficult to understand the Hindu psyche without taking into consideration the impact which the law of karma has on Hindus.

So, you see, whether I believe in it or not is of no account—although personally, I question its validity—particularly the one related to the cycle of birth and rebirth. For no one really knows what happens after death. And I am wary of speculating on questions to which there are as yet no definite answers. I don't know anyone here who can offer evidence that there is life after death.

LS: I wonder if that view really epitomises Eastern cultures. I wonder if it is more accurate to say that you speak of 'the' Indian culture and not 'the' Eastern culture. Has anyone commented about this?

PL: When I talk about Eastern culture I refer mainly to Indian culture. But since the similarities between Indian culture and other Eastern cultures are greater than the differences, it might seem appropriate to refer to them as Eastern cultures—although the law of karma does not figure in other religions.

LS: Let us now turn to psychotherapy and counselling—another major thread in your work. You have written extensively on critiquing counselling and psychotherapy on a number of levels, one being the hegemony of Western models of psychotherapy that require a lot of challenging and discussion. You have also raised a number of provocative ideas, some of which we can read a lot about and some, which you have articulated today. One that I think is very interesting is the issue of therapists raising moral issues and looking at the moral dilemmas underlying the distress of clients. I wonder if you have written about gender relations, violence, etc. What kind of moral imperatives would we have with our clients?

PL: I have not thought about these issues because for the present I am trying to clear the basic conceptual and philosophical issues. I am hoping that if I live long enough—hopefully another year or two—I might be able to spend some time looking at the issue of violence.

LS: So if I ask you to speculate on how we would raise this moral issue therapeutically, for example the issue of domestic violence, could you do that?

PL: I am working on a particular model at present. I call it *Moral-Dialectical Therapy*. I strongly believe that we, as responsible people, need to take moral issues—not only our own but more importantly those of our clients into very serious account. I feel it my duty to discuss the moral issues with our clients. We need to give the client an opportunity to think about them and discuss them in subsequent sessions. I believe that Socrates was right in arguing that most, if not all, human problems have an underlying moral base. Socrates adopted a dialectical approach to understanding wisdom. My approach is dialectical in terms of moral issues. Thus, I never hesitated to raise a moral problem with my clients.

LS: Does that imply that there is no moral relativism?

PL: No I am not saying that. I think this an issue on which I have no firm answers and I don't know of any philosopher with a firm answer in terms of morality being universal or morality being relativistic, morality being God-given, or morality being secular.

LS: So would you have any guidelines for how we should practice? You have talked about pseudo-therapies and you have talked about critiques of our Western modalities and their philosophical basis. You have also talked about culturally sensitive, multicultural therapies but have you been able to give us any guides in how to practice those?

PL: The Western approach to counselling and psychotherapy tends to operate on a horizontal model, which suggests that the client and therapist relate to one another on terms of *equality*. In Indian thinking, however, it is the other way around. Indian psychotherapeutic relationships operate on a model of verticality, where the therapist is seen as a guide, a guru, or even a demigod. The approach to therapy tends more to be didactic. The therapist leads and the client follows. Obviously it is not as clear-cut as that, but that is the general trend.

LS: You have also commented on the need for good and proper training for psychotherapists but at the same time we do not really have modalities or techniques, which you feel are valid. So how do we construct training models?

PL: This is a very, very important issue and I feel strongly about this. My own feeling is that there ought to be a greater concern among Western counsellors and therapists to understand the attitudes, beliefs and values of their clients from non-Western cultures. In other words, what makes people from other cultures 'tick'. But that does not seem to be the case—as I see it. Western therapists in general tend to see their own world and the world of their client from a Western perspective. And this makes it very difficult for them to crawl into the skin of someone from another culture and study the person from *that* point of view. Such a situation often leads to an impasse.

LS: What then is the solution?

PL: I think that it is important if therapy across cultures is to work, Westerners must show the humility and willingness to study cultures and intimately—not superficially as appears to be the case. One does not need to trade in stereotypes, for they are counterproductive in the long run. One needs a deeper understanding. I am sure there are many trained people in America and in Canada who are very knowledgeable about their cultures. It is those people with whom one would need to learn from. Failure to do that will be divisive and will remain divisive.

LS: Knowledge of a culture and proper understanding of a culture, however, does not necessarily lead us to know how to work with the culture. Can you reflect on what happens once we have the knowledge and the deep understanding? Will the culture lead us to interventions and modalities, for example, in indigenous work or non-traditional therapies? Is that the route we should be looking at?

PL: I have not given a great deal of thought to that particular issue. It would be useful for therapists from different cultures to work in tandem with therapists from Western cultures. One needs the willingness and the humility to learn from each other's cultures.

LS: So in your view, therapy is not just a Western concept?

PL: To help people in distress is a universal problem. And if helping people is to be labelled as therapy, then therapy is a universal concept.

LS: So we have things to learn from non-Western therapies?

PL: Just as the non-Westerners would have to learn from Western therapies.

LS: Would you say that what you have described now would be your current thinking about culturally sensitive therapies?

PL: Yes.

LS: If I could step back a few questions and follow up. What would you see the role of therapist advocacy and activism to be? Does the therapist have a role outside of the therapy?

PL: Do you mean professional role?

LS: Yes an advocacy role.

PL: Can you explain that?

LS: For the therapist working in areas of violence and gender relations and sexual abuse, for example. Many therapists take on larger roles in the fight against abuse. Do you have any views on this? Should therapists expand their work beyond the therapy room?

PL: I would not wish to legislate on that issue. It would depend on the individual competence of the therapist. But if a therapist wants to circumscribe the area of his/her work then I think it is best left there. If there was a violent incident with my client, …

LS: And would you have any view on the need for therapists to have therapy?

PL: I think Alan Roland is best qualified to say that; he is a psychoanalyst. And psychoanalysts do not become psychoanalysts without going into psychoanalysis themselves. To answer your question, I believe that some form of therapy would be of benefit.

LS: We are now coming to the end of our interview. Is there anything else you can reflect on to help us understand your journey here?

PL: By here, you mean?

LS: Here means now and at the time of receiving your Lifetime Achievement Award.

PL: Well as I said, I am still surprised, overwhelmed and humbled by the honour and the generosity of the award, which the University of Toronto has decided to confer upon me. I shall treasure this occasion for the rest of my days. I am glad I came to Canada, much against my doctors' orders in London and much to the distress and anxiety of my wife. As you know, my condition is very critical and it was touch and go as to whether I would make the journey to Toronto. I am here and hopefully I will make it back to London. It has been a great pleasure and great honour to be with you. I shall take away with me endless cherished memories.

LS: Thank you very much.

PL: Thank you for inviting me.

## REFERENCE

Roland, A. (1996). *Cultural pluralism and psychoanalysis: the Asian and North American experience.* New York: Routledge.

# PART TWO

# Playing Amongst the Pillars of East-West Psychology

# 5

# Cross-cultural Psychology: A Handmaiden to Mainstream Western Psychology

*Pittu Laungani*

## INTRODUCTION

**I** would like to start my paper on a personal note. I first went to England in the late-1960s. I was aware that psychology as an academic discipline was, to a very large extent, an American enterprise. I was aware too that, in terms of my own career prospects, I would have more opportunities and would stand a better chance of doing well in the US than in England. Yet I preferred England. There were at least three reasons why I elected to come to the United Kingdom.

### India's Historical Association with Britain

It might well be true that history, as Immanuel Kant pointed out, is nothing but a series of past mistakes. Be that as it may, one cannot deny the powerful influence and the impact which history in the broader sense of the term has on the shaping of one's personal, social and cultural psyche. Furthermore, as the Spanish philosopher George Santayana prophesized one cannot turn one's back on history; not to learn from one's past mistakes is to be condemned to repeating them.

Despite my love–hate relationship with Britain, England for me was the land of Shakespeare and Milton, Keats and Coleridge, Shelley and Wordsworth, Dickens and Austen, and all the other great writers on whom we were all weaned as children in school. (I confess to a Jesuit upbringing.) Then, as an undergraduate and postgraduate student, I was in awe of people such as Hume and Bacon, Mill and Russell, Darwin and Galton, and several others. Then, of course, came the stream of psychologists: McDougall, Spearman, Malinowski, Rivers, Bartlett, Freud (remember Freud spent the last few months of his life in England) and others, including Cyril Burt and Hans Eysenck, all of whom had a significant influence on my developing interests in psychology.

## The Playing Fields of Eton

If memory serves me right, it was Sir Arthur Wellesley who was reputed to have said that the wars of England are won on the playing fields of Eton. Taking this audacious remark further, it is hard to imagine any country where its people would devise a game that could be (and still is) played out in a leisurely manner over a period of five whole days, without it reaching a definite conclusion. Only the English had the time and the talent for inventing cricket! They were blessed with what Plato refers to as 'divine madness'. It is a game that the Americans find hard to understand and, therefore, difficult to come to terms with. Nor, I daresay, would they have the patience to endure such a leisurely game. But we excolonials, all around the world, were all socialized from an early age into playing cricket, and do rather well at it. Although this may sound like an exaggeration, I would like to believe that it was cricket that succeeded where other measures failed to unite the colonies into a Commonwealth.

## The New World

To me, America seemed like a bewildering new world. I was reasonably familiar with the works of many of the great American psychologists, ranging from William James and John Dewey, Titchner and Boring, Terman and Thurstone, Watson, Hull, Tolman and Skinner among many, many others. But my knowledge of America, its people and its culture was derived mainly from the great works of literature, drama, philosophy, poetry, and of course from Hollywood. Thus, I had paper knowledge and celluloid knowledge of the country, and although I admired them for their achievements and their technological conquest of the moon, I had no feelings of any real affinity with the United States. In India I had never met a single American in a face-to-face situation and besides, I knew not a soul in America. I felt intimidated by the idea of going to such a vast, vibrant, and varied country. One could easily lose one's way. What intimidated me further was the fact that I would be that much farther away from India, were I to have to return in an emergency or in a situation of personal or familial crisis.

## CULTURE SHOCK

My misplaced confidence notwithstanding, England, to me, came as a shock! I was bewildered by the English! There were as many accents there as there are dialects in India—or almost—each of them as though spoken in a different tongue, and a few even in forked tongues! It was difficult to distinguish between levity and seriousness, between jest and truth, between praise and censure, between affection and affectation, between acceptance and rejection. I found it exasperating not being able to read correctly their feelings and emotions when, on occasions, they chose to express them. In India I had been born into a particular caste and had learnt through childhood what was expected of me in a variety of social situations that involved a mingling of castes. But, with the English, it was difficult to place them in their appropriate class categories; the class divisions, it seemed to me, were blurred and not as clearly defined as the castes were (and to a large extent, still are) in India. I could not always work out what was expected of me in different situations and of different people. What distressed me even further was that hardly any of the English friends I made showed any curiosity concerning my own cultural origins and upbringing. They avoided personal exchanges as assiduously as an orthodox Brahmin might avoid an untouchable. Either they were too reticent to ask and find out, or they were totally uninterested. In my own state of paranoia, I chose to believe the latter. How, in the name of heaven, I kept asking myself in my increasing state of despair, will I ever begin to understand them and hopefully befriend a few of them?

Living in a foreign country, I soon realized, was like fighting a lone battle on several fronts: the weather, the climate, the preserved and processed food, the strange customs and conventions, the patterns of day-to-day life and, of course, the people. I committed unforgivable social blunders; I was guilty of all sorts of faux pas; I annoyed and exasperated people without meaning to. I asked questions which the English considered private, personal and sacrosanct. I volunteered information that they found difficult to handle. By the same token there were people who annoyed and even tormented me to such an extent that, in my state of anguish, I drove metaphorical stakes through their hearts! Although we spoke the same language, although we had past historical associations, although I had read the books that I had assumed they also would have read and although I dressed the way they did, I could tell that a vast ocean of differences separated me from them. (Interestingly enough, most of my fellow academics were almost entirely ignorant of both contemporary and classical Indian literature.) I felt alienated. I felt like Moses standing at the edge of the Red Sea. While the sea parted for Moses and his followers and they were able to cross to safety, I drowned and died a hundred deaths in the first waves of misunderstandings that engulfed me. I found that we were divided more by our differences than united by our similarities. Although Rudyard Kipling's observation that 'The East is East and the West is West and never the twain shall meet' was made almost a century ago, who would have imagined that his words were as appropriate then as they are today! Has anything changed over the years? Yes. Genuine intercultural understanding, which is painfully difficult and requires sustained and selfless effort, has given way to political correctness.

I soon began to realize that, in order to relate to the English and thus get on in a reasonable but superficial manner with them, it would be I who would be expected to make all the adjustments. Not they. In other words, I would have to learn to become assimilated into their culture—if I could get round to understanding it. I did not relish the idea of assimilation. Interestingly enough, the concept of assimilation, which had fallen into disrepute, is once again beginning to be debated in Britain and may soon reappear through the back door. If Parliament gets its way, foreigners with the right to live in Britain may be required to undertake an oath of allegiance to Britain. The naivety that unquestioning allegiance can be guaranteed by a signed document, the legality of which can be questioned by a 'tuppenny, hapenny' lawyer in a court of law, is beyond belief.

One might, in this context, recall the heart-rending moral crisis that E. M. Forster, the famous English novelist, was once tormented by, when he was asked what he would do if he had to choose between betraying a friend or betraying his country? At a personal level, I was totally opposed to the idea of learning to become like them—in speech patterns, in dress, in conversation, and all such characteristics that would have enabled me to be 'accepted' by them. I had no desire to become a metaphorical English clone. Even if I tried, I knew that I would only become a 2-dollar note—a counterfeit! I could not countenance such a move. For me, it would have meant a serious cultural compromise, an assault on my own notions of my 'self' and my 'identity', which I had developed, rightly or wrongly, over the years during the course of living in India. And, more importantly, such a compromise would have meant a sad loss of my own moral integrity.

It was then that it became clear to me that culture is an extremely complex and elusive concept (Berry et al., 1997). I also began to realize that most of our cross-cultural interactions—particularly when mutually unintelligible languages are involved in the interaction—are often based on superficial stereotypes, on inane smiles and meaningless but expansive gestures, on trite phrases, all of which lead nowhere. Moreover, such 'exchanges' may even succeed in compounding the misunderstandings and misperceptions. As soon as I saw my own life in cultural and historical terms, I became aware of the powerful influences that it had had on my growth and development, and on the way in which I saw myself and the world around me. Like the others, I too was handcuffed to my own culture by its past history. As I have stated elsewhere, we carry our culture as a tortoise with its shell. Destroy the shell and you destroy the tortoise (Palmer and Laungani, 1999). And that was how I got interested in cross-cultural psychology.

## MAINSTREAM WESTERN PSYCHOLOGY

Before we examine the issues related to cross-cultural psychology, we need to be clear about what is meant by mainstream Western psychology. In the later part of the 19th century, many psychologists were keen to free themselves from the abstract constraints of philosophy and turn psychology into a scientific discipline, which would have enormous practical applications (Boring, 1929/1950; Leahey, 1997). In addition to Darwin's monumental work on evolutionary theory, there were exciting discoveries being made in physiology, biology, statistics and neurophysiology. Psychologists in America and Britain, and to a certain extent in Europe, felt a compelling need to undertake precise, quantifiable, scientific research and, by so doing, hoped to discover laws of human behaviour that would have universal applicability and would be used in promoting human welfare (Miller, 1969). In their attempts to discover universal laws of human behaviour, every conceivable aspect of human behaviour—perception, cognition, motivation, intelligence, personality, memory, child-development, psychopathology, social behaviours, prejudice, diagnosis and treatment of mental disorders—was examined from a scientific perspective.

In their eagerness to turn psychology into a science, they espoused the natural science paradigm (Barnes, 1979; Laungani, 1996) and Western psychology came to be defined as the science of human and animal behaviour. The focus of psychology therefore was on two concepts: science and behaviour.

The natural science paradigm, they believed, would lead to a formulation of laws and discoveries that would apply not only to the American people but also to the rest of the world. Concepts such as purpose, consciousness, awareness, mind, self, identity, morality—concepts that give meaning and lend poignancy and substance to our lives—were seen as being redundant. They have long since been abandoned. They also dispensed with metaphysical abstractions, they jettisoned Freudian, Jungian and such other ideas; they discarded fundamental religious, existential, spiritual and such other human concerns from their scientific vocabularies. These terms were replaced by concepts such as positivism, operationism, empiricism, environmentalism, secularism, radicalism (a la Skinner), behaviourism, scientism and a few other isms, such as humanism, individualism and cognitivism. This is perhaps what tempted Sir Cyril Burt to comment that psychology at first bargained away its soul, it then lost all consciousness and awareness and, with the rise of behaviourism, it is in danger of losing its mind! There are three issues that are of concern to us here with regard to psychology's claim to be a science of behaviour.

First, in discarding all the metaphysical abstractions, they turned their backs on history. Turning one's back on history, as I mentioned earlier, is a potentially dangerous course of action. By denying and even denigrating the contributions of philosophy, religion, art, literature, all of which go toward constituting a culture, they created a psychology that, as ur-Rahman (1990) has eloquently argued, was sterile and fragmented. To a large extent, sterility replaced fecundity and triviality superseded profundity. Second, whether psychology can legitimately be called a science is in itself a debated issue. One should not be misled into believing that, just because there is a high degree of consensus among Western psychologists, psychology is a science. Consensus, as we know, is measure of reliability and not of validity. A thousand-year consensual belief in Ptolmey's geocentric model of the universe was struck a fatal blow by Galileo and was replaced by the heliocentric model of the universe.

The concern of Western psychologists that psychology is a study of behaviour—overt, observable, measurable, manipulatable, responsive behaviour—also raises very serious questions. It is extremely doubtful that the focus on overt, observable behaviour alone allows us to arrive at a comprehensive understanding of the human psyche. The human psyche consists of more than measurable behavioural responses. In Goethe's great epic, *Faust*, one might recall that Dr Faustus was prepared to barter away his soul to Mephistopheles for unparalleled knowledge. Although Faust's ethics were questionable, his aims were laudable and noble; there was in Dr Faustus an undeniable quality of greatness. But Western psychologists appear to have sold their souls for a far less worthy cause—for positivistic and 'scientific' psychology. Several eminent psychologists have rebelled against the very idea of a scientific psychology. Sigmund Koch, the great American psychologist, remarked that he would 'prefer a defective understanding of something of value over a safely defended description of something trite' (Robinson, 2001). William James, one of the greatest if not the greatest of the American psychologists, also refused to accept a psychology that won 'system' at the price of reality itself (Robinson, 2001).

Third, what is being argued here is this: the proper study of human beings and human nature would necessitate our having a wider, a more comprehensive view of what one means by humanity and what it means to be human. This involves our accepting the premise that we all live our lives at two inter-related levels—the outer level (that is the overt, behavioural level) and the inner level. In other words, there is the 'outer' self, or the social self, and the 'inner' self, or the private self. To concentrate on only the outer level—the social self—is to study human beings in one dimension, what Herbert Marcuse referred to as the 'One Dimensional Man'. It would therefore be essential to take the 'inner' person—the metaphysical and spiritual, the private and non-observable—and the 'outer' or 'observable' person as a whole and not separate them as appears to be the case at present. The two—the inner and the outer—are inextricably linked. To separate one's inner world from one's outer world is like trying to disentangle shadow from substance. Even the Neanderthal person, I daresay, must have had an inner life of some kind or other. Imagine a Neanderthal's first encounter with death. What did they make of death? Were they frightened? Were they wonder-struck? Were they in awe of what they had witnessed? Did they attempt to revive the dead? Did they mourn for the dead? Did they have any faint glimmerings of an 'afterlife'? Did they perform any rituals, ceremonies? Did they engage in any cannibalistic practices? Although we shall never know for certain, it makes sense to speculate on their inner speculations when confronted, for the first time in their lives, by the most extraordinary event.

However, all is not lost. Luckily, psychology has moved on, so to speak. Notwithstanding the 'die-hards', it is interesting to note that many of the metaphysical concepts that were sacrificed by the 'high priests' of psychology on the secular altar of scientific methodology are beginning to reappear through the back door, as it were, in the flourishing and exciting field of cognitive neuroscience. Psychology is beginning to turn full circle and has started to investigate the very topics that were abandoned in the earlier part of the 20th century—and with greater scientific rigour. The scientific rigour can be seen in the painstaking and meticulous attention that is paid to the design, construction and execution of complex multivariate research strategies, aided by statistical and mathematical models used in data analyses.

However, little attention has been paid to fundamental epistemological concerns. The importance of epistemological problems in any scientific research cannot be overstated. If one is genuinely concerned about 'discovering' objective 'truth', it is imperative that one takes on board the fundamental issues related to the philosophy of science. One therefore needs to be concerned with understanding the nature of science, the problems related to 'proof', 'falsification' and 'causality' (Popper, 1963, 1972), the nature of paradigms and paradigm shifts (Kuhn, 1996), the nature of 'progressive' and 'degenerative' research programmes (Lakatos, 1970), and, of course, the nature of 'truth' or objective knowledge. In undervaluing, if not ignoring, the fundamental epistemological problems related to the acquisition of objective knowledge, Western psychologists appear to have short-changed themselves in their eagerness to transform psychology into a science.

## THE IMPACT OF WESTERN PSYCHOLOGY ON CROSS-CULTURAL PSYCHOLOGY

To a large extent, the history of world psychology during the post-World War II era has been the history of American psychology. American psychology has continued to dominate world psychology. Such was the awesome power of

American psychology that, even during my own undergraduate and postgraduate days in India, we were fed and nourished on American psychology. This occurred despite the fact that many of the findings of American research lacked ecological validity, not just in non-Western cultures but, more importantly, even in their own culture. Admittedly, there were several powerful and vibrant European influences on the development of psychology that emerged from Germany, Austria, France, Switzerland, Britain and the Soviet Union. The spectacular contributions of the psychophysicists and the physiologists, the gestaltists and the genetic epistemologists, the neurologists and the biologists, the evolutionists and the Social Darwinists, the Freudians and the post-Freudians, instilled some doubts concerning the unchallenged superiority, if not hegemony of American psychology. But gradually the European influence on world psychology declined, partly because many of their writings were not translated and therefore not easily accessible, but largely because psychology in America outpaced growth in Germany (Leahey, 1997). Moreover, many of the European psychologists, in order to avoid Nazi persecution, emigrated to America where they lived and worked with their American colleagues in academic establishments, hospitals, psychiatric institutions, training centres, health clinics and such other places.

It seems reasonable to assume that all the European émigrés would have brought them not only their languages, their social patterns and family networks, their religious practices, but also their own cultural norms and values into which they had undoubtedly been socialized since childhood. It is strange and even bewildering that these salient features of their personal lives played—or seemed to have played—little part in their professional work in America! No doubt European psychology caused some minor twinges of conscience, but it did not create serious cognitive dissonance among the American psychologists. However, European psychology was soon assimilated into the mainstream of American psychology, which held total sway.

Yet the impression one gets is that Western psychologists tend to believe that the world is as they see it. They believe too that the rest of the people in the world also see the world as they see it—through Western spectacles. In other words, they were proposing what Berry et al. (1997) refer to as an absolutist position, which assumes that 'human phenomena are basically the same (qualitatively) in all cultures: honesty is honesty, and depression is depression, no matter where one observes it' (p. 1103).

What is it that they see? How do they construe the world? One might in this context refer to the famous account of Plato's cave. The prisoners described by Plato sit in the darkness of the cave with their backs to the entrance. The world they see is a world of flickering shadows. And thus, they mistake appearance for reality and shadows for substance. Western psychologists, in so far as their views of other cultures are concerned, have been like the chained prisoners in Plato's cave.

But doubts concerning the all-pervading power of American psychology began to spread among psychologists all around the world. They began to realize that many of the problems and issues that the Americans paid great attention to were of little or no concern to their own cultural needs. Yet for a while they retained a naive and trusting belief in the power of American psychology to solve most, if not all, human problems. Like the three wise men waiting to see the star of Bethlehem, they waited to see the peaceful solution of world human problems—thanks to the miracle of American psychology! But, unlike the wise men, they waited in vain. The expected miracle never occurred.

Doubts soon turned to disenchantment. They realized that the Americans themselves had not been able to put their own house in order. Human problems of the world remained unresolved. To a large extent they still are—mental illness, schizophrenia, depression, child maltreatment, international violence and aggression, terrorism, prejudice and xenophobia, to name but a few. To borrow the elegant title of a book edited by Crossman, American psychology was *The god that failed*.

## THE GROWTH AND DEVELOPMENT OF CROSS-CULTURAL PSYCHOLOGY

Cross-cultural psychology was just beginning to emerge as a fledgling discipline. Until about the late 1950s, psychologists, (including psychotherapists and counsellors) in Western countries, particularly in the United States and in Britain, remained 'culturally myopic'. Some, of course, were culture-blind. Cultural blindness, unlike colour blindness, is not a genetic abnormality. It is an inability, unwillingness, or failure on the part of an individual to recognize that some of the most obvious differences in beliefs, attitudes, values and behaviours among different groups of people are related to their own unique cultural backgrounds. If one is to make sense of their behaviours, their belief systems, the manner in which they perceive the world, one needs to take account of their cultural origins and the influence they have had on their growth and development. The acquired cultural blindness was due largely to the fact that Western psychologists in general and American psychologists in particular, either could not, did not or chose not to see the vital role that culture played in the development of the human psyche. I do not wish to convey the impression that the scientifically-'addicted' psychologists were totally naive about cultural issues; they were merely content to ignore them. The concept, culture, did not fit in with their vision of scientific psychology. The term, culture, was too complex and difficult to operationalize, viz., to define the concept in terms of measurable operations. Moreover, they failed to understand that the physicist Bridgman, who had first introduced the concept operationism, was himself wary of the concept. He believed that operationism, when pushed too far, results in scientific relativism. Since a concept was to be defined by the operations performed by the scientist, 'all science becomes my private science' (ur-Rahman, 1990: 55). They had inherited a legacy of 'scientism' from the 19th- and early 20th-century psychologists and, instead of shedding the legacy, which consisted of base metal, they endeavoured, like the alchemists of the past, to transmute it into gold.

What was even more astonishing was the arrogance displayed by some of the great anthropologists and psychologists of the past era, who condescended to study the lives of peoples of other cultures. Sir James Fraser (1954), who wrote the 12 volumes of the classic, *The golden bough*, which was a study in magic, superstitions, rites, rituals and religious practices across all societies in the world, boasted that he had never met nor indeed visited any of the lands of the people about whom he wrote (Beattie, 1964). It was around the 1960s that cross-cultural psychology, as Jahoda and Krewer (1997) point out, began to emerge as a distinct discipline. The 1960s witnessed an accelerated growth of cross-cultural psychology (Biesheuvel, 1969; Jahoda and Krewer, 1997). This was reflected in the growth of publication outlets and the creation of journals devoted especially to cross-cultural psychology. Prior to that, however, research in the field of cross-cultural psychology had been spasmodic.

In dribs and drabs, they turned away from the seeming enchantments of American psychology. Their salvation, as they saw it, lay in pursuing psychology from their own cultural standpoint. Durgan Sinha (1996) was the most outspoken champion, concerned with promoting indigenous psychology in India. He was convinced that Indians needed to break away from the stronghold of Western psychology. It was imperative that they started to examine psychological issues and problems, which reflected Indian perspectives and Indian themes. He was opposed to the idea of imitative and replicative studies of Western themes and problems, which were of little or no relevance to India. His sound and rational advice has not fallen upon deaf ears. What started as a trickle has already turned into a stream, and it will not be long before the tide turns, which when taken at its flood, will lead on to a new era in psychology. One can already see the mushrooming of several culturally diverse psychologies: cultural psychology, indigenous psychology and, of course, cross-cultural psychology, to name but a few. Whether the birth and development of such diverse psychologies will in any way diminish the stronghold that mainstream psychology exercises over world psychology remains a futuristic issue.

One laments the fact that psychologists from Western countries did not show a great deal of enthusiasm in venturing out of their own countries to test their theories in other parts of the world. This applies even more to Britain than to the United States. Since Britain had its colonies around the globe, it would have made cross-cultural research a viable and enterprising academic exercise. Exciting research opportunities went begging! Nonetheless, the early research created the groundwork for future developments. Although, in the last 40 years, cross-cultural psychology has 'come a long way' it still has not acquired the status of a separate discipline with its own epistemological, theoretical or content related features.

Cross-cultural psychology, as Brislin (1983) points out, is defined by its method. The emphasis has been, and continues to be, on the empirical testing of hypotheses, derived from mainstream psychological theories. Although cross-cultural psychologists are genuinely concerned about discovering behaviours that are 'universal' or culturally invariant and those that are influenced by factors within a given culture, strong emphasis is still paid to the methodology by which such discoveries can be made. Methodology, as one knows only too well, should serve the needs of theory. Not the other way round. To discuss the methodological issues related to cross-cultural psychology would require another paper. Suffice it to say that cross-cultural psychology has normally resorted to three standard methodological strategies:

## Constructing Taxonomies

To merely compile taxonomies that list differences and similarities between cultural groups may not help a great deal. Taxonomies, unless grounded in theory, tell us next to nothing about how such differences came into being and the impact of such differences on the beliefs, attitudes, values and behaviours of people of those cultures. Occasionally, however, taxonomies may lead to serendipitous 'discoveries', which might suggest a more profitable line of investigation.

## Using Psychometric Instruments

Similarly, to administer a battery of modified psychometric tests, originally constructed in America, to people of different cultures also tells us very little about genuine differences or similarities (Adair, 1973; Barber, 1976; Rosenthal and Rosnow, 1969). The use of psychometric tests has always posed serious theoretical and methodological problems. Psychometric tests are not constructed in a social vacuum; they reflect underlying values of the culture in which they are constructed, and in that sense, are cultural products. To use tests meaningfully in another culture, which in several ways may be completely different from the culture in which the tests were originally designed, may turn out to be a fruitless exercise for the simple reason that like is not being compared with like. This is not to suggest that psychometric tests cannot be modified and be made more relevant to the needs of the culture in which they are to be used; they can and often are. But problems remain. Yet the use of psychometric tests across cultures appears to be the standard methodological technique employed by cross-cultural psychologists (Laungani, 1996, 2001).

One of the main reasons for the continued use of psychometric tests in non-Western cultures, and particularly in India, is the sad fact that Indian psychologists find it easy to use these tests either in their original form or in translated versions on their research subjects. Consequently, it becomes easier for them to publish their research findings in Indian and other international journals. Quite often, the tests used are of little or no relevance to Indian conditions, themes, issues and problems. This kind of research by several Indian psychologists does not have a great deal to commend it: it is, to my mind, 'research for research's sake' and 'research for increasing one's publications'. As Kakar (1997) in another context reminds us, many Indian academics haven't quite succeeded in taking off the 'shackles' of the British Raj, to which they still appear to be chained!

### Experimental Studies

To replicate experiments done originally on American sophomores, on peoples of other cultures, who have never participated in a psychological experiment before and who have never been socialized into the rationale of a psychological experiment, may also turn out to be a fruitless exercise. The host of biases, ranging from demand characteristics and self-fulfilling prophecies to subject biases, may transform the experimental investigation into meaningless exercises (Rosenthal, 1976). In addition to the galaxy of biases that affect the validity of any experimental undertaking, there is also the unresolved issue concerning the relevance and the meaningfulness of experimental research in cross-cultural settings. Such an approach, although in keeping with the currently fashionable scientific methodology, in all likelihood leads to an epistemological cul-de-sac.

## CONCLUSION

I have now lived in England for more years of my life than I have in India. Although in the last 30 years or so I have been to America and Canada several times, I have never once regretted my initial decision to go to study, work, and live in England. I feel I have been fortunate enough to have imbibed and internalized the best of both worlds—the Western world and the Eastern world. Some of my outspoken friends have expressed the view that, in reality, I have imbibed the worst of both worlds. When I am in India, I am accused of being 'too English' (whatever that means) and in England, when the English can bring themselves to express an opinion—I am accused of being 'too Indian' (whatever that might mean). I am thus in a no-win situation.

This comment, trivial though it is, carries a powerful implication. It suggests that there exist not only several worlds in which we live but that different people construe their own worlds and the worlds of others differently. And within 'each world' there are different perceptions, different evaluations and different levels of understanding, which people bring to bear in their assessments. This raises a fundamental question, a question with which we are all concerned. What is a 'good' world? What constitutes a 'bad' world? Returning to Goethe's Faust for a moment, Faust exclaims that life on earth is hell. So does Schopenhauer, who states that 'this is the worst of all possible worlds'. Similar views have also been expressed by Voltaire, Nietzschze, Camus, Sartre and several other philosophers. Given the impossibility of choosing one's parents carefully (as Bertrand Russell, with an impish twinkle in his eye, was reputed to have advised those who wished to be 'happy'), one needs to start with what one is given, akin to being dealt a hand. Thus, the constraints exercised by one's genetic endowment, one's parentage, one's place of birth, one's culture, etc., need to be taken as given. Given these limitations, it becomes extremely difficult for psychology to predict how one will come to construe the world and the manner in which one will choose to live in it. And the fact that one's constructions and conceptions of the world are by no means static and keep changing makes such a prediction an impossible, if not a foolhardy, undertaking. (Yet Haley, working within the Newtonian research programme, was able to predict the return of what has come to be called Haley's comet with astonishing mathematical accuracy after a casual observation of the comet lasting no more than a few minutes!) It is clear, therefore, despite the valiant efforts of Western psychologists, with their emphasis on experimentation, testing, and the use of mathematical and statistical models to transform psychology into a science, that the major areas of human reality—consciousness, love, hate, greed, sorrow, to name but a few—cannot be convincingly investigated quantitatively. Quantitative models of mathematics and statistics, to a large extent, have enabled psychologists to acquire the 'trappings' of science; and like the prisoners in Plato's cave, they have accepted appearance for reality. In this context, it would be fitting to let Einstein (1954) have the last word: 'As far as the laws of mathematics refer to reality, they are not certain; and as far as they are certain, they do not refer to reality'.

## REFERENCES

Adair, J. (1973). *The human subject: The social psychology of the psychological experiment.* Boston: Little, Brown & Co.

Barber, T. X. (1976). *Pitfalls in human research: Ten pivotal points.* New York: Pergamon Press.

Barnes, J. A. (1979). *Who should know what? Social science, privacy and ethics.* New York: Cambridge University Press.

Beattie, J. (1964). *Other cultures: Aims, methods, achievements in social anthropology*. London: Routledge & Kegan Paul.

Berry, J. W., Poortinga, Y. H., Segall, M. H. and Dasen, P. R. (1997). *Cross-culture psychology: Research and applications*. New York: Cambridge University Press.

Biesheuvel, S. (Ed.) (1969). *Methods for the measurement of psychological performance*. International Biological Programme, No.10. Oxford: Blackwell Scientific Publications.

Boring, E. G. (1929/1950). *A history of experimental psychology*. New York: Appleton-Century-Crofts.

Brislin, R. W. (1983). Cross-cultural research in psychology. *Annual Review of Psychology, 34*, 363–400.

Einstein, A. (1954). *Ideas and opinions*. New York: The Modern Library.

Fraser, J. (1954). *The golden bough: A study in magic and religion*. London: Macmillan.

Jahoda, G. and Krewer, B. (1997). History of Cross-cultural Psychology and Cultural Psychology. In J.W. Berry, Y.H. Poortinga and J. Pandey (Eds), *Handbook of Cross-Cultural Psychology: Theory and Method*. Boston: Allyn & Bacon.

Kakar, S. (1997). Culture and psyche. Delhi: Oxford University Press.

Kuhn, T. S. (1996). The structure of scientific revolutions. Chicago: University of Chicago Press.

Lakatos, I. (1970). Falsification and the Methodology of Scientific Programmes. In I. Lakatos and A. Musgrave (Eds), *Criticism and the Growth of Knowledge*. London: Cambridge University Press.

Laungani, P. (1996). Cross-cultural investigations of stress: Conceptual and methodological considerations. *International Journal of Stress Management, 3*(1), 26–35.

———. (2001). Culture, cognition, and trauma: Crosscultural evaluations. In J. F. Schumaker and T. Ward (Eds), *Cultural cognition and psychopthology*. Westport, Conn: Praeger.

———. (in press). Measurement of stress: Conceptual, methodological and ethical problems. *International Journal of Health Promotion and Education*.

Leahey, T. H. (1997). *A history of psychology: Main currents in psychological thought*. New Jersey: Prentice Hall.

Miller, G. A. (1969). Psychology as a means of promoting human welfare. *American Psychologist, 24*, 1063–1075.

Palmer, S. and Laungani, P. (Eds) (1999). *Counselling in a multicultural society*. London: Sage Publications.

Popper, K. (1963). *Conjectures and refutations*. London: Routledge & Kegan Paul.

Popper, K. (1972). *Objective knowledge: An evolutionary approach*. Oxford: The Clarendon Press.

Robinson, D. N. (2001). Sigmund Koch—Philosophically speaking. *American Psychologist, 56*(5), 420–434.

Rosenthal, R. (1976). Experimenter effects in behavioral research. *Journal of Personality and Social Psychology, 34*, 966–977.

Rosenthal, R. and Rosnow, R. L. (Eds) (1969). *Artifact in behavioural research*. New York: Academic Press.

Sinha, D. (1993). Indigenization of psychology in India and its relevance. In U. Kim and J. W. Berry (Eds), *Indigenous psychologies: Research and experience in cultural context*, Thousand Oaks, CA: Sage Publications.

ur-Rahman, M. (1990). The Psychological Quest: From Socrates to Freud. Ontario, Canada: Captus University Publications.

# 6

# Unresolved Issues in Philosophy and Psychology: Implications for Therapy

*Pittu Laungani*

## INTRODUCTION

**Let** us start by examining the relationship between certain areas of philosophy and mainstream Western psychology. Psychology, as someone had remarked, has a short past but a long history, which can be traced to the early writings and speculations of the ancient Greek philosophers from the 6th century BCE. Philosophy, as Bertrand Russell (1946/1961) points out began with Thales who concerned himself with a variety of questions, including those related to the nature of human nature. Philosophy was seen as the prime discipline or the parent subject of all disciplines (Kenny, 1994; Leahey, 1997; Magee, 1998; Russell, 1946/1961). Virtually, all the contemporary scientific disciplines including physics, astronomy, chemistry, biology, genetics, physiology, medicine, neurology and mathematics grew out of or sprang from philosophy, or 'physical philosophy', as the scientific disciplines were then described. In breaking away, the diverse disciplines developed their own conceptual frameworks, their own research methodologies, and of course their epistemologies.

For over 2000 years psychology remained an integral part of philosophy. The ancient philosophers of Greece, Italy and Egypt from around the 7th century BC onwards, raised the perennial questions concerning the nature of nature, the nature of human nature, the mind, the soul, purpose, will, freedom, determinism, beliefs, values, happiness, hope, sorrow, despair, good, bad, moral, immoral, sin, virtue, beauty, ugliness, health, illness, life and death, and of course the nature of the human soul. There was not a psychological concept, which they did not consider and attempt to find answers to through reflection and argument. Their thinking was also influenced by their religious mythology, which played a significant role in their day-to-day lives (Kirk, 1974; Onians, 1951; Snell, 1960). Gradually, the theocentric models gave way to non-theistic and rational considerations in their quest for answers to cosmological and human problems. The Greeks laid the intellectual foundations on which future ideas and theories were constructed. It is fascinating to note that most of the issues of concern to ancient philosophers are as relevant today as they were in the past. For instance, issues related to the composition of matter, the nature of change and permanence, the relationship between mind (soul) and body, are debated as vigorously today as they were in the past. In the past, however, they were seen as the preserve of philosophy.

Until around the mid-19th century, psychology was seen as an integral part of philosophy. The two coexisted in reasonable harmony. It was only in the latter part of the 19th century that several psychologists in America and in Europe began to question what they felt were the 'constraints of philosophy' upon their fledgling discipline and started to consider the possibility of transforming psychology into a scientific discipline, thereby freeing it from the all-embracing influence of philosophy. The founding father of scientific psychology was Wilhelm Wundt who founded the first psychological laboratory at the University of Leipzig, in 1879. This stands out as an important landmark in the history of psychology. It was Wundt, a physician–philosopher who established psychology as an academic discipline (Boring, 1957). Thus was scientific psychology born, not as a 'pure' discipline but as philosophy garnished with physiology. It is interesting to note that Wundt held a chair in Philosophy and not in Psychology. Wundt defined psychology as the study of the mind and the role of the psychologist was to search for the laws that governed it. He firmly believed that the mind could be brought under the orbit of natural science, by the experimental method. Wundt's pioneering contributions to the growth and development of psychology have been of great historical significance. But the greatest thrust for the development of psychology (and other disciplines) came from two Victorian cousins: Sir Francis Galton and Charles Darwin. Galton's studies on the influence of hereditary factors on intelligence and Darwin's monumental work on evolutionary theory completely transformed human thinking the world over.

But it was not until the early part of 20th century that psychology began to be recognized as an independent academic discipline in Europe and in America. By then several competing 'schools' of psychology had developed in Europe and in America, including the Wurzburg, the structuralists, the psychophysicists, the Berlin school of gestalt psychology, the psychoanalytical, the functionalists, the pragmatists, the behaviourists and the radical behaviourist school of Skinner.

With the exception of one or two schools, which eschewed experimentation the rest espoused the natural science model and adopted an experimental approach in their research endeavours. Given the high status of science and the awe which science—not to mention the scientist—inspires, psychologists were keen to free themselves from the abstractions of philosophy to which they felt they had been shackled, and turn psychology into an independent scientific discipline (Boring, 1929/1950; Leahey, 1997; Nagel, 1965). They believed that it was only through the proper *scientific* study that they could hope to make the kinds of exciting discoveries that were being made in physics, biology, physiology, statistics, and neurophysiology and in evolutionary theory, to name but a few. Klineberg (1965) went as far as to suggest that the 'divorce (or emancipation) of psychology from philosophy has been accomplished…with relatively friendly feelings on both sides' (p. 114). But had it, really? For in the very next breath he pointed out that psychology owed a debt to philosophy, in the sense that many of the classical problems which were and still are of great concern to philosophers are of equal concern to psychologists. He warned that one should not ignore the contributions of philosophy. His warnings went unheeded.

It was not long before every conceivable area of human behaviour—perception, cognition, motivation, intelligence, personality, memory, child-development psychopathology, social behaviours, prejudice, diagnosis and treatment of mental disorders—was examined from a scientific perspective. Western psychology came to be defined as the science of human and animal behaviour. The emphasis was on the study of overt, observable, measurable behaviours. John B. Watson the founder of modern behaviourism was critical, if not scathing of concepts such as introspection, unconsciousness, mind, and all those, which could not be observed. Although he conceded that people displayed anxiety, depression, joy, happiness, etc., all these concepts acquired meaning only when one was able to observe their precise behavioural correlates. If not, they were best discarded. It was this form of ill-conceived reasoning that may perhaps have prompted Sir Cyril Burt to state that at first psychology lost its soul, it then bargained away its consciousness, and was now in danger of losing its mind! A compelling need drove psychologists to undertake precise, quantifiable, scientific research, in the hope of discovering immutable laws of human behaviour, which would have universal applicability and would be used in promoting human welfare (Miller, 1969). These grandiose claims were based on their unswerving faith in the ability of science, and in particular, the science of psychology to solve all human problems.

As though in keeping with Miller's hyped dream, the 1970s and the 1980s witnessed a significant change in the United States—a large number of psychologists, for a variety of reasons (it would require a separate paper to examine the reasons) opted out of academia and began to choose specialities outside their old core areas of experimental psychology. They moved into the major applied areas of human concern such as health, stress, trauma, counselling, psychotherapy, clinical psychology, child development, self-realization, advertising, marketing, motivation and management, among others. Many of them entered into private practice and consultancy. Others attempted to promote self-help groups, do-it-yourself groups, encounter groups, ran workshops of a similar nature, produced manuals ranging from training in positive growth and health, to creating a 'feel good' factor among individuals in search of a *personalized* existential meaning in their lives (Zilbergeld, 1983).

Psychology went public. Leahey (1997) argues, that as a result of the erosion of religious and metaphysical traditions people turned to science for moral and spiritual guidance, and this 'led them, inevitably, to [popular] psychology, the science of individual action' (Leahey, 1997: 471). Popular psychology, as though waiting in the wings rushed in, offering itself as an irresistible dish to people living in secular, 'godless' societies.

Not surprisingly, a variety of popular 'theories' took seed and sprouted like wild and colourful mushrooms on the hillside. The 'theories' of psychologists who had 'gone public' bore little resemblance to the theories and the research enterprises generated within the walls of academia. The former were seen as being pseudo-scientific and the latter as scientific. Scientific psychology, to a large extent came to be defined by its methodology, and not necessarily by its conceptual framework—a framework from which hypotheses could be deduced and tested empirically with the use of the most sophisticated methodological instruments. Methodology, however sophisticated and robust, needs to *follow* from a conceptual framework and not *precede* it (Gower, 1997). This factor was not given its due consideration. In their over-concern with methodology, they paid less attention to formulating clear, testable conceptual frameworks. This is not to suggest that blind empiricism guided their investigations. Blind empiricism, regardless of how accurately and perfectly the accumulated facts and data may have been gathered, does not lead to objective scientific knowledge. The telephone directory is an empirically gathered factual, precise document. It offers the most precise information; but such an investigation can hardly be said to be scientific. So is a railway timetable. There are several areas of empirical investigation, which lie completely outside the realms of science (Gjertsen, 1989). Empiricism alone is not enough. As Popper (1963) argues, empirical investigations in the absence of clearly formulated theoretical constructs need to be tempered with intuitions, hunches, guesses and conjectures, which may subsequently help in formulating a more rigorous theory. (One of the greatest moments in my own academic career was a 15 minute meeting I had with the great Jean Piaget, in Geneva, several years ago. In listening to the great man extolling the virtues of genetic epistemology, it became clear that his conceptual frameworks related to the stages of child development, were not, as is believed by many, a product of his 'experimental' studies on his children, but were based on his initial intuitive hunches and observations, which he 'tried out' on his children. There was, he explained, an interactive—or dialectical—process between theory construction and theory testing. And it was through this interactive process he argued, that one occasionally found one's way into exciting 'discoveries'.)

But one can never be *certain of the nature of the relationships* between the variables tested and the responses obtained. Even if such relationships were to be obtained repeatedly one would be unable to construct a general theory on this basis.

There are two reasons for this: First, as David Hume the great Scottish philosopher pointed out that even an unequivocal verification of a given hypotheses does not allow one to go 'beyond' the finding and make statements of a general nature. One can never be certain that (a) leads to (b), or that (b) follows from (a). All one has established is an observed relationship between (a) and (b), and not that (b) is caused by (a). Equally importantly, there is no guarantee that the same finding would be replicated on subsequent occasions, *ad infinitum*. To expect that is to expect a continuity of consistency—that tomorrow will be an exact replication of today, and today is the same as yesterday. There are no logical grounds for making such a prediction. Such an expectation or prediction leads us into an inductive trap, which David Hume drew the world's attention to. There appears to be no way of getting out of the inductive fallacy. Bertrand Russell in his book *The problems of philosophy* (1912), defends induction, but he does so by shifting from the high-ground of timeless certainty to the low-ground of probability, e.g., it is highly probable that the sun will rise tomorrow, but it is by no means *certain* that the sun will rise tomorrow. Several unknown factors could intervene, a hurtling meteor, which could upset the operation of the laws of motion.

Second, one needs to bear in mind that logically the same finding or prediction could have been explained by another hypothesis or sets of hypotheses. Logically, there may be an infinite number of hypotheses, which could explain the prediction. One might argue that the practice of Indian forms of meditation 'lead to' beneficial consequences—lowering of one's blood pressure, a slow down of one's heart rate, feelings of well-being, tranquillity, etc. However, similar responses can also be obtained by other variables. There is also a reverse feature to this side to this argument. Instead of obtaining the expected or predicted relationship one may actually obtain an *unpredicted*, or, *unintended* relationship: a meditating person may experience a fear, claustrophobia, boredom, aches and pains, etc.

It is clear therefore that all methodologies—from the crudest, involving a simple head-count to the most sophisticated, viz., the use of advanced measuring instruments, currently used in experimental research need to assume a conceptual framework of some kind or other. One needs to ensure that one does not construct complex methodological systems without having some awareness of the reasons underlying their usage and their feasibility.

Scientific research does not occur in a social and cultural vacuum. The dominant values prevailing in a culture have a bearing not only on the kind of research that is undertaken, the problems that are investigated, the manner in which it is undertaken but also the appropriateness of the research enterprise. The investigator is part of the historical and social context in which s/he works. Contemporary research in psychology therefore needs to be understood from within the framework of the dominant values prevalent in Western societies, such as individualism, secularism, environmentalism, liberalism, capitalism, the recognition and defence of human rights, the rule of law, political correctness, etc. All these dominant values define and establish limits as to what shall (or shall not) be investigated on whom, how, when, and under what conditions. For instance, the construction of an intelligence test needs to be seen within the context of the dominant values of the culture in which the test has been constructed. Not even the much publicized, Raven's Progressive Matrices—a non-verbal test of intelligence—is culture-free. The universal usage of an instrument can only be justified when it can be demonstrated that the instrument is not 'culture specific' but has 'universal applicability' and that what is being measured is a universal quality or attribute, and that, given certain considerations, one would be able to predict differences (directional, or one-tailed) in performances within and between different cultural groups. The clinical thermometer too serves as a good example. It has universal applicability. Regardless of where, when, how, and who constructed the clinical thermometer, it is clear that temperature in humans and animals is a universal attribute, which, given certain acceptable margins of errors, is measurable. But the precise calibrations of a thermometer became possible *only after the theory of thermodynamics was formulated.* In other words, methodology served the interests of theory and not the other way round.

## DEMISE OF METAPHYSICAL CONCEPTS

As was mentioned above, psychologists in their eagerness to transform psychology into a behavioural science, jettisoned metaphysical concepts, which were seen as being meaningless. Basic concepts such as will, purpose, consciousness, awareness, mind, self, identity, morality, goodness, virtue—concepts which give meaning and lend poignancy and substance to our lives—were seen as being redundant. Following in the footsteps of Rudolf Carnap and Wittgenstein—the champions of logical positivism and the recognized luminaries of the prestigious Vienna Circle—the psychologists argued that metaphysical propositions were neither true nor false. The meaningfulness of the statements could not be empirically verified. On the bases of their acceptance of the famous *verifiability principle*, they dismissed the entire field of metaphysics as meaningless nonsense.

Even Freudian and post-Freudians theories were put to the sword. Freud's theories were dismissed as being metaphysical, and therefore meaningless and nonsensical. It is true that many of Freud's writings are empirically unverifiable, such as the universality of the *Oedipus Complex*, notions of transference and counter transference, and a variety of defence mechanisms, including the mechanism of *reaction formation*, which can explain love and hatred with equal ease! It is also true that Freud had the remarkable ability of explaining away contradictions, which is *not* as is mistakenly believed by some of his followers, an asset but a great weakness of his theories. A theory, as Popper (1963) states, which explains everything, succeeds in explaining nothing. But despite its weaknesses, Freudian theory reveals many penetrating insights into the workings of the human psyche, which must make one pause and consider the importance of metaphysical concerns that guide and give meaning and substance to our lives. And although many Freudian concepts may fail to meet with rigid criteria set by the logical positivists, they offer explanations, which are not only plausible but worth pursuing. And as Aristotle remarked one should not expect greater precision of any subject than the nature of the subject permits (Gower, 1997).

But the logical positivists received their 'comeuppance' when they fell into the very pit they had dug for the metaphysicians. As Lavine (1989) points out, 'the verifiability principle fails its own test since it is not itself an empirically verifiable statement; it is therefore embarrassingly meaningless' (p. 401). By the end of World War II logical positivism died, and the Vienna Circle disintegrated.

But the ghost of logical positivism continues to haunt American mainstream psychology—as is evident from their obsessive attachment to the natural science paradigm and their continued insistence on 'evidence based' research obtained through empirical verification, a point to which, we shall return later.

In discarding metaphysical abstractions they turned their backs on history. To ignore the past and merely concentrate on the present, often leads to a distorted and even a simplistic understanding of the present. The Spanish philosopher, George Santayana believed that in turning one's back on history, one was likely to repeat the very mistakes, which one had made in the past. By denying and even denigrating the contributions of philosophy, religion, art, literature, all of which go toward constituting a culture, they created a psychology, which, as Mujeeb-ur-Rahman (1990) has eloquently argued, was sterile and fragmented. In their denial of the importance of metaphysical concepts, they tried to take away from humanity, the rules, the norms, and the ethical and moral values by which people attempt to understand and guide and regulate their own lives. Psychology does not (or pretends not to) concern itself with questions of *ought*, it offers no guide as to how we ought to lead our lives. It appears to be concerned with what *is*, and what can be observed, described, measured and analyzed, and not what *ought* to be. Yet, it is the questions of 'ought', which most of us wrestle with and attempt to find satisfactory answers to—answers that would make sense and give meaning to our lives, and allow us to become moral human beings. In their eagerness to discard metaphysical concepts, Western psychologists have exposed themselves to at least two potential dangers.

## DEBATES CONCERNING THE SCIENTIFIC STATUS OF PSYCHOLOGY

Whether psychology can legitimately be called a science is in itself a debated issue. One should not be misled into believing that because there is a high degree of consensus among Western psychologists that psychology is a science. Consensus, as we know, is measure of reliability and not of validity. A 1000-year consensual belief in Ptolemy's geocentric model of the Universe was struck a fatal blow by Galileo, and was replaced by the heliocentric model of the Universe, first articulated by Copernicus.

In their search for general laws of human behaviour psychologists have often assumed that there exist certain unchanging, invariant attributes, which all human beings share—what Plato refers to as 'essences'. Find those and you have discovered the key to understanding human behaviour! Thus the whole approach of 'scientifically orientated' psychologists is aimed at using methods, which ultimately will enable them to 'discover' this essence, a lawfulness of human nature, which is unchanging and common to humanity.

The belief in the lawfulness of human nature is a seriously debated issue. As Hull (1998) points out, there are no true human universals that can be traced to a common nature. One can hardly talk about human nature without at the same time considering the important role of nurture. Human beings are cultural animals. They are capable of modifying their behaviour based on learning. They are also able to pass that learning on to future generations in non-genetic, culturally transmitted ways (Eisenberg, 1972; Fukuyama, 2002). In keeping with Darwinian theory, it would be more correct to say that the variance in human behaviour is likely to be far greater than for virtually any other species. As Paul Ehrlich (2000) has argued that it is in human nature not to have a single nature. Human nature can be understood more by its variation than by its uniformity.

## MISPLACED EMPHASIS ON THE STUDY OF OBSERVABLE BEHAVIOUR

Even the Neanderthal person, I daresay, must have had an inner life of some kind or other. Imagine a Neanderthal's first encounter with death. What did they make of death? Were they frightened? Were they wonder-struck? Were they in awe of what they witnessed? Did they attempt to revive the dead? Did they mourn for the dead? Did they have any faint glimmerings of an 'after-life'? Did they perform any rituals, ceremonies? Did they feast of the dead and engage in any cannibalistic practices? Although we shall never know for certain it makes sense to speculate on their inner speculations when confronted for the first time in their lives by the most extraordinary event.

All is not well with the state of Western psychology. Psychologists, at the beginning of the 20th century, made all kinds of promises: psychology would usher in a new era; pressing human problems would be resolved, and people all over the world would live in peace, harmony, relative affluence and happiness. Hardly any of the promises has been honoured. It is difficult to chart the future course of psychology. In discarding the study of the 'inner' person, has psychology turned against itself? Apparently, not. Psychologists in the Western world are convinced even more so now than in the past that the solution to understanding human behaviour lies in pursuit of neurophysiology, neuroscience.

## THE RISE OF NEUROPHYSIOLOGY AND NEUROSCIENCE

Until about the early 1990s the liberal, 'nature-nurture' oriented psychologists, progressive intellectuals, feminists, and members of ethnic minorities rebelled against any biological, hereditary and genetic explanations of differences, (including male–female differences) in intelligence, personality, mental illness, depression, criminality, etc. Such explanations were seen as being reactionary and racist and socially divisive. Many psychologists engaged in such research (Burt, Eysenck, Jensen, Herrnstein, Murray and others) were accused, vilified, castigated in the press, in Courts of Law, in journals, and at National and International Conferences. Feminists too added their support, challenging suggestions that male–female differences were genetic rather than socially constructed (Hubbard, 1994). The controversy related to nature as the main determinant of human behaviour has far from died down. It continues. But in recent years many neurophysiologists, neuroscientists, psycho-pharmacologists, psychologists, psychiatrists and the promoters of the Human Genome Project have undertaken investigations to establish precise relationships between brain, genes, drugs and behaviour. Research in these areas is extensive, to say the least. Even metaphysical concepts have been subjected to experimental re-examinations without their being referred to as such. Concepts such as consciousness, awareness, memory, purpose (motivation) among others, are beginning to reappear in the field of cognitive-neuroscience. The liberal, radical, nurture-oriented psychologists were strongly opposed to biological, hereditarian and genetic explanations of human behaviours. But in recent years there has been a grudging acceptance, leading to an increasing emphasis on neurological, biological, genetic explanations of behaviour both within psychology and psychiatry. Cognition, a taboo word in psychology during the 1920s and 1930s, is now one of the major areas in the field of psychology. However the word cognition has acquired a different meaning, which subsumes a rejection of the theistic and non-theistic mind-body dualism. There is a belief that the concept of mind is untenable. What exists is matter.

But here we run into difficulties. What constitutes matter is in itself a debatable issue; this question has never been satisfactorily answered (Trefil, 1980). For centuries, both physicists and philosophers have wondered over the composition of matter. If matter consists of atoms, it appears that atoms are made of nuclei and electrons. Nuclei in turn are made up of protons and neutrons. What are protons and neutrons made of? Gell-Mann (Davies, 1990) coined the word quarks. But quarks are neither solid, nor liquid, nor gaseous; they have neither mass nor form. In other words the assumed solidity of matter may indeed turn out to be an abstraction, if not a myth (Davies, 1990). Heisenberg (1930) too, questioned the assumed solidity of matter in his famous research paper on indeterminacy principle in quantum theory, which he formulated in 1927. As Durant (1963) points out it would not be an exaggeration to say that as far as physics is concerned, matter appears to have dematerialized itself.

But leaving these abstract arguments aside, an acceptance of a materialist philosophy implies that each psychological concept or a psychological event must correspond to neurophysiological concepts. According to Davidson (1980), this is a mistaken belief. For instance, when a person admits to being happy and cheerful, we assume that the person making such an admission is rational, coherent and consistent. But if the actions of the person contradict and belie his articulated beliefs about himself, we may conclude that the person is inconsistent and irrational. Our conclusions concerning the person's inconsistency are based on our imposing conditions of rationality, coherence and consistency, as a prerequisite in our evaluations of human behaviour. And as Leahey (1997) points out, 'these conditions have no echo in physical theory' (Leahey, 1997: 461). This argument cuts both ways. There are some psychologists who argue—Churchland (1986) being one of them—that the very failure of psychology to find neurophysiological correlates 'proves' that psychological concepts are false. This is misplaced scientism at its imperial best! But there are others who argue in precisely the opposite fashion. Painstaking and meticulous attention is paid to the design, construction, and execution of complex multivariate research strategies, aided by statistical and mathematical models used in data analyses. Their main concern is to find evidence that will permanently put to rest notions of the mind and all the other concepts subsumed within it. This explains, to a large extent, the great concern of research workers with 'evidence-based' research—a term that is not quite easy to understand. To appreciate its full meaning, one needs to define clearly what one means by evidence. Does evidence-based research simply refer to random controlled trials (RCT) as appears to be the accepted procedure in medical and bio-medical research, as Pipitone argues? (2003, personal communication). Random controlled trials are meaningful, pertinent and even desirable with respect to certain types of research programmes in medicine. But whether the same justifications can be offered for research in neuropsychology and neuroscience is open to question. Seeking confirmatory evidence is seen as the first important step, an important step, which lays the foundations for other steps involved in verification and validation. But here we encounter a serious epistemological problem, raised by Karl Popper, who points out that 'It is easy to obtain confirmations, or verifications, for nearly every theory—*if we look for confirmations*' (1963: 36, emphasis added). Popper goes on to argue that confirmations paradoxically are far easier to obtain than refutations. Confirming evidence counts only when it is a genuine test of a theory, in other words, when the test has failed to falsify the theory. Thus the crucial test of a scientific theory lies in the extent to which it is falsifiable. Falsifiability is the criterion of scientific status of a theory.

Given the nature of evidence-based research one can see that it is concerned more with seeking confirmatory evidence and less with establishing refutations and falsifications. Generally research findings, which disconfirm and falsify hypotheses seldom, get a 'good press'. Disconfirmed findings are also unlikely to receive a sympathetic consideration by editors of relevant journals. From a financial point of view, even the most benevolent pharmaceutical companies, governmental agencies, charities and other multi-national organizations are unlikely to sponsor research projects where the stated aims of the research workers are to seek refutations of their hypotheses. It would seem therefore that a hasty confirmation is often preferable to a painstakingly obtained refutation. Lest one is inclined to believe that I am exaggerating, it might be worth referring to the controversy that erupted a year or two after Dr Peter Kramer's book, *Listening to prozac* (1993) was published. It was not the book that caused the controversy: it was the astounding claims, which the author had made concerning the miraculous effects of the antidepressant wonder drug Prozac. In the meantime, however, the drug had captured the imagination of almost 25 million Americans (Glenmullen, 2000) who loosened their purse strings, swallowed pills at regular intervals—adding to the fortunes of Eli Lilly, the pharmaceutical giants who had first produced and marketed the drug. Subsequent research into the uses and misuses of the drug (Breggin and Breggin, 1994; Glenmullen, 2000) was critical of the claims made by Peter Kramer. However, the criticisms were not given a sympathetic hearing, and if rumour is to be believed, concerted attempts were made to stifle, suppress, sabotage publications of the books by Breggin and Breggin (1994) and Glenmullen (2000).

To return to the point: Popper's views concerning the differentiation between science and non-science and between confirmation and refutation have by no means gone unchallenged (Lakatos, 1978; Godfrey-Smith, 2003; Kuhn, 1998).

Imagine a situation where systematic, stringent and long term attempts to falsify a theory fail. What then? How long would one need to continue with this 'eternal' quest? Popper offers no clear answers to this objection. He is concerned more about the discovery of truth in the Platonic sense—timeless and eternal—and perhaps less so about validity of a hypothesis, or sets of hypotheses. A validated hypothesis may reveal eternal truth, but according to Popper, this truth cannot be accepted unequivocally because its acceptance once again raises Hume's ghost of the inductive fallacy. What Popper provides us with is the *logic of scientific discovery* and not the psychology of scientific discovery. What he offers is a prescriptive working model, which allows us to distinguish between science and non-science, and in our case, deciding whether psychology is a science or a non-science.

Let me end this section by a brief reference to the work of Lakatos and Kuhn, the two contemporaries (now deceased) of Popper. Lakatos (1978) discusses the nature of science and the progress of science in terms of competing research programmes within which the scientific fraternity work. As an example from psychology one might construe the Freudian (psychoanalytical) and the behaviourist approaches as two competing research programmes, each with its own set of theoretical assumptions, methodologies, research designs and evaluative principles. The Lakatosian approach does not make it possible to judge the 'success' or the 'failure' of an individual scientist working within the framework of a given research programme. The entire research programme, over the years, may show signs of progress, leading to new discoveries, generation of more sophisticated theories, greater explanatory powers, etc. Lakatos refers to these as *progressive* programmes. Some programmes, on the other hand may show no progress and may tend to degenerate, which he refers to as *degenerative* research programmes. Thus, non-scientific and/or pseudo-scientific programmes would die away, and genuine scientific programmes flourish and progress. This view, as one can see, is strikingly different from Popper's.

Kuhn (1970, 1998) on the other hand argues that scientists work within an acceptable paradigm. As long as the paradigm does not run into problems, such as unexplained anomalies, insoluble methodological problems, work continues within that paradigm. Kuhn refers to this as 'normal science'. But when contradictory, anomalous, findings begin to increase, it causes unease among those working within the paradigm, and creates a crisis of confidence, leading many scientists to abandon the paradigm. This may trigger off a scientific revolution, which results in the old paradigm being rejected, and a new paradigm being accepted, gradually leading, once again to the practice of 'normal science'.

Where does mainstream Western psychology stand with respect to the three epistemological approaches that have been outlined? Do Western psychologists construe their research endeavours within sets of competing research programmes? Do they all see themselves as working within a Khunian paradigm? Or are their research enterprises to be evaluated individually from a Popperian perspective? To answer these questions meaningfully one needs to assume that psychologists do indeed work within single or multiple paradigms or research programmes. To answer these questions let us turn to the next section of the paper.

## THERAPIES AND PSYCHOLOGICAL SCIENCE

Mainstream Western psychology, as we have seen, lays claims to being a science—the chorus of dissent notwithstanding. Let us for a moment disregard the dissenting voices and assume for better or worse that psychology, not unlike physics, *is* a science. Let us further assume that the psychologists-turned-scientists work within the paradigm(s) and let us further assume that they are all engaged in what Thomas Kuhn describes as 'normal science'. Now if psychologists work within a paradigm it would be reasonable to assume that any applications in the discipline—in the areas of health, mental illness, stress, psychotherapy, testing, education, etc.—would be related to if not arise out of their theoretical constructs. As has been argued in the first section, applications in general *follow* from theory, thereby establishing a logical (even 'symbiotic') relationship between theory and practice. Such is what one would also expect in scientific psychology—a logical relationship of theory to practice. As an example, tests of intelligence make sense only when they conform to the acceptable theories of intelligence and arise out of the theoretical constructs. Whether the tests would have universal applicability or would be confined to the culture in which they were designed is also related to the articulated conceptual models. Otherwise the intelligence tests would have no meaning. Such relations can also be observed in other areas of psychology, e.g., biofeedback techniques, behaviour modification, to name but a few.

However, when one turns to psychotherapy, counselling, stress management, one finds that most therapies—with the exception of behaviour modification and a few others—concentrate on metaphysical concepts, which include fear, anger, guilt, forgiveness, vendetta, anxiety, depression, spirituality, mind, unhappiness, sorrow, self-realization—'things that happen in one's mind'. While such concepts are anathema to the scientifically oriented psychologist they are 'manna from heaven' for the therapist. The path taken by therapists follows a significantly different route from that traversed by scientifically oriented psychologists. In electing to concentrate on metaphysical concepts, therapists of virtually all persuasions and theoretical orientations have chosen to adopt a non-scientific approach in their work. It is of course refreshing to note that what the hard-nosed psychologists have disputed, denied and discarded, the therapists have extolled, embraced and enshrined in their own work. Scientific psychologists, dig into the inner regions of the brain in the hope of discovering precise mathematical relationships between brain and behaviour. Therapists on the other hand concerned with art and literature, myth and magic, custom and tradition, inner and outer selves, muse over the mysteries of the mind, probing into the depths of one's soul. There is an undeniable splendour in their work, as they weave the tapestry of humanity from the rich and exciting fabrics of past history, custom, tradition, art, poetry, literature and drama, religion and philosophy. Their language is sprinkled with the use of metaphors rather than cut and dried. Although many therapists deal with groups, offering varieties of group therapies, they hardly ever concern themselves with random controlled trials, complex data analyses and other evaluative techniques. This approach, as one can see, differs sharply from those followed by the scientific psychologists. A vast epistemological gulf separates the practitioners from the theorists. How has such a state come about?

For a start there is no unified paradigm to which therapists subscribe. In addition to the Rogerian, the Freudian, the neo-Freudian, the rational-emotive, and the existential models, there are several other models to which therapists subscribe, e.g., transactional, motivational, spiritual, and last, but not the least, eclectic. According to Herink (1980) there are more than 250 theories of counselling in America! This seems a conservative estimate to Howard (1996) who points out that Karasu (1986) has discovered more than 400 models of counselling and psychotherapy. Karasu's findings were reported in 1986. Over the last 17 years, the number of theories cannot but have increased.

Most of the so-called theories of counselling do not merit being called theories. They may best be construed as personal, private 'ramblings' of a counsellor, who may have come to believe that s/he has finally discovered the elixir of counselling, and with more haste and less prudence, rushes to promote and propagate the astounding discovery. As the Scottish philosopher David Hume would have remarked a couple of centuries ago, such theories are best consigned to flames. For a theory to be accepted as a good, sound theory, it must satisfy most, if not all, of the following criteria:

- A theory needs to be clearly and explicitly stated.
- It must be logically consistent and parsimonious.
- It should become possible to deduce a set of hypotheses arising out of the theory, which should be actually or potentially testable.
- A theory should be capable of being disconfirmed (or falsified).
- The acceptance or rejection of a theory is *unrelated* to the number of people subscribing to the theory.
- The popularity of a theory is not a legitimate criterion of its acceptance.

- Psychological factors such as beliefs, attitudes and values concerning a theory have nothing to do with the truth (validity) of a theory.
- A theory may be true (valid) even if no one believes in it, and conversely, a theory may be false even if everyone believes in it.
- Confirming evidence of a hypothesis does not establish a causal relationship between the theory and the hypothesis. (Logically, the confirming evidence could have been obtained by an infinite number of hypotheses.)
- The relationship between a theory and therapy needs to be clearly articulated.

In defence, one might argue that therapies cannot and ought not to be constrained within a single theoretical strait-jacket. Each client presents a different and unique set of problems, which each therapist learns to handle differently. Although a therapist may be partial to a particular theoretical approach and may tend to construe the problems of the client from that particular perspective, wisdom and expediency may necessitate alterations and changes during the course of therapy. But such an approach has a sting—or rather two stings—in its own tail.

- This is concerned with the validity of a given therapy. How does one establish the validity of a given therapy? How does one determine that the therapy actually works (or not as the case may be) and turns out to be beneficial to the health and psychological welfare of the client? By what criteria is one going to determine its efficacy?
- The second one is concerned with commensurability. Is there a way by which the efficacy (or otherwise) of one therapy be compared with another? This is an important issue not only from the client's point of view one but also from that of therapist and for all therapies in general.

Let us discuss these points briefly. The fact that a given therapy may not be amenable to any form of empirical testing should by no means be construed as an asset, an advantage or strength of that particular therapy. It is a singular weakness. It is of course possible that the manner in which a particular therapy is formulated and the assumptions from which it springs are not amenable to any form of rigorous empirical testing. Such a therapy may of course be valid and even true in a more general sense of the term. But we would still need to find ways of demonstrating its validity, viz., *how it works.* Explanations offered by the therapist, or emotional eulogies offered by satisfied clients, feelings of well-being by the client, are undoubtedly not without some merit. But one needs to go beyond such assessments and find objective ways of demonstrating their validity, or failing which, disconfirming their hypothesized relationships and predictions (Popper, 1963, 1972). It should be noted here that even if a rigorous empirical investigation were to confirm the predictions of the theory, it does not follow that one could then posit an unassailable relationship between the hypothesis and the obtained prediction. Logically it is possible for any other unspecified variables may account for the same prediction! In other words, any number of hypotheses could lead to the same prediction (Gower, 1997). This raises a question of serious concern. Should one continue to engage in (or permit the use of) untried, untested, unverifiable therapies?

As far as commensurability is concerned, this poses an even greater problem than testing the validity of a single therapy. Even under ideal circumstances, comparisons of theories are fraught with difficulties. For any meaningful comparisons to be made, one would need to agree on a common set of parameters. Some of the parameters against which comparative studies have been undertaken are:

- personality characteristics, including age, experience and gender of the therapist;
- clearly defined therapeutic methods to be used;
- agreed duration of therapy (3 months, 6 months, 1 year?);
- random control trials;
- measures of severity of the client's 'problem';
- outcome measures;
- follow up studies and relapse.

Several studies of this nature have been undertaken in the past (Bergin and Garfield, 1971; Bergin and Lambert, 1978; Eysenck, 1952, 1985; Luborsky et al., 1975, 1986; Sloane et al., 1975; Strupp, 1989), but according to Rachman and Wilson (1980) they suffer from severe conceptual and methodological weaknesses. Also, the hidden agenda of many such research projects has been to establish the superiority of one therapeutic approach over the other, making objective and unbiased comparisons even more problematic.

## CONCLUSION

Mainstream psychology in the West is not guided by any one or two major paradigms to which psychologists subscribe. There are several—ranging from models of neuroscience and bio-physiology to existential, humanist and spiritual models. There is glaring lack of consensus among psychologists concerning the nature of human nature and how it ought to be investigated. The controversy related to nature versus nurture has turned into a fierce battle, with no signs of truce between the two. The present divisions between theory and application in areas such as education, industry, counselling, therapy, child guidance, etc., appear to show no signs of decreasing, leading to vigorous defences of entrenched positions. The prolific popularisation of psychology in the form of 'do-it-yourself' books, videos, training courses, seminars, encounter groups, all of which lead to instant sexual, social, material, relational, financial success, health, wealth, happiness, beauty, etc., has merely served to increase the rift between mainstream psychology and its popular areas of applications.

Given the increasing demand for instant 'fix-its' in the Western world it would make sense to ask whether there are two distinct psychologies: one for the consumer on the street: popular, easy to access, understand, implement, and the other within the cloistered corridors of academia: technical, experimental, statistical, biological, physiological, neurological, which for the lay person may perhaps be as difficult to understand as the differential calculus to a non-mathematician. Which of the two, if either, merits being called a science?

History is replete with examples where disciplines deemed to be sciences—e.g., astrology, palmistry, alchemy, phrenology, water divination—turn out to pseudo-sciences, and disciplines deemed to be pseudo-sciences turn out to be genuine sciences, e.g., palaeontology, Darwinian theory. Should one therefore call psychology a science and hope that it does not one day turn out to be a pseudo-science, or should one look upon psychology as a pseudo-science and hope that one day it comes to be recognized as a genuine science of human and animal behaviour? It is best to let readers make up their own minds over this matter.

## REFERENCES

Bergin, A. E. and Garfield, S. L. (Eds) (1971). *Handbook of psychotherapy and change.* New York: Wiley & Sons.

Bergin, A. E. and Lambert, M. J. (1978). The evaluation of therapeutic outcomes. In S. L. Garfield and A. E. Bergin (Eds), *Handbook of psychotherapy and change: An empirical analysis.* New York: Wiley & Sons.

Boring, E. G. (1929/1950). *A history of experimental psychology* (2nd ed.). New York: Appleton-Century-Crofts.

Breggin, P. R. and Breggin, G. R. (1994). *Talking back to Prozac: What doctors won't tell you about today's most controversial drug.* New York: St. Martin's Press.

Churchland, P. M. (1986). *Neurophilosophy.* Cambridge, MA: MIT Press.

Davidson, D. (1980). *Essays on actions and events.* Oxford: Clarendon Press.

Davies, P. (1990). *God and the new physics.* London: Penguin Books.

Durant, W. (1963). *The pleasures of philosophy.* New York: Simon & Schuster.

Ehrlich, P. (2000). *Human natures: Genes, cultures, and human prospect.* Washington, DC: Island Press/Shearwater Books.

Eisenberg, L. (1972). The human nature of human nature. *Science, 176,* 123–128.

Eysenck, H. J. (1952). *Uses and abuses of psychology.* London: Penguin Books.

Eysenck, H. J. (1985). *Decline and fall of the Freudian empire.* London: Penguin Books.
Feyerabend, P. (1975). *Against method.* London: NLB.
Fukuyama, F. (2002). *Our posthuman future: Consequences of the biotechnology revolution.* London: Profile Books.
Gjertsen, D. (1989). *Science and philosophy: Past and present.* London: Penguin Books.
Glenmullen, J. (2000). *Prozac backlash: Overcoming the dangers of Prozac, Zoloft, Paxil, and other antidepressants with safe, effective alternatives.* New York: Simon & Schuster.
Godfrey-Smith, P. (2003). *In introduction to the philosophy of science: Theory and reality.* Chicago, IL: University of Chicago Press.
Gower, B. (1997). *Scientific method.* London: Routledge.
Heisenberg, W. (1930). *The physical principles of the quantum theory.* Berkeley, CA: University of California Press.
Herink, R (1980). *The psychotherapy handbook.* New York: Meridian.
Howard, A. (1996). *Challenges to counselling and psychotherapy.* London: Macmillan.
Hull, D. L. (1998). On human nature. In D. L. Hull and M. Ruse (Eds), *The philosophy of biology.* New York: Oxford University Press.
James, W. (1890/1983). *Principles of psychology.* Cambridge, MA: Harvard University Press.
Karasu, T. B. (1986). The psychotherapies: Benefits and limitations. *American Journal of Psychotherapy, 40,* 324–342.
Kenny, A. (1994). *The Oxford illustrated history of western philosophy.* New York: Oxford University Press.
Kirk, G. S. (1974). *The nature of Greek myths.* Harmondsworth: Penguin.
Klineberg, O. (1965). Some philosophical and methodological problems in Social Psychology. In E. Nagel (Ed.), *Scientific psychology: Principles and approaches.* New York: Basic Books.
Kramer, P. D. (1993). *Listening to Prozac.* New York: Penguin.
Kuhn, T. (1970). *The structure of scientific revolutions.* Princeton, NJ: Princeton University Press.
Kuhn, T. (1998). The nature and necessity of scientific revolutions. In M. Curd and J. A. Cover (Eds), *Philosophy of science: The central issues.* New York: W. W. Norton & Company.
Lakatos, I. (1978). Falsification and the methodology of scientific research programmes. In J. Worrall and G. Currie (Eds), *The methodology of scientific research.* Cambridge: Cambridge University Press.
Lavine, T. Z. (1989). *From Socrates to Sartre: The philosophic quest.* New York: Bantom Books.
Leahey, T. H. (1997). *A history of psychology: Main currents in psychological thought.* New Jersey: Prentice Hall.
Luborsky, L., Crits-Christoph, P., McLellan, A. T., Woody, G., Piper, W., Liberman, B., Imber, S. and Pikonis, P. (1986). Do therapists vary much in their success? Findings from four outcome studies. *American Journal of Orthopsychiatry, 56*(4), 501–512.
Luborsky, Lester, Singer, B. and Lubrosky, Lise (1975). Comparative studies of psychotherapies: Is it true that 'everyone has won and all must have prizes?'. *Archives of General Psychiatry, 32,* 995–1008.
Magee, B. (1998). *The story of philosophy.* London: Dorling Kindersley.
Miller, G. A. (1969). Psychology as a means of promoting human welfare. *American Psychologist, 24,* 1063–1075.
Rahman, M. (1990). *The psychological quest: From Socrates to Freud.* Ontario, Canada: Captus University Publications.
Nagel, E. (1965). Psychology and the philosophy of science. In E. Nagel (Ed.), *Scientific psychology: Principles and approaches.* New York: Basic Books.
Onians, R. B. (1951). *The origins of European thought.* Cambridge: Cambridge University Press.
Pipitone, N. (2003). Personal communication.
Popper, K. (1963). *Conjectures and refutations.* London: Routledge & Kegan Paul.

Popper, K. (1972). *Objective knowledge: An evolutionary approach.* Oxford: Clarendon Press.
Rachman, S. J. and Wilson, G. T. (1980). *The effects of psychological therapy.* London: Pergamon Press.
Robinson, D. N. (2001). Sigmund Koch—Philosophically speaking. *American Psychologist, 56,* 420–424.
Russell, B. (1912). The *problems of philosophy.* London: Oxford University Press.
———. (1946/1961). *History of western philosophy.* London: George Allen & Unwin.
Sloane, R. B., Staples, F. R., Cristol, A. H., Yorkston, N. J. and Whipple, K. (1975). *Psychotherapy versus behaviour therapy.* Cambridge, MA: Harvard University Press.
Snell, B. (1960). *The discovery of the mind: The Greek origins of european thought.* New York: Harper & Row.
Strupp, H. H. (1989). Psychotherapy: Can the practitioner learn from the researcher? *American Psychologist 44,* 717–724.
Trefil, J. (1980). *From atoms to quarks: An introduction to the strange world of particle physics.* London: Althone.
Zilbergeld, B. (1983). *The shrinking of America: Myths of psychological change.* Boston, MA: Little, Brown.

# 7

# Playing Amidst the Pillars: Pittu Laungani and Yogic Psychology

*Amrita Narayanan*

## INTRODUCTION

**Laungani** called into question the unilateral acceptance of Western models—particularly those that were not philosophically inclined—by pointing out the cultural bias implicit in such an approach (Laungani, 2001, 2002a, 2004a, 2004b). In this chapter, inspired by Laungani, I will describe some of the cultural differences between the Western (particularly American) and Yoga (Indian) approaches to psychology from a general perspective. I'll then respond to Laungani's (2002a) call for the indigenization of cross-cultural psychology by offering a framework for thinking about the psyche that originated in India's yoga psychology but takes an integrative approach that blends elements of Winnicottian and Launganic perspectives to delineate the potential of yoga as a cultural psychology.

## YOGA AS AN INDIGENOUS MODEL OF PSYCHOLOGY

Laungani (2001a, 2004a) was very much in favour of the indigenization of cross-cultural research. He felt that Western models were limited by culturally derived ontologies and epistemologies, and encouraged the development of indigenous models (Laungani, 2001b, 2002a, 2002b, 2004b). One tentative in the direction of indigenous model development has come from the Bihar school of Yoga in India, whose department of yoga psychology has called on psychologists world-wide to compile and operationalize the main concepts of yoga psychology[1] such that they can be clinically useful in today's international context (Bhushan, 1987).

Yoga psychology as a treatment modality is based on the fundamental idea that suffering occurs during deviations from a larger Self-awareness (Desikachar, 1987; Easwaran, 2000; Le Page, 2002a, 2002b). Health is associated with a full experience of diverse self-states as well as identification with a sense of unified wholeness amidst diverse self-states (Le Page, 2002a, 2002b; Narayanan, 2007). Though it is not the principal focus of this chapter, it is worth noting that the relationship between health and wholeness has been mirrored in the empirical literature not directly related to yoga. In their wheel of wellness model, for example, Myers et al., (2000) present empirical evidence that identifying with a range of characteristics and dimensions of personality is optimal for human health. In addition, some of the cognitive-behavioural research studies also suggest that over-focus on one dimension of the self—for example deriving self-worth largely from approval from others—can be detrimental to psychological health (Beck et al., 1983; Teasdale et al., 2002). Similarly, Kasser's research suggests that an 'over emphasis' on particular self-states—such as more materialistic self-states or those that demand more personal control—promotes suffering in the form of anxiety and depression in the human organism (Kasser, 2000).

Laungani has discussed in his writing, a concept from yoga psychology known as the *Kleshas* (loosely translated as 'stress' or 'causes of suffering'), pointing out that the very definition of stress and stressors differ vastly amidst diverse cultural milieus (Laungani, 2002c). This chapter looks at the *Kleshas*—the causes of suffering in the yoga paradigm—and identifies them as a unique paradigm of stress that is an alternative to the medical model. This tentative was inspired by Laungani's many papers questioning the scientific status of Western psychology (Laungani, 2002b, 2004b) as well as Bhushan (1987), Le Page (2002a, 2002b) and Saraswati's (1980) works on the importance of modernizing yoga psychology.

Although I am in a sense Westernizing an Indian concept by presenting its material in English and reading it through my own part-Western educated eyes, I will choose in my presentation style, to eschew the linear, solution-based approach that is characteristic of many of the modern Western models and take a more philosophical approach that mirrors the concept itself, for example, asking relevant questions rather than seeking to offer a set of concrete answers. In offering this model, I will acknowledge at the outset—as did Laungani (2002a)—that it is, like all other models, including the empirical model, inherently biased. Though indigenous in origin, it is influenced and shaped by the vision and education of the bicultural author—myself—who is elaborating upon it. In declaring the probable bias in this model, I am following Laungani's (2002a) and others' suggestion for an acknowledgement of value differences rather than an insistence on universality (Cornelissen, 2003; Laungani, 2002a).

## PSYCHIC STRESS IN EURO-AMERICAN AND YOGA PSYCHOLOGY

The word stress is used more generally by Western theorists to refer to a shift from system homeostasis—typically trigged by a threat—that is marked by biological indicators. Psychological stress has been a major focus of study in Euro-American models of psychology, and large volumes of literature can be found on the subject of stress and coping (Aldwin and Revenson, 1987; Sinha and Watson, 2007).

In considering psychological stress, psychodynamic theory has added to the understanding of the range of human response to psychic anxiety, biological psychiatry has enabled us to comprehend its underpinnings in the body and the brain, and cognitive-behavioural theory has offered methods and techniques geared towards the modification of these responses (Menninger, 1954). From a treatment perspective, change or growth means different things in each of these theories. Psychodynamic theory is interested in facilitating a deeper understanding of the sources of anxiety (La Planche and Pontalis, 1974), with an ultimate structural change in the organism such that what previously prompted a stress-based automatic reaction is now viewed with more insight. Biological psychiatry has been most focused on attenuating, controlling or preventing the non-normative responses to stress and on reducing their distress-producing effects (Laungani, 2002c). Cognitive-behaviourism has been most interested in changing maladaptive responses to stress and anxiety via actively re-writing and modifying the thoughts and the behaviours that are associated with the maladaptive response (Beck, 1975).

In contrast to the above described approaches, yoga psychology has been weighted not so much towards the exploration of stress and conflict in the human organism as much as the exploration of states of consciousness that lie beyond the stress response (Bhushan, 1998; Easwaran, 2000; Saraswati, 1980). Homeostatic well-being—and that which lies beyond it—not stress, is the main focus of yoga (Le Page, 2002a). Yoga can, in part, be thought of as the process of expansion of the human organism on various levels such that it can realize its maximum potential, beyond psychic homeostasis (Le Page, 2002a, 2002b). Stressors are important as obstacles to expansion, not simply because they produce distress. Within yoga psychology there is a field known as yoga *cikitsa*—yoga therapy—that is focused on treatment. In yoga therapy, as in yoga in general, *Kleshas* or obstacles to the state of yoga are the equivalent of psycho-social stressors in the Western tradition.

While yoga psychology became codified in the second century—the time period of Patanjali and Buddha—the body of knowledge that forms its core spans centuries of study and practice prior to and after that period (Feuerstein, 2005). The salient concepts in yoga psychology have been outlined in ancient texts, yet their form—verse, story and sutra—leave them open to some degree of interpretation (Narayanan, 2007). It has been suggested that this interpretable form has been purposeful—to describe timeless concepts in a way that leaves enough flexibility such that the concepts can be applied to diverse personalities and across historical epochs (Le Page, 2002a). Developing the field of yoga psychology includes the task of linking the concepts developed in different epochs, giving them meaning in a modern context and rendering them clinically useful (Narayanan, 2007). Despite the diverse origins of yogic knowledge and the need to make links across time, the research studies on yoga that have taken place in the last 20 years have used Western 'empirical' methodologies and Western paradigms to examine yoga with a resultant reductionism (Cornelissen, 2003; Laungani, 2001a and 2001b; Narayanan, 2007). In Laungani's words '[the] hasty and mindless approach of the natural science model have banished from [psychology's] newly acquired scientific vocabulary, concepts of the mind, awareness, consciousness, unconsciousness and of course the soul. In doing so they have severed our links with our past history' (Laungani, 2002b: 31).

## SELF-PSYCHOLOGY IN THE YOGA PARADIGM

Stepping outside of the Western paradigm and the natural science model allows the researcher to see not merely that perceptions of stress and methods of coping differ in India and the West but that the *Klesha*s are a stress paradigm in its own right. What follows is a discussion on the *Klesha*s situated in the context of yoga as a psychology of the self.

Yoga psychology is designed to facilitate Self-awareness.[2] A distinction is made between a quotidian self-awareness that is thought to be driven by circumstantial and interpersonal stressors and a larger awareness that is accessible in moments when reactions to stressors—both inner-psychic and environmental—are not automatic (Bhushan, 1998; Desikachar, 1987; Le Page, 2002a, 2002b). Self-awareness in its fullness is defined as knowledge of the self that is not limited to personal history and identifications like gender, ethnicity or even personality (Easwaran, 2000). The experience of this larger Self-awareness has been carefully operationalized in the 5-*Kosha* theory of the self—first presented in the centuries-old *Taiterreya Upanishad*—that describes the different types of self-awareness (Narayanan, 2007).

The 5-*Kosha* theory operationalizes self-awareness into five possible layers also described as 'selves', 'bodies' or 'sheaths', respectively: *Anamayakosha*, the self as a physical body, *Pranamayakosha*, the self as a body of breath, *Manomayokosha* the self as a mind-body, *Vijnyanamayakosha*, the self as a witnessing body and *Anandamayakosha* the self as a body of joy (Bhushan, 1987; Easwaran, 2000;

Le Page, 2002b; Saraswati, 1980). First told in the story of the *Taiterreya Upanishad*, the five *Koshas* are described as each their own type of knowledge, each meriting their own deep quest (Easwaran, 2000). In the story, the yoga[3] technique of meditation is suggested as a tool for the quest (Easwaran, 2000). The hero of the story, a young boy named Swethaketu who has prepared his whole life for this very quest journeys one by one into each of these layers of awareness (Easwaran, 2000). Each time he perceives he has found the extent of who he is, and each time his father who is his guide on the quest, encourages him to delve deeper and sure enough, Swethaketu finds yet another layer of the self within him (Easwaran, 2000). As the hero grows in self awareness, so does the reader of the story begin to understand the journey involved for seekers of self-awareness. The word yoga came to be used to describe the journey toward the state of complete self-awareness and the techniques of yoga—the breathing and physical exercisers among others—were considered tools to support this journey (Bhushan, 1987; Le Page, 2002a).

During the experience of one of the *Kleshas*[4] (stress-like phenomenon), awareness shrinks such that the self is perceived as a part rather than a whole greater than the sum of its parts. Yoga facilitates the journey back[5] to a unified Self-awareness with tools—such as exercises, breathing and psychotherapy—that promote an experience of wholeness that the therapist hopes will promote insight into the larger whole (Le Page, 2002a, 2002b; Saraswati, 1980). Continual practice of these techniques is thought to be part of the yoga journey of maintaining a sense of wholeness amidst inevitable fluctuations as well as growing in awareness—as did the young hero in the story—into deeper states of wholeness (Le Page, 2002a; Saraswati, 1980). Yoga as therapy fosters balanced growth in each of the *Koshas* (parts of the Self) by relating what is known as symptoms in the Western tradition to their perceived etiology in the form of gaps in self-awareness in specific or multiple *Koshas* (Le Page, 2002a, 2002b).

## AS THE SELF CONTRACTS, STRESS GROWS: UNDERSTANDING THE *KLESHAS*

The state of yoga is one of complete Self-awareness, and the exercises of yoga are directed towards developing this kind of holistic self-awareness. Human suffering in the yoga tradition is then thought to occur when there is a contraction of Self-awareness (Bhushan, 1998). *Kleshas*, previously described as 'stressors', are considered to be those phenomena that cause reductions in self-awareness or deviations from an individual's baseline state of holistic awareness. The *Kleshas* refer to phenomena that may be short term or character logical—though not unchangeable—that reduce the awareness of a larger whole. An example of a phenomenon that reduces awareness of the self is what is known in Western thought as the fight–flight syndrome (Le Page, 2002a). During the experience of fight–flight, the subject is less aware of his whole self and more aware of his need to escape or combat the situation.

The *Kleshas* are unique in their conceptualization of psychic stress because all psychic stress is situated in terms of fluctuations in Self-awareness. The mental, emotional, energetic and physical diversity that is the human experience is cradled in this model, as all beings are seen as moving in and out of states of self-awareness that are qualitatively more or less satisfying. Such acknowledgement of a multiplicity of self-states is very different from splitting the human population into the psychologically 'sick' and 'healthy' as may be the tendency in the DSM-IV diagnostic system (Laing, 1960; Okasha, 2008).

Each *Klesha*—*Avidya*, *Asmita*, *Raga*, *Dvesha* and *Abhinivesha* addresses what is arguably self-defining—and therefore cultural—questions: Who am I? What kind of influence do I wield in this world? What attracts me (desires, goals, motivations)? What repels me (aversions, traumas, fears)? How much time do I have for all this (death anxiety, time orientation and time anxiety)? The *Kleshas* conceptualize anxiety as a product of narrowing in self-awareness in relationship to these questions (Bhushan, 1987; Saraswati, 1980).

For example, the *Klesha Avidya* or 'ignorance' is typically translated as lack of Self-knowledge (Desikachar, 1987; Le Page, 2002a). In practice, *Avidya* refers to self-awareness versus Self-awareness, that is, a sense of self that is less whole than potentially possible. Yoga psychology distinguishes between a *Vidya*—an experiential internal sense of knowing that the Self is essentially whole and complex irrespective of life events—and *Avidya*—a sense of self that is strongly affected by life experiences such as personal profit or loss and the resultant highs and lows (Le Page, 2002a). *Avidya* is, in other words, a 'not knowing' or ignorance of the Self (Desikachar, 1987). A continuum can be established between *Vidya* and *Avidya*, where *Vidya* is an idealized state in which the individual has the ability to witness and consider all physical, mental and environmental events as part of a larger life-death-life cycle and *Avidya* is a state where these same events are experienced as chaotic, meaningless, personal attacks or reflections of an individual's worth and therefore stressful (Bhushan, 1987; Saraswati, 1980).

*Avidya* refers to either a chronic state of low self-awareness or to a collapse of the big picture of the Self during the course of mental, physical or environmental events (Bhushan, 1987; Saraswati, 1980). A collapse may occur or deepen during a particular stressful time period or may persist throughout the duration of a person's life to a greater or lesser extent. When an individual is closer to the *Avidya* end of the continuum he/she is more vulnerable to psychic stress due to a sensation of being so close to events that they feel unmanageable or intrusive. An individual may be thrown into a state of *Avidya* by an injury or disappointment of some kind, during which he or she is unable to situate the disappointment within the sphere of the whole picture of his/her life. In such a state, the disappointment dominates his/her vision of his/her life and may result in *Dhuka* or suffering (Desikachar, 1987).

Suffering is thought to be a part of life and a source of information of about *Avidya* (Bhushan, 1987; Saraswati, 1980). The experience of suffering is thought to be useful data about the construction of the mind and how it responds to suffering by changes in Self-awareness (Bhushan, 1987; Saraswati, 1980). An immediate effort to palliate suffering not only misses the opportunity to learn more about the shift in self-awareness that is considered to be at the root of the suffering, it might contribute to the *Avidya*, or limitation in self-perspective. For example, in the previous example the subject is suffering because of a disappointment. An approach that is based on the concept of *Avidya* as an obstacle to a healthy state would empathically explore why the person is experiencing the disappointment so keenly, allow the individual to situate themselves vis-à-vis the experience and eventually enrich their self-perspective until there is a fuller sense of Self that is able to integrate the disappointment rather than feeling diminished by it. An immediate effort to target the suffering that is the result of the disappointment—say by administering medication for depression—even if very successful in resolving the depression (suffering), might promote the *Avidya* (sense of self as small) and create the conditions for further suffering in the future (Desikachar, 2001). In this case, the *Avidya* is the incorrect self-knowledge that disappointment takes away from the essential wholeness of the self and *Vidya* is the sense that the self is still whole despite the disappointment. Medication that is administered simply with the goal of reducing the suffering without concurrent explorations of self-awareness may result in the maintenance of the idea that disappointment is to be avoided since it causes suffering. Such an approach is not philosophically aligned with the yoga focus on human growth. Laungani's (1992) paper and experience of focusing on the big picture during the period of his illness is a good example of maintaining a relative *Vidya* during a period where there is a great vulnerability for collapse into *Avidya*. Through his work, relationships and doubtless other psychic resources, Laungani was able to maintain a self-knowledge that more or less encompassed a sense of wholeness despite the strong circumstantial pull to identify himself completely with his illness (Laungani, 1992). This is an example of *Vidya* as conceptualized in a model of dynamic yoga psychology.

In a Western model the illness would be seen as a stressor, while in the yoga psychology model, only if the illness contracts or diminishes a person's sense of self is it considered stressful. In Laungani's words from another paper: 'Most intelligent and reflective people pass through similar torments, doubts and uncertainties concerning the nature and substance of their lives and meaning and purpose, which they could legitimately assign to their inner and outer existence' (Laungani, 2002d: 31). Laungani felt these searches for meaning with their accompanying torments, were not to be pathologized, even if co-occurring with what might be called 'symptoms' in the Western paradigm.

*Asmita*, the second *Klesha* or stressor is 'the sense of I' as an agent that can influence life events (Desikachar, 1987). *Asmita* is a pull to action and is considered to create a vulnerability to stress because it increases the responsibility on the individual self to a veritable level of omnipotence (Bhushan, 1987; Saraswati, 1980). In yoga psychology, the sense of self as a destiny fulfilling agent is thought to prompt action—fight or flight—versus reflection, a state that lies beyond fight or flight (Le Page, 2002a). For an example of *Asmita*, we can consider Laungani's (2002d) reference to the story *Samskara*, which describes the reaction of a village priest to an event that shatters social norms: the death of a high-caste man in the home of his mistress, a low-caste prostitute. In the story, this event is a stressor for the whole village that crystallizes around the logistics of how, where and by whom the funeral rites should be performed. The response of the priest who shoulders the responsibility of this event by virtue of his role in the funeral arrangements is a good example of *Asmita*. The priest feels that he must somehow solve this crisis, begins to feel an increasing identification with the event and a sense that his own self-esteem lies in solving this problem.

> Aware that the entire village looked up to him, he consulted all the religious texts, spoke to priests from other neighboring villages, but was unable to find a satisfactory solution. In the mean time of course the corpse remained in the house of the prostitute. The high priest in the village who was the most revered and respected member of the community felt totally traumatized by the event. He felt he had failed the villages, and despite his learning and erudition, had been unable to resolve the crisis...(he) was ultimately destroyed by the event. (Laungani, 2002d: 136)

The excerpt depicts the cycle of *Asmita*: a growing sense that the individual is personally responsible for the crisis at hand, that he alone is responsible for resolving it and the subsequent marshalling of individual and even community resources towards the end of problem-solving. The whole process leaves the individual vulnerable to suffering. *Avidya* represents a collapse of Self-awareness, so does *Asmita*. However, the quality of the collapse is slightly different. While *Avidya* or ignorance consists in identifying with an event that is not the whole me, *Asmita* is the identification with 'me' as the answer to the whole event. During the experience of *Asmita* the world appears to shrink, thereby infusing self-awareness with a sense of omnipotence (Bhushan, 1987; Le Page, 2002a; Saraswati, 1980). A consequent vulnerability to personal psychic injury and the inevitable disappointment that marks omnipotent grandeur results in *Dhuka* or suffering.

*Avidya* and *Asmita*—the contraction of awareness and the identification with a contracted awareness—lead to the next two *Kleshas*—*Raga* and *Dvesha* (Bhushan, 1987; Le Page, 2002a; Saraswati, 1980). The latter two *Kleshas* are thought of as efforts to find a solution to the sense of suffering that is the result of a contracted awareness (Bhushan, 1987; Saraswati, 1980). *Raga*, translated as 'desire' is not a wish but a highly driven, even desperate desire, that is chronic to the contracted state of self created in a situation of *Avidya* and *Asmita* (Bhushan, 1987). Desire may be triggered by psychic stress or perpetuate psychic stress and may be accompanied by biological indicators of increased autonomic arousal (fight syndrome) as the organism mobilizes to fulfil the desire (Le Page, 2002a). Desire drives the individual to action because the organism becomes dedicated to the service of the desire (Le Page, 2002a). There is a collapse of the reflective capacity to consider the relative need for desire fulfilment prior to engaging the system to work for it (Le Page, 2002a).

*Raga* as a *Klesha* does not mean that all desires are pathologized as they were in the case of renunciates such as the Buddha (Le Page, 2002a). Rather, *Raga* as a *Klesha* for the average person is probably well-understood as the relentless pursuit of a desire in the absence of reflection on the source of the desire, from a contracted self-space and with little or no ability to contemplate or moderate that pursuit (Saraswati, 1986). Possessiveness, fear of loss, the perception of desired objects as unique, frequent expectations of reward and identification with the *Raga* objects are some of the effects of *Raga* as a *Klesha* (Bhushan, 1996).

*Dvesha*, the fourth *Klesha* is the flight response representing psychic tasks that are avoided and experiences that are feared (Bhushan, 1996; Le Page, 2002a). *Dveshas* occur because of a contracted sense of Self, caused either by *Avidya* (identifying with an event) or *Asmita* (omnipotent problem-solving). *Dveshas* may occur in the short- or long-term or on different scales—from avoiding someone who is anxiety provoking, to avoiding a whole arena of life, both considered to also perpetuate a contracted state of self. An example is described by Laungani in his work on death and bereavement in which he discusses the extent to which identity among upper caste is built around avoiding certain tasks such as those related to death. In his words: 'No high-caste Hindu would wish to set up a funeral director's business because it would mean loosing one's caste. To lose caste is to lose identity and the sense of communal security that *jati* (caste) brings' (Laungani, 1996: 193). When the self is experienced as contracted—that is, not whole—severe limitations upon its self-perceived capacities may arise and these also fall under the *rubrique* of *Dveshas*. In the previous example, the cycle of *Avidya–Asmita–Dvesha* can be seen by a contracted sense of self or *Avidya* (inflexible experience of self as high-caste), a personal responsibility or *Asmita* (strong feeling that one has to protect one's caste status) and action oriented, non-reflective avoidance behaviour or *Dvesha* (avoiding funeral director's position). Like *Ragas*, all *Dveshas* need not be pathologized, rather the emphasis is on an awareness of their existence and a reflective process around them regardless of behavioural outcome.

Finally, the fifth *Klesha, Abhinivesha* is translated as death-anxiety (Desikachar, 1987). During *Abhinivesha,* there is an impetus to action that stems from a sense of an acute shortage of time, stemming from the sense that death is imminent. In recalling a purely biological model, an animal under fear of death at the hands of a predator tends to move as fast as possible in order to escape death (Le Page, 2002a). In yoga psychology, *Abhinivesha* or death-anxiety pushes individuals to move as fast as possible—in the process running towards their *Raga*s or away from their *Dveshas*—in an effort to deal with their feelings of *Abhinivesha* (Le Page, 2002a). In addition, *Abhinivesha* may occur long-term across the life-span wherein an individual feels like certain ambitions or tasks must be completed as soon as possible due to a collapse of time experienced by the imminence of death. This may be particularly acute in someone experiencing severe illness or in a severely traumatized individual.

At the heart of yoga psychology are the following central concepts: first the importance of a larger sense of wholeness of the mind-body-breath and spirit, second, the criticality of the reflective function in maintaining and growing this larger self-awareness and finally, the importance of maintaining a meaningful relationship to time (collapsed in fight-flight and death anxiety) in order to support the process of enlarging self-awareness.

## PLAYING AMIDST THE PILLARS: CULTURE, SELF-AWARENESS AND THE *KLESHAS*

In a psychology that centres around Self-awareness—as does yoga psychology—culture is important because much of what we consider to be our 'self' involves culturally derived shared beliefs, values and norms that tend to construct the self (Kitamaya et al., 1997). However, a clearly stated theoretical relationship between yoga and culture is absent from the literature, other than of course the fact that yoga is culturally Indian in origin (Narayanan, 2007). In this section of the chapter, I will situate yoga psychology in the larger sphere of cultural psychology by using Winnicott's definition of culture and Laungani's cultural pillars (Laungani, 1996, 2001b) to further elaborate on the *Klesha*s not only as a part of yoga's self-psychology but also as a theory of cultural psychology.

British psychologist Winnicott defined culture as those phenomena that develop in the space between inner-psychic and external reality (Winnicott, 1971). Culture, in Winnicottian terms, is distinct from values which are more clearly a part of internal or external reality. Laungani's work however focuses on cultural values, which he describes as 'the currently held normative expectations that underlie individual and social conduct' (Laungani, 2001a: 345). In his essay on cultural pillars that describe expectable patterns of behaviour in India and England, Laungani states that 'Salient beliefs concerning right and wrong, good and bad, normal and abnormal, appropriate and inappropriate, proper and improper and the like, are to a large extent influenced by the values operative in the culture' (Laungani, 2001a: 345). Laungani's cultural pillars of expectable behaviour—such as individualism and materialism among people from British culture and spiritualism and collectivism from those raised in the Indian tradition are presented as static elements.

While other theorists have defined culture differently based on their individual epistemological preferences, there are several reasons for integrating Winnicott's definition of culture into the field of yogic psychology. First, Winnicott's definition is particularly applicable to yogic psychology because it locates cultural experience in the first sensation of self-ness as distinct from 'union with the mother' (Winnicott, 1971: 97). Winnicott writes that 'Culture is first and foremost created at an instinctual level in the area of potential space between the mother and the baby' (Winnicott, 1971: 51). Winnicott's concept of 'union with the mother' that predates a sense of separateness is the closest concept I know of in Western language and psychology that approximates the concept of the unified Self in yogic psychology. Second, Winnicott's definition of 'potential space' (Winnicott, 1971: 41) in which there is room for play and therefore culture to develop bears some resemblance to the concept of the expanded self in yoga psychology. Just as the collapse of the expanded self results in the impetus to action without the reflective function and resultant psychic suffering (Bhushan, 1987), so does the potential space and the playing ability when collapsed, result in psychic distress (Winnicott, 1971). Just as the yoga psychologist's task is to facilitate a return to baseline wholeness and eventually a growth towards a more expanded self (Le Page, 2002a), the Winnicottian therapist's role is in 'bringing the patient from a state of not being able to play into a state of being able to play' through an increase in the potential space for play (Winnicott, 1971: 38). Third, Winnicott's definition of culture is meaningful in an understanding of the psyche as it locates cultural experience as a potential bridge between inner and outer worlds. Winnicott accords a particular peculiarity to cultural experience that cannot be accounted for by inner-psychic reality or external reality but is some kind of intermediate area between the two (Winnicott, 1971). This aspect of Winnicott's definition allows a distinction between culture and values. Fourth, Winnicott's definition views a mutually constitutive dynamic between the individual and culture such that the individual is not merely born into a culture but becomes into and plays with elements that serve as his or her culture (Winnicott, 1971). Other authors have even conceptualized mental illness as accountable, to some measure, to a failure of certain individuals to successfully negotiate the cultural paradigm

(Laing, 1960). Finally, Winnicott's definition concurs with research findings that suggest that individuals are not born into cultural paradigms so much as they negotiate, learn to fit into—and occasionally transform—through experience, their relationship to cultural paradigms. For example, Sinha et al.'s (2002) study showed that individuals in a 'collectivist culture' in India still have individualistic needs that must then be played with and negotiated such that they may find fruitful cultural expression (Sinha et al., 2002).

Just as in an individual model of psychic stress there is a tension between the 'id' and the 'superego', in a cultural model of psychic stress, there is a tension between the needs of the individual's inner-psychic reality and the demands of external reality (Winnicott, 1971). Such a model of stress keeps the inner–outer dialectic that is implicit in the id–superego conflict without limiting the dialectic exclusively to the Western cultural symbols of id and superego. Culture, as Winnicott defines, is a solution to the internal and external needs and demands via playful and symbolic experience (Winnicott, 1971). An individual's journey, in relationship to culture is in some sense a process of testing and evaluating through personal experience what aspects of culturally agreed upon truth feels individually true and what aspects of individual truth may find cultural validity.

The journey to the discovery of the culturally meaningful self from the culturally constructed self parallels in many ways the journey towards a multi-dimensional (5-*Kosha*) Self in the yoga tradition. In considering these journeys towards more authentic selves, social values are of consideration because bridges between inner and outer worlds cannot occur in isolation of a larger social setting in which the Winnicottian mother finds herself, nor can yoga as a technology—with the exception of renunciates—take place outside of the context of social relationships (Desikachar, 1999; Le Page, 2002a, 2002b). Without a certain degree of social acceptance, individuals suffer from 'ontological insecurity' (Laing, 1960). Cultural norms and values represent group-sanctioned bridges between internal and external reality that may be differentially utilized by any particular individual within a culture. Cultural pillars—such as the ones described by Laungani (2002a)—are descriptors of deeply ingrained values that individuals must negotiate in the architectural construction of the cultural self.

The above two concepts—culture as a bridge between the inside and outside (Winnicott, 1971) and cultural pillars (Laungani, 2002a, b) that mark historically successful and socially sanctioned bridges between inner and outer realities—are easily situated within the yoga psychology framework of the *Klesha*s (Desikachar, 1999; Le Page, 2002a).

I had stated in the previous section that at the heart of yoga psychology are two concepts: first the importance of a larger self-awareness of wholeness of the mind-body-breath and spirit and second, the primacy of the reflective function in maintaining, growing and deepening this larger self-awareness. Winnicott's 'potential space' in which culture arises can only exist, I believe, when there is a larger self-awareness akin to that described in the yoga tradition. In Winnicott's potential space as well as in yoga psychology's expanded self-awareness there is the possibility of a 'reflective' (Le Page, 2002a; Saraswati, 1980) or 'playing' (Winnicott, 1971) function. Culture in the absence of play and reflection is probably better described as a value and indeed may become a type of *Klesha* or obstacle to an expanded self-awareness. 'Culture', in this frozen state might closely approximate static pillars or values. During a contraction of the self and the shutting-down of the reflective function, as is often the case in an acute stress state, an automatic deferment to cultural pillars may take place as a defence, creating a *Klesha* or obstacle to an expanded state of awareness. I would describe this as a collapse of the journey of cultural play as well as the journey of yoga and a potential area for intervention by the multicultural or yoga psychologist. Such an occurrence could take place in individualist or collectivist cultures or families. To be able to step back and be able to reflect upon a choice versus proceeding forward without thoughtfulness would fall under the category of the *Klesha Avidya* (lack of self knowledge). Proceeding without reflection creates a vulnerability to the stress response because there the collapse of the reflective function creates a tendency to action—fight or flight—which in this example could mean a flight away from cultural norms (the *Klesha Dvesha*) or a fight for traditionalism or modernity amidst those norms (the *Klesha Raga*). Neither of these fight–flight states is considered yogic in state or in technique since they denote an absence of the reflective function and a *modus operandi* that takes place from a contracted state of self (Saraswati, 1980). Following reflection, the action itself is less important and a culturally accommodative action may very well be chosen.

Static culture that is integrated without the element of play—including dominant cultural trends such as individualism, collectivism, materialism and spiritualism—can contribute to the *Klesha Avidya* and the use of cultural pillars as a defence. For example, in a culture of individualism, community needs may be neglected not so much by choice but by blind participation in the 'culture of individualism' (Kasser, 2002). Participation in the culture of individualism delineates the 'self' by the boundaries of the body, or the self's achievements or goals creating a vulnerability to stress that is very different for someone who defines 'self' as community (Kasser, 2002). In both cases, there may be a tendency for certain individual or community needs to be suppressed or go unrecognized because they fall outside the cultural norm of individualism.

In a model of psychology based on Self-awareness and the dynamics surrounding self-awareness, Laungani's cultural pillars are particularly useful in defining the norms based on which people make cultural negotiations and play between internal and external reality. To use a visual image, it may be useful to think of the pillars themselves as columns within a larger space that depicts the whole Self. Rather than define cultures as being characterized by pillars, today's multicultural context suggests that an interest for the multicultural psychologist may lay in the negotiations that individuals, families and societies make occur in the cultural spaces between the pillars. Different situations, ethno-geographical locations, time periods in history, economic stressors and a constellation of other factors pull for negotiations in one direction or another. 'Playing' and potential space for culture to arise amidst the pillars describes ongoing negotiations whereas a static state where pillars represent the person or culture speaks more to situations where cultural values have become *Kleshas* or obstacles to the state of yoga.

## IMPLICATIONS FOR MULTICULTURAL PSYCHOTHERAPY AND COUNSELLING

Drawing upon the works of Bhushan (1987, 1996, 1998), Laungani (1994, 2001a, 2001b, 2002b, 2002c and 2004a, 2004b) and Winnicott (1971) to offer an integrative model of psychic stress that has originated in the yoga psychology tradition but is influenced by multicultural and psychodynamic perspectives is an exercise in playing with as well as placing 'cultures on equal terms' (Laungani, 2002: 151). Such an exercise has implications for multicultural psychotherapy and counselling both in terms of content and process as I will describe here.

From a content perspective, birthing yogic psychology into a form that is comprehensible and in part Western in descriptive structure, is a step in Laungani's call for an indigenization of cross-cultural therapy (Laungani, 2002a). Focusing primarily on concepts of awareness and consciousness rather than on measurable behaviours is a shift away from the Western natural science approach and therefore part of the process of liberating cross-cultural psychological topics from being 'handmaidens' to mainstream Western psychology (Laungani, 2002a: 385). Integrating an inquiry into the meaning of culture from a Western psychologist (Winnicott) marks a return to the philosophical heritage of Western psychology that, as Laungani describes, 'forms an integral part of one's subjective and existential world and of therapeutic process' (Laungani, 2004b: 107). Finally, marrying theories from the Indian tradition and the perspective of British psychologists, invites a proliferation of boundaries in a way that does not believe in a mutual exclusion of culture-based epistemological and ontological realities.

From a process perspective, the implications for multicultural psychotherapy and counselling arise from a conscious integration of culturally relevant methodologies in the body of the chapter as I will now describe. First, I purposefully chose to address philosophical and conceptual issues rather than bring the yogic psychology perspectives to equal terms with the Western perspectives on the basis of 'scientific' findings. Second, I used traditional yogic techniques, such as philosophical inquiry, metaphor and storytelling in this chapter to suggest that these processes also have their own legitimacy in both Indian and British culture inasmuch as do double-blind randomized clinical trials. Third, while there was a measure of my own creative analytical process in the chapter, I named—as is the tradition in India—at the outset, the expert teachers and visionaries—Bhushan, Le Page, Laungani and Winnicott—whose works had inspired and exhorted this piece of writing versus presenting it as an objective work. Fourth, I based my justification for the use of Winnicott's definition of culture alongside a yogic psychology conceptual framework on reasons that are both emotional (feels like a fit) and cognitive/logical (as per the detailed explanation I provided in that section). Finally, in the process of writing this chapter, I used narrative as much as logical techniques in an effort to blend poly-cultural variables thereby to some extent mirroring in the process of the chapter some of the cultural negotiations I described in the content.

## CONCLUSION

In this chapter, I have presented some concepts from yoga psychology notably the *Kleshas*—obstacles to yoga, and the *Koshas*—multidimensional aspects of an expanded sense of self. I have also discussed these concepts within the context of culture using a particular definition of culture from Winnicott to situate and contextualize both the definition of culture and the definition of values as distinct from culture. Playing amidst the pillars is a visual image I have offered for the journey to and from different states of self-awareness in which the cultural pillars are topographical realities in the external world with correlates in the internal world and a cultural journey includes negotiations that take place between inner and external worlds, pillars and different states of self-awareness. The image allows for both a rigid adherence to the pillars—which may be particularly relevant during periods of acute stress or to cultural groups in general—as well as a 'playing between the pillars', that may be facilitated by cultural yoga psychologists where there is some measure of flexibility, choice and playful reflection around culture from a state of expanded self-awareness.

Having used traditional, modern as well as Indian and Euro-American perspectives in both the process and content of this work, I believe the above exploration settles into the potential space of multicultural psychology which involves having choices that are not binary but rather potentially more complex and spacious (Laungani, 2002a, b, 2004a, b; Winnicott, 1971). Rather than espouse the proposed scientific and objective status of psychologists who do not identify as multicultural, I believe this piece accepts the invitation to multicultural psychologists to enjoy the benefits of methodological complexity and celebrate the legitimacy of epistemological diversity in the footsteps of pioneers such as Laungani.

## NOTES

1. Here and throughout the chapter, I will use 'yoga psychology' to mean the 'science of mind' as explored in India's contemplative tradition (Bhushan, 1987: 1). The question of what falls under the rubrique of yoga psychology is open to ongoing development and codification during the renaissance of yoga that has been ongoing over the last few decades (Bhushan, 1987). The 'yoga psychology' spoken of in this chapter draws from different periods in the history of yoga but is most influenced by the Tantra yoga period (Saraswati, 1980) whose integration of mutiple dualities in a single whole reality through direct experience embodies the most studied concepts in yoga psychology today (Bhushan, 1987; Easwaran, 2000).
2. The word Self is written with a capitalized S to distinguish the self (small s) from the Self that is written about in the yoga tradition. While the self (small s) refers to self-perception—the Self refers to a 'something else' that remains unchanged amidst fluctuations in self-perception (Easwaran, 2000).
3. The formal codification of meditation as a yoga technique did not occur till several centuries later when Patanjali collected this information in his Yoga Sutras (Desikachar, 1999).
4. This may be the appropriate time in the chapter to point out that *Kleshas* are loosely defined as stressors (Ramachandra, 1983), but more strictly defined as obstacles to the state of yoga (Desikachar, 1999) and defined in yoga psychology as 'self-contracting' thoughts, feelings, environments and experiences (Bhushan, 1987).
5. Yoga psychology is both positive and normative in that it encourages growth and change while simultaneously suggesting that this growth or change is not a 'becoming' something else but a 'being what is'. Thus, paradoxically, the journey of yoga is 'becoming who we are' (Bhushan, 1998; Le Page, 2002a, 2002b).

## REFERENCES

Aldwin, C. M. and Revenson, T. A. (1987). Does coping help? A re-examination of the relationship between coping and mental health. *Journal of Personality and Social Psychology, 53*, 337–348.

Beck, A. T. (1975). *Cognitive therapy and the emotional disorders*. New York: International Universities Press Inc.

Beck, A. T., Epstein, N. and Harrison, R. (1983). Cognitions, attitudes and personality imensions in depression. *British Journal of Cognitive Therapy, 1*, 1–16.

Bhushan, L. I. (1987). Yoga psychology: A re-emerging Field [Electronic Version]. *Bihar School of Yoga Magazine*, July 1987.

———. (1994). A yogic model of mental health [Electronic Version]. *Indian Journal of Psychological Issues, 1*(3), 1–5.

———. (1996). Asakti-Anasakti: A model of mental health [Electronic Version] *Bihar School of Yoga Magazine*, January 1996.

———. (1998). Yoga: An instrument of psychological transformation [Electronic Version]. *Bihar School of Yoga Magazine*, September 1998.

Cornelissen, M. (2003). The need for the Indian tradition. *Psychological Studies, 48*, 38–52.

Desikachar, T. K. V. (1987). *The yoga sutras of Patanjali (a translation).* New Delhi, India: East-West Books.

———. (1999). *The Heart of Yoga: Developing a Personal Practice* (Revised Edition). USA: Inner Traditions International.

———. (2001). *The yoga of Krishnamacharya.* Symposium conducted at the Krishnamacharya Yoga Mandiram, Chennai, India.

Easwaran, E. (2000). *The Upanishads.* India: Penguin Books.

Feuerstein, G. (2005). *The Yoga tradition: Its history, literature, philosophy and practice.* New Delhi: Motilal Banarsidass.

Kasser, T. (2002). *The high price of materialism.* Cambridge, MA: MIT Press.

Kitamaya, S., Matsumoto, H., Markus, H. and Norasakkunit, V. (1997). Individual and collective process in the construction of the Self: Self-enhancement in the United States and self-criticism in Japan. *Journal of Personality and Social Psychology, 72*(6), 1245–1267.

La Planche, J. and Ponalis, J. B. (1974). *The language of psychoanalysis.* New York: Norton Press.

Laing, R. D. (1960). *The divided self: An existential study in sanity and madness.* Harmondsworth: Penguin.

Laungani, P. (1992). *It Shouldn't Happen To A Patient.* London: Whiting & Birch Ltd.

———. (1994). Cultural differences in Stress: India and England. *Counselling Psychology Review, 9*(4), 25–37.

———. (1996). Cross-cultural investigations of stress: Conceptual and methodological considerations. *International Journal of Stress Management, 3*(1), 25–35.

———. (2001a). The influence of culture on stress: India and England. In Adler, L. L. and Gielen, U. P. (Eds), *Cross-cultural topics in psychology (2nd ed.).* Westport, CT, US: Praeger Publishers/Greenwood Publishing Group.

———. (2001b). Understanding mental illness across cultures. In S. Palmer (Ed.), *Multicultural counselling: A reader, part II: Theory and practice of multicultural counselling.* London: Sage Publications.

———. (2002a). Cross-cultural psychology: A handmaiden to mainstream western psychology. *Counselling Psychology Quarterly, 15*(4), 385–397.

———. (2002b). Mindless psychiatry and dubious ethics. *Counselling Psychology Quarterly, 15*(1), 23–33.

———. (2002c). Stress, trauma and coping strategies: Cross-cultural variations. *International Journal of Group Tensions, 21*(2), 127–153.

———. (2002d). Hindu spirituality in life, death, and bereavement. In J. D. Morgan and P. Laungani (Eds), *Death and bereavement around the world* (Vol. 1, pp. 9–38). Amityville, NY: Baywood.

———. (2004a). Counselling and therapy in a multi-cultural setting. *Counselling Psychology Quarterly, 17*(2), 195–207.

———. (2004b). Some unresolved issues in philosophy and psychology: Their implications for therapy. *Counselling Psychology Quarterly, 17*(1), 107–123.

Le Page, J. (2002a). *Yoga therapy*. Brazil: Integrative Yoga Therapy Press.

———. (2002b). Creating yoga therapy classes and individual sessions that work. *International Journal of Yoga Therapy, 1,* 1–14.

Menninger, K. A. (1954). Regulatory devices of the ego under major stress. *Journal of the American Psychoanalytic Association, 2*(2), 280–310.

Myers, J. E., Sweeney, T. J. and Witmer, J. M. (2000). The wheel of wellness counseling for wellness: A holistic model for treatment planning. *Journal of Counseling and Development, 78*(3), 251–266.

Narayanan, A. (2007). What empirical evidence is available for the impact of a yoga practice on different aspects of the self? Can Brahman be operationalized? Psy.D. Dissertation, Pacific Graduate School of Psychology-Stanford Universtiy Psy.D. consortium, Dissertation Abstracts International, B 68, 07.

Okasha, S. (2008). *Us and them: The fundamental bias in the therapeutic relationship.* Paper presented at the Richmond Area Multi-Services Cultural Competency Project, San Francisco, CA.

Ramachandra, R. S. K. (1983). The conception of stress in Indian thought: The theoretical aspects of stress in Samkhya and Yoga systems. *NIMHANS Journal, 1,* 115–121.

Saraswati, S. S. (1980). *Yoga from shore to shore* (3rd ed.). Munger, India: Bihar School of Yoga Press.

———. (1981). *A systematic course in the ancient tantric teachings of Yoga and Kriya*. Munger, India: Bihar School of Yoga Press.

———. (1986). Antar Mouna [Electronic Version]. *Bihar School of Yoga Magazine,* September 1996.

Sinha, B. K. and Watson, D. C. (2007). Stress, coping and psychological illness: A cross-cultural study. *International Journal of Stress Management, 14*(4), 386–397.

Sinha J. B. P., Vohra N., Singhal S. and Sinha R. (2002). Normative predictions of collectivist-individualist intentions and behaviour of Indians. *International Journal of Psychology, 37*(5), 309–319.

Teasdale, J., Moore, R., Hayhurst, H., Pope, M., Williams, S. and Segal, Z. (2002). Metacognitive awareness and prevention of relapse in depression: Empirical evidence. *Journal of Consulting and Clinical Psychology, 70*(2), 275–287.

Winnicottt, D. W. (1971). *Playing and reality*. London: Tavistock Publications.

# 8

# South Asian Traditional Healing in Counselling: Laungani's Search for a Transcultural Approach

*Aanchal Rai and Roy Moodley*

## INTRODUCTION

**In** recent decades, South Asian communities in the West have been steadily increasing as a result of immigration and population growth (Citizenship and Immigration Canada, 2006; National Statistics, 2005). The health and mental health needs of these communities are numerous and varied, but are not being adequately met by the mainstream health care providers. The reasons are complex, but in general, health and mental health care practices are seen as culturally insensitive, discriminatory and lacking in cultural competencies and knowledge (Bhugra and Bhui, 2007; Commander et al., 1999; Sue and Sue, 1990). Consequently, it results in the underutilization, premature termination and poor outcomes for those who use the services (Alexander, 1999; Gill-Badesha, 2004; Herring, 1999; Laungani, 2002a).

Numerous efforts have been made to address the inequalities and difficulties faced by South Asians. For example, there has been an increase in employing medical doctors in hospitals and clinics; the inclusion of interpreters in health and mental health care services; culture sensitive practices, such as the availability of appropriate food (for example, *halal*, vegetarian, and so on) and the increasing accessibility to counselling psychology and psychotherapy services. However, there still remain some major areas of contention, such as dissimilar beliefs about illness and cure seeking, differing world views and the emphasis of a universal approach to health and mental health care (Laungani, 2002a; Moodley,

2000a; Moodley, 2000b). A strong critique has already been made against counselling psychology and psychotherapy (Laungani 1997; Moodley, 1999a). For example, Pittu Laungani (1997) argued that a culture-centred approach was more appropriate than a client-centred approach for South Asian clients, which contextualizes the client in his or her culture during therapy. He identified many incongruencies between counselling psychology and psychotherapy and the mental health needs of South Asian clients. In formulating a culture-based theory in therapy, Pittu Laungani not only interrogated the individualistic and Eurocentric ways in which counselling and psychotherapy is provided, but sought to inform counselling psychology of new and innovative ways in which all clients could benefit from therapy. His emphasis on cultural contexts, differing belief systems, and culturally sanctioned ways of representing and presenting illness are critical features in his work.

Furthermore, Pittu Laungani believed that therapists can only gain access to clients' pain and discomfort through meaningful intercultural communication. He argued that an impasse in therapy occurs when a therapist and client are unable to have a 'meaningful intercultural communication' (Laungani, 1997: 343), which is based on a common language, common verbal and non-verbal meanings, ethical standards and/or political ideas (Laungani, 1997). Since East-West cultures differ to a great extent, based on their values and belief systems which are incorporated into a person's daily functioning and world view, it makes the communication process much more complex and difficult. As Laungani says, 'Our beliefs and behaviours do not arise in a social vacuum...[they are] to a large measure influenced by the dominant values prevalent in our culture...[and] in that sense we are all prisoners of our own culture, handcuffed to it' (Laungani, 2004a: 56). In acknowledging the importance and the limitations of culture, Pittu Laungani clearly maintains that any form of communication in counselling and psychotherapy is heavily laden with pitfalls and challenges, to the extent that each person can be 'handcuffed to culture' and therefore unable to be free of it. For a therapist, this will mean navigating negative countertransference feelings related to individual and group stereotyping, cultural generalizations and racist thoughts. By respecting and acknowledging a client's culture and value system, therapists can promote a meaningful and problem-solving experience for their clients (Laungani, 1997).

In this chapter, we discuss the issues that Pittu Laungani raises concerning the current gap between the counselling and psychotherapy practices and South Asian mental health needs. In order to bridge the gap, Pittu Laungani proposed a transcultural approach within which spirituality, religion and South Asian indigenous and traditional healing[1] methods can be integrated and infused into counselling. But first we begin with a discussion of Laungani's critique on Western counselling and psychotherapy.

## THE EAST-WEST GAP IN COUNSELLING PSYCHOLOGY

According to Laungani, the Western value system underlies the foundation of Western psychology and becomes the primary reason for leading to a chasm between its theories and practices, and the needs of South Asian clients. It is crucial to note that a gap is formed, primarily when counselling psychologists and mental health practitioners fail to acknowledge and value the belief systems of their clients. Laungani labels this phenomenon as 'cultural blindness', saying that it is

> an inability, unwillingness or failure to recognize that some of the most obvious differences in beliefs, attitudes, values and behaviours among different groups of people are related to their own unique cultural backgrounds...[this] blindness was due to the fact that Western psychologists in general...either could not, did not or chose not to see the vital role that culture played in the development of the psyche. (Laungani, 2002a: 392–393)

Indeed, this is a strong argument by Laungani for culture and one that still remains relevant for the mainstream of counselling and psychotherapy. However, Laungani's view that Western psychologists are 'culturally blind' is a personal one, and one that is continuously being challenged by multicultural counselling, critical multicultural practices, the concept of 'colouring in the white' and the notion of replacing multiculturalism in counselling and psychotherapy (Moodley, 2007).

Pittu Laungani's critique was not focused on Western psychologists only, he also examined client-centred therapy for its relevance to South Asian clients, which resulted in his 'culture-centered and not client-centered' article (Laungani, 1997); suggesting that crucial differences exist between the fundamental cultural assumptions held by counsellors and those by South Asian clients, thus leading to a wide chasm. According to Laungani (1997), 'clients do not understand or share the fundamental assumptions of the counsellors. As a result, client-centred counselling becomes irrelevant' (Laungani, 1997: 343). He goes on to describe the specific tenets of counselling that maintain and foster the gap between counselling and South Asian mental health needs. The factors inherent to counselling that have been identified by Laungani include: emphasis of separate selves in Western counselling; the focus on an individual self in Western therapy; the belief of a necessity for maintaining an equitable relationship between the counsellor and the client; the belief that relationships are contractual and time-limited, and that psychological theories are universal and generically applicable to all cultures (Laungani, 2004a). These factors are discussed in the following:

## Division and Splitting of the 'Self' in Therapy

Western forms of healing have often differentiated between the body, mind and spirit of a person (Pachuta, 1993). Consequently, these aspects of a person are assessed and treated in different disciplines of Western health care. For example, Western counsellors often deal with clients who suffer from disturbances related to mind and emotions, but not the physical self (Moodley and West, 2005). According to Laungani, Western counselling follows the principle of individualism, where, 'mental illness is related to the emphasis on self-reliance, complemented by a belief in free will, which asserts that one must trust one's own ability to solve one's problems by logical, rational and scientific means' (Laungani, 2002b: 146).

This logical and rational understanding of the self is contradictory to the holistic concept, which underpins South Asian world view and concept of the self. In addition to the concept of holism, a related concept is that of harmony between the various selves of a person. In South Asian philosophy of health and well-being, harmony between the holistic self and the nature/environment reflects a state of health and well-being. According to Bojuwoye (2001), disharmony with the nature/environment signifies illness; a point that Alladin (1999) makes when he says that a person's 'inner experience of self should be clearly delineated from the outside' (Alladin, 1999: 92). Indeed, the concept of harmony of the physical, mental and spiritual self with nature/environment is not a common occurrence in Western forms of therapy (Laungani, 2002b; West, 2005). Therefore, Western counselling which primarily focuses on a specific aspect of a person—the mind and emotion—could easily be a challenge for some South Asian clients who construct 'the self' in a holistic way. Consequently, Western therapists' interpretations and analysis tends to be in conflict with South Asian clients who construct their illness representation and presentations in a holistic way.

The concept of the individual 'self' in therapy may differ in the ways that many ethnic minority clients see themselves and the way this concept is understood in therapy. The evolution of the self is a highly complex process and is culturally constructed, thus making it problematic for South Asian clients in therapy. For example, in therapy, clients' needs are discussed and reflected on; their own concerns are valued and emphasized in the problem-solving conversation with the counsellor. Additionally, the focus in counselling lies, primarily, on the person and not on his or her family, work or social environment (D'Ardenne and Mahtani, 1989; Sue and Sue, 1977). This structure constructs a particular focus for clients; the resolution of issues pertain to their own lives. This concept differs from the 'self system' of South Asian clients who see themselves as an integral part of their families and extended families. For example, in India and Pakistan families are emotionally interdependent and values such as interpersonal empathy, closeness, loyalty and interdependence are commonly shared among the family members (Jacobson, 1995; Weiss, 1994). Laungani (2002b), also, adds that for Indian clients, their familial, social, emotional and religious conditions play a crucial role in their understanding of psychological disturbances. Therefore, a South Asian client who reports being distressed would often refer to himself or herself in the context of the complexity and disruption in his/her relationships, especially the familial relationships.

The idea of a relational self also reflects the interdependent nature of relationships, where family members seek assistance from each other, often de-necessitating the act of seeking outside help for distresses (Gill-Badesha, 2004; Laungani, 2004a; Sharma, 1994). Furthermore, according to South Asian cultural values, disclosure of personal distress to others, and especially to strangers, is considered taboo. Laungani (2004a) aptly captures the essence of this taboo in his statement: 'Indians do not wash their dirty laundry in public' (Laungani, 2004a: 74). According to Laungani (2004a, 2004b), breaking this taboo brings disgrace upon the individual and his or her family since the person has decided to break the cultural norm of resolving issues within the four walls of the household. Seeking mental health assistance is often rare and is labelled as a 'strange' concept among South Asian groups (Chandras et al., 1999). Therefore, the focus on the individual self in the counselling session and the taboo associated with the concept of counselling become problematic factors for many South Asian clients whose cultural beliefs, self constructs and world view are distinct from those of the majority groups and Western mental health care.

## Universality of Psychological Theories

The principal belief in Western counselling and psychotherapy of a 'universality of psychological theories and concepts' (Sue et al., 1982: 47) has prevented the exploration of the culture and belief systems of ethno-cultural groups. As a result, the theories and practices of counselling and psychotherapy are dominant paradigms in the health and mental health provision in the West (Bojuwoye, 2001; Laungani, 2004a, 2004b). For example, the Western meanings attached to mental health, illness and well-being are categorized into several groups based on the characteristics of conditions such as depression, anxiety, schizophrenia, and so on. However, among South Asian groups, these various categories do not exist as they do in the Diagnostic and Statistical Manual of Mental Disorders (DSM)-IV manual. According to Shon and Ja, South Asians tend to dichotomize people as either 'normal' or 'crazy' (Shon and Ja, as cited in Sharma, 1994: 31), making it possible for some South Asians to harbour negative connotations about psychological distress, thus forcing him/her to abandon the idea of counselling altogether.

As discussed earlier, many South Asian individuals on the other hand, construct and perceive the person as a whole, where the mental, physical and social selves are not divided into separate categories (Kakar, 1982), thus the direct application of Western counselling theories and techniques to South Asian clients becomes impossible, if not difficult, in the clinical management of the client. Furthermore, such applications can lead to disruptive and unproductive counselling sessions due to differences in world views and cultural values and beliefs systems (Atkinson, 1985; Laungani, 2005; Sharma, 1994; Vontress, 1996).

## Counsellor–Client Relationship in Western Counselling

The process of the counsellor–client relationship has in recent years been advanced as one of the most important variables in counselling and psychotherapy. Given its neutral stance, congruence and non-judgemental presence, it has been argued, particularly in client-centred counselling that the process is ethical, equitable and democratic. However, Laungani (1999) and D'Ardenne and Mahtani (1989) have argued that this tenet of Western counselling is an illusion and mystifies the power relations in therapy. It promotes and maintains this position through the idea of individualism within which the client is expected to 'pursue their own clearly defined goals, take responsibility for their actions, cope with their problems, take credit for their successes and accept blame for any failure encountered on the way' (Laungani, 1999: 143).

This process can be seen to be incongruous with the South Asian belief system, where relationships are based on hierarchies and people in positions of authority, such as a doctor, an elder or a healer are respected and revered. Furthermore, people in positions of authority are expected to be directive in the relationship, where they mostly guide, instruct and advice the individual (D'Ardenne and Mahtani, 1989; Laungani, 1999). Similarly, South Asian clients also expect their counsellor to adopt a role of authority and guide them to use their own skills and expertize (Roland, 1988). This belief stands in sharp contradiction to the Western belief in a neutral counsellor–client relationship. For example, seeing a client as a daughter or addressing the counsellor as a mother is unacceptable in counselling and psychotherapy, and may be limited to the transference or countertransference relationship. If this issue arises then it is addressed in therapy. But, South Asian clients may intuitively view and respect a counsellor as an authority figure; as an older member of the extended family (Laungani, 2004a).

The way in which South Asian clients construct the counsellor–client relationship is an important factor in positive outcomes. According to Laungani (2004a), Western counselling follows the principles of cognitivism, which includes values such as: rational thought processes, restricted expression of emotions, emphasis on work and activity and the belief that relationships outside family life are by-products of work environments. On the other hand, Laungani argues that South Asian clients tend to follow the philosophy of emotionalism that include intuitions, feelings, the free expression of emotions, emphasis on relationships and the belief that work grows out of relationships (Laungani, 1997, 2004a). While this may appear to be a gross generalization of South Asian clients and Western counselling, it nevertheless is an important issue to consider since some South Asian clients may seek an emotional bond with their counsellors, constructing the relationship at a familial level, where the counsellor can also be given the status of a family member such as a father, uncle, brother and sister (Laungani, 2004a; Roland, 1988;). Indeed, this concept appears to be in sharp contrast to Western counselling, which is bound by ethical principles and policies that questions the idea of a dual relationship with the client (Koocher and Keith-Spiegel, 2008). Similarly, an expression of feelings and emotions by a South Asian client may seem obvious to them as a means to convey their pain, as opposed to conveying their concerns through thoughts, as expected in counselling and psychotherapy.

## SOUTH ASIAN TRADITIONAL HEALING IN TRANSCULTURAL COUNSELLING

In *Asian perspectives in counselling* (2004a), Pittu Laungani suggests that many South Asian clients often visit traditional healers for their concerns, distresses and illnesses because traditional healers are considered and acknowledged within their communities as possessing special insight, awareness, knowledge and skills that grow out of timeless wisdom (Lee and Armstrong, 1995). Since South Asian traditional healing methods tend to encompass all the three aspects of a person—the mind, body and spirit—clients may feel more comfortable in this kind of cure-seeking strategy (Alladin, 1999; Kakar, 1982; Laungani, 2002b, 2004a). According to Laungani (2002b), South Asian clients, 'may resort to formulations where the material and spiritual, physical and metaphysical, natural and supernatural explanations of phenomena coexist with one another' (p. 139–140). He suggests that attaining knowledge of these systems can 'provide different cultures with exciting opportunities to learn valuable lessons from one another…[and] lead to a better understanding of healing strategies [and] bring cultures together' (Laungani, 2005: 146). Laungani discusses a number of indigenous therapies that are often utilized by South Asians, such as Ayurveda,[2] Yoga,[3] Vedic Astrology[4] and religious counselling.[5]

Although Laungani did not explore the integration of traditional healing into counselling and psychotherapy in much detail, except for making a suggestion of increasing awareness about South Asian healing practices, he makes constant reference to Hindu spirituality, religion and traditional healing as an essential ingredient in the health and mental health of many South Asian clients. The studies conducted in the West reveal that many South Asians use traditional healing methods for their afflictions and prefer seeking assistance for their psychological disturbances from South Asian traditional healers (Chandras et al., 1999; Hilton et al., 2001; Kumar et al., 2005; Rao, 2006). For example, Hilton et al. (2001) found that many South Asian women in Canada seek traditional healers for coping with their illnesses and also tend to hide this resource from Western health care professionals for fear of being chided or 'disregarded as mere superstitions'. Also, Rao (2006) found that the assistance of traditional healers is not sought for every concern or illness, and not by all South Asian clients either. He cautions against making an assumption that all South Asians seek traditional healing over mainstream medicine. Other researchers in the UK and Australia have also noticed similar trends and have documented the prevalence and preference of traditional healers over mainstream health care practitioners by South Asians (Cochrane and Sashidharan, 1996; Dein and Sembhi, 2001; Greenwood et al., 2000; Hussain and Cochrane, 2004; Moodley, 1999b).

## MEANS BY WHICH COLLABORATION CAN BE BROUGHT ABOUT

Although the idea of collaboration is desirable and in some cases possible, it is however extremely difficult to achieve with particular groups of healers, and some types of healing practices. The history of Colonialism and the prevailing attitude towards ethnic minority health care practices have created much distrust and concerns between counsellors and traditional healers. Traditional healing is seen as 'scientifically invalid', 'superstitions' and a 'new age' engagement with very little or no conclusive health outcomes. Clearly this is a myth, and an erroneous assumption of an age-old healing tradition. Researchers throughout the world, as discussed earlier, have shown that traditional healers and healing are used by many people in many metropolitan cities in the West (Moodley and West, 2005). Moreover, recent research by Aanchal Rai (2008) in Toronto on South Asian traditional healers and their healing in counselling has shown that the traditional healers have been inundated with clients from all cultures and communities seeking help for all types of illness and distresses. This seems to suggest that the traditional healers are much more open than was previously thought. Indeed, it is now up to Western counsellors to understand and appreciate alternative world views (Myers et al., 2005), thus making collaboration highly possible.

There are a number of ways in which collaboration can be achieved: first, counsellors need to be aware of the role of traditional healers in counselling, health promotion and education, and vice versa. Second, both groups of practitioners need to have an understanding and appreciation of the theories and philosophies of each other's disciplines. Third, issues that govern the clinical practices would need to be shared with each other, such as assessment, ethics, treatment, boundaries, and so on. Many of these processes can be undertaken at seminars, workshops and conferences. Moreover, it can provide counsellors and healers to connect and form alliances, and create a referral system, where Western mental health care practitioners can refer their clients to traditional healers and vice versa. Another important outcome for a collaborative alliance is the possibility of engaging in joint research on all kinds of areas that interest traditional healers and counsellors. The results of this kind of collaboration would have consequences for further research, curriculum change, counsel or training and education, and supervision.

## CONCLUSION

Pittu Laungani highlighted the crucial role that culture plays in the mental health needs of South Asians in the West. These needs are often not met by counselling and psychotherapy due to the differences between the South Asian clients' world view and the Western psychotherapeutic paradigm. As a result, South Asians underutilize or abandon the counselling services offered to them.

Throughout his work, Pittu Laungani attempted to raise the status of ethnic minority cultural practices, particularly South Asian traditional healing in counselling and psychotherapy. He argued that a collaborative approach between traditional healers and counsellors would be beneficial for clients, irrespective of their ethno-cultural histories (Moodley and West, 2005). Through collaboration, South Asian traditional healers and Western counsellors can promote a deeper understanding and appreciation of an alternative world view of healing; understand the differences and similarities of the various approaches they use; become aware of the relationship between spirituality and religion, and the work of the healers; and facilitate a referral and consultation process. Overall, an alliance between the traditional healers and counsellors can magnify the trust and comfort level of South Asian clients with their counsellors. As Sue (1999) says, '[alliance with healers provides] knowledge and insights into cultural populations which would prove to value the delivery of counselling services...[and] enhance the cultural credibility of counselors' (p. 148).

Indeed, counsellors' cultural credibility can be greatly enhanced if they collaborate with traditional healers, even at a minimal level of gaining knowledge and insights into the different cultural and ethnic groups. Towards this end, it is clear that Pittu Laungani has made a tremendous contribution to the theory and practice of transcultural counselling psychology and psychotherapy; bringing to our attention the critical importance of culture, traditional healing, spirituality and religion. He is now seen as one of the pioneers of the multicultural counselling movement alongside significant elders, such as Clemmont E. Vontress, Paul Pedersen, Joseph Trimble, Juris G. Draguns, Anthony J. Marsella and many others.

## NOTES

1. Traditional healing has been defined as 'helping beliefs and practices that originate over extended time within the culture, that are not transported from other regions, and that are designed for treating the inhabitants of the given group' (Sue, 1999: 143). These healing methods are often dispensed by a helper who is a respected elder member of the family or community (Sue, 1999).
2. Ayurveda refers to 'an ancient Indian system of holistic medicine drawn from Vedic literature that seeks to balance individual imbalances through adjustments in diet, exercise and sleep and involving herbs, aromas, meditation and yoga to address health issues' (*Webster's New Millennium Dictionary of English*, 'Ayurveda', 2007).
3. Yoga refers to '*1.* A Hindu discipline aimed at training the consciousness for a state of perfect spiritual insight and tranquility, and/or *2.* A system of exercises practiced as part of this discipline to promote control of the body and mind' (*The American Heritage Dictionary of the English Language*, 'Yoga', 2007).
4. Vedic Astrology or *Jyotisha* is the oldest form of astrology prevalent in India. It is based on the stellar constellations and emphasizes that life is interplay of both fate and free will—fate being the reaction to our previous exercise of free will. It originates from the Vedas, the oldest scriptures from the sages of the Vedic culture in India (Dasa, 1993).
5. Religious counselling according to Laungani refers to the ascription of 'illness, distress and afflictions' to God, where the belief system and God's prowess is sought for the purpose of healing (Laungani, 2004b).

## REFERENCES

Alladin, W. (1999). Models of counselling and psychotherapy for a multiethnic society. In S. Palmer and P. Laungani (Eds), *Counselling in a multicultural society* (pp. 90–112). New Delhi: Sage Publications.

Alexander, Z. (1999). *Study of Black Asian and ethnic minority issues.* London: The Department of Health.

Atkinson, D. R. (1985). A meta-review of research on cross-cultural counseling and psychotherapy. *Journal of Multicultural Counseling and Development, 13*(4), 138–153.

Ayurveda. (n.d.). *Webster's new millennium dictionary of English,* preview edition *(v 0.9.7).* Retrieved 15 August, 2007 from Dictionary.com website: http://dictionary.reference.com/browse/ayurveda

Bhugra, D. and Bhui, K. (2007). *Textbook of cultural psychiatry.* UK: Cambridge University Press.

Bojuwoye, O. (2001). Crossing cultural boundaries in counselling. *International Journal for the Advancement of Counselling, 23*(1), 31–50.

Chandras, K. V., Eddy, J. P. and Spaulding, D. J. (1999). Counseling Asian Americans: Implications for training. *Education, 120*(2), 239.

Citizenship and Immigration Canada. (2006). Facts and figures 2006—immigration overview: Permanent and temporary residents. *In Canada—permanent residents by top source countries.* Retrieved 13 August 2007 from, http://www.cic.gc.ca/english/resources/statistics/facts2006/permanent/12.asp

Cochrane, R. and Sashidharan, S. P. (1996). Mental health and ethnic minorities: A review of the literature and service implications. In *Ethnicity and health: Reviews of literature and guidance for purchasers in the areas of cardiovascular disease, mental health and haemoglobinopathies.* CRD Report 5, NHS Centre for Reviews and Dissemination Social Policy Research Unit, University of York.

Commander, M. J., Cochrane, R., Sashidharan, S. P., Akilu, F. and Wildsmith, E. (1999). Mental health care for Asian, black and white patients with non-affective psychoses: Pathways to the psychiatric hospital, in-patient and after-care. *Social Psychiatry and Psychiatric Epidemiology, 34*(9), 484–491.

D'Ardenne, P. and Mahtani, A. (1989). *Transcultural counselling in action.* London: Sage Publications.

Dasa, S. (1993). What is vedic astrology? *Bhaktivedanta college—Online journal and article database.* Retrieved on 19 August 2007, from http://www.bhaktivedantacollege.org/bvc_site/resources_services/articles/jyotish/what_is_vedic_astrology/what_is_vedic_astrology_1.html.

Dein, S. and Sembhi, S. (2001). The use of traditional healing in South Asian psychiatric patients in the U.K.: Interactions between professional and folk psychiatries. *Transcultural Psychiatry, 38*(2), 243–257.

Gill-Badesha, D. (2004). Attitudes of south Asian immigrants toward utilizing counselling services. *Masters Abstracts International, 42*(6).

Greenwood, N., Hussain, F., Burns, T. and Raphael, F. (2000). Asian in-patient and carer views of mental health care. Asian views of mental health care. *Journal of Mental Health, 9*(4), 397–408.

Herring, R. (1999). Counselling native American Indians and Alaska natives. Thousand Oaks, CA: Sage Publications.

Hilton, B. A., Grewal, S., Popatia, N., Bottorff, J. L., Johnson, J. L., Clarke, H., Venables, L. J., Bilkhu, S. and Sumel, P. (2001). The Desi ways: Traditional health practices of South Asian women in Canada. *Health Care for Women International, 22*(6), 553–567.

Hussain, F. and Cochrane, R. (2004). Depression in South Asian women living in the UK: A review of the literature with implications for service provision. *Transcultural Psychiatry, 41*(2), 253–270.

Jacobson, D. (1995). Social systems. In J. Heitzman and R. L. Worden (Eds), *A country study: India.* Washington: Library of Congress.

Kakar, S. (1982). *Shamans, mystics, and doctors: A psychological inquiry into India and its healing traditions.* Delhi: Oxford University Press.

Koocher, G. P. and Keith-Spiegel, P. (2008). *Ethics in psychology and the mental health professions.* New York: Oxford University Press.

Kumar, M., Bhugra, D. and Singh, J. (2005). South Asian (Indian) traditional healing: Ayurvedic, shamanic, and sahaja therapy. In R. Moodley and W. West (Eds), *Integrating traditional healing practices into counselling and psychotherapy.* (pp. 112–121). Thousand Oaks, CA: Sage Publications.

Laungani, P. (1997). Replacing client-centered counselling with culture-centered counselling. *Counselling Psychology Quarterly, 10*(4), 343–351.

———. (1999). Client centered or culture centered counselling? In S. Palmer and P. Laungani (Eds), *Counselling in a multicultural society* (pp. 133–152). New Delhi: Sage Publications.

———. (2002a). Cross-cultural psychology: A handmaiden to mainstream Western Psychology. *Counselling Psychology Quarterly, 15*(1), 385–397.

Laungani, P. (2002b). Understanding mental illness across cultures. In S. Palmer (Ed.), *Multicultural counselling: A reader* (pp. 129–154). Thousand Oaks, CA: Sage Publications.

———. (2004a). *Asian perspectives in counselling and psychotherapy*. New York: Brunner-Routledge.

———. (2004b). Counselling and therapy in a multi-cultural setting. *Counselling Psychology Quarterly, 17*(2), 195–207.

———. (2005). Building multicultural counselling bridges: The holy grail or a poisoned chalice? *Counselling Psychology Quarterly. Special Issue: Dedicated to Dr Pittu Laungani, 18*(4), 247–259.

Lee, C. C. and Armstrong, K. L. (1995). *Indigenous models of mental health intervention: Lessons from traditional healers.* Thousand Oaks, CA: Sage Publications.

Moodley, R. (1999a). Psychotherapy with ethnic minorities. A critical review. *Changes, International Journal of Psychology and Psychotherapy, 17*(2), 109–125.

———. (1999b). Challenges and transformations: Counselling in a multicultural context. *International Journal for the Advancement of Counselling, 21*(2), 139–152.

———. (2000a). Counselling and psychotherapy in a multicultural context: Some training issues, Part One. *Counselling, Journal of the British Association for Counselling, 11*(3), 154–157.

———. (2000b). Counselling and psychotherapy in a multicultural context: Some training issues, Part Two. *Counselling, Journal of the British Association for Counselling, 11*(4), 221–224.

———. (2007). Re-placing multiculturalism in counselling and psychotherapy. *British Journal of Guidance and Counselling, 35*(1), 1–22.

Moodley, R. and West, W. (2005). *Integrating traditional healing practices into counseling and psychotherapy.* Thousand Oaks, California: Sage Publications.

Myers, L. J., Obasi, E. M., Jefferson, M., Anderson, M., Godfrey, T. and Purnell, J. Q. (2005). Building multicultural competence around indigenous healing practices: A strategy and model for implementing APA's multicultural guidelines. In D. W. Sue and M. G. Constantine (Eds), *Strategies for building multicultural competence in mental health and educational settings* (pp. 109–125). New York: Wiley.

National Statistics. (2005). Focus on ethnicity and identity. Office for National Statistics, London, U.K. Retrieved 29 May 2009 from http://www.statistics.gov.uk/downloads/theme_compendia/foe2004/Ethnicity.pdf

Pachuta, D. M. (1993). Chinese medicine: The law of five elements. In A. A. Sheikh and K. S. Sheikh (Eds), *Eastern & Western approaches to healing: Ancient wisdom & modern knowledge* (pp. 64–90). New York: Wiley.

Rai, A. (2008). *Role of South Asian traditional healers in counselling.* M.A. Thesis, Ontario Institute for Studies in Education, September 2008.

Rao, D. (2006). Choice of medicine and hierarchy of resort to different health alternatives among Asian Indian migrants in a metropolitan city in the USA. *Ethnicity & health, 11*(2), 153–167.

Roland, A. (1988). *In search of self in India and Japan: Toward a cross-cultural psychology.* New Jersey: Princeton University Press.

Sharma, P. (1994). Asian Indian attitudes toward seeking professional psychological help. ProQuest Information & Learning. *Dissertation Abstracts International: Section B: The Sciences and Engineering, 55*(10), 4614.

Shon, S. P. and Ja, D. Y. (1982). Asian Families. In M. McGoldrick, J. K. Pearce and J. Giordano (Eds), *Ethnicity and family therapy* (pp. 208–228). New York: Guilford.

Sue, D. W. (1999). Advocacy and indigenous methods of healing. In J. Lewis and B. Loretta (Eds), *Advocacy in counseling: Counselors, clients, & community* (pp. 143–148). Greensboro, NC: Counseling and Student Services Clearinghouse.

Sue, D. W., Bernier, J. E., Durran, A., Feinberg, L., Pedersen, P., Smith, E. J. and Vasquez-Nuttal, E. (1982). Position paper: Cross-cultural counselling competencies, *10*(2) 45–52.

Sue, D. W. and Sue, D. (1977). Barriers to effective cross-cultural counseling. *Journal of Counseling Psychology, 24*(5), 420–429.

Sue, D. W. and Sue, D. (1990). *Counseling the culturally different: Theory and practice* (2nd ed.). New York: John Wiley & Sons.

———. (1999). *Counseling the culturally different* (3rd ed.). New York: Wiley.

Vontress, C. E. (1996). A personal retrospective on cross-cultural counseling. *Journal of Multicultural Counseling and Development, 24*(3), 156–166.

Weiss, A. M. (1994). Society and its environment. In P. Blood (Ed.), *Pakistan: A country study.* Washington: Library of Congress.

West, W. (2005). Crossing the line between talking therapies and spiritual healing. In R. Moodley and W. West (Eds), *Integrating traditional healing practices into counseling and psychotherapy.* (pp. 38–49). Thousand Oaks, CA: Sage Publications.

Yoga (n.d.). *The American Heritage Dictionary of the English Language, Fourth Edition.* Retrieved 1 November 2007, from Dictionary.com website: http://dictionary.reference.com/browse/Yoga

# 9

# East-West Journey in Counselling Psychology: An Interview with Pittu Laungani

*Roy Moodley*

## INTRODUCTION

**Pittu Laungani** was well known internationally for his work on cross-cultural psychology but perhaps remained relatively less well known in England where he spent most of his life. He was a friendly, direct, reflective man who when given the opportunity did not shy away from speaking his mind and was totally unafraid to share his views on culture, psychology and Western counselling and psychotherapy. He argued for a vigorous, conceptual, philosophical and theoretical basis to all scientific endeavours, yet remained a very compassionate and sensitive academic psychologist with a deep interest in the health and well-being of his students and peers. Whilst he was involved with the practice of counselling psychology, this did not deter him from being equally focused on theoretical and conceptual matters in his discipline. Pittu's academic work assesses and analyses the difficulties that cross-cultural psychology is currently experiencing; interrogates its practices and offers many critical interventions in cultural inclusiveness. Laungani made numerous recommendations for transformation of a discourse that is embedded in Eurocentric ideas and theories. He also became involved in cross-cultural psychological aspects of death and bereavement, stress and emotion and mental health issues. Additionally, he spoke about his research and writings with several scholars and these interviews were published in many of the leading psychology and counselling journals (Collard, 2005; Stermac, 2005, also chapter 4 of this volume; West, 2004). In my conversation with Pittu, we talked about personal issues since he had explored further aspects of his work in the other interviews. Only a small part of these discussions are presented in this chapter.

My conversation with Pittu took place on the 2nd and 3rd of July 2004 at the Holiday Inn, Bloor Street West, Toronto in his hotel room. He had come to Toronto to receive the Lifetime Achievement Award for cross-cultural psychology and multicultural counselling from the Centre for Diversity in Counselling and Psychotherapy (CDCP), Ontario Institute for Studies in Education (OISE), University of Toronto. He talked very personally about his early childhood along with his passion for academic and creative writing. Pittu spoke of his love for literature and science; the pleasure that writing plays and novels give him and the intellectual fulfilment and connection with other academics his work enabled him to enjoy and pursue. In his interview, he engaged in frank talking about his personal life; his younger single life, marriage and his relationships with people. He shared the loss and sadness he felt about the death of his colleague John Morgan with whom he co-edited four volumes on death and bereavement. John Morgan was due to speak at the Toronto Conference where Pittu Laungani received his Award, but tragically died shortly before this.

Pittu Laungani's conversations were not only a personal narrative but also a journey across cultures and continents. Not withstanding his failing health, he nevertheless made the trip to Toronto to receive the Lifetime Achievement Award; an occasion that pleased him greatly since he felt that his scholarship and writing was eventually being recognized.

On the trip to Toronto, Pittu was accompanied by his wife, Ann (a registered nurse in an earlier life) and joined by a close family friend, Isobel Rodriguez (a general practitioner from Portugal). He risked the journey to North America from London despite his deteriorating health. Meticulous arrangements were made with the airline for oxygen to be made available on the flight and for a Toronto health care agency nurse to meet him at the airport with a further supply of portable oxygen cylinders. He offered his keynote speech the next day, accompanied inevitably by the portable oxygen cylinder. The audience of 250 people were inspired and struck by the passion he had for his discipline. The presentation of the Lifetime Achievement Award by the then Right Hon. Alvin Curling, the Speaker of the House of the Ontario Parliament, was at an evening ceremony held at the University of Toronto, Faculty Club.

My conversations with Pittu were held over two days as his stamina was limited and failing. Every now and then we paused while he took more oxygen before continuing. When he was really tired we stopped for the day. I left his hotel and went on my way with his invitation to continue the next day. The second interview was conducted in much the same way—we began where he had stopped earlier and whilst he talked, he took doses of oxygen and continued till he was exhausted. We concluded the second day with the idea that we would cover some of the issues that he alluded to and wanted to say more about, but at another time, perhaps on a later occasion back at his home in London. This never happened because Pittu died before I could get to see him again.

## INTERVIEW: PITTU LAUNGANI IN CONVERSATION WITH ROY MOODLEY

Pittu Laungani (PL): I was born in Bombay, India when the British were still ruling over India. I was from a large family; 16 children but 11 died very early. I'm the youngest but I have no recollection of those early years. My siblings had left home by the time I became conscious of family so I had no recollection of those that were alive or the one's that died. We lived in a small flat which was near a cinema, Metro cinema, and that's where I grew up, in a block of flats. Apart from that I don't have any vivid recollections of my infancy. Because I was the youngest and my brother who was older than me was about 12 years older so there was no contact in terms of siblings because he was too old and he wouldn't play with me. So in a sense I grew up as an almost only child but had friends in the building we lived in. We were on the fifth floor, there was an English family on the fourth because it was pre-independence time, and there was a lad called Ronny or Ronald and his father I think was a Royal Navy officer, so I used to play with him. Then there was a Chinese family, a Singaporean family on the third floor, I knew them. Then there were Catholic families on the fourth floor, third floor, and second floor. Also there were many Gujaratis, and Punjabis. A mix of families, all different groups all living together. These are the people I associated with. So this is the way we were united you know.

Roy Moodley (RM): And I guess you also went to school together?

PL: Yes. When I reached the age of five, my parents decided to send me to a Jesuit school which was walking distance from where we lived and it was considered to be the most prestigious Catholic school in Bombay, and I think also in the country. Being a Jesuit school, the medium of instruction was English, so I learnt to speak English at a very early age, and in fact I became more fluent in speaking English than I did my own language which was Sindhi and the other Indian language, Hindi. My parents only spoke Sindhi and a little bit of Hindi which made communication between us difficult. My family came from Sindh, which is now a part of Pakistan. My father, mother and all my brothers and sisters were born in Sindh. The reason why I was born in Bombay was because my father left Sindh, went to Karachi and eventually made his way to Bombay to make his fortune. We were landowners in Sindh. But partitioning changed all that.

RM: Partitioning! That must have been a very painful time for you?

PL: I was about nine years old when India got its independence. And being nine at the time and thinking about what was happening at the border between Sindh and India. We had property there and some of my relatives were still in Sindh. I believe one or two are still living there, my father went to Pakistan or just before it became Pakistan in the hope of selling his property; recovering what money he could, but I think he was unable to sell his property so he came back, and then we lost everything. Many people lost their property in Sindh; just as many Muslims lost property in India when they were forced to leave or voluntarily left India.

RM: But before we can get to that painful history, because it takes us into the politics of how the British governed, ruled and eventually left India, and the complexity and problems of the partition. Can you talk a little more about the communication difficulty you mentioned earlier between you and your family.

PL: Yes. I spoke English, and at home they didn't speak English. Going to a Jesuit school, I read different kinds of English books and since my family could only speak Sindhi and Hindi, I was unable to talk about my interests. That impeded my relationship with them you see. What also did not help was the fact that Hinduism as a religion didn't have any impact on me. My parents were conventional Hindus by which I mean they did their *pooja* (prayer) at home; they went to the temple on Sunday but they had a fairly laissez-faire attitude to religion. They didn't go through the kind of rituals which you would expect an orthodox Hindu family to go through and there were no compulsions upon me to go to the temple with them, no compulsions to observe the rituals, no compulsions to have fasts and so on and so forth. So in a sense it didn't really have an impact on my life, and there was nothing from that point of view to tie me to my family. The books I read even as a young boy were books that were mainly written by English authors; and so because my parents couldn't read English, they didn't know what I read…and so in a sense I was an only child from a psychological point of view rather than a child that had four brothers and sisters.

RM: Did your parents have a plan for your future? In other words, what were their ambitions for you?

PL: I don't think. I'm being honest, I don't think I was ever asked what I wanted to become. What I was told was what I should not become. I wanted to play cricket. I wanted to become a cricket player. They said 'no'. Then I thought I wanted to be a film star. They said 'no'. In fact I even got a contract from a film star which I had to turn down because my father said he would thrash me to my skin if I joined the film industry. I would have made a lot of money, I'm sure. Then I couldn't play cricket because I wasn't good enough. I couldn't play cricket at a very high level. I didn't practice enough. Also I wasn't given the facilities, because you know to play cricket the parents must encourage you and they would have to buy me boots and gloves and so on, which I knew they were unwilling to do because they thought I would be wasting my time playing cricket rather than studying. So there was that conflict. By the time I reached the age of 12 or 13, I had very little contact with my parents although I did live in the house because I was financially and materially dependent on them. And when I passed my matriculation my brother, I remember very clearly, said that you are the only one in the family who's actually passed the matriculation and now we can find a good job for you. My father found a job for me as a clerk in a company. And I said that I wanted to go to college and he was very reluctant for me to go to college, and so I wasted my time working as a clerk in an office. Then I got a bit fed up with that, and again I said that I wanted to go to college and we had a bit of a tussle. And he said that he has never been to college and I said that you haven't been to college there is no reason why I shouldn't go to college. He said, 'well I have done very well in life', and I said, 'it's not a question of doing very well. I just want to go to university and you wouldn't allow me to'. And I think my father said, 'I think you are difficult to handle here. We will teach you a lesson by sending you to Hong Kong'. So he sent me to Hong Kong.

RM: And you accepted this decision? Just went along with it?

PL: Well...because, you see, I wanted to rebel but I didn't have any support from anyone in the family so I knew I would be on my own and my father could be quite stern. Second, I was frightened of running away from the house. I didn't know where to go. I didn't have any money. So I think it an act of cowardice on my part rebelling to an extent without having left home. And...I was intrigued by the idea of going abroad you see. So I was packed off and sent to Hong Kong. My father had some friends there who ran shops there. I worked in a departmental store, and in Hong Kong and at that time when you work for another Indian company, they give you accommodation as well. I spent a year in Hong Kong and then went back home. I think I went back because I was bored with the kind of work I was doing and I still was hankering after wanting to go to university; and I felt the longer I stayed, the more difficult it will become for me to leave. Obviously my father was displeased at my sudden arrival but there was little he could do and then I joined the university, graduated and then I went on to do a masters degree in psychology. But luckily, the professor in the department of psychology offered me a job. So I worked there for about three years, and I did some research there, but I was somehow not very happy.

RM: You eventually got what you wanted—a college education. Why were you unhappy?

PL: I wanted to know what my chances were of becoming a professor. He said, 'hardly any because the university is controlled by professors who are high-caste Hindu Brahmins'. And I don't come from that caste so he said that it would be difficult for me to get a professorship, and so he suggested that I should leave and perhaps go to England or the United States or Australia or Canada to make my fortune and an academic career there. I applied for a work permit given my masters degree. I got it in six weeks and I went to London. For about a year or so I couldn't do any kind of teaching job, so I worked as a clerk in an office. And for about another year I worked as a school teacher which I really hated, and then after that I got a teaching job in a college which was not attached to a university, but nonetheless it was a college of education. Because I had to compete with a large number of white lecturers and I didn't want to show that I was given a job out of charity, and I wanted to be on equal terms, I had to work very hard at my lectures, doing a lot of background reading, a lot of preparation, marking and so on. No time for anything else. But, eventually, I decided to undertake a Ph.D. at the Institute of Education, London University. It was a cross-cultural study; looking at personality differences between cultures and differences in conformity between cultures. So I designed a conformity test which I used in Bombay to interview and test college students. I collected a sample of 1,500 students in Bombay in two months, going there twice in two years. And, similarly, I collected a sample of English students and did a comparative analysis. I got my Ph.D. and I stayed there at the university.

RM: So academically you made the East-West journey it seems in psychology. You received a psychology master's degree in India, and then a doctorate in London. You achieved your dream. The rebel in you—against your father—had won. But let's go back a bit in this wonderful story. When you arrived in England: what was your sense of this new country, its people and culture?

PL: I found England very tough because I was unused to the weather for a start; the cold really bothered me quite a lot. That was one problem, and the second problem was that there was a struggle for money. You know so it was difficult to live the kind of life that I was living in Bombay because my father was rich, I could drive a car; there was no problem there. But luckily I had one or two Indian friends from Bombay who were living in England, and they sheltered me for a while...in a sense, that I could see them and meet them regularly, and so on.

RM: I see you avoided my question on British culture and its people? However... there you were in London; a city of culture and theatre and the arts. What did this mean to you?

PL: I used to go to the theatre from time to time.

RM: Did this early exposure lead to your play writing adventures?

PL: The idea of writing a play had never occurred to me and I just admired the plays of other writers. In those days, I saw plays rather than wrote them because that was not in my consciousness. No, the idea was totally alien to me.

RM: I guess you were busy with academic research and scholarly publications.

PL: Yes, I published a few papers but the idea of telling a story through the novel form intrigued me. When I was working as a clerk, I did not know how to spend my time in the office because the work they gave me was so easy I finished the work in a couple of hours and so I started to write a novel. The novel was based on a friend of mine from Bombay who came to London to study and work. I used to meet him regularly and he fascinated me because he was a very eccentric individual. Also, I felt that he wouldn't be able to survive living in England. I had the intuitive feeling that he wouldn't be able to cope and sooner or later he'd go back. So that's the first novel I wrote; that gave me some enthusiasm for writing in a more fluid style than in a more academic style. It was pretty hard work but I enjoyed doing it.

RM: This fluidity of style comes across in your later academic work. It seems you are converging all your talents, i.e., scholarly research, play writing skills and writing novels, to a point where they have influenced a particular style in your academic papers and books. Indeed, the dialogue style in your case studies is close to what counselling and psychotherapy sessions are like in the clinical room. Many of these case studies have offered us an in-depth analysis of your understanding of the cultural complexity between the West and the East.

PL: Yes. A theme I followed in my second novel. It's called an Indian wife.

RM: An Indian wife! Were you trying to explore the idea of culture and marriage or cross-cultural relationships, or the idea of immigrants and their search for partners from their home countries? What were the issues?

PL: Basically the theme of the novel is when foreigners like us live in a foreign country, say England, and when crisis occurs in life; when the chips are down, you immediately go back to the womb of your own culture; that's the culture which offers you security.

RM: So what you're saying is that when crisis occurs in multicultural kinds of relationships people always go back to their cultural ways of thinking and being—a cultural womb. Is that really going back metaphorically to the origin of some early childhood experience somehow?

PL: Well going back to your own culture offers you security.

RM: But can there be a going back whether metaphorically or in reality in that cultural origin. Culture is dynamic and is constantly in flux. Can the person who is in distress really get to a place culturally that offers this sense of security?

PL: Yes. Let me illustrate. In my fourth novel, The Chameleon I explore the relationship between an Indian man and his white English girlfriend. And they have their fights and quarrels. Shall we get married, shall we not get married, and it goes on and on, and eventually she walks out on him. The title Chameleon is put forward in order to demonstrate that to live in two cultures one must have two personas—the English persona and the Indian persona. The Indian persona you keep to yourself and you only disclose that when you're with other fellow compatriots or unless you have friends who accept your personas. And you have an English persona which you display as a public face, you see.

RM: I find that concept problematic. Sounds like a schizophrenic split? That leads to a bicultural fragmentation of the ego, with possible consequences for the psyche. A very unhealthy psychology, I think?

PL: Oh No!...No...it doesn't. I can change the persona whenever I want to. So if I want to get angry with an English friend, I just behave like an Indian. And, you know, most of them who are good friends of mine will have learnt to accept that and they say, 'oh! He's only being Indian'. You see. And the advantage there is that you, you can engage both cultures at your choosing; have the best of both worlds. Sometimes it gets me into trouble because people are not prepared to accept, you know, my Indianness, if you like and similarly sometimes I behave like an English person with Indians and they are not prepared to accept my Englishness, as an Indian. And sometimes the white English also find it difficult to accept my Englishness.

RM: Are you saying that there may have been issues at the university for you? Did you experience any racism at work?

PL: I don't think so, but I think they withheld my promotion...I applied for a chair, they wouldn't give it to me and they said my work was too theoretical. I said, look, that is the most important work you can do...anyone can do empirical work...anyway, I think there was an element of racism there. I could have taken them to court. I could have gone to the race relations board, but...I operate on the assumption that even if I did win and get a chair, I was not prepared to enter into a fight, you see. So I let it go.

RM: How does that make you feel, the fact the institution didn't give you the recognition?

PL: Well, I was, how should I put it, I have a very phlegmatic attitude to problems, you see. I mean initially I was upset. Then I said, you know, that's how they operate, that's how they operate, I'm not going to fight it. Like you know this Lifetime Achievement Award that I was given. My university still hasn't sent me a congratulatory letter. You can see that. It's a shame, even though two of my colleagues sent a letter to the chief executive of the university, that I got the award, not a single letter. You see, I would have expected the university to write to me. So I tend to develop a kind of a duck's back, you know. The water off a duck's back, and don't worry about it because if I worry about it then I'll do something about it which means I will waste my energies in dealing with that problem rather than the problems which are more important to me, which is to write.

RM: Yet, you are getting the opposite response from the major journals in the UK. For example, the *British Journal of Guidance and Counselling* has done a special issue on your work. So too will the *Counselling Psychology Quarterly* journal will be doing a special issue on your Lifetime Achievement Award event. (Editors note: The reader can find these in the *Journal of Counselling Psychology Quarterly*, Volume 18(4), December 2005, and the *International Journal of Health Promotion and Education* (IJHPE), Volume 44(1), 2006.)

PL: I find that quite gratifying. My pleasure comes out of writing. I enjoy it very much...if it gets published, that's fine. I've had many rejections of my research papers from different journals.

RM: You have written prolifically in various areas of psychology—numerous papers, book chapters and books; many novels and plays; and now you received the Lifetime Achievement Award from the University of Toronto. What's your understanding of your contribution to future generation of psychologists?

PL: But you see, I have a feeling, maybe I'm wrong; I think most books die in about three months or six months after publication; most books, academic books in general. Even novels die, you know, death. And so they sink; they sink into oblivion. And it's a lucky writer who can get his books read after two years, or three years or four years you see, that's my feeling. So I have no grand illusions about my contribution. I still write, it gives me a lot of pleasure, it's nice to see my name in print, it's nice to go to a bookshop and see my books there. But I have no illusions that it's going to last, you see. As I said, if it dies, it dies.

RM: Many of your books if not all of them have survived that average four year period that you mention. Even the death and dying ones, excuse my pun, they too have not died.

PL: They haven't died, yes. But I don't expect the books will become, you know, noted...to me the pleasure lies in the activity, and the pleasure lies in the writing...what happens to it afterwards, I don't really care.

RM: I guess that is part of the writing process. The writer has no control once the ideas are in the public domain; they have a life of their own. And one sees the ideas filtering through in different ways, informing new ideas, and engaging people in a debate or controversy.

PL: Well that's the whole point of an idea, of whether it'll happen or not, and once I'm dead, I don't know what happens in any case. So, I don't think that, that worries me. I have no intimations of immortality and I think like most other ordinary individuals one is born, one lives, maybe one contributes a bit and one dies and one is forgotten, and that's it, you know. And that's how I see it.

RM: This is an interesting philosophy. Is your interest and focus on death and dying underpinned by these ideas? The issue that seemed very interesting to me and maybe you would like to reflect on—is something you said earlier in this conversation about your family, your siblings. You said there were 11 siblings who died. Could it be that your interest in death and dying starts here? Is there a search for you to make a connection with them or to understand their absence or presence?

PL: Personally, I don't see a connection, because it's impossible for me to visualize a person who is nonexistent, because as I said they were old. I think I had one sister who was older than me by about 2 years, and I knew her when I was very young and she died of an illness. That's my only recollection of her. But apart from that I have no recollection of any other members. It's impossible for me to because they died before I was born you see. I think my interest in death and bereavement started by accident than by design. There was a conference in the early 1990s. I was recovering from a very serious illness. I relearned how to walk…paralyzed…I couldn't walk at all, and someone phoned me to say that there was a conference in Edinburgh, an international conference on death and dying. Would I be interested to read a paper on death and bereavement. So I said, 'I don't know anything about death and bereavement, and the only thing I know about death and bereavement is my impending death'. So we'll talk about that she said. I thought she was being silly so I just ignored it. She phoned me again, I don't know who she was. So I said, 'okay'. She said, 'Do you know anything about Indian funerals?' I said, 'well, yes, you know being an Indian, having lived in India, I know enough'. She said, 'Why don't you talk about Indian funerals'. I said, 'okay'. So I prepared a paper on Indian funerals, and then another paper on my own illness. So I read two papers there, and the audience was absolutely stunned by those papers, and I received about 50 letters. These were before the days of e-mails you see, and then more invitations to do more papers on death, dying and bereavement. So that's what got me interested in death…and…bereavement…

(Pittu Laungani began to experience difficulties with his breathing. He puts his oxygen nasal spectacles on). Excuse me.

RM: Okay. We can stop now. Thank you for talking with me.

# REFERENCES

Collard, P. (2005). An Interview with Dr. Pittu Laungani. *Counselling Psychology Quarterly*, *18*(1), 7–18.

Stermac, L. (2005). In the therapist's chair: Professor Lana Stermac in conversation with Dr. Pittu Laungani. *Counselling Psychology Quarterly*, *18*(4), 261–276.

West, W. (2004). Pittu Laungani in conversation with William West. *British Journal of Guidance and Counselling*, *32*, 1–14.

# PART THREE

# Towards Wisdom in the Practice of Counselling and Therapy

# 10

# Transcending the Boundaries of Counselling: Pittu Laungani as Master Counsellor

*Juris G. Draguns*

## INTRODUCTION

**In** Pittu Laungani's own pithy definition, 'counselling is helping people help themselves' (Laungani, 2004a). In the course of his productive and eventful life, this endeavour was the focus of his effort and concern. In the process, Pittu Laungani extended the scope of counselling, transformed it and pointed it towards new aspirations and vistas. Above all, he audaciously crossed boundaries and transcended restrictions. It is as a bridge-builder and integrator that Pittu Laungani will be remembered. In this chapter, I would like to trace his innovative and, occasionally, iconoclastic contributions. To this end, I would like to address the following themes that have been central to Pittu Laungani's work: comparing and analyzing Eastern and Western assumptions, expectations and practices of counselling in order to identify its cultural and universal components, using his personal experience, including suffering and illness, in enhancing the sensitivity of counselling operations, making death and dying the central concerns of psychology both as a body of knowledge and as a fountainhead of application in counselling and elsewhere and linking the practical concern of counselling with the basic issues of epistemology and philosophy of science. These sections will be preceded by a personal and subjective reaction to Pittu Laungani as a person and scholar, and they will be followed by a brief epilogue.

## PITTU LAUNGANI AS A PERSON: A RECONSTRUCTION

My personal contacts with Pittu Laungani were limited to the last four years of his life; I have not had the privilege of meeting Pittu Laungani in person and our communication remained exclusively electronic. The initially terse exchanges of e-mails evolved into lengthy, reflective and wide-ranging messages not tied to any practical or concrete purpose. Somewhat like a mosaic, an image of Pittu Laungani gradually emerged, then fused with the impressions gleaned from his published writings. In the process, the boundary between the public and the private facets of his life got blurred and eventually faded. Thus, a relationship came into being with a live and vibrant human being, not just with his thoughts but with his feelings, even though it was based on the exchange of written messages.

What impressed me about Pittu Laungani was how his formidable erudition and expertise were seamlessly blended with his personal experience and with his resulting wisdom. Many prominent contributors to psychology dazzle us with the brilliance of their formulations, their methodological acumen and the elegance of their research. Their contributions continue to reverberate across decades and generations; yet their originators remain shadowy and curiously disembodied figures. Try as one might, little or nothing is learned about the authors from their books and articles or even from their addresses and public presentations. What animates him or her? What does he or she live by? What matters to him or her? Quite often these questions remain unanswered.

Not so with Pittu Laungani. Whatever he wrote—a one page letter or a monograph extending over several hundred pages—was informed by his personal experience, his values, aspirations and enthusiasms, all of them spontaneously expressed and communicated in a close approximation of a person-to-person dialogue. Pittu Laungani just refused to succumb to the compartmentalization of experience, to the airtight separation of the academic persona from the private self, a stricture that is virtually imposed upon contemporary scholars. Nothing that Pittu Laungani did was detached and impersonal. His books and articles constituted an important avenue of self-expression, and his personal, all too often literally painful, experiences were fused into an integrated whole that was composed of his observations, reflections and knowledge. Thus, everything that he knew became personal and everything in his experience enriched his knowledge. It is therefore not surprising then that Pittu Laungani transcended the conventional formats of scientific communication and explored new modes and venues. Social scientists are not expected to be playwrights, but Pittu Laungani was, with two produced and successful plays, *The Strange Affliction of Hamlet, Prince of Denmark* and *Pillars of Wisdom.* The latter title, incidentally, was incorporated into Pittu Laungani's e-mail address, another reminder that everything that he wrote was a meaningful self-expression. I have read the manuscript of Pittu Laungani's short story, *Einstein's Nephew,* a remarkably perceptive and gripping narrative based on a real-life encounter in which Pittu Laungani's gift of capturing another person's uniqueness comes through as much as it does in his published clinical case studies (Laungani, 2005a).

Similarly, in a natural and seemingly effortless manner, Pittu Laungani ranged across domains of knowledge and traditions of inquiry from psychology through sociology, anthropology, literature and history to philosophy, and especially epistemology, the study of knowledge. What we know and how we know was the key question to which Pittu Laungani constantly returned, and his erudition made him immune to the insecurities of so many scientists who confine themselves to the established, but restrictive, formats of reporting and explaining their findings.

Thus, Pittu Laungani's personal qualities are conveyed spontaneously through his writings. What stands out is his human warmth, his genuine empathy with people of all cultural backgrounds, his stoicism in the face of suffering, his ardent concern with the major issues and perils faced by the human species or parts thereof at this point in history, his fascination with the achievements of the human mind, his excitement and curiosity, his concern about humanity's prospects and his sense of awe and wonder over human potential. Above all, Pittu Laungani had a way of relating to each correspondent and interlocutor on a one-to-one basis: each exchange, oral or written, would become an encounter with an authentic and responsive human being.

Let us now proceed from this vignette of Pittu Laungani as a person to the mark that he left through his scientific and professional activity as embodied in his writings.

## COUNSELLING EAST AND WEST: ITS CULTURALLY DISTINCTIVE AND UNIVERSAL FEATURES

Let us begin at the beginning. Here is a retrospective account of young Pittu Laungani's (2002) first encounter with England in the 1960s:

> England to me came as a shock! There were as many accents there as there are dialects in India—or almost. Each of them as though spoke in a different tongue, and a few, even in forked tongues! It was difficult to distinguish between levity and seriousness, between jest and truth, between praise and censure, between affection and affectation, between acceptance and rejection. I found it exasperating not being able to read correctly their feelings and emotions on the rare occasions they chose to express them. In India I had been born into a particular caste and had learned through childhood what was expected of me in a variety of social situations, which involved a mingling of castes. But with the English it was difficult

> to place them in their appropriate class categories: the class divisions, it seemed to me, were blurred and not as clearly defined as the castes were (and to a large extent still are) in India. I could not always work out what was expected of me in different situations and of different people. (Laungani, 2002: 387)
>
> Living in a foreign country I soon realized was like fighting a lone battle on several fronts: the weather, the climate, the preserved and processed food, the strange customs and conventions, the patterns of everyday life, and of course the people. (Ibid.: 387)
>
> Although we spoke the same language, although we had past historical associations, although I had read the books, which I assumed they would have also read, and although I dressed the way they did, I could tell that a vast ocean of differences separated me from them. I felt alienated. (Ibid.: 388)

An extraordinarily perceptive description of culture shock! Note that the writer focused on subtle differences that he spotted, which a less discriminating observer may have overlooked. The stressful experiences that he described launched Pittu Laungani on the tortuous and difficult path of a participant observer of the culture of his host country, England, and enabled him to take a fresh look from an outsider's perspective of his country of origin, India. Late in life, he reflected:

> I have now lived in England for more years of my life than I have in India. Although in the 30 years or so I have been to America and Canada several times, I have never once regretted my initial decision to go to study, work, and live in England. I feel I have been fortunate enough to have imbibed and internalized the best of both worlds—the Western world and the Eastern world. (Laungani, 2002: 395)

As Laungani acquired skill and experience as a British-trained counselling psychologist, both of his cultural outlooks were brought to bear upon identifying the hidden contrasts in human services in the two countries. In a somewhat daring manner, Pittu Laungani implicitly generalized these differences to East and West, the former encompassing not only the Indian subcontinent but also the East Asian countries at the Pacific rim down to Indonesia and Indochina, the latter descriptive of the English-speaking countries of the Old and the New Worlds, but also applicable, perhaps with modifications and to varying degrees, to the nations of Continental Europe.

Eventually, Laungani (2004a) identified four axes on which Eastern and Western cultures could be placed at the opposite poles: communalism–individualism, emotionalism–rationalism, determinism–free will and materialism–spiritualism. India and other countries of the region tend towards communal, family-centred values, practices and social and economic organization; the United Kingdom and other related nations in Europe, North America and Australia celebrate the individual and his or her self-assertion and self-actualization. In South Asia and regions around it, belief, feeling and intuition hold sway; Western civilizations from the ancient Greeks to the modern Britons and Americans extol reason, logic and control. Somewhat paradoxically, Indians and their neighbours accept fate and determinism as the natural order of the world while Westerners, although accepting intellectually the deterministic tenets of modern science, operate in their daily lives on the basis of the principle of free will, which is deeply embedded in the implicit belief system of the Western culture. Finally, spiritualism, prevalent in India, posits the primacy of contemplation and reflection and values subjective illumination over objective information. Euro-Americans characteristically opt for empirical observation, comprehension and mastery of external and material reality.

These concepts, however, should be regarded as reference points rather than as mutually exclusive categories. Nonetheless, they are relevant to counselling in a multicultural environment in a host of subtle ways. In their interaction with clients, British counsellors emphasize neutrality or objectivity, cognitive control and empathy. Counsellors are cast in the role of facilitators who enable clients to choose their preferred courses of action in an acceptant and non-judgemental atmosphere, free of pressures of the outside world (Laungani, 2004a). The expectations of Indian counsellees are altogether different. Indian clients seek, and Indian counsellors strive to provide, wisdom and enlightenment, which a counsellor or a guru is expected to dispense in a decisive and authoritative manner. Thus, the ethos of the counselling profession in Britain and North America tends towards egalitarianism and horizontal relationships; in India and perhaps elsewhere in Asia interactions tend to be hierarchical, based on the perception and expectation of the counsellor's moral superiority and greater wisdom (Laungani, 2004a). In relation to the goals that the clients bring to counselling and psychotherapy, Western clients expect counsellors' help in freeing them *to* realize their aspirations and to reach their goals. In contrast, Asian clients seek freedom *from* distress, disruption and turmoil as they strive for social harmony and serenity.

Eschewing both a nihilistic moral relativism and a righteous absolutism, Laungani also rejects the extremes of both directive and laissez faire approaches in preparing counsellors to serve a heterogeneous and multicultural clientele. He admits that there is no prospect of finding a perfect solution to the challenge of values in counselling, even though 'the incompatibility of values [between the counsellor and the counsellee], if left unresolved, may become a source of acute psychological distress for the therapist' (Laungani, 2004a: 87). One might also add that such a disparity would adversely affect the client by making him or her disoriented, confused and insecure. In the last years of his life, Pittu Laungani was working on addressing moral dilemmas and concerns by means of a new model of intervention which he termed Moral-Dialectical Therapy, and he believed that ethics and morality are relevant to all counselling and psychotherapy, but especially so when these services are rendered across culture lines. Regardless of a client's cultural background,

> the problem which each of them brings to the therapist is concerned, in the final analysis, with making sense of one's life...What constitutes a 'meaningful life' might of course be worded and described differently, but in essence it is concerned with the sentiment expressed in the fourth century BC, when [Socrates] posed the question: 'How shall we lead our lives?' (Laungani, 2004a: 228)

These philosophical considerations inevitably affect counsellors' *modus operandi.* British, and by extension Western, counsellors emphasize in their interaction with clients neutrality or objectivity, cognitive control and empathy. The *raison d'être* of the counselling profession as it evolved in Europe and America posits its basis is science, and neutrality and objectivity are the hallmarks of scientific observation. Closely related to this emphasis is the requirement that the counsellor's behaviour in the professional encounter be always under rational and volitional control. The client is invited to be spontaneously expressive; the counsellor keeps a tight lid over his or her personal reactions. The possible impression of coldness and indifference that neutrality and non-expressiveness of the counsellor may convey is counteracted by empathy which the Western counsellors are trained not only to experience but also to communicate to their clients. As Pittu Laungani points out, objectivity cognitive control and empathy cannot be automatically applied to encounters with Indian clients who expect to be guided, instructed and directed by their 'counsellors', whatever their historical and cultural designation may be. Indian counsellees easily slip into an expectant, receptive and dependent role and look up to their counsellors as active and decisive purveyors of traditional yet living wisdom. A reversal of such expectations is built into the Western rationale of counselling operations: it is the counsellee who is expected to assume an active, self-initiated and self-directed role while the counsellor abides by a non-directive stance and consistently refrains from telling the counsellee what to do.

In comparison to cognitive control and objectivity, empathy appears to be the more robust ingredient of counselling regardless of culture. Laungani (2004a) explicitly recognizes its key role and allows for its different modes of expression and communication across cultures. His published case studies of his clients, British and Indian, are highly empathetic portrayals of human condition (Laungani, 2003a, 2004a, 2005a). They may serve as models of empathetic experience and interaction for counsellors in the years to come, based on Pittu Laungani's explicit recognition and intuitive knowledge of the universals of human existence, above all of the ubiquity of human distress and of the striving to counteract it by the serenity that comes from finding or imposing meaning on human existence.

Distilling conclusions from his personal observations and from his professional experience, Laungani (2004a) formulated a set of seven general rules in order to make counsellors more sensitive and more effective whenever cultural boundaries are crossed. They deserve to be reproduced in his words, in their entirety:

Rule 1: Do not use the term culture as a wastebasket to discard anomalies and unexplained behaviours (Laungani, 2004a: 223).
Rule 2: Even within a single culture, people may be divided more by their differences than united by their similarities (Laungani, 2004a: 224).
Rule 3: Always expect the unexpected and prepare to be taken by surprise (Laungani, 2004a: 225).
Rule 4: The universal popularity of a theoretical model neither guarantees its usefulness nor its validity. The two are independent (Laungani, 2004a: 225).
Rule 5: There are no standardized norms for dealing with clients from different cultures. What may be relevant in the West may have little or no meaning in the East and vice versa (Laungani, 2004a: 226).
Rule 6: Wisdom lies in recognizing and accepting the culturally relevant beliefs and practices of one's clients (Laungani, 2004a: 226).
Rule 7: Ask not what you can teach other therapists. Ask instead what you might *learn from* other therapists (Laungani, 2004a: 227). (Italics in the original.)

Based on one perceptive counsellor's cumulative professional and personal experience, these seven rules provide general guidelines for culturally competent and sensitive counselling regardless of place or time.

## EXPERIENCING ILLNESS: SUFFERING, ENDURING, COPING AND TRANSCENDING

Pittu Laungani never separated his personal life from his academic, scholarly and scientific endeavours. Thus, during the last 18 years of life, while his body was being ravished by a debilitating muscular disease, Pittu Laungani coped with it as he did with all of the exigencies of his life: he observed, reflected, recorded and continued to live fully, meaningfully and productively, even serenely. In the face of these traumatic events, many, perhaps most, people would have given up and retreated to dependence, helplessness and passivity. Others would have tried to cope by curtailing and rationing their energy expenditure and activity level. In Pittu Laungani's life, however, this trying and literally, as well as figuratively, painful period was marked by a flowering of productivity and creativity. Moreover, looking back upon these years, Laungani (2005b: iii) wrote: 'Despite my terminal condition, they have been the happiest, the most peaceful, and the most productive years of my life.'

Significant, innovative and integrative, contributions—well over 50 articles, chapters and monographs—appeared in 1990s and 2000s, including all of Laungani's writings that are referred to in this chapter. I wonder how many of the readers of these articles and books were aware of the author's suffering and pain that he endured while writing them as he was battling an irreversible illness!

Pittu Laungani not only defied his illness, he described and conceptualized it and imbued it with meaning. He did that by using his suffering as 'raw material' for two remarkably lucid and unsparing factual accounts of his medical condition and of his subjective experiences (Laungani, 1992, 2003b). From this intensive introspective study with an 'N of 1', he was able to derive eight rules, with an equal number of corollaries that are both philosophical and pragmatic. Informed by personal experience, enriched by the heritage of Western and Eastern thought, they contain applicable hypotheses and provide sources for pilot research programmes for helping people cope with pain, avert despair and find solace. Moreover, these experientially based suggestions for creating meaning and purpose and even extracting 'as much fun and pleasure out of it as possible' (Laungani, 2003b: 162) may be useful to counsellors and to patients suffering from intractable, disabling and painful conditions. In Laungani's own words, these rules and their respective corollaries are as follows:

Rule 1: Focus all your energies on what you *can* do rather than on what you would like to do.
Corollary to Rule 1: Do not even think about what you cannot do! Concentrate only on what you can do (Laungani, 2003b: 167–168).

Rule 2: Recognize that your own illness is unique to you.
Corollary to Rule 2: Your perceptions, your own understanding, your own beliefs concerning your own illness are unique. They are unlikely to be understood, appreciated, or shared by most doctors (Laungani, 2003b: 169).

Rule 3. Pain is an internal part of the human condition. Learn to accept it.
Corollary to Rule 3: Try hard enough and it becomes easier to accept and cope with physical pain than any other kind of pain, particularly, the pain related to destitution and loss of meaning, purpose and integrity (Laungani, 2003b: 171).

Rule 4: Find an activity in which you can get passionately absorbed.
Corollary to Rule 4: The activity should be challenging, time-consuming, and well within your natural inclinations, talent and physical capabilities (Laungani, 2003b: 174).

Rule 5: Train yourself to see the funny side in every situation.
Corollary to Rule 5: Remember, humour acts as an antidote to depression. Humour keeps one alive and makes life worth living (Laungani, 2003b: 175).

Rule 6: There is very little purpose in worrying about external events that are entirely beyond one's sphere of control.
Corollary to Rule 6: Accepting the probable consequences of one's actions is often better than avoiding the action altogether (Laungani, 2003b: 177).

Rule 7: Learn to create room for hope in your life. The last thing that came tumbling out of Pandora's box was hope.
Corollary to Rule 7: Never forget that all your hopes must be guided by reality (Laungani, 2003b: 180).

Rule 8: It is necessary to come to terms with one's mortality.
Corollary to Rule 8: Acknowledgement of one's mortality acts as a liberating influence in one's life (Laungani, 2003b: 180).

In formulating these eight rules and their corollaries, Pittu Laungani enriched the repertoire of counselling and psychotherapy practice, much of which is concerned with the alleviation of personal and physical suffering and with the anxieties and uncertainties regarding mortality, another example of transmuting distress into hope and helplessness into helpfulness.

## ACCEPTING DEATH AND NOT DREADING IT

For most of the last two decades of his life, Pittu Laungani lived in the shadow and at the edge of death. His philosophical erudition and his immersion in the Hindu tradition of accepting death as a never-ending cycle of renewal and rebirth served to immunize him from the powerful contemporary Western trend of denying death rather than coming to terms with its inevitability on both cognitive and emotional planes. Logically, Laungani (2003b) asks, why should death be dreaded? Indeed, on the basis of personal experience he asserts that for people who suffer from chronic life-threatening conditions, the prospect of a likely early death can potentially be a liberating experience. Once the inevitability of death is truly accepted and its probability clearly envisaged, the person is free to live more fully and intensely, more reflectively and more meaningfully, by casting trivialities aside and concentrating on those aspects of life that matter.

Laungani reminds his readers of Martin Heidegger's dictum that coming to grips with the reality of death and its meaning helps people understand how to live. Rather whimsically, Laungani echoed Woody Allen in referring to life as a terminal disease. 'Given the indisputable certainty of death,' he exclaimed, 'is it not strange that the heart denies what the head affirms and knows to be true?' (Laungani 2007: 211). Death and dying are the ultimate issues of human existence, to be faced, understood and accepted and not to be dreaded. Yet, countless people in all cultures, including England and India, are hounded by the fear of death.

In the West, secularization, medicalization and sanitization of death have divested it of its awe-inspiring features and have removed its stark, physical reality from public view. Seemingly, these trends should have reduced the fear of death. Instead, they have only fostered an avoidant attitude towards it. Traditional religious rituals that used to provide catharsis and comfort in the past centuries have come to be less universally practiced and have lost much of their emotional impact for a great many people. No consensually agreed upon or socially validated rituals have replaced these age-old ceremonies, with the survivors left to improvise secular funerals, which quite often fail to provide closure and meaning to the same extent that the traditional rituals did (Laungani, 2005b).

The situation is quite different in India where funerals are community and family affairs, death is public and emotions are freely displayed rather than suppressed. Death is viewed as a natural, predetermined process rather than a tragic, devastating event. Therefore, it is not only accepted but even celebrated. A great many old people go to great lengths to prepare and even to accelerate their death—without any euthanasic or suicidal intent. Their overriding intention is to die well, at the right place and at the right time, after the performance of traditional preparatory rituals. Indian immigrants to Britain find themselves in a stressful and frustrating situation since there is no way of staging a spectacular Indian funeral in the host country (Laungani, 2003b, 2005b).

To my knowledge, Pittu Laungani never spelled out the counselling implications of these two contrasting modes of marking death. He would, however, have probably agreed that, by virtue of its central place in according meaning to life, death is, or should be, an essential theme in counselling. Moreover, in Europe and North America counsellors and counsellees more often skirt or avoid it than confront or incorporate it into counselling. Laungani (2007) did regret the 'de-ritualizing' of death in modern and post-modern Western societies, thereby leaving the survivors without an important and time-tested source of social and spiritual support. He agreed with the eminent contemporary theologian, Jaroslav Pelikan (1974), that tradition is the living faith of the dead, [and] traditionalism is the dead faith of the living.

Few counsellors or psychotherapists have addressed the healing role of living tradition which overlaps with religious belief and spiritual concerns, but is not identical to them. Pittu Laungani would probably agree that the interventions of modern counsellors complement the rituals and traditions associated with death and burial, but are not equipped to replace them.

## THE INTERDISCIPLINARY NATURE OF COUNSELLING: ITS PHILOSOPHICAL FOUNDATIONS

Pittu Laungani was committed to scientifically based counselling, yet he was not beholden to science as the only road to knowledge. Analyzing the growth of counselling in the United Kingdom (Laungani, 2004b), he noted the widespread lack of awareness of the theoretical bases of counselling among some working members of the profession. Thus, there is more often a lack of fit between theory and practice in counselling than there is correspondence. In particular, Laungani observed widespread naiveté and cultural blindness among the members of the counselling profession about the counselling needs of actual and potential clients who had immigrated to the United Kingdom, including those who came from the Indian subcontinent. By virtue of his own bicultural background and his prodigious interdisciplinary scholarship, Laungani was uniquely equipped to contribute to the resolution of the two problems he had identified, and he proceeded to examine the theoretical underpinnings of counselling in general and those of its application in the multicultural arena.

Laungani's (2004a, 2007) last two books provide a clear and highly readable account of the interaction between culture and behaviour in various domains, including those that are relevant to counselling. Laungani (2004a, 2007) traced these links to the socialization practices in various cultures, followed the divergence of values as a result of these early as well as subsequent experiences and spelled out the implications of these characteristics for various domains of behaviour. In particular, cultures shape the experience of stress and the response to it. Laungani's writings spell out such contrasts between East and West in considerable detail and specificity; they have already been touched upon in the earlier sections of this chapter.

Impressed as Laungani was by the importance and scope of cultural differences in behaviour and experience, he counterbalanced his account of these features with warnings against stereotyping members of the other culture by fitting all of them into a uniform mould. Stereotyping occurs when trends are reified into types and when nuances and exceptions are glossed over and individuals are pigeonholed into categories based on their ethnocultural labels. Stereotypes are often applied to the members of out-groups, especially when they are different in their physical appearance, attire, customs and practices. Instead of succumbing to stereotypes, investigators and counsellors should use empirically based information on cultural differences cautiously and tentatively, and should studiously avoid the mindless leap from the group to its members. It is worth noting that Laungani emphasized culturally shared values and culturally characteristic themes rather than circumscribed fixed traits and specific behavioural acts. Stereotyping members of out-groups and engaging in a blanket refusal to recognize cultural differences in behaviour and experience are the twin obstacles to cultural perceptiveness and sensitivity.

What cultural characteristics are worth investigating, heeding and eventually incorporating into culturally sensitive counselling programmes and practices? Laungani (2004c) was an outspoken opponent of blind, atheoretical empiricism involving haphazard collection of data in the vain hope that these data might yield a coherent and meaningful pattern. Instead, Laungani (2007) advocated proceeding thoughtfully and systematically from the analysis of the recognized features of culture to its observable manifestations, especially as they are gathered by bicultural or multicultural individuals. Pittu Laungani was such a person *par excellence*, and his life can be construed as a cumulative process of reflective culture learning, by contact and juxtaposition, in India and in Britain and by alternating insider's and outsider's perspectives. It is thus that the dimensions of values and subjective experience that set apart the two cultures were identified. They are then amenable to be more formally and rigorously tested and to be eventually applied, tentatively and cautiously, to relevant real-life situations, as exemplified by personal counselling.

As Laungani (2007) has reminded us, cross-cultural psychology is a young science that is still searching for its paradigm. Is cross-cultural psychology but an offshoot of 'mainstream' psychology originated in Germany and North America, based on the experimental method, and now extended to the study of observable behaviour and reportable experience of all humans? Or does it require innovative methods in order to do justice to the dazzling variety of phenomena that cross-cultural psychology is called upon to investigate? Is cross-cultural psychology methodologically pluralistic or eclectic?

Laungani's answers to the above three questions are complex. He gently criticized cross-cultural psychology that gradually came into being in North America and Western Europe in the 1960s and 1970s for being excessively beholden to Western models in both conceptualization and methodology. In particular, '*all theories of personality that we have knowledge of are Western constructions. They have been formulated, designed, and tested by Western psychologists, largely on Western subjects*' (Laungani, 2007: 106) (Italics in the original). Laungani favoured greater pluralism in both theory and method, using, but not exclusively relying on, emic or culturally indigenous concepts and developing and adapting culturally syntonic methods and/or concepts if necessary. The objective is to balance cultural sensitivity with intercultural comparability, which can only be accomplished by a flexible, multimethod approach. Within this inclusive orientation there is room for exploratory, descriptive studies as well as for more rigorous, hypothesis-testing research. The challenge is to keep these differences between the varieties of investigation in mind, and to draw appropriate conclusions from them.

In one of his last publications, Laungani (2004b) took a searching look at the status of counselling in relation to science and concluded that it falls short of Popper's (1963, 1972) criterion of falsifiability. Moreover, counselling is but loosely tied to theory. In a rigorous sense, the scientific status of all psychology and certainly that of counselling is in doubt. The question is:

> Should one therefore call psychology a science and hope that it does not one day turn out to be a pseudo-science, or should one look at psychology as a pseudo-science and hope that one day it comes to be recognized as a genuine science of human and animal behaviour? (Laungani, 2004c: 122)

However, Laungani was well aware that science is not the only fountainhead of knowledge. Philosophy, art, literature, poetry and personal experience provide valuable information and guidance, and all of these served as bases for Pittu Laungani's insights that he shared through his writings. Steeped in science, Laungani steered clear of scientism, and committed though he was to empirical observation, he was not shackled to empiricism.

## PITTU LAUNGANI AS A PIONEER OF MULTICULTURAL COUNSELLING AND A GUIDE TO ITS FUTURE

Through his contributions over close to four decades, Pittu Laungani has virtually shaped the field of multicultural counselling in Great Britain, and his impact and influence have extended far beyond the United Kingdom. At the time when he embarked upon this venture, a substantial database for it did not yet exist. Pittu Laungani's singular contribution was informed by his interdisciplinary scholarship and erudition and by his rich and varied personal experience in immersing himself into the British culture while never loosening or severing his ties to India. The events of his life, and especially his physical disability and suffering, provided additional valuable and unique inputs and sparked contemplation that he shared with his colleagues, students and readers.

The goal of multicultural counselling has traditionally been focused on helping individuals adjust to the culturally distinctive environment in which they find themselves, and to enable them to cope more effectively with the challenges that they encounter. Pittu Laungani encouraged counsellees, by personal contact and through his writings, to go beyond these objectives and to live fully by enduring and enjoying whatever the vicissitudes of life might bring. Being able to do that comes close to attaining wisdom. Wisdom has variously been defined in terms of both questions and answers. Thus, it 'addresses important and difficult questions and strategies about the conduct and meaning of life'

(Baltes et al., 2005: 330), but also 'represents a truly superior level of knowledge, judgment, and advice' (Baltes et al., 2005: 330). Above all, 'wisdom involves a perfect synergy of mind and character, that is an orchestration of knowledge and virtue' (Ibid.). Although wisdom as a term rarely if ever occurs in Laungani's writings and is not to be found in the index of his two last books (Laungani, 2004a, 2007), as a concept it implicitly suffuses his thinking, especially about the goals and objectives of counselling. Wisdom cannot be taught, but it can be modelled and facilitated, and Laungani has certainly provided guidance on how to live serenely even when the slings of fortune batter us mercilessly. In addition to overcoming adversity, wisdom also comes from integrating the various disparate threads of one's experience and from reconciling apparent contradictions. Pittu Laungani has done all of that. At the beginning of this chapter, I called Pittu Laungani a bridge-builder. Specifically, he has connected cultures, narrowed the gulf between reason and faith in philosophy and in life, observed the external world and learned from inner experience, shuttled between the abstract issues of humanity and the concrete concerns of his clients and has invariably done it with grace. A product of both East and West, Pittu Laungani merits being called a guru and a Renaissance man. Traditionally, counselling has aimed to enable clients to remove internal and external obstacles so as to facilitate adjustment and coping and to increase competence. To this objective, positive psychologists have added the promotion of happiness (Seligman, 2005). Pittu Laungani took a further step: by integrating the diverse threads of his knowledge and experience in the service of counselling, Pittu Laungani has launched counselling on the quest for personal wisdom.

## REFERENCES

Baltes, P. B., Gluck, J. and Kuntzmann, U. (2005). Wisdom: Its structure and function in regulating successful life span development. In C. R. Snyder and S. J. Lopez (Eds), *Handbook of positive psychology* (pp. 327–347). New York: Oxford University Press.

Laungani, P. (1992). *It shouldn't happen to a patient: A survivor's guide to fighting life-threatening disease.* London: Whiting & Birch.

———. (2002). Cross-cultural psychology: A handmaiden to mainstream western psychology. *Counselling Psychology Quarterly, 15*(1), 385–397.

———. (2003a). Sexual abuse in an Asian family. *Counselling Psychology Quarterly, 16*(4), 385–401.

———. (2003b). Therapeutic strategies for coping with a life-threatening illness: A personal testament. *Illness, Crisis, & Loss, 11*(2), 162–182.

———. (2004a). *Asian perspectives in counselling and psychotherapy.* Hove, East Sussex: Brunner-Routledge.

———. (2004b). Counselling and therapy in a multicultural setting. *Counselling Psychology Quarterly, 17*(2), 195–207.

———. (2004c). Some unresolved issues in philosophy and psychology: Their implications for therapy. *Counselling Psychology Quarterly, 17*(1), 107–123.

Laungani, P. (2005a). Caste, class, and culture: A case study. *Counselling Psychology Quarterly, 18*(1), 61–71.

———. (2005b). Cultural considerations in Hindu funerals in India and England. In J. D. Morgan and P. Laungani (Eds), *Death and bereavement around the world. Volume 4: Asia, Australia, and New Zealand* (pp. 39--64). Amityville, NY: Baywood.

———. (2007). *Understanding cross-cultural psychology.* London: Sage Publications.

Pelikan, J. (1974). *The spirit of Eastern Christiandom: 1600–1700.* Chicago: University of Chicago Press.

Popper, K. (1963). *Conjectures and refutations.* London: Routledge & Kegan Paul.

———. (1972). *Objective knowledge: An evolutionary approach.* Oxford: Clarendon.

Seligman, M. E. R. (2005). Positive psychology, positive prevention, and positive therapy. In C. R. Snyder and S. J. Lopez (Eds), *Handbook of positive psychology* (pp. 3–12). New York: Oxford University Press.

# 11

# Caste, Class and Culture: A Case Study

*Pittu Laungani*

## INTRODUCTION

**This** is a cross-cultural case study. It revolves round two persons. Although they are the main *dramatis personae*, so to speak, it would be unwise to ignore several other persons who enter into the 'drama', whose influence upon the lives of the two persons is not inconsiderable. It needs to be emphasized that I have done my utmost to safeguard the identity and the anonymity of the two persons involved in the case study. To prevent any recognition several details have been altered and false names and false places have replaced true names and true places. It is my belief that they will remain unrecognized not only by their closest friends but also by their own kith and kin. The 'facts' of the case, however, have not been altered. In placing the word facts in inverted commas, I would like to make it clear to the reader that facts often involve some form of interpretation and judgement. It is important to bear in mind that the event(s) to which I refer took place in the early years of the 1980s. I would urge the reader to see the case study from its historical perspective, and not from the fresh light of the 21st century.

Sailesh Chatterjee is a medical doctor. He originally comes from Calcutta, in India, which is where he was born and where his parents live. He is a young man in his mid-30s, working in a London teaching hospital as a Registrar. He had come to England about 15 years ago to study medicine. After getting his medical degree he stayed on in England for a few years to get some first hand work experience and also complete his MRCP before returning to Calcutta. Although he has been to Calcutta on a few occasions during the last 15 years, much to the dismay of his parents, he has shown not the slightest sign of returning home.

## THE FIRST MEETING

Prior to our meeting, Dr Chatterji phoned me at home and asked if he could come and see me professionally. How he had got hold of my number, I do not know. Nor did I inquire. There is, as I have mentioned in one of my earlier case studies, a network of Indian contacts, which, like God, works in mysterious ways! As I got to know him better he told me that he knew someone who knew someone who knew someone, and so on...and eventually, my name had cropped up. And then he recalled having met me once. It appears that I had first met Dr Chatterji and Ms Mayhew at a friend's party, several years ago, although I have no recollection of that meeting.

I laid down a set of ground rules, which I stressed he would have to follow if we were to continue with our meetings. I have always avoided using words such as therapy, treatment and counselling, because of the negative connotations, which are often built around such terms I often tend to use the neutral term such as problem-solving. (I have borrowed the term from the writings of Sir Karl Popper, who looks upon all life as 'problem-solving'.) The term problem-solving has a more positive ring about it because problems can be construed in abstract, rational and intellectual terms. They can also be visualized in the form of propositions from which hypotheses can be teased out and tested, and moreover, problems can involve the combined talents of many persons, who may bring their own perspectives and levels of expertize to bear on finding satisfactory solutions.

First, I could not promise that I would take him on as a client. That to a large extent, I explained, would depend on our first meeting. I would need to be sure in my mind that I was the right person whose help he had solicited, and that it was within my province to help him. By the same token, he too would need to be sure and have the required confidence and trust in me and in my ability to be of some help. I insisted too that I was a 'stickler' for time; he would therefore need to make sure that he was punctual and did not miss any appointments, if we agreed to continue our meetings. To bring the point home, I added with a mild touch of sarcasm, that while medical doctors often kept their patients waiting, I would not keep him waiting! I stressed the fact that the first meeting was extremely crucial. There were a few other ground rules, which I said, I would explain to him when we met in person.

Dr Chatterji arrived on time. He was a tall, lean and good-looking man, very smartly dressed in a double-breasted grey, woollen suit, a silk shirt, and a silver grey tie to match. He sat in a chair, crossed his legs, ran his hands through his long and curly hair, cleared his throat, looked at me a bit uncertainly as though waiting for me to 'open the proceedings'. I remained silent. I 'busied' myself, rearranging some of the bric-a-brac, cluttering my desk, waiting for him to make a start.

Addressing me by my title, he said, 'I have a problem'. Once again, he lapsed into silence. I was pleased at his use of the word 'problem'—although he had given the word its own personalized meaning, which probably included a gamut of emotions and feelings, anxieties and tensions, uncertainties and indecisions. I waited.

'My life is in a mess!' he added after a while.

'Let me ask you a few questions, if I may,' I said, ignoring his emotional statement. 'These are what I call quick-fire questions. And I would like quick-fire answers. They help to clear the air, so to speak. Don't try and elaborate. And don't think too long about any question I ask you. Just say, "yes", "no", or "don't know". I am asking you to give me the first response that comes to your lips. Is that okay?' (Hearing myself speak, I was beginning to sound like a 'humanized' personality test.) At least for the present I would like to treat it as a game.'

'Okay.' He seemed doubtful, though.

What I was trying out on Chatterji was a variation of the 'word-association' test. The word-association test is an improvisation of the ideas underlying the technique of 'free-association', which was first introduced by Freud in his psychoanalytic encounters with his patients. Many psychoanalysts still follow the free-association technique in the course of their work. The formulation of the word-association test has been attributed to Carl Jung; but there are others who believe that the test was designed by Kent-Rosanoff. What is important in the word-association test is the time taken between hearing the word (receiving the stimulus) and the answer (the response) given by the person being tested. One can measure the time-sequence to each response electronically, and then focus on the delayed responses, with the assumption that those areas might be worth probing.

But I had no intention of using the word association test. Instead of asking him to respond to a set of words I wanted him to respond as quickly as possible to a set of questions which I thought would perhaps help me in two ways. One, to rule out the 'non-problematic' areas in his life and two, give me a clue to the areas in his life, which he said had turned his life into a 'mess'.

'Let's start. How old are you?'

'34.'

'Married?'

'No.'

'Girlfriend?'

'That is the problem.'

'You mean you haven't got one?'

Once again, he lapsed into a stony silence. I waited.

'That's the problem. Had one. She's walked out on me. Three months ago.'

'I see.'

'What do you see? You see nothing! You don't even know what the facts are! Yet you claim to be able to see'

'I'm sorry. I didn't say I understood your problem. I was merely acknowledging your problem.' I made a mental note of his anger and hurt and decided not to pursue it at that moment. He'd come to it when he was ready. 'Would you say, you were a good doctor?' I asked, changing the subject.

'Don't know.' A slight pause. 'My patients think quite well of me, though' he added as an afterthought.

'Any specialist area of medicine that is of interest to you?'

'No. I am a General Physician.'

'You're a Registrar, I take it.'

'Yes.'

'What's the next step?'

He hesitated for a while. 'Senior Registrar. That is on its way' he said as though stating a fact.

'Then?'

He sighed. 'I can't even contemplate the idea…'

'of being a consultant?'

He nodded.

I continued with this line of questioning for a few more minutes. We sat silently, looking at each other.

'Let me summarize what we have talked about so far. You are an ambitious young doctor and you like working as a General Physician. You've already got Part I of your MRCP but have failed in your first attempt at getting Part II. But you are planning to have another go. You seem very keen to "move on", get a consultancy somewhere, but you've had a problem with your girlfriend, who's walked out on you'.

'Yes.'

'Now, before we go any further, I would like to know a bit more about yourself, your family and whatever else you consider relevant.'

He looked at me, blinked a few times, wiped his face with a handkerchief and nodded gently. It took him a while to get started. At first he spoke of irrelevancies, such as from where he bought his clothes. He said he always bought his suits and shirts and ties from a smart West End tailoring shop. He said he enjoyed dressing smartly. That to him was one of the joys of living in England. One could wear wonderful suits. India didn't have the climate for wearing smart suits; it was too hot and too humid. And he didn't particularly care for the traditional Indian pyjamas and kurtas—whether they were made of silk, polyester or cotton. I noticed that his suit was beautifully tailored and extremely well pressed. Before I could wonder how he could afford to dress with such expensive elegance, he came up with the answer.

His parents, he said, came from an old established family, which went back several generations. His father had been a major shareholder in a large Shipping Corporation, based in Calcutta, and also its Managing Director. The Company had a fleet of cargo ships.

'So money, obviously, is not a problem.'

'Right.'

'What is it then?'

After a long, strained silence, he explained that his father and his mother would have preferred him to get married and settle down in India. They had all the right connections: financial, social, cultural and historical; his grandfather had been a personal friend of the Nobel laureate Tagore and had also been deeply influenced by the liberal reformism of Ram Mohan Roy, the founder of the *Brahmo Samaj*. And given their familial connections they would have found for him an appropriate match. But he had shown not the slightest inclination to consider their proposals. He fobbed them off by arguing that he was eager to finish his MRCP and try and become a consultant in General Medicine in one of the teaching hospitals in London. He said he had no intentions of returning to India and getting married to a nice, demure, rich Bengali girl that came from an aristocratic family.

His main reason for wanting to continue living in England had to do with his girlfriend Jennifer Mayhew, of whose existence his parents until recently were unaware. Although his father was an extremely liberal person in many ways, he was certain that under no circumstances would he countenance the idea of Sailesh, his only son, marrying an English girl, or any foreigner for that matter.

Jennifer Mayhew he explained was 30: 4 years younger than he. She had read English at University College, in London, but did not work for a living; to keep her hand in, she did a bit of Extra-Mural teaching; that is all. There was little need for her to find work. She was comfortably off. She was the only child of her parents, who lived in Dorset. They owned vast acres of farmland, which they had inherited from their parents, who in turn, inherited it from their parents, going down a few generations. She had just completed writing her first novel and was making some attempts to get it published. Despite her 'connections' in the publishing world, she was keen not to exploit them. She would prefer her novel to be published on its merits—or not at all. In a few words, Sailesh had painted a good, clear picture of Jennifer Mayhew.

There were, I felt, several other pieces to the jigsaw puzzle, which when assembled together in the right shape, form, and order would give me a clearer understanding of his problems than I had at the moment. But I had the distinct impression that Jennifer's walking out on him had something to do with his father. But he had told me enough for me to brood over until our next appointment.

## SUBSEQUENT MEETINGS

Dr Chatterji arrived on time. As usual, he was immaculately dressed; everything matched with everything else—even the silk handkerchief peeping out of the breast pocket of his woollen jacket.

'How do you feel today, Dr Chatterji?' I asked him, when he sat down in a chair across my desk.

He spoke of his work at the hospital, and the 16–18 hours a day workload that he and most other doctors who were expected to carry out.

'You must be incredibly fit,' I said.

'Does that make me incredibly competent too? I doubt it. Mistakes can be made. Serious mistakes.'

I could see that he was eager to get involved in a discussion or even an argument on the failing health of the National Health Service, but I gradually got him round to talking of his personal problems—which of course, was what he had come to see me about.

I asked him about Jennifer. It appears that Jennifer and he had been seeing each other for over 6 years and had started living together for the last 2 years. It was hardly surprising that he had been unwilling to consider any marriage proposals, which his father might have put in his way. About 6 months ago, Jennifer and he had decided to get married. The decision, he explained had not been easy on both sides; they had gone through their doubts, their uncertainties, their understandings and misunderstandings, their quarrels and their reconciliation, their remorse and their recriminations, their 'Indianness' and their 'Englishness', over and over again. But they both knew that the idea of *not* living together (as man and wife) was far more painful and intolerable than living together as man and wife. They both loved children and neither of them had any desire to bring up illegitimate children, Jennifer for religious reasons, and Sailesh because he came from a culture where illegitimacy was considered vile and loathsome.

In so far as Jennifer was concerned, she had made no secret of her relationship with Sailesh. Her parents knew. Whether her parents approved of her 'cross-cultural' choice for a husband, I was unable to find out. But from the accounts, which Sailesh offered at our subsequent meetings, I was convinced that her parents had no strong feelings about this issue, if anything, they looked forward to having a resident doctor in the house! They had met Sailesh on more than a few occasions, and it would appear, had been suitably impressed.

Sailesh, on the other hand, had been unable to bring himself to disclose his relationship with Jennifer to his parents. He was, as I gradually pieced the information together, quite intimidated by his father, which made it exceedingly difficult, not to say painful, to discuss or disclose any issue which might involve a major change in his own personal life. It was not as though he did not love his father. He had a deep enduring affection for him; but he was also not a little in awe of him. Like most Hindu children, he too had been brought up to love and fear his father. Roland (1988) in his magnificent book *In search of self in India and Japan* discusses this ambivalent theme from a psychoanalytical perspective.

Even the idea that Sailesh ought to do a medical degree in England had been his father's. Luckily, for Sailesh it was a choice he had welcomed open-heartedly, pouncing on the offer with alacrity. So long as Sailesh fell in with his father's 'grand plans' he and his father got along well with each other and there were no problems But if Sailesh expressed a wish or a desire, which his father took exception to, disliked, or disapproved of in any way, it was understood that Sailesh, sooner or later, would be expected to back down—which of course he did. Sailesh could never bring himself to confront his father. Obedience, like blood, coursed through his veins.

Given the rigid, hierarchical and patriarchic structure of Indian society I understood some of the subtle dynamics affecting their relationships. But Jennifer (whom sadly, I never got to meet) must have been quite bewildered by the 'Jekyll and Hyde' persona presented by Sailesh in this situation. As a medical doctor, he could take major, life-saving (or life-threatening) decisions and defend them: yet he could not bring himself to inform his parents of his choice of a marital partner.

For me to try and convince him that he was an independent being, that he had his own future, his life and happiness to consider, that he had to learn to take decisions which on certain occasions, may go against the expressed wishes of his father, that he had to train himself to 'live' with such difficult and painful decisions, is the stuff which Western therapy is composed of. Wedded to the philosophy of Individualism, garbed in the guise of rationalism a western therapist would in general attempt to persuade him to adopt an attitude, which would focus more on his own personal needs and problems and less on the consequences of his actions on other significant persons in his life. This was precisely what I avoided doing. It was culturally alienating, and in the long run, it could easily turn out to be counter-productive, if not destructive. At any rate, the event which he had described, had preceded in its recounting by more than three months.

Jennifer did not exactly push him into a corner, but she did make her position clear. If they married in England, she wanted *his* parents to be present at their wedding or alternatively, her parents being present at their wedding if they decided to get married in India. On the one hand Jennifer would have preferred to have got married in England, surrounded by all her family members, her relatives, and friends. On the other, she was enchanted by idea of getting married in India—the exotic splendour of Sailesh's sisters' weddings, the lavish parties, which went on for several days, had, 'turned her head' so to speak. But she was insistent that Sailesh notified his parents of the event.

Finally, Sailesh wrote to his parents, informing them of his decision. He received no reply. Jennifer and Sailesh in the meanwhile decided to get engaged, and arranged a lavish party, which Jennifer's parents had volunteered to hold. A few weeks later, Sailesh sent his parents a card, inviting them to his engagement party. Once again, there was no reply to the invitation. He had been unable to gather the courage to phone his parents in Calcutta.

'What did you do?' I inquired when he reached the end of his narrative.

'My father died. He died of a massive heart attack.'

I was stunned. It was so sudden, so cold, so brutal.

'When did it happen?'

'Two days before our engagement party. *Just 2 days!* He ruined everything!'

It was then that he started to sob and cry. I pushed forward a box of tissues, but he was oblivious to the box or to my presence. I sat brooding. This was the first occasion on which he had blamed his father. There were in his tears, years of frozen anger, hurt and hatred, which, like a melting glacier, overwhelmed him entirely. His anger and hatred was not unmixed with terrible feelings of guilt and remorse. From time to time, he kept moaning and blaming himself for his father's death; at other times, he cursed him for having ruined his life. He was like a manic-depressive psychotic on a seesaw, which swung perilously from guilt to rage, rage to guilt, without coming to a standstill.

I could not rule out the possibility that his father may have been ill, suffering from a cardiac problem, and that the time of his fatal seizure may have been a pure coincidence, unrelated to Sailesh's invitation. But in this too, I was proven wrong. For I learnt that his father had always enjoyed excellent health; in fact, he played a rigorous three-set game of tennis every morning at his Club. Ironically, it was on the tennis court, where he was waiting to play his first game that he had a seizure from which he never recovered.

His father's sudden death created a major problem in the lives of Sailesh and Jennifer. As the only son, (and therefore the oldest) it was expected that in accordance with the teachings of Hindu religion, it would be his sacred duty—*dharma*—to attend his father's funeral, abide by all the sacred rites and rituals and light the funeral pyre, which would ensure the final repose of his father's soul. And after the 10–12 days of mourning, he would have been expected to perform the final rites and ceremonies, which would involve the immersion of his father's ashes in the Ganges. For a son not to participate in the final funeral rites (Laungani, 1997, 1999, 2000, 2004) is to commit a grave sin, a sacrilege. The wrath of one's entire family, one's community (*baradari*) one's caste, would descend upon the evildoer with the force and the power of a meteor hurtling down from outer space.

By ancient tradition, women have never been allowed to participate in the final funeral rites in the crematorium. Although his two sisters may have been willing to perform the last rites they would not have been permitted to do so.

This is what led to the final rift between Sailesh and Jennifer. Understandably, she was sympathetic to his father's tragic death; yet from her own point of view, she was angry, hurt, and disappointed that Sailesh's departure to Calcutta would mean the cancellation of their engagement party. Each blamed the other. Sailesh blamed Jennifer for having forced his hand into writing to his parents, instead of giving him time to sort matters out in his own way. She blamed him for allowing himself to be cowed down by his father and not standing up to him as every man would. With each unthinking insult hurled at the other, the cultural differences between the two widened; like rapiers, their mutual recriminations drew blood, each 'hit' exposing a festering stereotype, such as 'You English this…you Indians that', and ripped apart the paper-thin veneer of cultural sophistication, tolerance and understanding which they both believed they had acquired over the years, which no doubt they had. But given a situation of crises, neither of them was able to hold on to their newly acquired cultural sophistication.

Sailesh attended his father's funeral. Jennifer called off the engagement. In-between his tears Sailesh confessed that he did not know what to do with his life anymore. He confessed that he was still desperately in love with Jennifer. He confessed too that he had no regrets about having been to India for his father's funeral, although he still hated his father for having died when he did. 'It was as though he had planned it. Stage-managed his death to teach his son a lesson he'd never forget'.

'Have you tried getting in touch with her?'

'Yes. I have phoned her, left messages for her, even phoned her parents…'

'Do you think she feels guilty about your father's death.'

'I don't know…but I don't think so. There is no reason for her to feel guilty.'

'What about your mother?'

'Naturally, she has taken it very badly. But luckily, both my sisters live in Calcutta, and she's been staying with my elder sister and her family. And we have a large, extended family—uncles, aunts, cousins—they all come and see her regularly.'

I asked him if he had made any plans for his future, now that he was on his own.

'All my plans were tied up with Jennifer's plans.'

'Even the MRCP? Jennifer would hate it if you didn't complete it.'

'What's the point?'

Sailesh had given me a lot to think about. I needed time to mull over what had transpired, replay in my mind's eye, all the meetings that we had had so far. I felt that I had now obtained an insight into most of the problems, which deeply disturbed Sailesh. My own regret was the fact that I had not met Jennifer; but whether it would have helped me to arrive at a better understanding of the present situation, I could not tell. But she would have had to be something out of the ordinary for Sailesh to feel the way he did about her.

I suggested that we should meet one more time, twice, if it became absolutely necessary. At our next meeting, I wanted him to come up with written 'solutions' to his problems The solutions could be temporary, short-term, or long-term. I assured him that my role was not to judge the quality of his proffered solutions. I would concern myself with their feasibility. It did not matter to me whether the solutions seemed bizarre, irrational, self-damaging or whatever. And since I had no wish to put any words or thoughts in his mouth and mind, I would not offer any 'solutions' of my own until I had gone over what he had to say about them. Once again, I assured him that there would be nothing startling or unique or earth shattering about my own 'solutions' to his problems; they would merely be a re-working of his own solutions, from perspectives, which he may not have considered.

The final meeting, if it became necessary, would be a summing-up meeting.

## THE LAST TWO MEETINGS

On his arrival the following week, Sailesh put a printed sheet of paper on my desk. He said that he had spent an agonizing week thinking about his problems; he had to find a solution—a sound, workable solution—or else he'd go out of his mind. 'I can't go on like this: my work at the hospital is beginning to suffer.'

I studied the sheet of paper in front of me. It was very cleverly composed. It was clear that he had spent a lot of time and energy thinking over all the possible avenues that were open to him and those which were not open to him. He had divided the sheet into two major headings:

- Returning to India.
- Staying On.

Under each heading he had worked out what seemed to him the advantages and disadvantages of returning to India or staying on in England. His father whom he loved and feared had died. His mother, although presently living at her daughter's house, was now a widow. She would need comforting and looking after. His girlfriend Jennifer had called off their engagement or in other words, his future marriage had died before being solemnized. He had also failed the second part of his MRCP. There didn't seem much point in his staying in England. He was young enough to start afresh, get married to a young beautiful, and talented woman of his own caste and class. And given the prestigious family background which he came from he would have little difficulty in finding a consultancy in one of the well-known teaching hospitals in Calcutta. It was obvious there were good reasons for him to return. Without actually putting it into words, he had begun to sound homesick. His explanations carried the implication that it would be nice once again to be among his own people, in the city of his birth, surrounded by his friends, his family members, and all the familiar sights, sounds, and places that he had grown up to love. I had the distinct impression that he was not averse to the idea of returning home.

But he had also given a great deal of thought to the issues underlying the second heading, 'Staying On'. His use of the phrase staying on, reminded me of novel of the same name, by Paul Scott (1977) in which Mrs Tusker who, upon the death of her husband in India has to decide whether she stays on in India where she and her husband have lived for several years, or whether it was time for her to return 'home'. Sailesh too, I could see, was torn by a similar conflict. He had been living in England for several years and had got used to an English way of life. England, as he once remarked, had got into his soul. It was like the blistering Arctic wind that got into one's bones, which one was never able to shake oneself out of. His father had died and there was little that he could do about it. The problems related to sorting out the probate, the will, and ensuring the happiness and comfort of his widowed mother could be sorted out by and by, without his having to 'burn his boats'. And if he left, he would have left without having completed his MRCP. His dead father, he was sure, would never forgive him for that. He owed it to his father to complete his MRCP; it was after all at his father's behest that he had come to England. Although it seemed hopeless at the moment, he felt that there was still a possibility that Jennifer and he would get together; one doesn't give up a 6-year relationship that easily!

Despite the cogency of his arguments, he had been unable to take a firm decision. Just as I was beginning to wonder, what kind of decision he would take, when he turned to me.

'What do you think I should do?'

Gently but firmly, I warned him that if he was waiting for me to take a decision on his behalf so that he could act upon it, he was mistaken. 'It is not for me to decide what you should do or how you should live your life, or, more to the point, where you should live. I cannot even say to you what *I* would do in your situation because you might take that as the course of action to follow. I am afraid this is one decision which *you* will have to take on your own.'

At this, he became quite angry, an anger which I had not seen before. 'What was the point of my coming to see you then, if you are unable to help me?' He went on in this vein for a few more minutes and finally lapsed into a strained silence.

'I am more than willing to listen to you and hopefully even help you to understand your own dilemmas. I am quite happy to clarify any confusions or conundrums that trouble you at this time. But in the last analysis, my friend, it is *you, you, and you alone* who will have to decide what you would like to do.' I picked up his sheet of paper and pointed to an interesting entry, which he had made under the first heading: 'return to India *after* obtaining my MRCP'. I suggested that he should see the MRCP as being independent of the problems related to Jennifer, the sudden death of his father, and the uncertain future of his widowed mother.

I let him talk through the point about his returning to India with or without completing his MRCP. He exhausted himself as he went over the same points again and again and again, trying to work out the best solution. I suggested that he should think over these points during the course of the week, so that we could discuss them at our final meeting the following week.

Decision was written large on his face when he came to see me a week later. 'You have decided to do your MRCP,' I stated as he sat in his chair.

'How did you know?'

'It wasn't too difficult to guess. Now you can knuckle down, and get your teeth into getting that precious qualification, which you have been hankering after for a few years.'

'Yes, I need to prove to myself that I can do it.' He offered elaborate explanations as to why he had decided to pursue this course of action. All the other problems, he explained were less urgent; his mother was being looked after by his sisters, probates in India could take years to be sorted out, he still had an interesting job at the hospital, he had good working colleagues, and he was appreciated by his patients. He had the blessings of his consultant at the hospital, and it seemed more than sensible that he should concentrate all his energies in acquiring that elusive qualification. He could then decide on other courses of action.

'It might even redeem you in the eyes of your father.'

'Yes. I will have earned his confidence.'

Once again, addressing me by my title, he said that it had been nice meeting me, and he was glad to have made my acquaintance. He would, if I permitted it, like to keep in touch with me.

'If I should fall seriously ill, I shall make it a point to come and see you.'

'I sincerely hope that never happens—I mean that you never fall seriously ill.'

## CONCLUSION

Twenty years have gone by since I first met Dr Sailesh Chatterji. True to his word, he kept in regular touch with me. His relationship with Jennifer restarted, continued for a while, but foundered once again. Eventually they lost touch with each other. He returned to India, where he stayed for three years, during which period, in accordance with his father's wishes, he married an attractive Bengali woman from his own caste and class. But finding it difficult to settle down in Calcutta, he and his wife returned to England. He is now working as a Consultant in a teaching hospital in Bristol.

## REFERENCES


Laungani, P. (1997). Death in a Hindu family. In C. M. Parkes, P. Laungani and B. Young (Eds), *Death and bereavement across cultures*. London: Brunner-Routledge.

———. (1999). Death among Hindus in India and England. *International Journal of Group Tensions, 28*, 85–114.

———. (2000). The changing patterns of Hindu funerals in Britain: Cultural and psychological implications. *Asian Journal of Psychology and Education, 38*, 2–14.

———. (2004). *Asian perspectives in counselling and psychotherapy*. London: Brunner-Routledge.

Roland, A. (1988). *In search of self in India and Japan: Toward a cross-cultural psychology*. Princeton, NJ: Princeton University Press.

Scott, P. (1977). *Staying on*. London: William Heinemann.

# 12

# Pittu Laungani, a Bicultural Psychologist: Commentary on 'Caste, Class and Culture'

*Alan Roland*

**It** is a rare delight to encounter a psychotherapist who can really write. Pittu Laungani, who was a playwright on the side, is by far one of the most gifted writers in our profession. He employs dramatic tension, leaving the reader eager to know how the case will unfold, fascinated with its unexpected, dramatic turns, and closely participating in Pittu Laungani's own inner process of thinking and reacting as well as with the client, Dr Chatterji. How different this is from most case studies that are simply descriptive and analytic.

He is also novelistic through detailing Dr Chatterji's physical appearance, posture, dress, manner of speaking, family background, location, and such. One builds up quite a picture of the client. While the case description is undoubtedly psychologically accurate, Laungani has creatively fictionalized all of these details to thoroughly disguise the client. There may be one billion people in India but among these urban, educated elite, everyone seems to know everyone else. So my guess is that this tall, thin doctor from an old, Calcutta Brahmin aristocratic family with immaculate English suits of such and such a colour was really a relatively short, squat, upper caste Hindu or Parsee or Muslim man, perhaps a lawyer or engineer, from a wealthy family in what was then Bombay, Madras or even Ahmedabad or Pune. But you do get a textured picture of a man who is Anglicized on one level but with a deep, inner core self from a traditional, well-to-do Indian extended family that is also partly Westernized. This is no mean feat to pull off so well.

## PITTU LAUNGANI AS A BICULTURAL PSYCHOTHERAPIST

Pittu Laungani as a psychotherapist is both Western and Eastern in approach, sometimes simultaneously both, at other times clearly one or the other. As a cognitive psychologist employing Karl Popper's (1988) rational problem-solving approach, he is distinctly Anglo-American in orientation. But his rationale for using this is also Indian, as he tries to avoid any association to psychotherapy or counselling as being implicitly too shameful for the client. Until only the last decade or so, even the Indian urban educated were highly reluctant to come for any kind of psychotherapy or counselling because of shame, that having emotional problems or mental illness would reflect poorly on the reputation of the extended family.[1] This in turn would impact on the possibility of a good marriage for their children. In Bombay in the 1980s, at a time when this client was being seen by Pittu Laungani, anyone going into psychotherapy would almost never go to a therapist from their own community out of dread that word would leak out into the community.

Laungani also combines Western and Indian approaches in his laying down strict rules on time, promptness and missed sessions. He is very Western, especially in terms of the northern European/North American culture belt, in laying down the law that one condition of working together is that the client must come exactly on time. Indian notions of time are much looser where coming late to appointments or meetings is often the case. Promptness is not an imperative. An interesting exception to this is when a meeting is to take place at an auspicious time, usually decided by astrological readings, which is then strictly observed (personal communication, Rajesh Kumar).[2] On the other hand, the manner in which Pittu Laungani states his condition of promptness conveys the image of an authoritative Indian father-figure who strictly sets the rules in the hierarchical relationship. It is assumed in Indian hierarchical relationships, which are ubiquitously present, that the superior, especially the father-figure, is strict in his rules but with caring, responsible and nurturing attitudes towards his subordinates. This is very different from Western hierarchical relationships which are much more contractual, emphasizing rights and obligations.

Pittu Laungani's strong emphasis on insisting that his client make his own decisions rather than being told what to do, in other words, maintaining and enhancing the client's autonomy in decision-making, is very Western in approach.[3] Indian patients ordinarily seek advice and guidance from a therapist as they are used to receiving from a variety of family elders and other superiors. They rely on this to guide them through the subtle complexities of multiple extended family and other hierarchical relationships. Different Indian therapists handle this in different ways. A Mumbai psychoanalyst, Udayan Patel, (personal communication, October, 1977), simply tells his patients that I am here to help you understand yourself not to tell you what to do. Another, Alexander (1979), working with patients from rural areas would cite a lotus pond with bubbles coming to the surface. He tells his patients that if you simply try to skim the bubbles off, they will reappear. But if you delve deeply into the pond to get to the source of the bubbles, you can then solve the problem. Pittu Laungani's approach is basically to help the patient in his or her own decision-making process in solving their problems, not to tell them what to do.

In any case, Laungani's emphasis on autonomy of decision-making and rationality are cardinal tenets of the modern Western culture of individualism, and permeate all of the psychotherapies to one extent or another. I would suggest that his Westernized college education in Bombay and particularly his moving to England were spurs to this part of his bicultural self.

## INDIAN SENSIBILITY

Then, there is the other cultural/psychological side of Pittu Laungani, his Indian sensibility. First, there is the matter of how the client came to Pittu Laungani. He rightly mentions the unseen networks in Indian society that work in mysterious ways.[4]

More important is Laungani's awareness of social change in the area of the arranged marriage. He asks the reader to remember that he saw his client in the 1980s and not in 2005 when the paper was published, implying that attitudes towards the arranged marriage have changed considerably in the intervening years in the urban educated middle and upper middle classes. In more current times, marriages in this group are often arranged marriages by introduction where the couple can see each other as long as they wish, and each has veto power (Mathew, 2008). Or not infrequently, a couple may arrange their own marriage but almost always with family approval as it is extremely difficult to function in India without strong family ties.

In the 1980s, marriages were still largely arranged by the family with often only the young men being given veto power over family choices. Thus, it would not have been unusual for this family to expect their son, Pittu Laungani's client, to agree to a suitable arranged marriage, and for him to expect them to be very upset if he married a foreigner.[5] Since then, much has changed. It is crucial for the therapist or counsellor to be aware of these changing expectations and practices as Pittu Laungani was.

I mention this at some length because in the usual discussion of cross-cultural psychology differences are mainly emphasized; that is, the psychological makeup of the person from another culture is what is customarily talked about. Rarely is the issue of social change as it is incorporated in the psyche analyzed.

For clients from any culture there is often a layering of values and attitudes from childhood and adolescence that are deeply internalized, and which may or may not be congruent with the values and expectations one has incorporated from contemporary society (Roland and Harris, 1978). This can sometimes generate considerable inner conflict. Thus, Dr Chatterji's contemporary self had modern, liberal attitudes towards marrying a foreigner but he was also deeply attached to his parents and their traditional attitudes towards the arranged marriage.

Of considerable importance is Laungani's understanding of Indian familial relationships and particularly the complexities and subtleties of the father–son hierarchical relationship. He rightly recognizes the importance of strong emotional ties to the family and the merit of considering the welfare of family members. Implicit in this recognition is an Indian 'we-self' in contrast to the Western individualistic 'I-self' and the salience of esteem or 'we-self esteem' in the guarding and enhancing of family reputation (Roland, 1988, 1996). Whenever the self is mentioned in any Western psychological text of whichever school of thought, it is always implicitly assumed to be an 'I-self,' in a dualistic relationship to another or others. This contrasts with an Indian (and generally Asian) 'we-self', where the self is experienced in an I–we relationship to the other(s), especially in insider familial relationships. Here, there is partial merger with the other with more permeable outer ego boundaries. This we-self fluctuates according to the relationship but is balanced by a highly private self that can harbour all kinds of feelings, thoughts and fantasies that are kept more secret than most Euro-Americans are capable of.[6]

Laungani also understands the complex nature of the father–son hierarchical relationship where there is overt distance and authority but a more covert close emotional attachment. He characterizes the Indian hierarchical relationship as rigid, implying authoritarian, but I wonder if this pejorative way of looking at it indicates certain Westernization on Pittu Laungani's part. Fathers expect obedience, deference and loyalty from their sons but there are equal expectations that fathers be nurturing and responsible to their sons. It is interesting to note that the two times when Dr Chatterji was full of rage in session were: *(a)* his recounting his father dying two days before his engagement party that spoiled everything; and *(b)* when Dr Chatterji perceived Pittu Laungani as not being of help to him in his making a decision. Both the times Dr Chatterji felt that a father-figure had failed him.

Central to the Indian father–son emotional connectedness is that, each reflects well on the other, each supporting and enhancing the other's we-self esteem. In Indian and other Asian relationships, esteem is far more salient than in the United States of America, and I suspect England too.[7] Pittu Laungani was certainly aware of this dynamic of father–son we-self esteem by his strongly supporting Dr Chatterji's choice to stay in England to complete his medical exams, something his late father had dearly wanted, and that in Dr Chatterji's mind would earn him his father's respect as well as reflect well on his father. That his father was no longer alive, in no way interfered with this kind of psychology. I have heard reports of men still striving to earn their fathers' respect many years after their fathers had died.

This issue of maintaining a high degree of we-self esteem can become problematic in Indian hierarchical relationships when one or the other fails to respect the other. But it is more problematic with Indians and other Asians in American hierarchical relationships where the centrality of maintaining and enhancing each other's esteem is much less important. Where exploitation occurs in American corporate or higher educational situations, the Euro-American therapist tends to see it as basically an abrogation of the contractual relationship where rights and obligations are basic.[8]

In general, with Indians and other Asians in American-style hierarchical relationships, there is often considerable hurt over the superior being blunt in any critiques, again feeling hurt and threatened in their self-esteem. In addition, they often do not experience the superior as being as nurturing and caring as they are used to in their indigenous hierarchical relationships. A simple example is of an Indian man with two graduate degrees who worked very hard and competently in his first year at a bank. When he learned that he was not given a raise, he was quite hurt. He then found out that to get a raise, he had to ask for it. This was quite different from expecting the superior to have him in mind and to give a raise without his having to ask.

To return to the case study, there is the rather important matter of how a therapist or counsellor understands and responds to Dr Chatterji's problematic relationship with his father. Was it simply the case that Dr Chatterjee became more Westernized and Anglicized than his father had anticipated, and had fallen in love with a very interesting English woman whom he wanted to marry? This would, of course, have the unintended consequence of conflict with his father since he knew his father would have great difficulty accepting his marrying a foreigner. It would be something like the Sholem Aleichem short story (1999) of a poor Jewish family living in a shtetl, who saved their every ruble to send their brilliant son to a good school in Moscow. There he learned the latest theories, became enamoured with radical social thought, participated in demonstrations, and was then thrown out of school. His family had wanted him to get an excellent education but never anticipated that he would acquire a whole new value system. Perhaps this is similar to Dr Chatterji's family's expectations, that he would go to England for medical training but still remain a traditional urban upper class Hindu who is partly Westernized. Or was it the case that within the usual Indian father–son hierarchical relationship that Dr Chatterji's father was on the more extreme side, more intimidating and unbending than is usually the case, idiosyncratically out-of-kilter with the usual Indian father–son relationship from that milieu. If this were so, it would explain Dr Chatterji's intense pent-up rage at his father's sudden death and indicate that there was probably more than a little unconscious rebellion in Dr Chatterji once he went to England and felt freer from his father. No wonder then that he hadn't returned in 15 years to India and became involved with an English woman. Perhaps his failing the MRCP exam was also part of an unconscious rebellion against his father, that he not have to return to India since he had not passed this major exam, a gateway to becoming a consultant, that was part of his father's agenda. Failing the exam would also reflect poorly on his father. It is not so easy for a therapist to evaluate which of these two scenarios is more relevant, yet it is crucial to do so. In the latter scenario, this kind of evaluation is even more daunting for a non-Indian counsellor or therapist because first he or she has to be aware of the nature of Indian father–son hierarchical relationships; and then to what extent this relationship is idiosyncratically askew (Roland, 1996). In any case, these kinds of judgements are central to what tack a therapist or counsellor takes with the client. Counsellors and therapists working with their own indigenous clients in their own country are also making judgements of their clients' problems in the context of their understanding of what usually goes or doesn't go in their own culture.

Pittu Laungani, himself, adhered to Indian familial rather than Western individualistic values in not siding with Dr Chatterji's former girlfriend, Jennifer Mayhew. She felt that Dr Chatterji should have stood up to his father and assert his right to marry a woman of his choice. This is a stance that Laungani believed most Western psychotherapists and counsellors would take, and which is profoundly related to the culture of individualism. Pittu Laungani recognized that Dr Chatterji was deeply concerned over the negative impact on his father that his choice might have, and wanted to convey it in a way that would preserve the father–son relationship.

Still another facet of the father–son relationship emerged in Dr Chatterji periodically staying in touch with Pittu Laungani over the years once the counselling sessions had ended. Once a relationship is formed, in whatever context, Indians often try to incorporate the other person into becoming a member of their extended family.[9] With a male patient and therapist, such as Dr Chatterji and Pittu Laungani, this also would be modelled on the father–son hierarchical relationship.

A therapist would also try to evaluate what kind of transferences were going on in the therapy and other relationships. If, indeed, Dr Chatterji had a particularly intimidating and difficult father, Dr Chatterji's way of reacting to him would be unconsciously carried over to other relationships with male authority figures including the therapist. This might even include Dr Chatterji's returning to settle in England years later after he had passed his MRCP, had returned to India and married a suitable woman from his community, and had a consultancy there. Perhaps, unresolved issues with his father unconsciously surfaced again in his reactions to Indian hierarchical relationships at work.

## CROSSING CULTURES AND THE BICULTURAL SELF

Pittu Laungani was astutely aware of the profound cultural/psychological misunderstandings that occurred between Dr Chatterji and his girlfriend, Jennifer Mayhew. As alluded to earlier, she insisted he should assert himself with father and family by telling them of his upcoming engagement to her; he felt that she should have backed off, giving him more space to communicate his decision eventually to his family to preserve the relationship with his father. Pittu Laungani saw these different attitudes and misunderstandings as her being rooted in an individualistic approach of looking at what is best for oneself and standing up for it; and he being embedded in a familial-oriented culture and psychology where one is constantly concerned about the welfare and esteem of family members. Apparently, over a period of years, they had ironed out many difficulties over their differing value orientations and ways of doing things. But on the crucial issue of marriage, things fell apart for them once his father had suddenly died.

Compounding the problem after his father's sudden heart attack and death two days before their lavish engagement party was that Dr Chatterji had to return to India immediately, not only for the funeral but more important, as his father's only son to perform certain rites of the dead. Only he could do them. Again, Pittu Laungani suggests that cultural misunderstandings led her to call off not simply the engagement party but the engagement, itself. She apparently had not appreciated the necessity of his spending time in India performing these rituals. She may well have thought that compared to his family she was not important to him.

But there is another major facet to crossing cultures, and that is Dr Chatterji's bicultural self. Pittu Laungani clearly spells out that in dress and manners, Dr Chatterji had become very English, that as he remarked, 'England had gotten into his soul.' Thus, Dr Chatterji, like many other Indian and Asian immigrants to England and the United States, develop a bicultural self. The indigenous cultural self is basic but there is the contemporary self of the new culture that can have very different values and ways of relating. This often creates conflict, hurt and turmoil on one hand, and an expanding self that is able to make new kinds of integrations and ways of thinking and doing things (Roland, 1996).

## CONCLUSION

Pittu Laungani is recognized as a writer extraordinaire in the psychotherapy field, and as a bicultural psychologist who combines Western methods and approaches with Indian sensibilities. This has enabled him to elucidate cross-cultural psychological issues in an insightful and extremely helpful way. Pittu Laungani was also able to appreciate the cultural/psychological misunderstandings and the inner struggles of the Indian immigrant, as he wrote about in this case study. And most important, he has been able to convey to a whole generation of counsellors and psychotherapists through his imaginative, lucid writing the important clinical issues involved in crossing cultures psychologically.

However, there are other facets of the bicultural self of Indians and other Asians that are loaded with conflict and turmoil. From a psychoanalytic perspective, culture is not simply out there influencing behaviour but is profoundly internalized, affecting a person's whole emotional makeup and life. When persons from radically different cultures immigrate to Western countries, they incorporate certain values, attitudes and ways of relating into their self. If this conflicts with their earlier indigenous self, there can be intense inner turmoil and conflict, not uncommon in Indian immigrant in the United States. Values and ways of relating can be diametrically opposite.[10] Related conflicts also take place in the second generation born in the United States, and in a somewhat different vein in the 1.5s; those who grew up in their indigenous country in early childhood but then came with parents and went through American schooling. These 1.5s and second generation Indian Americans often refer to themselves as ABCD, American Born Confused Desi (Indians). I would like to give a few brief examples of this, particularly from my Indian women patients. The 1.5s who often immigrate with their parents during their childhood have a self that is formed initially in a completely indigenous culture. They then develop a bicultural self earlier than adult immigrants by growing up in schools in Anglo or American society. A simple example of this is that I find the 1.5s can easily ask questions or even challenge a teacher in American schools, something the adult immigrant has difficulty doing. The 1.5s differ from the second generation in having more of an indigenous self and are exposed not as early to American or English children and culture.

In one case, an Indian American mother, Veena, a 1.5, was in a Clinical Psychology Ph.D. programme with a psychoanalytic orientation. She complained in session that she is a very poor mother, that she cannot set limits on her two-year-old toddler. Knowing about Indian child-rearing, I raised the question of whether she, herself, was raised as a toddler in India by being distracted with something good whenever she would do something that could be dangerous or otherwise forbidden. She reflected that that was exactly how she was raised, not with the setting of limits that is characteristic of Euro-American child rearing and the norms in most of our psychology books. These distinctions made it easier for her when her child later went to nursery school. The teacher told Veena that her child was a wonderful child but tended to annoy the other children by touching and hugging them. Veena then told her child that among their Indian friends it was perfectly fine to touch and hug them but that American children are not used to it, so it would be better not to do it at school.

Another woman, Meena, an immigrant, was still disturbed a year later from a class she had in her graduate school at Princeton University. The teacher assistant (TA) had apparently given her a hard time but she was unable to stand up to the TA. She felt it was some emotional disturbance within her that prevented her from asserting herself with this difficulty. I finally interpreted to her that she probably couldn't stand up to the TA because the latter was a superior, and in Indian hierarchical relationships, you absolutely do not confront a superior. She then let me know that the TA gave everyone a difficult time but the Euro-American students let her have it, so much so that the TA complained to the professor that the students were ganging up on her. She realized that her own deeper expectations around hierarchical relationships differed more than she knew from the newer American ones.

## NOTES

1. Since 1995 (approximately), there has been a mushrooming demand for counselling and psychotherapy in all of the major Indian cities according to counsellors and psychotherapists. They believe, this is due to the changing roles of urban educated women, who often have good jobs and want changes in the hierarchical relationships with both husbands and in-laws.
2. This emerged at a meeting, 'Understanding India,' at the Aarhus School of Business in Denmark, November 2005.
3. In psychoanalysis, various authors, including Phyllis Greenacre (1959) and Erik Erikson (1950) have emphasized the need to preserve the patient's autonomy, especially in making decisions.
4. I shall never forget how on a visit to Mumbai in 1991, a man rang the doorbell one evening at a flat where we were renting two rooms. He stated that I should be ready in a half hour so that he could drive me to a suburb of Mumbai where Professor Chakraborty (1987) of the Calcutta Indian Institute of Management was giving a weekend management seminar at a Godrej plant. I have no idea how he or they learned where I was staying or that I would indeed be interested in meeting Professor Chakraborty. He simply seemed to appear out of the blue.
5. I am reminded of what happened to an Indian professor of mine, M. N. Chatterjee of Antioch College, when he related that he sent back word to his family in India around the time of World War I that he was marrying a Scottish woman whom he had met in Edinburgh while doing an engineering degree. His family wrote back that they had just performed the rites of the dead for him.
6. Most social scientists rarely cite the highly private self of Indians and other Asians, instead emphasizing a collective self. I first encountered the private self elaborated psychologically in an article by Anandalakshmi (1978), then Chair of the Postgraduate Child Development Programme at Lady Irwin College in New Delhi. It collaborated what I had observed in my clinical experience with Indians.
7. I know of an instance when the Indian son went to study in college abroad but had to endure a great deal of deprivation, even to the extent of sleeping on park benches. He later said that he was able to take it in stride because he felt he was reflecting well on his father. Conversely, a son may wish to get even with his father over a great wrong but the way this is often done is by failing.

8. I have had Indian patients who were furious at being greatly exploited. I initially saw it as a gross breaking of their contract which they had every right to be angry at. In one case, the patient was being short-changed in their pay for certain work. In another one, an Indian woman was called up to work much longer hours in a medical fellowship programme than was clearly spelled out in her contract, which was to do the fellowship half time for double the length of period. Further, she had to repeat rotations that she already had had, also against contractual rules. In both cases, their rage was not at the breaking of the contractual agreement as I had initially seen it. Rather, they kept repeating over and over, 'they do not respect me.' The salience of being esteemed was far more important than the breaking of the contract, per se. In both cases, they asserted themselves to eventually get things straightened out. But they lost respect for their superiors, also basic to Indian hierarchical relationships.
9. In Mumbai, I have experienced a number of patients seen in short-term psychoanalytic therapy wanting to invite me to tea or a dinner at their home. Thus, professional relationships, such as in counselling or psychotherapy, are not only professional but become personal and familial as well.
10. For instance, being modest and self-effacing are traditionally important values for Indian women; whereas to function in many American work milieus, a woman has to be assertive, articulate, and at times self promoting.

## REFERENCES


Aleichem, S. (1999). *Tevya's Daughters: Collected Stories of Sholom Aleichem.* J.B.H. of Peconic.

Alexander, V. K. (1979). Rural psychotherapeutic process. In M. Kapur, K. Sathyavathi and R. L. Kapur, (Eds), *Psychotherapeutic processes* (pp. 39–40). Bangalore: National Institute of Mental Health and Neuro Sciences.

Anandalakshmi. (1978). *Socialization for competence.* Delhi: Indian Council for Social Science Research.

Chakraborty, S. K. (1987). *Managerial effectiveness and quality of worklife: Indian insights.* New Delhi: Tata McGraw-Hill.

Erikson, E. (1950). *Childhood and society.* New York: W. W. Norton.

Greenacre, P. (1959). Certain technical problems in the transference relationship. *Journal of the American Psychoanalytic Association, 7,* 484–502.

Mathew, R. (2008). *Evolving traditions in America: South Asians and arranged marriages.* Youngstown, New York: Cambria Press.

Popper, K. (1988). *The open universe: An argument for indeterminism.* London: Hutchinson.

Roland, A. (1988). *In search of self in India and Japan: Toward a cross-cultural psychology.* Princeton: Princeton University Press.

———. (1996). *Cultural pluralism and psychoanalysis: The Asian and North American experience.* New York: Routledge.

Roland, A. and Harris, B. (Eds) (1978). *Career and motherhood: Struggles for a new identity.* New York: Human Sciences Press.

# 13

# Solitude of Unbearable Shame: An Analysis of Two Case Studies by Pittu Laungani

*Sabar Rustomjee*

## INTRODUCTION

**The** feeling of 'Shame' is a universal experience which is encountered frequently, in varying degrees and in numerous situations in our everyday lives. It needs to be recognized that every shame-producing event both challenges as well as threatens the core sense of integrity in ourselves. Shame is the most personal and private of all feelings. As '*Shame lurks unseen*' (Mollon 2002: xii), one needs to be vigilant in identifying Shame in unsuccessful therapy cases. One can clearly distinguish two presentations of shame, namely bearable and unbearable shame. Bearable shame can be described as an emotion which enables the recipient to be able to put it under scrutiny, and gain benefit through learning from the experience. Bearable shame can be normalized as being a part of everyday living. It can then felt to be no more than a temporary embarrassment which is dismissed and soon forgotten.[1] On the other hand, unbearable shame arises when one feels emotionally overwhelming humiliation, accompanied by the conviction that one's credibility, honour and very sense of self-worth has been totally destroyed forever.

'Shame' and 'Guilt' are basically very different from one another. Nevertheless the same person can experience both emotions under different circumstances. For example, in most persons at different periods, we may see episodes of guilt which are amenable to reparation. The same person may also on another occasion present with unbearable shame, which presents with much greater severity and is resistant to the usual methods of counselling or psychotherapy. For example, following an episode of childhood humiliation when during play, an 'unruly' donkey unseated him and his face was scratched all over by thorns, Nelson Mandela (1994: 11–12) says, 'I had lost face among my friends. Even though it was a donkey that unseated me, I learned that to humiliate another person is to make him suffer an unnecessarily cruel fate. Even as a boy I defeated my opponents without dishonouring them.'

It is now well acknowledged that working with unbearable shame is of crucial importance. This is because it can result in lethal consequences when left untreated. Moreover, whether such untreated shame presents itself in an acute or chronic form, it could keep on re-emerging with lifelong recurrences (Lewis, H. B. 1971). The purpose of this chapter is to highlight the centrality of unbearable shame and its tragic consequences when left untreated. The differences in outcomes between bearable and unbearable shame as well as between shame and guilt are clarified using examples from Asian mythology.

Two case histories of Pittu Laungani's work with sexual abuse victims and their immediate family are analyzed. The first concerns a 15-year-old Punjabi female, Jaswant, who was treated very successfully with tremendous empathy and sensitivity in a culture-centred approach (Laungani, 2003b: 385–401). The second was a longstanding friend of Pittu Laungani, named Harry, a marine engineer, whose wife was brutally raped (Laungani, 2004b: 200–221). Pittu Laungani felt this case was unsuccessful. Possible reasons for the different outcomes are discussed, especially with regards to solitude, silencing of shame, narcissism and shame, and absence of support from their community, family and friends.

## UNBEARABLE SHAME

Pittu Laungani, in his work with unbearable shame has pointed out, very painstakingly, important examples of the above. His knowledge and experience in the field of cross-cultural research in this matter, as well as his personal life experiences and competence in Indian cultural and religious issues, has provided us with the opportunity of studying his writings and exploring our own horizons further in this field.

The wisdom he offers is very relevant to all areas of personal crisis, including unbearable shame. He says, following his 16 years of personal battle with polymyositis, that he learned on his Road to Recovery (Laungani, 2003a: 166), that, 'Do not even think about what you cannot do.' Also, that 'you need to recognise that your illness is unique to you and your beliefs are unlikely to be understood, appreciated or shared…' (Laungani, 2003a: 169). Moreover that, 'accepting possible consequences, is often better than avoiding action altogether' (Ibid.: 177). He also recognizes the value of humour.

Shame is about losing ones's honour. Cassio in Shakespeare's *Othello* says, 'Oh! I have lost my reputation—lost the immortal part of myself and what remains is the bestial' (Shakespeare, 1968). In this context, loss of honour is compared to soul murder. Hence, it is no wonder that we as human beings try our utmost to avoid a confrontation with Shame. Instead we put up numerous resistances, often the commonly used defence mechanisms of the ego. Some of these include denial of shame, repression of shame, rationalization of Shame and disavowal of Shame which means turning a blind eye.

It is important for us now to distinguish between shame and guilt. It needs to be kept in mind that guilt has a capacity of being repaired. This is very different from unbearable shame which attacks the very core of an individual and if allowed to remain without helpful intervention, it can become soul destroying.

**Guilt:** As there are numerous points of view about guilt as well, I personally apply the understanding of the origins of guilt from Melanie Klein's seminal paper *Love, Guilt and Reparation* (1937) in which she states that, 'love and gratitude arise spontaneously in the baby in response to the love and care of the mother'. However, 'the power of love is there in the baby as well as destructive impulses.' Guilt can arise in young babies and children from the perfectly normal fantasy of destroying the mother, when the mother appears to frustrate the child by not complying with immediate gratification. The guilt can then be resolved through reparative measures between both mother and child.

An example of guilt in Asian mythology, described below, very clearly describes how even guilt arising from a cold and calculated attempt by a queen to murder her own son at birth, is able to be resolved through love, reparation and forgiveness. As can be seen, although the guilt caused great pain and suffering, it was not soul destroying for either.[2]

Helen Block Lewis (1971) discovered a very high frequency of unexplored and untreated shame markers when looking through transcripts of a large number of cases who had not achieved therapeutic success. It seemed obvious during her research with Witkin et al. (1954) that the topic of shame had not been openly discussed by these therapists at the time. Some years later, when shame was able to be discussed more openly, there was much better understanding of the dynamics associated with the events that had occurred then. Unfortunately by this time these patients had returned with new complaints of even greater intensity.

Donald Nathanson (1987) in *The many faces of shame*, states that 'Shame guards the boundaries of the self' and implores therapists to explore the 'centrality of shame,' during therapy.[3] Of the same opinion have been Alexander (1938), M. Lewis (1992), Wurmser (1997) and others. This issue has been kept in the forefront of this chapter.

# TWO CASE HISTORIES OF SEXUAL ABUSE LEADING TO UNBEARABLE SHAME TREATED BY PITTU LAUNGANI

**Case Study 1** 'Sexual abuse in an Asian Family' (Laungani, 2003b), is a case of sexual abuse in an Asian family of Punjabi origin, where three children, between the ages of 13 and 15 were all sexually abused by the same uncle—the husband of an aunt, for a period of over 10 years. The most severely affected was a young female, Jaswant aged 15 who was the oldest. The other two were boys.

The following essential guidelines were put into place by Pittu Laungani. The most vital one being confidentiality. Pittu Laungani in all his written case material, without fail, reassures the reader that all possible recognizable features have been meticulously distorted by him without jeopardizing the essence of the work. This enables us to trust his authenticity. Even when discussing the fact that he received a call from a certain police station, he says it was from, 'let's say—in Ealing' He then qualifies it further, 'I have never been to Ealing Police Station. I do not even know where it is' (p. 386). He restricts himself to the given task. Pittu was initially requested to help the police obtain a comprehensive history from the two fathers of the rape victims, through his knowledge of Indian languages and Indian culture. He writes 'My role was clearly defined. To enter into an argument on the moral and legal issues...was not my brief, regardless of how I might have viewed the problem privately' (p. 387). Later on, when the police requested him to change roles from being a cultural and linguistic expert, and work with Jaswant, the 15-year-old female in his capacity as a counsellor, then he did so. He worked strictly within boundaries, explaining guidelines clearly to Jaswant, hoping that no unrealistic expectations would be made on both sides. When requested later by Jaswant's father to start counselling her, Pittu, being well aware that he had not counselled an adolescent before, writes, 'However, I promised nothing, not even a specific number of sessions' (p. 390). Instead Pittu clarified that both Jaswant and he would be 'free to withdraw' if either was unhappy or dissatisfied and she may then agree to be transferred to another 'more competent and experienced' counsellor (p. 390). This lessened the burden on the therapist to perform, as well as giving freedom of movement to the client (Please note, this is their very first interview).

## The Therapeutic Skills of Pittu Laungani

Pittu always describes in the beginning, how and why each referral was made. In this case, Scotland Yard had contacted him previously regarding his work, in cross-cultural research into child abuse among Asian children, and had invited him to give lectures to their child protection team. Hence, he was acknowledged by them as an expert in the field. Pittu Laungani's observations, interventions and communication skills have always been admired by all his colleagues. He refrains from using the term 'transference' or 'counter transference', but describes clearly and vividly the depth of emotions expressed by the persons involved towards him as well as his own feelings at relevant moments towards them. An example of this is Pittu Laungani's astute observation of the two brothers, who were also fathers of the molested children. On being introduced to Pittu Laungani, they 'waived' their hands in a dismissive manner, away from him, as if his presence was inconsequential. They then angrily expressed, that nothing constructive could emerge from this interview, which was felt to be an unnecessary ordeal, and that the issue of child molestations was a family matter which only they, the brothers would decide as to what the outcome would be. Here an experienced clinician like Pittu Laungani recognized the attempted superficial omnipotence of the brothers arising from a deeper position of helplessness and rage. It is possible that an inexperienced counsellor may well have become personally offended and wrongly interpreted it as a negative response. It is also possible such a counsellor may have nursed his/her own narcissistic injury rather than observing the distress and suffering of the two brothers. Laungani instead, observed the pouring of sweat on the brothers' faces, which they kept on wiping off their foreheads. He identified their rage, despair and helplessness which was their true feelings at the time, and worked empathically with them.

Attunement to culture-centred counselling is also one of Pittu Laungani's great strengths. He openly described his admiration of both brothers' fears of how all family members including their traumatized daughter and sons would be affected by such a public revelation by the media, as well as the detrimental effects it would have to their family business. Laungani indicates very vividly how much he was in tune with (that is, culturally attuned to) the overwhelming feelings described by both brothers, for example, wanting revenge, 'an eye for an eye'...(Laungani, 2003b: 389) on the one hand, but also fearful on the other of the consequences of public humiliation on the family. In his objective and humble manner, rather than influencing the brothers in any way, he nevertheless confides with the readers saying, 'I saw it all too clearly' Laungani, (2003b), realizing how traumatic the situation was for them, and the internal conflicts they as Indian Sikhs suffered, in deciding to take a family member to court. Another example was him, making a huge effort to understand her religion. He started studying hymns from Jaswant's revered Sikh religious text 'Adi Granth'. This then provided a common ground for discussion between them, and she and her family gradually appreciated all the efforts made to reach her. Here we note how he changes the focus from client-centred therapy to a culture-centred orientation (Laungani, 1997). He also kept in mind, the culturally relevant stressful life events (Laungani, 1996: 29).

## Self-Awareness of His Personal Feelings

Pittu's strength in his awareness of his own emotional reactions, during his work is admirable. He says very descriptively, 'It was as if some malevolent demons had dug their sharp claws into me and wrenched my soul apart. I sat in a daze' (Laungani, 1996: 388).[4] His ability to be so open and honest about his deepest and most painful feelings is an excellent role model to follow. Obviously Pittu could protect himself from vicarious traumatization, while at the same time, used it constructively. Through acknowledging his own personal pain on listening to Jaswant's grief, he Pittu Laungani, who had not treated a single sexually abused adolescent female before, was now able to allow himself to understand and empathize with her, in a very sensitive manner. Once again, not every counsellor or therapist is able to put himself in this position, whilst benefitting his client and himself.

## An Empathic Therapeutic Process

The key features of the counselling were an absence of demands from Pittu, allowing Jaswant to be in total control of what she did say, or deliberately appeared to avoid saying, thereby nurturing a culture of mutual self respect, Pittu was also able to accept her idealization of him and seeing him as her only life line for a period of time after her grandmother's death. This capacity is described as 'holding and containing' (Winnicott, 1960a: 44; Winnicott, 1963: 240; Bion, 1970). Pittu Laungani was able to integrate and work successfully with very strong conflicting emotions and thoughts.

During the termination period, Jaswant was able to be tearful, acknowledging the loss she would feel with the closure of sessions. The happy ending for Pittu Laungani was when seven or eight years later he received an invitation from Jaswant's father to her wedding! Two major components in Jaswant's recovery were the genuine and tremendous family support she received as well as very appropriate management. Laungani (2004a) describes the necessity for clinicians to be experienced in multicultural counselling as 'Indian society not unlike other eastern societies is a family-based and community-orientated society' (Ibid.: 62).

The case study of Jaswant in India in the astute, empathic and experienced hands of Laungani, along with her family support, is in sharp contrast with cases of unbearable shame leading to suicide in places where very little such support is available. This is especially so when the family is fragmented and the local community in that area is more persecutory than compassionate. An example is the play written by Hendrick Ibsen, 'The Wild Duck' (1826–1906).[5]

**Case Study 2** 'Asian Perspectives in Counselling and Psychotherapy' (Laungani, 2004b: 200–221) is another example of silent suffering following shame. Laungani initially grapples with whether to refer to this very 'unique case' as a 'tragedy' of a person named Harry who was a long-term friend, or to describe him as a 'case study' as Harry did engage in therapy with Pittu Laungani, but for a very limited period of time. In my experience, combining friendship and therapy is fraught with complications invariably resulting in the therapist feeling cheated, and the client floating around without adequate boundaries to hold and contain difficult thoughts and feelings (Bion, 1970; Winnicott, 1963: 240; Winnicott, 1960a: 44). Hence it is no wonder that as a reader I could sense Pittu Laungani's overwhelming emotional pain, while his client/friend remained oblivious of Pittu Laungani's unspoken feelings which, through his years of experience, he was able to contain admirably.

Harry was a restless marine engineer who enjoyed the naval lifestyle of living in various exotic cities (ports) for varying periods of time. It came as somewhat of a surprise when at his parents' recommendation he agreed to a marriage. His wife Reema had lived in Delhi, and had a university degree. They moved from Delhi to live in a fashionable area of the city of Mumbai near the sea (to accommodate Harry's work commitments).

On the outside, Reema appeared to fit in well with a group of new friends. Later it became apparent that she was presenting what is termed as a *False Self* to the world (Winnicott, 1960b).[6] In Asian culture, it is referred to as *saving face* (Hu, 1944). Inwardly she was unhappy to have moved away from her own parents, and having to live alone when Harry was away from her for long periods at sea. She would beg him to take a job on land, but he would refuse, being oblivious to her unhappiness. A decision was finally made to move to Sydney hoping this would reduce time away from each other. Unfortunately, this led to additional cultural and racial difficulties for Reema. Very unfortunately, in addition, Reema suffered two miscarriages, during which she could have no help from her own family. During this entire period, it seems that Harry continued to gratify his own emotional and work needs despite her numerous pleas to change his job and settle in one place with her. A crisis then occurs while he is in Japan on work and Reema is alone in Sydney, leading a life of silent solitude not having community or family support. He is abruptly informed by the police that his wife is in hospital. He discovers that she has been brutally raped and also had a third miscarriage with future infertility as a consequence.

He feels totally devastated and suffers severe narcissistic injury. In an attempt at denial of his grief, he starts to mistrust Reema's faithfulness. Reema sinks into a deep depression probably contributed to by long standing shame, the miscarriages and living alone in a very stressful situation, and traumatized by even her husband turning away from her (Laungani, 2002). It is possible that both Harry and Reema, both now suffered unbearable shame, feeling total failures in life.

Harry then sabotages his only potentially helpful relationship with his friend Pittu by creating a four-year period of total break in contact after initially telling him fragments of the crisis. He leaves Pittu Laungani extremely worried, helpless and powerless to help him. Harry then suddenly out of the blue, without any explanation for the long break in contact, arrives in London and contacts Pittu Laungani. Consciously or unconsciously, Harry may have finally realized that he and his wife needed Pittu Laungani's help. His narcissism however did not allow him to acknowledge his own need for therapy and instead he put the major focus of their grief, on his wife's depression. They both benefited from a few sessions with Pittu Laungani, but he did not stay long. As was Harry's norm, he then abruptly departed from London for the Pacific Islands where he hopefully did enjoy some precious months with his wife. Some months later, Pittu Laungani heard the very tragic news that Harry had suffered a sudden heart attack and died.

Reema herself had then felt able to return to India in the capacity of a widow, which is much more acceptable in Indian society, than a female with three miscarriages, in addition to having been raped! Reema had also obviously overcome her fears of loss of face (Hu, 1944) which had prevented her return to India earlier.

## CONCLUSION

Perhaps the details of the cases provided by Pittu Laungani, may encourage one to read more of Kohut (1978) and H. B. Lewis (1987) regarding the intricacies of helping a traumatized person with significant narcissistic rage and possible underlying unbearable, long standing shame (Scheff, 1987). In the second case study, Harry defended against exposure of these feelings partly by outwardly controlling those around him, being constantly on the move, as well as presenting a rigid, insensitive exterior to cover up a very vulnerable inner self (Freud, 1914). In addition, Freud (1914–1916) in helping us to understand the psychology of guilt discusses the possibility that there already exist in the 'Pale Criminal' (p. 332–333) a sense of guilt long before the crime was committed. Hopefully, routinely exploring cases of unbearable shame will pave the way for further exploration of a pre-existing sense of shame. In order to do so, we need to become more aware of our own hidden shame, our guilt, our vulnerabilities, our love and our hate, so we can help towards cultivating a culture in which society can respond with attunement rather than abandon with shame. Among all of Pittu Laungani's words of wisdom, regarding cross-cultural psychology (Laungani, 2007: 179), I will always remember the ones below:

'Ask not if white will glisten, and black will fade.

Ask instead if the two will form a glorious pattern of light and shade.'

## NOTES

1. Bearable shame, for example, when exposed to a mildly embarrassing situation, is relatively easily overcome by reassuring thoughts. Michael Lewis (1992) writes that there are two types of embarrassment—one involves no evaluation and is related to exposure, and the other is related to evaluation.
2. Okonogi, in the book *Asian Culture and Psychotherapy*, edited by Wen-Shing Tseng, Suk Choo Chang and Masahisa Nishizono (2005), describes the Ajase Complex, originally written by Heisaku Kosawa, a Japanese psychoanalyst in 1953, it describes how Queen Idaike organizes the murder of a hermit, followed by an attempted murder of her own son Ajase, both of which were finally resolved through remorse and sacrifice. She seeks and follows the advice of Lord Buddha, and devotes herself totally to the care of her son who had discovered her past crimes, had then become murderously enraged towards her and fallen ill. He became covered by foul smelling sores. Ajase with his mother's remorse, love and dedication, recovers and forgives her. Following his father's death, he becomes 'an enlightened sovereign'. In this case, reparation following guilt contributed to a successful outcome. Kosawa has also written a paper titled 'Two Kinds of Guilty Conscience' (1932), one being a comparison of paranoid and depressive guilt and the movement from a punitive to a reparative guilt (Okonogi, 1967, 1978.) The Indian myth of Ganesha has a similar theme, but here it is his father who after cutting off his son's head, feels intense guilt and remorse, and replaces it with the head of an elephant. Ganesha is now a revered figure in Hindu homes, and considered to bring good luck. So, once again we see a successful outcome following remorse after initial guilt.
3. D. Nathanson, (1987: 3) writes, 'While it is true that each of us knows what it is like to be embarrassed or humiliated, we do not know with any certainty what another person means to express when using the same words.'
4. Pittu Laungani's experience reminded me of James Gilligan (2000) who wrote about Shame. 'Without a minimal amount of self esteem, the self collapses and the soul dies. When we cannot protect ourselves…something gets killed within us—our souls are murdered' (p. 48).
5. Ibsen describes how rather than the family supporting a 14-year-old fragile young Norwegian girl, whose sight was failing, instead inflict upon her their own personal uncontained suffering which is transgenerational. This leads to her tragic suicide along with her much loved pet 'Wild Duck'. This resulted from the unbearable shame at believing that she had disappointed her father.
6. Winnicott describes the *False* and the *True Self*, being the authentic self of the person who can verbalize true thoughts and emotions at their own free will and discretion. The *False Self* is the part of the self which is projected to the outside world for purposes of creating a required image of oneself.

## REFERENCES

Alexander, F. (1938). Remarks about the relation of inferiority feelings to guilt feelings. *International Journal of Psychoanalysis, 19,* 41–48.

Bion, W. R. (1970). Container and contained. *Attention and interpretation.* London: Maresfield Reprints.

Freud, S. (1914). *On narcissism: An introduction* (Std. ed. 14). London: Hogarth Press.

———. (1914–1916). *Criminals from a sense of guilt.* (Std. edn. 14). London: Hogarth Press.

Gilligan, J. (2000). Violence—Reflections on our deadliest epidemic. London: Jessica Kingsley Publishers.

Hu, H. C. (1944). The Chinese concepts of 'Face'. *American Anthropologist, 46,* 45–64.

Ibsen, H. (1950). The Wild Duck. In *Hedda Gabler and other plays* (1826–1906) (pp. 139–260). London: Penguin.

Klein, M. (1937). Love, Guilt and Reparation and other works 1921–1945. In Masud Khan (Ed.), *The Writings of Melanie Klein Vol. 1.* The International Psychoanalytic Library No 103. London, U. K.: Hogarth Press.

Kohut, H. (1978). Thoughts on narcissism and narcissistic rage. In P. H. Ornstein (Ed.), *The search for the self: Selected writings of Kohut, H.* (1950–1978, Vol. 2) (pp. 155–175). New York: International Universities Press.

Kosawa, H. (1932). Two kinds of guilty conscience—The Ajase complex. *Journal of Japan Psychoanalytical Association, 1*(14), 5–9.

Laungani, P. (1996). Cross-cultural investigations of stress conceptual and methodological considerations. *International Journal of Stress Management, 3*(1), 25–35.

———. (1997). Replacing client-centred counselling with culture-centred counselling. *Counselling Psychology Quarterly, 10*(4), 343–351.

———. (2002). Stress, trauma and coping strategies: Cross-cultural variations. *International Journal of group Tensions, 31*(2), 127–154.

———. (2003a). Therapeutic strategies for coping with a life-threatening illness. A personal testament. *Illness, Crisis & Loss, 11*(2), 162–182.

———. (2003b). Sexual abuse in an Asian family. *Counselling Psychology Quarterly, 16*(4), 385–401.

———. (2004a). Counselling and therapy in a multicultural setting. *Counselling Psychology Quarterly, 17*(2), 195–207.

———. (2004b). Case Study 2. *Asian perspectives in counselling and psychotherapy.* London: Brunner-Routledge.

———. (2007). *Understanding cross cultural psychology.* London: Sage Publications.

Lewis, H. B. (1971). *Shame and guilt in neurosis.* New York: Int. Uni. Press.

———. (1987). Shame and the narcissistic personality. In D. Nathanson (Ed.), *The many faces of shame* (pp. 133–169). New York: Guilford Press.

Lewis, M. (1992). *Shame the exposed self.* New York: The Free Press.

Mandela, N. (1994). *Long walk to freedom.* London: Abacus.

Mollon, P. (2002). Shame and jealousy. In I. Wise and P. Williams (Eds), *The hidden turmoils Series.* London: Karnac.

Nathanson, D. L. (1987). A timetable for shame. *The many faces of shame.* New York: The Guildford Press.

Okonogi, K. (1967). Some comments on psychoanalysis in Japan. *Journal of Japanese Psychoanalytic Society, 7,* 297.

———. (1978). The Ajase Complex of the Japanese. The Depth Psychology of moratorium people. *Japan Echo, 6*(1), 104–118 (In Japanese).

Scheff, T. J. (1987). The shame/rage spiral. In H. B. Lewis and N. J. Hillsdale (Eds), *The role of shame in symptom formation* (pp. 109–149). New Jersey, USA: Lawrence Earlbaum Associates.

Shakespeare, W. (1968). *Othello.* London: New Penguin Shakespeare.

Wen-Shing T., Suk C. C. and Masahisa, N. (2005). *Asian culture and psychotherapy.* Hawaii: University of Hawaii Press Honolulu.

Winnicott, D. W. (1960a). *The maturational processes and the facilitating environment.* London: Hogarth Press.

Winnicott, D. W. (1960b). *The maturational process and the facilitating environment.* London: Hogarth Press.

Winnicott, D. W. (1963). *The maturational process and the facilitating environment.* London: Hogarth Press.

Witkin, H., Lewis, H., Hertzman, M., Machover, K., Meissner, P. and Wapner, S. (1954). *Personality through perception.* New York: Wiley.

Wurmser, L. (1997). The shame about existing: A comment about the analysis of 'Moral' masochism. In M. R. Lansky, A. P. Morriso and N. J. Hillsdale (Eds), *The widening scope of shame.* New York: Analytic Press.

# 14

# Becoming a Cultural Chameleon: Pittu Laungani, Western Counsellors and Multicultural Clients

*William West*

## INTRODUCTION

**In** this chapter[1] I will draw upon the work of Pittu Laungani, especially his ideas about counselling across cultures and in particular, white counsellors working with culturally diverse clients. Before considering Pittu Laungani's work on culture and counselling, I want to make a comment on Pittu Laungani's way of speaking. He was a tender, courteous man always interested in people, their lives and their families. However, he had a rhetorical habit of passionately and forcefully making his points and he was also intolerant of sloppy or lazy thinking which he was always willing to challenge. All in all a formidable opponent in debate! In addition, he had high expectations both of himself and you. If you were a counsellor he expected to see your real concern for people, if you were an academic then show your learning!

Each section of what follows is, in effect, in two parts. First, I present Pittu Laungani's ideas about the shortcomings of Western counselling as it is currently practiced for non-Western clients and second, what strategies would help develop cross-cultural counselling. These include: Pittu Laungani's critique of Western counselling approaches, an avoidance of discussing religious issues, cultural ignorance among counsellors and language barriers. I will then briefly explore the implications of Pittu Laungani's work for the development of counselling in India. Finally, as a conclusion to this chapter, I will discuss Pittu Laungani's personal solution to the problem of living in England as an Indian. He saw this as about becoming a chameleon and this clearly has application to the counselling process.

Before considering Pittu Laungani's ideas on Western counselling it is important to reflect, however briefly, on the nature and status of multicultural counselling in Britain. Even the term 'multicultural' is open to challenge since terms such as cross-cultural, Afro-centric, transcultural, black feminist, intercultural and anti-racist have been used (Palmer, 2002) (for further discussion see also Moodley, 1999).

However, whatever term is used and however differently it is understood, there are different cultures and subcultures in varying degrees of tension within Britain, especially in the urban areas. The dominant majority culture is white and it is within this culture that modern counselling has largely developed, and the value system underpinning white Western counselling reflects this truth. This truth had little to say about different cultures and cultural differences.

McLeod[2] suggests that in the 1960s and the 1970s counselling and psychotherapy responded to the 'equal opportunities movement and debates over racism and equality by developing strategies for building a greater awareness of cultural issues into counselling training and practice' (McLeod, 2003: 244). He saw this as an attempt to assimilate a cultural dimension into mainstream practice. More recently a new multicultural approach has emerged that 'places the concept of "culture" at the centre of its "image of the person"' (McLeod, 2003: 244). Membership of a culture is thus seen as a key influence on personal identity and how relationships, morality and the 'good life' are understood. However, I would maintain that there is still too little exploration of such ideas of culture among counsellors in Britain.

McLeod's more social constructionist view of culture 'Counselling represents one of many ways in which cultural norms and values of a society are affirmed, and operates as a means of helping individuals to negotiate their own relationship with these cultural norms' (McLeod, 2001: 589) suddenly becomes troubling when we ask: Which culture? In our postmodern multicultural society what are the cultural norms? How can we support our clients living with cultural and sub-cultural tensions?

This is precisely the territory that Pittu occupied in which he invites us to reflect on some very basic differences between British and Indian cultures across four key dimensions of individualism/collectivism, cognitivism/emotionalism, free will/determinism and materialism/spiritualism (Laungani, 2004). Pittu had a real and appropriate contempt for any counsellor who would work with a South Asian client without this basic broad stroke cultural awareness. Indeed Pittu Laungani cautions us:

> An unintentional error that counsellors—and indeed the majority of Westerners all over the Western world—make is to be misled by the perceived Westernization of their Indian clients. Should they meet with an Indian who speaks English fluently and colloquially, one who dresses in a Western manner, is involved in a professional occupation and for all appearances gives the impression of being a Westerner,

> they also assume the Indian to be a Westerner. *The Indian is then imbued with a Western mind!* [Pittu Laungani's emphasis] He/she is then divested of most, if not all, his/her cultural inheritance. (Laungani, 1997: 349–350)

## MY RELATIONSHIP WITH PITTU LAUNGANI

I was privileged to meet Pittu Laungani[3] on a number of occasions following our first meeting in May 2003 and we frequently exchanged e-mails from then on until his death in February 2007. On two occasions I met Pittu more formally and audio taped interviews/conversations with him. The first interview[4] was published in 2004 (West, 2004) and created quite a stir indeed; several papers were published in response (Chantler, 2006; Lago, 2006; Wilkins, 2006) and a further paper Moodley (2007) was written partially inspired by the ideas in the interview. In the second interview, Pittu Laungani responded to these papers and further developed his thinking. This second interview which occurred in Autumn 2006 has not yet been published. In this chapter, I draw on both interviews to explore Pittu Laungani's thinking.

In his first interview with me he describes his experience of first moving to England in poignant terms, 'Shock after shock reverberated through the depths of my soul' (West, 2004: 427). Further more,

> One was born into a given culture, and imbibed its norms, yet one possessed the qualities that enabled one to make the necessary adaptions to the changing social and political world one inhabited. Yet I was at my wits end. I did not know what to do. (West, 2004: 427)

Here was Pittu Laungani, a capable, sensitive and young man at the time, struggling to cope with life in England or rather struggling with life with the English.

Pittu Laungani also faced that dreadful experience that newcomers to a country face as they become somewhat assimilated and then return home on a visit.

> When I am in India, I am accused of being too English (whatever that means) and in England, when the English can bring themselves to express an opinion, I am accused of being 'too Indian' (whatever that might mean). I am thus in a no-win situation. (Laungani, 2002: 21)

In the academic world, Pittu found the unwritten expectations, such as that he should be very familiar with Western classical music and art, hard to bear, 'I have seen sly and "knowing" looks exchanged whenever I have been unable to identify a piece of music, or tell a Hogarth from a Constable' (West, 2004: 425). Pittu grew accustomed to this conditional acceptance but initially 'it hurt like hell'.

What was equally painful to Pittu was the lack of interest shown in his culture, so that the cultural learning and sharing was a one way process. Pittu pointed out to me on another occasion that ethnic groups are usually non-white. For example, we never discuss, or even see, the Australian, New Zealand or Canadian as white minority groups in England.

His critique of multicultural was based on it largely being defined by white people, especially in recent times by politicians. 'Multiculturalism is as defined by the Westerners...people who come to this country have their own views on multiculturalism' (West, 2006: 9). He was keen to present India as a multicultural society with many faiths, ethnic groups and languages although not uncritically.

Finally, in terms of my relationship with Pittu Laungani, he said something in my first interview with him that I found surprising, if not shocking, indeed I was moved to tears by what he said:

> I still find I don't understand them [the English], as I might intuitively understand an Indian or a Pakistani or a Sri Lankan. I suspect one of the main problems as I see it is their lack of 'openness'—particularly among the kind of persons I know and meet and entertain. There is among many of them a reluctance, an inhibition, or even a horror of showing their feelings easily and without artifice. That's my view, and nothing would please me more than to be proven wrong. You know, William, without wishing to cause any embarrassment you are one of the rare exceptions that I've met. (West, 2006: 426)

## PITTU LAUNGANI'S CRITIQUE OF WESTERN COUNSELLING APPROACHES

Pittu Laungani's critique of Western counselling approaches cannot be separated from his experiences of living and working both in India and Britain. The refusal of most white British people, educated or not, to learn about non-Western cultures horrified him. This attitude, mostly unconscious and recognized, which amounts to a form of cultural superiority, I believe, is embedded in counselling theory practice, training and supervision. From such a perspective there is nothing white counselling can learn from centuries of traditional helping in non-Western cultures.

Pittu Laungani referred to this as the gold standard,

> There is a widespread Eurocentric belief that all developing countries over time will be influenced by Western science, technology and know-how, to such an extent that in the process they, too, will become Westernized and indistinguishable, from other Western countries. The West sets, so to speak, the gold standard which

> developing nations attempt to achieve. If developing nations and/or members of ethnic minorities living in Western nations are all driven to become Westernized, there is hardly any point in trying to understand an Indian from his/her own unique cultural perspective. (Laungani, 1997: 350)

Pittu Laungani was, in particular, very critical of the person-centred approach (Laungani, 1997) as practised in Britain and provoked some strong responses from a number of quarters (Chantler, 2006; Lago, 2006a). I think this should be seen in context. First, the person-centred approach is by far the most common form of training that counsellors receive in Britain, and rightly or wrongly many people's view of counselling is based upon their view of this approach. Second, I think that many of Pittu Laungani's deep empathic responses to his clients and their cultures embodied the best of a person-centred viewpoint although Pittu would not like me saying so! Third, I think it is the case that we often save the strongest criticism for those we are closest to. Perhaps it is the person-centred counsellors who are most likely to be influenced by Pittu Laungani's work. Finally, the strength of the responses to him may lie in a recognition of the uncomfortable truths he was asking us to face.

There is evidence that clients from ethnic minority groups have good experiences of counselling in Britain (Netto et al., 2001). However, clients from ethnic minority groups are still under-using counselling. Indeed, there is still widespread suspicion about how culturally sensitive counsellors are likely to be. For example, Edge and Rogers report from their research among black Caribbean women in Manchester 'In this study, beliefs that "counselling" was unlikely to be culturally sensitive and therefore incapable of meeting their needs were also evident' (Edge and Rogers, 2005: 22).

People from ethnic minority groups in Britain are less likely to access talking therapies and more likely to receive drug treatment and hospitalization for their mental health needs (Edge and Rogers, 2006; Farsimadan et al., 2007). When ethnic minority people do get access to counselling they usually have similar outcomes to white people. Those who specifically want to be counselled by people from their own ethnic background do have better outcomes than those who are not ethnically matched (Farsimadan et al., 2007).

So the perceptions that ethnic minority groups have about how culturally sensitive counsellors are likely to matches Pittu's critical stance. Perhaps it is not surprising that in a racist society, black people expect their counsellors also to be racist. Of course training more ethnic minority counsellors would help but the models of counselling need to be developed to transcend their white origins. Our notions of good life, often only implicit in our counselling models, need to be explored and made explicit. While much counselling theory and practice still denigrates religion and spirituality and promotes secularity, there is still plenty of work to be done!

## AN AVOIDANCE OF DISCUSSING RELIGIOUS ISSUES

Pittu insists that counselling tends to be discussed almost exclusively along secular and overly rational lines, with hardly any attention being paid to the religious issues, which may have a strong bearing on the outcome of counselling. Counselling like psychotherapy has often been in denial of the often healthy nature of many people's engagement with religion and spirituality. For example, many Black Caribbean women in Britain draw on their spirituality, including prayer, reading the Bible and using the church for practical, emotional and pastoral support to combat depression and black churches have group processes akin to group psychotherapy (Edge and Rogers, 2005).

Indeed, counselling training in Britain stills lacks an adequate exploration of religion and spirituality (West, 2000, 2004). Indeed religion is often considered in counsellor training in England, as is race and ethnicity, under the heading of diversity. The implication being that being religious is other than the norm which is white, secular and heterosexual.

However, despite this secular culture of counselling and psychotherapy many therapists are themselves religious (Gubi, 2002). Pittu Laungani comments on the curious phenomena of religious-minded counsellors not working with their clients' spirituality: 'There are a large number of counsellors particularly American who are church goers…and yet when they have the counselling sessions God is taken out of the picture. I find it absolutely strange' (Laungani, 2006: 7).

Pittu, though not religious, recognized the value of religious and other rituals in people's lives. He was always ready to engage with his clients' religious and spiritual lives. In his second interview with me, he briefly refers to an Irish friend of his who spoke of intending to go to church to light some candles in response to his difficulties. Pittu Laungani asked his friend to light one for him even though both knew Pittu Laungani was not a believer. His friend was pleased if puzzled, '"I thought you don't believe." I said, "I believe what you believe and I'm going to join the queue in your belief"' (West, 2006: 13). To Pittu Laungani this was one way of establishing a bond between him and his Irish friend.

## CULTURAL IGNORANCE AMONG COUNSELLORS

Pittu Laungani regarded what he called the 'abysmal' unfamiliarity that many Western counsellors have for non-Western cultural issues faced by their clients as a serious impediment in the progress of counselling. He had no time for counsellors who were unwilling to learn about other cultures especially those who expected their clients to teach them about the clients' culture. He was clear that it was naturally important to listen very carefully to the clients' cultural experience but not to approach any client with total ignorance of their culture. Indeed Pittu Laungani would actively seek information after a session in relation to say a metaphor or quote from the Koran or the Bible used by a client.

What is striking is how many black people never consider seeking counselling because they don't expect counsellors to be culturally sensitive. For example, in Dawn Edge's research into perinatal depression among black Caribbean women in England she found 'in this study, beliefs that "counselling" was unlikely to be culturally sensitive and therefore incapable of meeting their needs were also evident' (Edge and Rogers, 2005: 22). So how do counsellors change this assumption among ethnic minority groups and to what extent is this assumption born out of practice?

Although training counsellors from ethnic minority groups is important, this wont in itself, I believe, have a huge impact on access to counselling by such groups. Work needs to be done on how counselling might fit into other services available to such groups, including the role of churches, self help groups, and so on (West, 2007).

To Pittu Laungani the solution was obvious, namely for the counsellor to: learn about the clients' culture, before, during and after the session. But this was only possible *if* the counsellor was at all interested:

> I wonder if Western counsellors and therapists even feel the need to acquire this kind of information, which is not easily found in textbooks or research journals. One acquires this form of intimate information through living, observing, and gradually piecing it together in a coherent, meaningful and organised manner. (West, 2004: 422)

This is perhaps the crux of the matter, it is risky as Pittu realized 'people are frightened of treading into uncharted territory' (West, 2004: 435), and it takes courage, but what can be fearful and anxiety provoking can also, with a bit of insight, become a source of joy and even excitement.

## LANGUAGE BARRIERS

Pittu Laungani's view was that Western psychotherapists should 'come clean' and admit their lack of understanding of other cultures and even learn other languages for 'the very fact that you're making an attempt to talk in the language of the client…brings the client close to your heart' (West, 2006: 3).

To understand the challenge white counsellors face in understanding their clients' language and culture it might help to consider the challenge immigrants face when they come to Britain even when they already speak English. As Pittu stated:

> England, to me, came as a shock! I was bewildered by the English! There were as many accents as there are dialects in India—or almost. Each of them as though spoken in a different tongue, a few even in forked tongues! It was difficult to distinguish between levity and seriousness, between jest and truth, between praise and censure, between affection and affectation, between acceptance and rejection. (Laungani, 2002: 387)

Counselling often makes powerful use of metaphors. Pittu Laungani invites us to think about how we use metaphors and that these are often cultural specific and class based too. '[I]f you're an educated Muslim you use educated metaphors often based on the Koran, if you're unaware of them you miss certain important points they're trying to make' (Laungani, 2006: 3).

On another occasion Pittu reminisced about his early childhood in India.

> We were all great friends, the English boys and all the other Indians kids who lived in the building...We could all speak English and several Indian languages. To us words were like any other sounds, which hung in the atmosphere; we picked them up without trying...But our English friends appeared to be more insulated: none of them could speak any of the Indian languages—although like us, they had all been born and brought up in India and were exposed to the same sounds, which assailed our ears repeatedly. (West, 2004: 419–420)

Pittu Laungani is raising several key points in the above quote: first, how natural it is for children to acquire languages; but second somehow English children get discouraged from learning other languages. It seems to me that many British people do consider learning to speak a foreign language as an act of inferiority. Curiously, high status education for children in England used to include learning of the 'classic' languages that no-one actually spoke, like Latin and Ancient Greek!

## CHALLENGES AND FUTURE DIRECTIONS

I believe that Pittu Laungani's work represents a developing challenge to the theory and practice of (white) Western counselling that is part of a larger critical current including Dupont-Joshua (2003), Lago (2006), Moodley (2007) and Palmer (2002). This has implications on many levels, including theory, training and practice.

There is much that an individual counsellor could do to learn more about non-Western culture before non-Western clients cross the threshold of the counselling room. The quality that seems to be lacking, or perhaps hidden under a blanket of fear, is the quality of curiosity of wanting to know, of wanting to learn about another culture. With such a quality to the fore, the counsellor would be better prepared for their non-Western clients and would communicate a true interest in their client's culture. It would be natural, following such an approach, to seek further knowledge of their clients' particular culture during and after the counselling session.

Such a counsellor would be better suited to offer appropriate training and supervision. However, this is just a beginning and on a small and individual scale. How might Western theories of counselling change in ways not only to better help non-Western clients but also potentially be more useful to Western clients? This would be the most interesting and exciting development and fitting outcome from Pittu Laungani's life's work.

Meanwhile we must train counsellors from as wide a cultural background as possible in order to offer at least some appropriate choices for non-Western clients. Such diversity needs to be reflected in counsellor trainers, supervisors, membership of relevant professional bodies and researchers. Progress is being made but it is also too slow.

## IMPLICATIONS OF PITTU LAUNGANI'S WORK FOR THE DEVELOPMENT OF COUNSELLING IN INDIA

Pittu Laungani's work has had some considerable impact on counselling theory and practice within Britain and North America. As yet, his work has not been widely made available within India. However, I can foresee a key contribution that his work could make to the development of a variation of counselling best suited to India.

Shreck wrote in 1964 that counselling theory and practice had largely been imported in India directly from the West and in doing so ignored important cultural differences which meant that clients for counselling would be seeking and expecting guidance from their counsellor. Indeed writing at about the same time (1964) Krishnamurthy maintained that in Indian theory, there were three kinds of counsellors: an authority figure who gives orders; a friend who influences the person to do good deeds or a spouse or intimate friend who uses all methods to influence the client's behaviour.

In reflecting on the impact of Western therapies, Kumar et al., write how

> the vast repertoire of traditional healing practices prevalent in India reflects certain common, shared philosophies and therapeutic methodologies. These practices mirror the health beliefs and explanatory models of the Indian population. These models vary significantly from the Western health belief model, which excludes the spiritual dimension and promotes body-mind dualism to some extent. (Kumar et al., 2005: 120)

Arulmani (2007), while acknowledging the growth of counselling in India especially within schools, discusses the psychology apparent in the traditional Indian culture and suggests the possibility of a creative meeting between this and Western approaches. This is, I believe, the spirit of the counselling psychology programme at De Montforte College in Bangalore.[5]

The notion of using Western counselling methods within an Indian cultural framework came naturally to Pittu Laungani. Indeed, it epitomizes the spirit of his work with clients from an Indian background in Britain. By a careful reading of Pittu Laungani's many case studies (Laungani, 2004), it is possible to begin to construct a model of combining Western and Eastern approaches for the Indian context.

Such a model has to begin with an acceptance of, and a deep knowledge of, the client's Indian cultural background both in terms of its broad sweep and also the particular regional, religious, local and personal variations. This includes some awareness of the impact of Westernization or rather globalization of the client and their family and community. The possibility then arises of what Pittu Laungani (1997) referred to as 'culture-centred counselling'.

## CONCLUSION

Pittu Laungani argues that counsellors must learn the art of becoming a chameleon 'so whatever the client defines themselves in they should be able to blend in with client' (Laungani, 2006: 5). I understand this to mean that the counsellor works at getting into the client's frame of reference, including the cultural role of the helper within the client's culture. As Pittu Laungani makes clear for South Asian people 'The sick and infirm often consult religious personages, gurus and pundits, diviners and astrologers, fakes and fraudsters, fakirs and faith healers, spiritualists and herbalists, with far greater fervour than they do medical doctors and psychiatrists' (Laungani, 2004: 421). Roy Moodley (1999) maintains that it is not uncommon for South Asians in Britain to consult traditional healers simultaneously with consulting counsellors. Pittu Laungani was convinced that this art of becoming a chameleon 'is difficult to acquire, you only acquire it if you can admit to yourself that there is something lacking in you...there's a gap that you need to fill' (Laungani, 2006: 5).

However, becoming a chameleon is not without its side affects, witness Pittu Laungani's comments quoted earlier about being too English in India and too Indian in England. So there is perhaps a price to pay in developing such mobility between cultures. Despite the costs of this, I don't think Pittu would have said it was not worthwhile. It also occurs to me that what the world most needs now is more and more people able to truly become global citizens, truly able to transcend differences of culture. Pittu Laungani's writings and even his own life experiences point to this possibility.

However, I want to add a brief and personal caveat. En route to a meeting with Pittu Laungani for what, I did not realize at the time, was to be the final one I developed a fantasy. In this fantasy, I was a follower about to visit my Eastern guru or holy man—Pittu Laungani, and his physical frailness by then only added to this image. I told Pittu Laungani about this notion but he was not taken with it by any means and merely laughed. However, it does point to the cultural issue of many white English people thinking that Indian people have the spiritual solutions to the meaning of life. So maybe as Indian people come to England in search of the good Western life there is also a move in the other direction.[6] We have much to learn from each other about the good life—material and spiritual.

I have a dream of a form of cross-cultural counselling and healing that is not rooted in a Western model but instead is based on an integrative model that is pan-cultural. A model broad enough, and humble enough, to encompass the time-honoured learnings from traditional healing and the best of modern approaches wherever they are occurring; an approach that profoundly respects the clients' culture, both macro and micro. Pittu Laungani's work in many ways offers us some useful pointers towards bringing this dream to reality.

## ACKNOWLEDGEMENTS

This chapter would not have been possible without the encouragement and guidance of the editors. The part played by Pittu Laungani is also self evident. There are other people who should be acknowledged: Lynda Ankrah, Fevronia Christodoulidi, Kam Dhillon, Dawn Edge, Susan James, Abdullah Popoola, Rebecca Sima, David Smith, David Spence and Dori Yusef.

## NOTES

1. The title of this chapter comes from an e-mail sent to me by Pittu just before our second interview.
2. John McLeod is arguably Britain's leading academic writer and researcher on counselling.
3. Since I consider myself a friend of Pittu Laungani, it is natural and respectful for me to also use his first name rather the academic convention of only using surnames when making reference to others' work.
4. Pittu Laungani and I, re-created the interview live at the 10th BACP Annual Counselling Research Conference held in London in May 2005.
5. For further details visit www.sampurnamontfort.com. Students on their Masters in Counselling Psychology programme study Indian and transpersonal psychology and holistic and alternative approaches as well as the more usual Western counselling theories.

6. This 'move in the other direction' became a reality for me when I visited India for the first time in January 2008 to attend a conference in Bangalore at which Pittu Laungani would have spoken. For a flavour of my visit see Christodoulidi (2008).

# REFERENCES

Arulmani, G. (2007). Counselling psychology in India: At the confluence of two traditions. *Applied Psychology: An International Review, 56*(1), 69–82.

Chantler, K. (2006). Pittu Laungani in conversation with William West. *British Journal of Guidance and Counselling, 34*(3), 385–390.

Christodoulidi, F. (2008). *Namaste, thresholds: Counselling with spirit*, Spring, 6–9.

Dupont-Joshua, A. (Ed.) (2003). *Working inter-culturally in counselling settings*. East Sussex: Brunner-Routledge.

Edge, D. and Rogers, A. (2005). Dealing with it: Black Caribbean women's response to adversity and psychological distress associated with pregnancy, childbirth, and early motherhood. *Social Science and Medicine, 61*, 15–25.

Farsimadan, F., Draghi-Lorenz, R. and Ellis, J. (2007). Process and outcome of therapy in ethnically similar and dissimilar therapeutic dyads. *Psychotherapy Research, 17*(5), 567–575.

Gubi, P. (2002). Practice behind closed doors: Challenging the taboo of prayer in mainstream counselling culture. *Journal of Critical Psychology, Counselling and Psychotherapy, 2*(2), 97–104.

Krishnamurthy, N. (1964). Counselling as we find it in the Gita. *Transactions of All-India Institute of Mental Health, 4*, 42–49.

Kumar, M., Bhugra, D. and Singh, J. (2005). South Asian (Indian) traditional healing: Ayurvedic, Shamanic and Sahaja Therapy. In R. Moodley and W. West (Eds), *Integrating traditional healing practices into counselling and psychotherapy* (pp. 112–121). Thousand Oaks CA: Sage Publications.

Lago, C. (2006a). *Race, culture and counselling: The ongoing challenge*. Maidenhead: Open University Press.

———. (2006b). Pittu Laungani in conversation with William West: Personal reflections, (some) considered thoughts and emotional impacts. *British Journal of Guidance and Counselling, 34*(3), 391–402.

Laungani, P. (1997). Replacing client-centred counselling with culture-centred counselling. *Counselling Psychology Quarterly, 10*(4), 343–351.

———. (2002). Cross-cultural psychology: A handmaiden to mainstream Western Psychology. *Counselling Psychology Quarterly, 15*(1), 385–397.

———. (2004). *Asian perspectives in counselling and psychotherapy*. London: Brunner-Routledge.

McLeod, J. (2001). Counselling as a social process. In P. Milner and S. Palmer (Eds), *The BAC Reader, Vol. 2* (pp. 589–598). London: Sage Publications.

———. (2003). *Introduction to counselling*, 3rd *Edition*. Buckingham: Open University Press.

Moodley, R. (1999). Challenges and transformations: Counselling in a multicultural context. *International Journal for the Advancement of Counselling, 21*, 139–152.

———. (2007). (Re)placing multiculturalism in counselling and psychotherapy. *British Journal of Guidance and Counselling, 35*(1), 1–22.

Netto, G., Gaag, S. and Thanki, M. (2001). *Perceptions and experiences of counselling services among Asian people*. York: Joseph Rowntree Foundation.

Palmer, S. (2002). *Multicultural counselling: A reader*. London: Sage Publications.

Shreck, T. C. (1964). Counselling theory: Some cultural implications. *Journal of Vocational and Educational Guidance, 10*(1), 15–20.

West, W. (2000). *Psychotherapy and spirituality: crossing the line between therapy and religion.* London: Sage Publications.

———. (2004) Pittu Laungani in conversation with William West. *British Journal of Guidance and Counselling, 32*(3), 419–435.

———. (2006). Pittu Laungani in further conversation with William West, unpublished manuscript.

———. (2007). Faith, hope and communities: Counselling in a context of cultures, keynote speech to COSCA Counselling Conference 'Talking cures as social action', Dunblane, Scotland, 27 November.

Wilkins, P. (2006). Responding to Pittu Laungani. *British Journal of Guidance and Counselling, 34*(3), 383–384.

# PART FOUR

# Multicultural Transitions and Therapeutic Relationships

# 15

# Counselling and Therapy in a Multicultural Setting

*Pittu Laungani*

## INTRODUCTION

**It** all comes down to words: words, words and more words! All reputable theories of counselling, all forms of ancient, traditional and modern psychotherapies share this very powerful feature in common. Freud in fact called his form of therapy the 'talking cure'. Such is also the case with the post-Freudian, neo-Freudian, and other talking therapies: transactional, Gestalt, existential, behavioural, cognitive-behavioural, person-centred, narrative, to name but a few. The differences in the theories lie, not necessarily in the words used but in the assumptions that underlie each theory and the interpretations and explanations that follow there from. Thus although words serve as the basic tools of most therapies, they hold different meanings for different therapists. Even a simple and trivial statement is open to different interpretations. For instance, let us state: 'Bush and Blair eat well'. This simple statement is open to at least three different interpretations, which are:

Bush and Blair eat sumptuously, lavishly and elegantly.
Bush and Blair chew and masticate their food before swallowing.
Bush and Blair eat good, healthy, nutritive food.

The question is: Can one be certain which statement(s) applies to them both? Bush may eat sumptuously, but may not eat healthy food. Blair might chew and masticate his food before swallowing, but not eat lavishly. On the other hand they may both be concerned with eating healthy, nutritive food. It is also possible that all the three statements are relevant to each of them. Given a dozen dispassionate observers of this 'scenario', can one assume a high degree of observer reliability? Finally, would their assessments correspond with the subjective assessment of the *dramatis personae?* Despite their triviality these questions are by no means easy to answer with any degree of certainty.

The problem, as one can see, is compounded when a therapist listening to a client attempts to interpret the client's statements, which are often charged with powerful emotional undercurrents. Yet, it is largely through words that a client articulates his/her confusions and conundrums, anxieties and angst, or whatever else that might lie at the root of the client's problem(s). Words are an integral part of the communication process.

There are other factors too, which play an important role in the communication process. Darwin in his famous book, *Expression of the emotions in man and animal* (1872) demonstrates the means by which animals communicate with members of their own species: through facial expressions, gestures, grunts, noises, sighs, and a variety of other non-verbal physical movements. Subsequent studies by ethnologists, including Lorenz, Hinde, Ekman, and others, made clear that communication, both among animals and humans is an extremely subtle and complex process. In certain instances, failure to perceive subtle non-verbal and/or bodily cues with accuracy can mean the difference between life and death. This caveat applies not just to animals but in certain circumstances also to humans. Bruno Bettelheim in his book *The informed heart* (1986) based on his experiences in the Nazi concentration camps in Dachau and Buchenwald records in harrowing detail the cues that the inmates of the camp had to perceive with unfailing accuracy to survive the brutality of the guards patrolling the camps. This of course is an extreme example that is of no relevance to a counselling and/or a therapeutic encounter. The example does however illustrate the point that regardless of the situation one finds oneself in, one needs to be eternally vigilant in order to make sense of even a casual social encounter. Eternal vigilance is not just the price of democracy. It is of invaluable help to both the client and the counsellor in promoting a deeper understanding of the client's problems. Since counselling situations are often charged with a variety of emotions, it is not always easy to perceive them correctly. The situation assumes even greater importance when a therapeutic encounter occurs between counsellors and clients of different cultural backgrounds. It is imperative for the parties concerned, in particular the therapist, to be vigilant and sensitive enough to read correctly the differential forms of verbal, non-verbal, and other physical cues the client knowingly or unknowingly may display to the therapist. Failure to acquire such skills would condemn the therapist to remain chained like the prisoners in Plato's cave, who mistake appearance for reality and shadows for substance.

At an empirical level though, it is worth asking if therapists do really acquire such astute observational, intuitive, empathetic and interpretative powers. Or do therapists, given the very nature of their professional work imbue themselves with such highly desirable observational and interpretive skills? Do we *really* understand and interpret correctly? Is the private world of the client that we attempt to enter the world the client recognizes and inhabits, or is the world of the client a figment of the therapist's imagination? Such questions are extremely difficult to answer. However, they should not lull us into believing that therapists acquire—'*that something extra*'—which an ordinary mortal lacks.

In this paper the author is concerned more with words and their uses and abuses and less with non-verbal and physical manifestations of behaviour. Words, as the famous semanticist Hayakawa (1965) pointed out contain special, idiosyncratic meanings and messages for each of us. We all construe words differently—specially, those which reverberate with feelings and emotions. Beauty, in that sense, is in the eye of the beholder! So is ugliness! Given the tyranny of words, it seems a virtual miracle that we are able to communicate with one another reasonably successfully. How many of us would dare explain Freud's concept of 'cathexis of energy' as Freud conceptualized it! Do we really understand what a therapist means when s/he points out that the client's problems can be traced to 'the anal explicative or anal retentive psychic tendencies, which manifest themselves in an overtly hostile but covertly passive unconscious oedipal relationships with his/her significant others'. This is high-sounding rubbish on a grand scale! The art of talking nonsense with distinction! How can the poor client even begin to comprehend the meanings attached to the above statement!

## THE TYRANNY OF WORDS

Words, as Osgood et al. (1957) in their research into psycholinguistics have demonstrated, carry two distinct types of meanings which they have identified as *denotative* and *connotative*, or in other words, objective and subjective. Meanings of words according to them can also be perceived along three major dimensions, which they refer to as *evaluative*, *potency* and *activity*. Even the word table, which should arouse little confusion in its objective definition may inspire different subjective evaluations; a Victorian table, a Chippendale table, old grandma's table, or the table which Eddington visualized in terms of an unpredictable dance of sub-atomic particles, floating in space.

For therapy to progress in a 'satisfactory' manner—I shall abandon any attempt at defining the word 'satisfactory'—it would be beneficial both for the client and for the therapist to understand the diverse emotive and cognitive meanings which each of them assigns to words. It is only through a close correspondence in understanding the subtle nuances of words, which form the basis of therapy, that some genuine progress can be achieved. This is not to suggest that a therapist will rely solely on the statements of the client. As has been stated earlier an astute and experienced therapist would respond to a repertoire of other subtle cues, such as gestures, physical demeanour, facial expressions, eye contact, extent of gaze, tone of voice, silences, etc., in order to create a gestalt configuration. But the words and the choice of words and what they mean to the client have a major role to play in a therapeutic encounter. As has been mentioned earlier one can testify to this by trying to imagine what it must feel like to be engaged in a therapeutic encounter with a deaf mute: not impossible, but difficult.

All languages make use of metaphors. A proper use of language also involves the use of similes, culture-specific phrases, proverbs, and an injection of new phrases and words that for a variety of reasons become fashionable. All these form an integral part of the process of communication.

## THE USE OF METAPHORS

Metaphors help us to articulate, interpret and reinterpret our own world of experience to ourselves and hopefully share it with others. Each culture produces its own sources of metaphor. They facilitate communication among its members. The use of metaphors also enables us to interpret our own world of experience. To understand a given culture it thus becomes necessary to understand the metaphors commonly used in that culture. For instance would it ever be possible to understand Islamic culture without some knowledge of the Koran? Or a Hindu's unshakable belief in an after-life, without some knowledge and understanding of the workings of the 'law of karma'? Religion provides most cultures with a central area of metaphor. Gombrich (1979) argues that a society, which fails to embellish its language by reaching out into the sources of metaphor, would cease to be a society. It is of course possible that one may be unfamiliar with the classical origins of metaphors as such and yet be familiar with the subtle meanings underlying them. Gombrich argues that children brought up in homes where such metaphors are common parlance, learn to see them as part of everyday communication. Children brought up in such homes appear to have no difficulty in understanding and indeed using metaphors, such as *Trojan horse, Draconian laws, Caesar's wife, 'seems madam?', stoic endurance, Quixotic, Dionysian, Apollonian, Faustian, Kafkaesque, Oedipal, Confucian, Elysian, Darwinian, the playing fields of Eton, meeting one's Waterloo, being in limbo, the patience of Job*, etc. The use of such metaphors does not necessarily reflect classical education. It is through repeated usage of such metaphors within the home that their underlying meanings become clear.

Another point to be noted here is this: the types of metaphors one employs in conversation to a large measure are class-related. The above metaphors reflect a certain kind of learning and upbringing and are less likely to be understood by all and sundry. On the other hand metaphors such as *it's not cricket, he had a good innings, a sticky wicket, pull your finger out, between the devil and the deep blue sea, sour grapes, up the creek without a paddle, thick as two short planks, a lemon*, etc., are more commonly employed metaphors. Thus, metaphors range from the very simple to the very complex—even elitist.

All metaphors have their own historical origins and are culture-specific. Metaphors such as *imaan, haraam, halal, izzat, shudha, pavitra, apavitra, vairaag, punya, joothaa, shubha, dharma, karma, gyani*, are part of common lore in India. Indian society is structured along caste-divisions and not along class-divisions. Interestingly enough most of the above metaphors cut across caste boundaries and are used with equal facility by all and sundry. The origins of the above metaphors do not necessarily reflect classical learning. They arise out of the popular stories from the ancient Indian epics, such as the *Mahabharata* and the *Ramayana*, which are told and retold to children as an important part of their socialization and upbringing. Through constant exposure, the metaphors get internalized, becoming part of everyday speech, for instance, the word *shudha*, which translated literally means pure. However, the word *shudha* carries with it a host of other meanings, such as spiritual purity, pure (uncontaminated) food, a pure, truthful, honest, trustworthy person, etc. Many esteemed figures from Hindu religion and mythology—*Satyavan Savitri*, Yudhisthira, Rama, Sita, Arjuna, Krishna—also come to be used as metaphors. At the same time there are a host of caste-related metaphors which reflect negative connotations, such as when a person is referred to as a *bhangi* (a sweeper), a *hajaam* (a barber), a *dasu* (a demon), a *chandaal* (an untouchable) and so on. Seemingly there appears to be no common thread running through Eastern and Western metaphors, but a closer examination reveals that in both cases, names become metaphors regardless of whether the names originate from mythology and literature (as many Western names do) or from mythology and religion (as many Eastern names do). Each name over time becomes part of folklore, creating new, rich and varied avenues of shared experience. Metaphors are part of everyday speech, a form of shorthand, which strengthen a mutual sharing and understanding of common modes of communication, thus facilitating interaction at a deeper and more meaningful level. This would apply at a client-therapist level too. To get a 'flavour' of a cross-cultural therapeutic encounter, let us visualize a scenario. Let us hide behind a *metaphorical* arras—not the one behind which Polonius stood while eavesdropping on Hamlet's encounter with his mother—and eavesdrop on an encounter between a white English (or American) therapist and an Indian (Muslim) client facing him on the other side of the desk.

*Client:* Well. Doctor *Sahib*, what should I do? (*He wrings his hands in a gesture of despair and looks imploringly at the therapist.*)

*Therapist:* (*With a mask of neutrality over his expressionless face*) What do *you* think you should do?

*Client:* (*Rather peeved, even angry.*) Every time I am asking you a question you are throwing the question back at me!

*Therapist:* Oh, am I?

*Client:* (*Exasperated.*) You have done it again! Look Doctor *Sahib*. You are the expert. I have come to you for help. If I knew how to help myself surely I would not come to see you.

*Therapist:* (*Not in the least put out*) Mr Ahmed, it is really for you to decide what you should do. I cannot decide for you.

*Client:* (*Acutely disturbed and even bewildered.*) I understand. But I am not asking you to *decide* for me, Doctor. I am asking your opinion. I have come to you for help. I don't understand why you should not help me. You should be guiding me. Helping me. Showing me the way. I am like a Bedouin, lost in the sand dunes of Arabia. But you don't want to help me to decide what I should do.

*Therapist:* (*Defensively*) That is not quite true.

*Client:* When I go to see my GP, he tells me what I should do, what medicines I should take, how long for, and so on—and then leaves it to me to decide whether I will take them or not. But you don't even tell me what I *should* do! (*Looks at the therapist.*) If you were a brain surgeon, would you be asking me to perform my own operation?

*Therapist:* (*In spite of himself*) No, of course not!

*Client:* What's the difference? So if you were a brain surgeon you would perform brain surgery on me. You are a surgeon of the mind and yet you will not perform psychosurgery—which you can!

*Therapist:* (*Reluctantly gets drawn into an argument*) It is not my role to tell you what you should do, or even what you ought to do. My role, as I see it, is to interpret, or throw some light on your problems, to help you to see your problems.

*Client:* I am not asking you to tell me what my problems are. I *know* what my problems are! I am asking for advice, *how to overcome my problems.*

*Therapist:* (*Remains silent*)

*Client:* You know what I think, doctor. (*Pointing his index finger to his forehead*) It is fate. It is Allah's will. It is my *kismet*, my '*taqdeer*'. What was to happen has happened. Who can fight against one's fate, against what is written! (*Here he quotes the well-known couplet from the Persian poet Omar Khayyam* [translated by Edward Fitzgerald]

*The Moving Finger writes; and having writ,*
*Moves on: nor all thy Piety nor Wit,*
*Shall lure it back to cancel half a Line*
*Nor all thy Tears wash out a Word of it.*)

*Therapist:* (*Totally at a loss as he hears the poem, which his client has recited in Persian: sits in embarrassed silence, unable to decide what he should say.*)

Even without any specific knowledge as to the nature of the problem, one can see that there is a gulf between the client and the therapist. Both of them are locked into their own private cultural worlds. They are either unable or unwilling to step out of them.

Even the manner in which they relate to one another reveals their unique cultural biases. This is not an unusual therapeutic situation; and one can see that there is a genuine clash of cultural values between the therapist and the client. Let us now analyze the above encounter in psycho-cultural terms.

## THE CLIENT'S WORLDVIEW

The client fails to understand why the therapist remains so distant, aloof—and even quite cold. The failure or the unwillingness on the part of the therapist to offer specific guidance is a source of acute disappointment for the client. For one would expect a trained therapist to have a reasonably astute awareness of his client's subjective world. One can see that the encounter between the therapist and the client is getting nowhere. They are, without putting too fine a point on it at *cultural crossroads*, with no meeting ground in sight. They appear to have reached an impasse. For not only have they encountered linguistic, spiritual and religious difficulties but have displayed serious cross-cultural differences that impede progress. The client would prefer to adopt a 'vertical' model, which posits a hierarchical but informal relationship between himself and the therapist. The client is eager to seek guidance (and success) from the therapist, which the therapist is unwilling to offer; the therapist desires of his client 'self-guidance', which the client is unable to comprehend or work toward. His own cultural model from which he operates cherishes a clear and didactic guidance from the therapist. The client lives in a world, where one's life appears to be preordained. There is in him a belief that one needs to submit unconditionally to the Will of Allah, and hope that the almighty Allah will take mercy upon his lost soul. At the same time he looks upon the therapist, albeit in a minor sort of way, as an 'intermediary' who might intercede on his behalf and bring him success. The client's belief in the ability of the therapist to 'solve' his problems arises out of the unswerving faith, esteem and deference in which, therapists, healers and gurus are held by people from Eastern cultures (Hoch, 1974; Kakar, 1982; Roland, 1988). He sees his therapist as a spiritual guide, even as a guru, or a *pir*, whose magico-religious-spiritual powers will cure him of his problems. Second, seeking *unconditional* guidance from one's healer is seen as an integral part of both Islamic and Hindu culture.

## THE THERAPIST'S WORLDVIEW

The therapist however does not share the worldview of the client. It is clear that the therapist operates from a euro-centric model, which posits a 'horizontal', non-hierarchical, but formal interpersonal relationship that emphasizes individualism. It is not part of the therapist's remit to offer direct help, which might enable the client to resolve his problems. The therapist, to a large measure sees his role as that of a facilitator, a catalyst—a clarifier of confusions, conflicts and conundrums. But finding solutions to his client's problems does not fit in with his own value orientations which subscribe to the belief that human beings are self-determining creatures who have the ability and the necessary cognitive and emotional skills to realize, self-actualize their own personalities. His own world is at variance with his client's and his personal philosophy has little room in it for a deterministic formulation. Life to the therapist is not ordained or preordained. One has control. One has free will. One has choice. It is through the exercise of one's free will that one is able to bring about the desired changes in one's life. Thus it is to the advantage of the therapist to adopt a stance of neutrality. In so doing the therapist might be 'playing out' his own internalized value systems to which, he is handcuffed since childhood. The notion of freewill is so strongly embedded in the Western psyche that even Sartre felt compelled to state that all human beings are ultimately *condemned* to be *free*. The notion that there is no escaping from one's freedom to act acquires meaning only when seen from a euro-centric perspective.

Thus, he would be unwilling to play a directive role in the therapeutic process, which his Muslim client expects of him. While he is willing to play the role of an empathetic but dispassionate observer, and even a 'sounding board', he is unwilling to guide and direct the client in terms of the kind of decisions the client should or ought to take.

What can be done? The question is this: can the clash of cultural values be overcome? Are there legitimate ways by which one might transcend cultural boundaries and perhaps even formulate a super structure that would digest all the cultural variations and anomalies? The search for an answer leads us into the controversies and paradoxes related to notions of multiculturalism and homogenization of cultures. Let us examine them briefly.

## MULTICULTURALISM OR HOMOGENIZATION?

In recent years several economists and political scientists have argued that given the present emphasis of the first world, particularly of the US on economic and material globalization, it is possible that over time the value systems of diverse cultures, particularly those in the third world will become homogenized (Friedman, 2000; Grondona, 2000; Harrison, 2000). This subsumes a belief that the impact of science and technology combined with large-scale multinational financial aid and investments will foster the growth of material affluence and economic prosperity, which in turn, will transform the values of the third world countries and bring them in line, so to speak, with those of the West. Furthermore, globalization will lead to a process of Westernization and modernization and all the developing countries will eventually come to imbibe Western values of *individualism, humanism, empiricism, secularism* and *scientism*, and will become indistinguishable from other Western countries. Since the West will set the 'gold standard' all developing countries will aspire to achieve such a standard, thus, completing the process of homogenization. The East shall no longer be East, and the West, West. The twain will meet and become culturally unified and homogenized.

The idea underlying homogenization, as Parikh (2000) points out, is based on the belief that 'there is only one correct, true or normal way to understand and structure the relevant areas of life' (p. 1). That *of course*—as the 'experts' never tire of reminding us—is the Western way! Like 'coca-colonization'—a cynical sociological phrase—the dreamed of globalization will lead to a homogenization of beliefs and values (Friedman, 2000). There are as many protagonists of this argument as there are dissenters (refer Das, 2002; Friedman, 2000; Laungani, 2003; Roy, 2001; Sen, 2000; Stiglitz, 2002, for a comprehensive analysis).

From a psychological point of view it needs to be stressed that although all human beings share a variety of common biological, physical, and psychological characteristics and behaviours, they have uniquely different, diverse and idiosyncratic ways of responding to their environment and to their own world. Human behaviour is neither static nor a 'finished' product. It evolves. It reconstitutes itself culturally. Human behaviour is self-reflective and diversified. Human beings, regardless of their cultural origins, have the ability to share certain common values and agree to common commitments. It does not therefore follow that such consensual agreements will necessarily lead to a corrosion of one's traditional values, one's cultural identity, leading to the acquisition of a 'universal' Western identity. Despite economic prosperity, (or economic deprivation) people do not jettison their own cultural identity. Human beings, like chameleons, have the distinct ability to adapt and incorporate the changes within their cultural identity, without wrecking their ancient structure.

Let us take an example of India. Given the long history of foreign rule over India, extending over 1200 years—the Turks, the Moguls, the Dutch, the Germans, the French, the Portuguese, and last but by no means the least, the English—Indians have still managed to retain their unique caste-system, their law of karma, their languages, their multiple pantheistic gods, their patterns of worship, their diverse languages, and their characteristic extended family networks, and to a significant extent, their ancient values. Even the concerted attempts initially by the Muslim rulers and a few hundred years later by missionaries to convert Hindus (particularly from the lowest caste) to Islam and Christianity respectively, did not meet with great success. (To put this in the context of numbers, the present Christian population in India is just over 6 per cent, whereas, the Dalits (previously known as untouchables) constitute over 17 per cent of the total Indian population.) Buddhism too, despite its origins in India, has failed to make the same impact in India as it has done in Sri Lanka and China.

Here in lies an interesting paradox. On the one hand there is increasing emphasis on promoting multiculturalism in Western cultures, and on the other, a gaining belief in the very same Western countries in the eventual homogenization of cultures, the world over. It is difficult to reconcile these two polarized views logically. Yet it would be unwise to underestimate or ignore the impact of globalization on developing countries, in terms of the cultural identity, their pattern of life and the structure of family life.

If homogenization of Eastern and Western cultures becomes a reality, then the issue of transcending cultural boundaries becomes redundant. But whether such a metamorphosis takes place or is yet another form of 'wishful thinking' amongst people in the West, remains to be seen. What seems more likely to happen over time would be the acquisition of a hodgepodge of conflicting values, as is evident in many Eastern cultures today (Laungani, 2003). Bearing these factors in mind let us now return to the issues concerned with transcending cultural boundaries in counselling and psychotherapy.

It needs to be reiterated that no theory, no therapy, is ever constructed in a social vacuum. The therapist or the theoretician is part of the historical and social context in which he/she works. These factors influence the formulation of a therapy and/or a theory. For instance the belief in exorcism was seen as legitimate during the Middle Ages because of the prevalent beliefs in witchcraft. It would be difficult to sustain such a belief in the 21st century. Nor can theories be constructed wholly on logic. A total reliance on the logic of theory construction is a mistaken view, despite what many epistemologists might argue. It seems unwise to deny the impact of social and historical factors on the construction of therapies and theories. The theoretician and/or the therapist are/is part of the historical and other social forces and is inevitably influenced by these forces in any work that s/he engages in.

## WESTERN VALUES AND THERAPY: PAST AND PRESENT

It is not the task of this paper to describe the contemporary models of therapy and counselling that are used. My main interest is to consider the process of therapy against the background of the major value systems, which have had a marked influence on contemporary therapies.

Counselling and psychotherapy have a long past but a short history. Many of the problems, which clients bring into the consulting rooms of counsellors and psychotherapists, are problems of living, or, in other words, relational, sexual, existential, moral, material and spiritual problems. Socrates, in or around 400 BCE, asked the most fundamental question of all times: 'What constitutes a good life?' Or: 'How shall we lead our lives?' These questions are as relevant today as they were almost 3000 years ago. Several philosophers, theologians, scientists, psychiatrists, psychologists and scholars from other related disciplines, concerned with these fundamental questions, have attempted to provide answers but the quest for satisfactory answers continues. The fact that for the last 3000 years or so we have been asking the same questions over and over again, would seem to suggest that the existential needs of people over the centuries have remained unchanged.

In the distant past, one turned to one's aged aunt or granny, one's friends and relatives, or one's neighbours and associates, one's vicar, and a host of other people, such as palmists, astrologers, spiritualists, soothsayers for guidance and help. Given the communal structure of social life, which fostered its own network of interdependence, it was not at all difficult to find just the kind of person or persons whom one could turn to for guidance and help. One had faith and confidence in the ability of one's helpers. One relied on their experience, their knowledge and their wisdom.

In addition to the communal avenues of help that were open to virtually all and sundry, religion, acted as glue, which united societies and brought people together. The medieval superstructure of Christianity provided by St. Thomas Acquinas, enshrined custom, guided behaviour, promoted ritual, perpetuated tradition and assailed doubts—thus creating a certain degree of stability in society. Religion formed an integral part of one's daily life within one's community. But gradually as a result of scientific and technological innovations, extending over several centuries, religion was ex-communicated by the secular papacy (Laungani, 2004).

The 20th century has ushered in a new era of *secularism*, *individualism*, *humanism*, *materialism*, *empiricism* and *scientism*—the dominant values around which life revolves in the West. It is only within the framework of these prevalent value systems that one can attempt to understand the types of therapies that are currently in use. The therapies, wittingly or unwittingly are designed to 'defend' the value systems, and in so doing, aim to preserve a *status quo* in Western society.

That there is a serious downside to the present value-systems is undeniable, but to discuss these issues in any depth is to go beyond the scope of this paper. However, one point deserves some attention. The decline in religious beliefs and the secularization of society has created as several psychologists have pointed out, a spiritual vacuum in society. Second, the philosophy of individualism does not offer a guide to meaningful living neither with one's fellow human beings nor indeed with oneself. Leahey (1997) argues, that as a result of the erosion of religious and metaphysical traditions people turned to science (or scientism) for moral and spiritual guidance, and this 'led them, inevitably, to psychology, the science of individual action' (p. 471). Despite the monumental inputs of psychologists to solve human problems all is not well with the state of Western psychology, nor for that matter with the state of the world. The 20th century, as Fukuyama (2002) has argued, has been the most volatile and violent century of all times. It has struggled through two world wars, and this is not counting the acts of international aggression, one has witnessed virtually in all countries all over the world, including by America. The disclaimers made by President Bush when he said 'The United States of America. The most free nation in the world. A nation built on fundamental values; that rejects hate, that rejects violence, that rejects murderers and rejects evil' (Bush, 2001) have no truth in them whatever. In the last six decades starting with World War II America has been at war with and bombed over 22 countries! These include Japan, China, Korea, Indonesia, Cuba, Vietnam, Cambodia, Grenada, Panama, Bosnia, Iraq, Afghanistan, among others (Roy, 2001). The world has witnessed the collapse of the mighty Soviet Union, the emergence of new authoritarian states, religious and sectarian warfare in Europe, Africa, Asia and other countries. The list is virtually endless.

Psychologists, at the beginning of the 20th century, made all kinds of promises: psychology would usher in a new era; pressing human problems would be resolved, and people all over the world would live in peace, harmony, relative affluence and happiness. Hardly any of the promises has been honoured. It is difficult to see what psychology has achieved. It is impossible to chart the future course of psychology.

## EASTERN VALUES AND THERAPY

Are the Eastern approaches to therapy any different? Or are they a poor imitation of Western approaches? In the not too distant past the trend was one of imitation and aping Western approaches, Western theories, and the use of

Western psychometric instruments. Whether this was due to an inability or an unwillingness on the part of academics and therapists to rid themselves of their past colonial mentality, as Kakar (1997) has argued, or there were other factors at work is debatable. It is of course possible that there are several other factors at work. Imitation, the best form of flattery, provided opportunities for scholarships and sponsorship and collaborative research enterprises in European and American countries. They also provided publication avenues in European and American journals.

But the situation in the last two decades or so has gradually begun to undergo a change. Although Western models of therapy continue to be used among the small Westernized clientele to be found mainly in large metropolitan cities, the therapists in Eastern cultures have almost reinvented their ancient indigenous approaches, which range from Astrology and Palmistry, Ayurvedic and Homoeopathic treatment, religious therapy pilgrimages, shamanism and exorcism, to yogic exercises and meditation (Laungani, 2004). The indigenous approaches are in keeping with the fundamental value systems of Eastern cultures, which in contradistinction to Western value systems can be described in terms of communalism (collectivism) religiosity, determinism, emotionalism and spiritualism. For instance, the philosophy of individualism, which plays an extremely dominant role in Western thinking, is of little value in Eastern thinking. Easterners in general tend to organize their private and social lives, which include their beliefs, attitudes and values along communal lines. Communal goals often take precedence over individual goals. This is noticeable even within family structures where the goals of an individual are often subordinated to the goals of the family (Laungani, 2003). In the West while there is a clear demarcation between the sacred and the secular, the lines between the two are blurred in the East (Klostermaier, 1998; Koller, 1982; Lannoy, 1976).

And as we saw from the brief case study, people in Eastern cultures tend to construe their life in terms of it being ordained. The Muslims believe strongly in the Will of Allah, in the 'day of reckoning' (*qauamat*), whereas the Hindus subscribe to the Law of Karma, which forms an integral part of their psyche. For any therapist, Western or Eastern to disregard the above beliefs and values embedded within the Eastern psyche would seriously impede the therapist in engaging in a genuine and meaningful cross-cultural therapeutic encounter.

## CONCLUSION

The final question is this: Is there a way by which one might transcend the cultural boundaries in counselling and psychotherapy? The answer is a cautious yes. To achieve such an end it is essential that the following factors be given serious consideration.

- The East and the West would need to meet as joint and equal partners and work together to promote a clearer understanding of differences and similarities in the value systems of Eastern and Western cultures.
- There is a paramount need to design intensive, meaningful and relevant training courses, which would serve the mutual interests of therapists both from the West and the East when dealing with multicultural issues.
- The therapists would need to be concerned not just about the idiosyncrasies of different psychotherapies, but find ways of 'weeding out' a vast number of pseudo therapies which are often unleashed upon unsuspecting clients (Laungani, 2004).
- In working together, the therapists would need to examine the major problems which threaten the world, and in so doing construct the means which would enable people to transcend over physical, psychological and cultural boundaries and hopefully usher in a new era where people shall live in peace, mutual trust and harmony.

But so long as counsellors, therapists, academics remain entrenched within their own cultural boundaries such a dream is unlikely to be realized.

## REFERENCES

Bettelheim, B. (1986). *The Informed Heart.* London: Pergrine.

Bush, G. W. (2001). Remarks made by President George W. Bush at an anti-terrorism event. Washington DC—Federal News Service, 10 October.

Darwin, C. (1872). *The expression of the emotions in man and animals: Introduction, afterword and commentaries by Paul Ekman.* London: Harper Collins Publishers.

Das, C. (2002). *The elephant paradigm: India wrestles with change.* New Delhi: Penguin.

Fitzgerald, E. (1859). *Rubaiyat of Omar Khayyam.* London: Book Club Associates.

Friedman, T. (2000). *The lexus and the olive tree.* London: Harper/Collins.

Fukuyama, F. (2002). *The end of history and the last man.* New York: Perennial.

Gombrich, E. H. (1979). *Ideals and idols: Essays on values in history and in art.* Oxford: Phaidon Press Ltd.

Grondona, M. (2000). A cultural typology of economic development. In L. E. Harrison and S. P. Huntington (Eds), *Culture matters: How values shape human progress.* New York: Basic Books.

Harrison, L. E. (2000). Promoting progressive cultural change. In L. E. Harrison and S. P. Huntington (Eds), *Culture matters: How values shape human progress.* New York: Basic Books.

Hayakawa, S. I. (1965). *Language in thought and action.* London: George Allen & Unwin.

Hoch, E. M. (1974). Pir, fakir, and psychotherapist. *The Human Context, 6*, 668–676.

Kakar, S. (1982). *Shamans, mystics and doctors.* London: Unwin Paperbacks.

Kakar, S. (1997). *Culture and psyche: Selected essays.* New Delhi: Oxford University Press.

Klostermaier, K. K. (1998). *A short introduction to hinduism.* Oxford: One World Press.

Koller, J. M. (1982). *The Indian way: Perspectives.* London: Collier Macmillan.

Lannoy, R. (1976). *The speaking tree.* Oxford: Oxford University Press.

Laungani, P. (2003). Family life in India. In J. L. Roopnarine and U. P. Gielen (Eds), *Families in global perspective.* Boston: Allyn & Bacon.

———. (2004). *Asian perspectives in counselling and psychotherapy.* London: Routledge.

Leahey, T. H. (1997). *A history of psychology: Main currents in psychological thought.* New Jersey: Prentice Hall.

Osgood, C. E., Suci, G. J. and Tannenbaum, P. H. (1957). *The measurement of meaning.* Urbana, II: University of Illinois Press.

Parikh, B. (2000). *Rethinking multiculturalism: Cultural diversity and political theory.* New York: Palgrave.

Roland, A. (1988). *In search of self in India and Japan.* Princeton, NJ: Princeton University Press.

Roy, A. (2001). *The algebra of infinite justice.* New Delhi: Penguin.

Sen, A. (2000). *Development as freedom.* New Delhi: Oxford University Press.

Stiglitz, J. (2002). *Globalization and its discontents.* London: Allen Lane.

# 16

# Migration, Cultural Values and the Medical Model: Pittu Laungani and Psychotherapy

*Ruth M. Lijtmaer*

## INTRODUCTION

**Within** a culture, there are beliefs about the purpose of life, symbolic rituals, concepts of time and space, causation of events, the persons' responsibility for those events to occur and how mind and body work (Dana, 1993). The aspects of our cultural introjects are values, attitudes and conventional ways of behaving that are based on these ethnocultural roots. These introjects develop from early life experiences, influence our world view (Schechter, 1992), contribute to our internal emotional states and consequently to the therapeutic relationship. There is a commonality of defences and conflicts that are both provided and facilitated by a particular culture. Considering this, psychopathology is a universal phenomenon. Anxiety, depression, defence mechanisms, dreams, all are present in all human beings of different cultures. Nevertheless, their modes of expression may differ in diverse cultures. Even analyzing the interaction between socio-cultural background and mental illness influences the way patients relate to mental health professionals. We may misjudge the behaviour and the verbalizations of the patient if we attribute the patient's behaviour only to pathology neglecting the patient's cultural background.

In this chapter, I will consider Pittu Laungani in the context of counselling, psychotherapy and psychiatry in the USA. I will explore and compare Laungani's work on cross-cultural issues that coincide or are discrepant with the work of American cross-cultural psychology. The themes that I chose to discuss that are relevant to both countries are: migration and culture shock when people migrate and the use of language (Laungani, 2002a), and Eastern and Western cultural values in psychotherapy (Laungani, 2002a, 2004a, 2004b).

## MIGRATION AND LANGUAGE

In his paper published in 2002, Laungani described his personal account of choosing to migrate to England instead of the USA, and how he experienced culture shock as an Indian immigrant. He stated, 'We carry our culture as a tortoise shell. Destroy the shell and you destroy the tortoise' (Laungani, 2002a: 388). Laungani told of his struggles as an immigrant 'fighting a lone fight on several fronts: the weather, the food, the customs and conventions, the patterns of day-to-day life and the people' (Laungani, 2002a: 388). Laungani's candour at describing his 'unforgivable social blunders' (Laungani, 2002a: 387) is telling us that he is not alone in this culture disparity. Our patients as well as immigrant therapists had similar experiences. Another concept that he proposed was the idea of assimilation and losing his culture and personal history. By doing that would have meant a 'sad loss of my own moral integrity' (Laungani, 2002a: 388).

The immigrant experience has been more fully described in the American literature starting in the 1980s, even though there were other works before that. More recently, due to a greater flux of immigrants to the USA, more articles have appeared. Most of them emphasize how migration is a complex psychosocial process involving profound losses with long-standing effects in the individual. At times, the psychic depletion depends, among other factors, if the person arrives in a new country as an immigrant or an exile. Whatever the circumstances, these changes entail periods of disorganization, pain, frustration and produces a catastrophic loss. As a result of continuous contact with a new culture, the migration experience unchains a process that leads to the transformation of internal structures and internalized object relations. The emotional impact of changing cultures is based on the emotional symbolic association between the present cultural experience and the early relationship of the child with the primary caretaker. It is no coincidence that people talk about the 'mother country' (Lijtmaer, 2000).

Significant psychological processes occur during this traumatic experience. As a result of cultural relocation and the loss of the primary object, 'mother country', the individual is deprived of the 'holding functions' (Winnicott, 1953) of the native country that had provided a feeling of safety and connectedness to others. The immigrants lose this environment and cultural space, and find themselves in an unknown territory peopled with strangers whose expectations and habits are often very different of what the immigrant knows (Marlin, 1994). Because of this, there is an overvaluation of the old cultural symbols (for example, conventions, language and food) and a devaluation of the new ones. This splitting process results from a retrospective idealization of the lost object, the motherland, and can be used defensively to protect the ego from painful effect (Lijtmaer, 2000).

Another psychic experience in migration is nostalgia. Following Akhtar (1999), nostalgia helps the immigrant defend against the aggression resulting from current frustrations. The feeling of nostalgia can also be used to protect the ego from inadequacy.

Only few works on the experience of the immigrant therapist appeared that are similar to the experience of the patients (Akhtar, 2006; Lijtmaer, 2006b). However, issues of training, supervision and the therapist's own therapy add another dimension to the clinician's immigrant experience that is missing in the literature.

In terms of language usage (bilingualism) in the therapeutic dyad, articles appeared in the USA, particularly starting in the 1970s. Since then until now, many studies have shown the effects of second language on the therapeutic relationship. Issues like language independence and the defence mechanism of splitting (Marcos and Alpert, 1976); language choice and language switching in the treatment situation (Marcos et al., 1977); misinterpreting or misdiagnosing a patient due to a language barrier as well as misinterpretation by the patient (Marcos and Urcuyo, 1979); the 'detachment effect' or language switching to serve defensive purposes when content becomes too threatening (Rozensky and Gomez, 1983) and the influence of language choice in the transference (Lijtmaer, 1999, 2000).

Some studies demonstrated that lack of common language may result in a diagnosis of more severe psychopathology, decreased patient self-disclosure, lower ratings of patient–analyst rapport and lower ratings of analysts' empathy and effectiveness (Leong 1986, in Flaskerud and Lui, 1990). Other studies suggested that bilingual patients are able to access early memories with more emotional intensity when encouraged to recount those experiences in their mother tongue. Even though they may relate and remember those experiences in the second language, the intensity of the emotion may be lost (Bauxbaum, 1949; for references, see Lijtmaer, 1999; Zac De Filc, 1992).

Laungani describes that there are many Indian accents and dialects that can be neglected by the counsellor. Talking about his personal experience he stated,

> It was difficult to distinguish between levity and seriousness, between jest and truth, between praise and censure, between affection and affectation, between acceptance and rejection. I found it exasperating not being able to read correctly their feelings and emotions when, on occasions, they chose to express them. (Laungani, 2002a: 387)

These difficulties in understanding different languages, is similar to what happens in the USA. For example, mainstream American culture homogenizes Spanish-speaking peoples into one ethnic group: Latinos or Hispanics. Yet, such a group involves dozens of different countries, each with a particular socio-political history and unique versions of the Spanish language. Similarly, Laungani's concept of individualism and collectivism (referring to Western and Eastern cultures) is also reflected in language usage. Since language is representational of the cultural context in which the therapist and the patient live, the American cultural pattern that emphasizes the individual is reflected in our capitalization of the word 'I', conveying importance. However, in Spanish, the word for I is 'yo', with a small 'y', implying the individual is less important, and the group or family is valued. The complexity of language expression as an indicator of cultural values becomes apparent when we begin to consider the clinical implications of the difference between 'I' and 'yo' (Chamorro, 2003; Lijtmaer, 2006b).

Laungani also considers the importance of metaphors in treatment. He describes how metaphors are class-related, have their own origin, are culture-specific and its effects in the therapeutic relationship. He stated,

> Metaphors help us to articulate, interpret and reinterpret our own world of experience to ourselves and hopefully share it with others. Each culture produces its own sources of metaphor. They facilitate communication among its members. The use of metaphors also enables us to interpret our own world of experience. (Laungani, 2004b: 198–199)

After a short vignette, Laungani demonstrates how therapist and patient are 'locked in their own private cultural worlds. They are either unable or unwilling to step out of them' (Laungani, 2004b: 200).

## EASTERN AND WESTERN VALUES IN PSYCHOTHERAPY

Even though somewhat changing, still there is cultural blindness and stereotypes in the USA (Laungani, 2002a). Therefore, the issue of stereotypes (Laungani, 2002a: 388) is alive and well in India and Britain as well as in the USA. Laungani (2002a) criticized Western psychology and particularly American psychology. He stated that Western psychologists tend to believe that the world is as they see it, 'They believe too that the rest of the people in the world also see it as they see it—through Western Spectacles' (Laungani, 2002a: 392). In terms of America, he said that the Americans paid little or no attention to their own cultural needs and remained trusting the power of their psychology to solve most, if not all of human problems (Laungani, 2002a: 392). His explanation for this phenomenon is that the acquired cultural blindness is due to the fact that Western psychologies and American psychology in particular, could not, did not or chose not to see that vital role of culture in personality development

(Laungani, 2002a: 292–293). From my perspective, the issue at stake is that American psychology and psychoanalysis had until quite recently focused on the White population; therapy being a treatment for the powerful and the few (Altman, 2000, 2006). Fortunately, things are slowly changing now. There is more research and papers on the minority population. In the USA, the ethnic issue that is more prevalent is with African-Americans and Hispanics, due to the big percentage of that population.

In the last years, more psychoanalytic papers appeared on race (see references in Lijtmaer, 2001a). Some of the psychoanalytic papers talk about countertransference and the therapist's responses when working with someone different from them (see references in Lijtmaer, 2006a). Laungani (2004b) mentions the Western therapist's work, even though he does not use the word countertransference. He stated that 'The therapist operates from a euro-centric model, which posits a "horizontal", non-hierarchical, but formal interpersonal relationship that emphasizes individualism' (Laungani, 2004b: 201). This can be a problem for a patient of Eastern culture. He also cautions to therapists' 'playing out' their own internalized value system that will influence his/her work (Laungani, 2004b: 201). This fact can happen in any place in the world, when patient and therapist are of Eastern and Western cultures. Particularly, when we think of some cultural values like individualism, materialism, secularism compared to communalism, religiosity, determinism, emotionalism and spiritualism that are tenets of Eastern cultures (Laungani, 2004b: 205).

As an example, I personally experienced conflict when I, a Latina/Hispanic therapist working in Eastern USA treated my first Chinese patient. My metapsychology and the Western values of mental health with which I trained, were shaken by this patient. I had to adjust my treating modality to fit the patient's needs. For example, I frequently had to question the patient in order to clarify cultural practices and meanings related to her ethnic background. My candid ethnic illiteracy and attunement to 'difference' constituted a powerful vehicle towards effecting psychic change. I also had to be more didactic and had to assume the role of teacher which went against the psychodynamic philosophy in which I was trained (Lijtmaer, 2000).

On the West coast of USA, due to the strong Asian population (particularly Chinese and Korean) the works of Cheng and Lo (1991), Flaskerud and Lui (1990), Tang (1992), Tang and Gardner (1999) and Tung (1991) among others, are used. These authors emphasize the different cultural norms of the Eastern and the Western cultures and its effect in the treatment process, particularly when therapist and patient are of different ethnicity. However, being of the same ethnicity can also pose problems. For example, Tang and Gardner (1999) describe the possibility of a strong identification with the patient. This identification based on personal experiences of being misunderstood, can lead the therapist to work harder with the patient. He suggests an empathic-introspective approach that requires the therapist to self-reflect on his/her subjective organizing principles, including assumptions, thoughts, ideas and feelings that are culturally based (Yi, 1995, 1998). Another example of over-identification with a patient is the case of a Black patient–therapist dyad, in an inner city clinic. The patient criticized some of his co-workers and labelled them as discriminating against him. The therapist did not inquire more about the patient's ideas and feelings about this. Instead, he started telling the patient things he could do. The therapist felt uncomfortable with this response to the patient. Later, he realized that at a deeper level, he felt discriminated himself. This example of over-identification (Comas-Diaz and Jacobsen, 1991) indicates how some therapists from ethnic minorities change their technical stance and become more supportive and active with patients from ethnic minorities. Their technical change is the result of an unconscious fear of over-identification with intrapsychic aspects of their patients' problems. This is particularly more prevalent among groups who have a history of oppression and discrimination. Another case in point is cultural myopia. Gottesfeld (1978, cited in Comas-Diaz and Jacobsen, 1991), an Italian analyst, found that she developed some blind spots towards an Italian patient. She unconsciously did not explore certain conflict areas out of a sense that it was natural for the patient to behave the way she did. Thus, Gottesfeld accepted the patient's unwillingness to expose family secrets and having a secret life because she colluded with the conviction that the powerful closeness of the Italian family must be maintained at all costs. This illustration of 'cultural myopia' indicates how the therapist, due to cultural similarities may find himself/herself unable to question the patient's responses, leaving significant material uncovered which can be accompanied by an unconscious collusion.

## IMPLICATIONS FOR MULTICULTURAL COUNSELLING

While migratory processes have been a universal phenomenon since the beginning of mankind, with the recent global changes in ideological and political perspectives, wars and economic collapse, migration is quite prevalent. Moving to another land disrupts people's connections with their contexts of significance: their land, language, customs, culture, sense of community, concepts of time and space and their way of life. Therefore, migrating to another land is a complex psychosocial situation involving profound losses with long standing effects in the individual. It is a dynamic, open-ended process in which the individual's ego capacities and overall personality integration are severely tested (Marlin, 1994). Because of people's destiny to move from one place to another, the issue of multicultural counselling has become quite significant. How much do we know of the 'other', this stranger that may have different values, ways of thinking and language different from us, the therapists?

How many of you have come across a cab driver, a maid or a seamstress who was also a relatively new immigrant? Would you have thought that the Latino maid was a nurse in her native country, or the cab driver was an engineer in his native land? What I am referring to is how heterogeneous we are and as mental health providers are we prepared to help this diverse population?

In the medical context, migrants or ethnic minorities are often misdiagnosed and over-medicated because professionals do not understand nor search for contexts that provide meaning to their presenting symptoms. Furthermore, their idioms of distress are sometimes interpreted as signs of psychosis, craziness or malingering (Guarnaccia et al., 1990, cited in Alvarez, 1995). Since language is a powerful tool utilized by people in positions of power to define others and to ascribe meanings to their experiences, our use of language can sometimes control and shame others for being different (Irigaray, 1993; Jordan, 1989; Miller, 1896, cited in Alvarez, 1995). Because English is not the native tongue of many immigrants, they cannot define or communicate well their stories of distress. As a result of this, they are frequently misunderstood, mistreated and reduced to categories of inferiority. It is not unusual for immigrant women to experience degradation or sexual harassment in the workplace. However, many suffer silently for fear of losing their jobs or having their illegal status exposed.

Within the family context, the family structure, roles and dynamics are often pathologized by social service, educational and legal systems. The fact that many families try to maintain elements of their native culture can be highly criticized.

In the school context, immigrant children and/or children born to immigrant parents do not escape categorizations. These children's cooperative versus competitive nature and deferential manners are often misinterpreted and categorized as shy, insecure and dependent. Bilingualism and differences in learning styles tend to be construed as cognitive deficiencies since these children may not do well on standardized tests. Another significant point is that children of immigrant parents may be left in their native country separated from their parents. A child's reaction to this loss may include withdrawal, acting out and even self-destructive behaviour. These are the children that are often medicated. While medications can alleviate symptoms of depression, this treatment modality is not helpful for people with migration experiences (Alvarez, 1995).

## CONCLUSION

Summarizing the implications for multicultural counselling; culture is such an embedded part of our lives that the psychotherapeutic setting does not produce a culture-free interaction. Both patient and therapist influence and are influenced by their own cultural background or ethnicity. Herron (cited in Javier and Rendon, 1995) postulated that every culture has its own unique form of unconscious that may have powerful effects on the therapeutic process. He stated that the ethnic unconscious refers to 'repressed material that each generation shares with the next and is shared by most people in that ethnic group' (Javier and Rendon, 1995: 513). Seen in this way, ethnicity and culture can touch deep unconscious feelings in most individuals and may become targets for projection by both patient and therapist. Our inability to be aware of cultural differences, may lead us to misunderstand the patient's world if we attribute the patient's behaviour only to pathology neglecting the developmental cultural background that the patient comes to treatment with. In the case of cultural differences, the disparities are often a source of mutual subjective arousal, sidestepping exploration of the patient's observations. The more disparate the respective worlds of the dyad, the more work have to be undertaken as a joint exploration for understanding.

Finally, I would like to emphasize how Laungani's work had parallels in the USA. His works on immigration, Eastern and Western values and his advocate for psychological treatment had its followers in clinicians in the USA who are sensitive, open-minded and caring for the individual well-being, the way he was. I will like to end by quoting Laungani, '...as long as counsellors, therapists, academics remain entrenched within their own cultural boundaries such a dream is unlikely to be realized' (Laungani, 2004b: 206).

## NOTE

Multiculturalism does not encompass only the four primarily ethnic minority groups. Rather, it includes many of us—in one way or another. This conceptualization assumes a dialectical relationship between understanding people as individuals and also as representatives of the groups with which they identify. What needs to be explicit in discussing multicultural psychotherapy is that the therapist at times may respond inappropriately to the patient for reasons that are not, in essence, due to internal conflicts. Some of the therapist's failures in understanding and empathizing with the patient can be due to lack of knowledge of the patient's culture, (Gorkin, 1987: 70), and/or our ideas about mental health which are biased by our own culture and metapsychology. Issues that we believe are pathological may not be so in the patient's world. Normality is in the eyes of the observer. The concept of normality is different in different cultures. Accordingly, it is neither the task nor the goal of the therapist to help people conform to any culture but rather to help them develop their own potentialities. In cultures where interdependence is encouraged and is essential for survival, the therapist's attempt to work towards independence and individuation is doomed to failure or, worst produces an ambivalence and cultural confusion in the mind of the patient. In societies where interdependence and interpersonal surveillance exist, the society develops shame-orientation (Neki, 1976, cited in Lloyd and Bhugra, 1993: 299). Therefore, in this multicultural world, a clinician's awareness of difference in the therapeutic relationship is paramount for a successful treatment.

## REFERENCES


Akhtar, S. (1999). The immigrant, the exile, and the experience of nostalgia. *Journal of Applied Psychoanalytic Studies, 1*(2), 123–130.

———. (2006). Technical challenges faced by the immigrant analyst. *The Psychoanalytic Quarterly, 75*(1), 21–44.

Altman, N. (2000). Black and white thinking: A psychoanalyst reconsiders race. *Psychoanalytic Dialogues, 10*(4), 589–605.

———. (2006). Whiteness. *The Psychoanalytic Quarterly, 75*(1), 45–72.

Alvarez, M. (1995). *The experience of migration: A relational approach in therapy. Work in Progress*, No. 71. Wellesley, MA: Stone Center Working Paper Series.

Bauxbaum, Edith. (1949). The role of a second language in the formation of ego and super-ego. *Psychoanalytic Quarterly, 18*, 279–387.

Chamorro, R. (2003). From the other side: Countertransference in Spanish-speaking dyads. *Journal for the Psychoanalysis of Culture and Society, 8*(1), 84–87.

Cheng, L. and Lo, H. (1991). On the advantages of cross-cultural psychotherapy: The minority therapist/mainstream patient dyad. *Psychiatry, 54*(4), 386–396.

Comas-Diaz, Lillian and Jacobsen, Frederick M. (1991). Ethnocultural transference and countertransference in the therapeutic dyad. *American Journal of Orthopsychiatry, 6*(13), 392–402.

Dana, R. H. (1993). *Multicultural assessment perspectives for professional Psychology*. Massachusetts: Allyn and Bacon.

Fisher, N. (1971). An interracial analysis: Transference and countertransference significance. *Journal of the American Psychoanalytic Association, 19*, 736–745

Flaskerud, J. and Lui, P. (1990). Influence of analyst ethnicity and languages on therapy outcomes of Southeast Asians clients. *The International Journal of Social Psychiatry, 36*(1), 18–29.

Gorkin, M. (1987). *The Uses of Countertransference*. Northvale, New Jersey: Jason Aronson, Inc.

Hall, R. (2001). Biracial sensitive practice: Expanding social services to an invisible population. *Journal of Sociology and Social Welfare, 28*(2), 23–36.

Helms, J. E. and Cook, D. A. (1999). *Using race and culture in counselling and psychotherapy: Theory and process*. Needham Heights, MA: Allyn & Bacon.

Holmes, E. (1992). Race and transference in psychoanalysis and psychotherapy. *International Journal of Psychoanalysis, 73*, 187–219.

———. (1999). Race and countertransference: Two 'blind spots' in psychoanalytic perception. *Journal of Applied Psychoanalytic Studies, 1*(4), 319–332.

Javier, R. and Rendon, M. (1995). The ethnic unconscious and its role in transference, resistance and countertransference: An introduction. *Psychoanalytic Psychology, Special Section: Ethnicity and Psychoanalysis, 12*(4), 513–520.

Laungani, P. (2002a). Cross-cultural psychology: A handmaiden to mainstream Western Psychology. *Counselling Psychology Quarterly. 15*(4), 385–397.

———. (2002b). Mindless psychiatry and dubious ethics. *Counselling Psychology Quarterly, 15*(1), 23–33.

———. (2004a). Some unresolved issues in philosophy and psychology: Their implications for therapy. *Counselling Psychology Quarterly, 1*(7), 107–123.

———. (2004b). Counselling and therapy in a multicultural setting. *Counselling Psychology Quarterly, 17*(2), 195–207.

Leary, K. (1995). 'Interpreting in the dark': Race and ethnicity in Psychoanalytic psychotherapy. *Psychoanalytic Psychology, 12*(1), 127–140.

———. (1997). Race, self-disclosure, and 'forbidden talk': Race and ethnicity in contemporary clinical practice. *Psychoanalytic Quarterly, 66*, 163–189.

———. (2000). Racial enactments in dynamic treatment. *Psychoanalytic Dialogues, 10*(4), 639–653.

Lijtmaer, R. (1999). Language shift in bilinguals: Transference and countertransference implications. *Journal of the American Academy of Psychoanalysis, 27*(4), 611–624.

———. (2000). Psychotherapy with multicultural populations. *Issues in Psychoanalytic Psychotherapy, 22*(2), 35–42.

———. (2001a). Countertransference and ethnicity: The analyst's psychic change. *Journal of the American Academy of Psychoanalysis, 29*(1), 73–84.

———. (2000, 2001b). Splitting and nostalgia in recent immigrants: Psychodynamic considerations. *Journal of the American Academy of Psychoanalysis, 29*(3), 427–438.

———. (2006a). Black, White, Hispanic and both: Issues in bi-racial identity and its effects in the transference-countertransference. In R. Moodley and S. Palmer (Eds), *Race, culture and psychotherapy: Critical perspectives in multicultural practice*. London: Brunner-Routledge.

———. (2006b). *The immigrant analyst's bilingual/bicultural self.* Paper presented at IFPE (International Federation for Psychoanalytic Education) 16th Annual Interdisciplinary Conference 2–20–06 to 2–24–06, Queretaro, Mexico.

Lloyd and Bhugra. (1993). Cross-cultural aspects of psychiatry. *International Review of Psychiatry, 5*(2–3), 291–304.

Marcos, L. R. (1976). Bilinguals in psychotherapy: language as an emotional barrier. *American Journal of Psychotherapy, 30*(4), 552–559.

Marcos, L. R. and Alpert, M. (1976). Strategies and risks in psychotherapy with bilingual patients. *American Journal of Psychiatry, 133*(11), 1275–1278.

Marcos, L. R., Eisma, J, E. and Guimon, J. (1977). Bilingualism and sense of self. *The American Journal of Psychoanalysis, 37*(4), 285–290.

Marcos, L. R. and Urcuyo, L. (1979). Dynamic psychotherapy with the bilingual patient. *American Journal of Psychotherapy, 33*(3), 331–338.

Marlin, O. (1994). Special issue in the analytic treatment of immigrants and refugees. *Issues in Psychoanalytic Psychology, 16*(1), 7–16.

Rockquemore, K. (1998). Between black and white, exploring the 'Biracial' experience. *Race & Society, 1*(2), 197–212.

———. (2003). Multiple realities: A relational narrative approach in therapy with Black-white mixed-race clients. *Family Relations: Interdisciplinary Journal of Applied Family Studies, 52,* 119–128.

Root, M. P. P (1998a). Resolving 'other' status. Identity development of biracial individuals. In P. Oragnista, K. Chun and G. Marin (Eds), *Readings in ethnic psychology* (pp. 100–112). New York: Routledge.

———. (1998b). Experiences and processes affecting racial identity development: Preliminary results from biracial sibling project. *Cultural Diversity and Mental Health, 4*(3) 237–247.

Rozensky, R. H. and Gomez, M. Y. (1983). Language switching in psychotherapy with bilinguals: Two problems, two models and case examples. *Psychotherapy: Theory, Research and Practice, 20*(2), 152–160.

Schachter, J. and Butts, H. (1968). Transference and countertransference in interracial analysis. *American Psychoanalytic Association Journal, 16*(4), 782–808.

Schechter, A. (1992). Voice of a hidden minority: Identification and countertransference in the cross-cultural working alliance. *The Amer. J. of Psychoanalysis, 53*(4), 63–81.

Tang, N. (1992). Some implications of Chinese philosophy and child-rearing practices. *Psychoanalytic Study of the Child, 47,* 371–390.

Tang, N. and Gardner, J. (1999). Race, culture, and psychotherapy: Transference to minority therapists. *Psychoanalytic Quarterly, 68*(1), 1–20.

Tummala-Narra, P. (2007). Skin color and the therapeutic relationship. *Psychoanalytic Psychology, 24*(2), 255–270.

Tung, M. (1991). Insight oriented psychotherapy and the Chinese patient. *American Journal of Orthopsychiatry, 6*(2), 186–194.

Winnicott, D. W. (1953). Transitional objects and transitional phenomena: A study of the first not-me possession. *International Journal of Psychoanalysis, 34*, 89–97.
Yi, C. (1995). Psychoanalytic psychotherapy with Asian clients: Transference and therapeutic considerations. *Psychotherapy, 32*(2), 308–316.
———. (1998). Transference and Race: An Intersubjective Conceptualization. *Psychoanalytic Psychology, 15*(2), 245–265.
Zac De Filc, Sara. (1992). Psychic change in the analyst. *Internat. J. Psychoanalysis, 73*(2), 323–328.

# 17

# Tortoises and Turtles: Pittu Laungani, Cultural Transitions and Therapeutic Relationships

*Fevronia Christodoulidi and Colin Lago*

## INTRODUCTION

**The** world of today is profoundly multicultural, multiethnic and multinational. Many millions of people worldwide are continually on the move to new cultures, new places to live, to work and to seek shelter. Indeed, it is estimated that one in every 35 people in the world today is an international migrant (Koser, 2007). Such 'geographic' moves are frequently chosen in the hope that a new life in another place will offer enhanced work and life possibilities. Others, sadly, are subject to forceful relinquishing of their countries of origin. Both categories of people, whether choosing or forced to migrate, have to face considerable personal, cultural, linguistic, social and spiritual challenges, which are rarely anticipated and rarely acknowledged in the public domain (Madison, 2006). A number of significant personal processes will inevitably occur for such people, both sojourners and settlers in a new country, in relation to re-defining their personal and cultural identities as well as re-discovering a comfortable territory where a sense of 'at-homeness' can be built again, whether temporary or permanent. Given the complexities such populations face at so many levels, the therapeutic task of offering them a supportive empathic relationship can also be challenging for the therapist.

Laungani's contribution to the field of professional therapeutic practice in the UK is difficult to assess accurately. Stephen Palmer (2007) in his obituary of Pittu Laungani, notes that: '...his work in the field of cross cultural counselling... caused controversy among his colleagues. He had an aversion to what is known as person-centred counselling believing that this reflective Western approach was not suitable for clients from the Indian subcontinent'.

In separate interviews with us, Pittu Laungani expressed a disdain for the apparent simplicity of most counselling courses curricula and was critical of working practices such as the recognition of boundary maintenance. His strong critique of 'person-centred' approaches is also difficult to comprehend in that in his article 'The Counselling Interview: First Impressions', he articulates and recommends some of the principles underlying person-centred theory but fails to reference or attribute them! (Christodoulidi, 2006; Lago, 2005). For Laungani, (again quoting from his obituary), 'the problem with the western approach to psychotherapy was that it tended to operate on a horizontal model and assumed equality, whereas, in his view, an Indian model would be vertical, with the therapist as the guru or guide' (Palmer, 2007). These assertions of Laungani are supported by the extensive research work of Hofstede (1980), who identified contrasts between the two cultures in relation to two main dimensions, that is, 'power–distance' and 'individualism–collectivism'. On the dimension of 'power–distance' (a term used to describe the extent to which a society accepts the fact that power in institutions and organizations is distributed unequally), India scored much higher than the UK, that is, formal relationships in India would reflect this sense of differentiation of position and respect would be attributed to the authority of those in power (for example, psychotherapists). In contrast, in the UK, a cultural belief exists that inequalities in society should be minimized and all should have equal rights. This value base inevitably also underpins the practice of humanistic approaches to psychotherapy in the West. On the cultural dimension of 'collectivism–individualism', the British society was strongly biased towards individualism (a belief that identity is based on the individual and individual decisions are valued highly), whereas, in contrast, Indian culture operated in a more balanced way between the demands of the collective, (family, local community) and the individual.

The central theme of this paper of how to assist the culturally different client manage the transition and integration of original and host culture, we are reminded of the image of the tortoise carrying its shell, carrying its 'home' on its back and moving along with it for a lifetime. It is certainly the fact that, short of a great trauma, the tortoise, wherever it is, can seek refuge in its own home (shell) at any time. As Laungani and Palmer state (cited in Laungani, 2002a) 'we carry our culture like the tortoise carries its shell; destroy the shell and you destroy the tortoise' (p. 388). In relation to this aspect of the metaphor, we are reminded of the tortoise's normal functioning: That is, it has the habit/behaviour of withdrawal rather than confrontation when attacked. Closely related to the tortoise, the turtle is also able to live in two environments, able to move on land and in water…it can live in two 'cultures'. So, if we extend that metaphor to human ability for change and resilience, it would mean that we can actually manage living in more that one environment or culture comfortably and with a 'whole' sense of self. But, if we see the tortoise's shell as related to its sense of home, how do things change when there is a move away from 'home'?

## THE MOVE FROM 'HOME'

Globalization and multiculturalism have created an opportunity where both individuals and groups of people are facing the challenge to understand their ever changing identities and the world around them. The topics of 'cultural adaptation' and the impact of 'mobility across cultures' have been examined in the literature from a number of disciplines (Adler, 1987; Furnham and Bochner, 1986; Kim, 1988; Palmer and Laungani, 1999). The painful consequences of such transitions have been summarized by Schram and Lauver (cited by Leong and Chou, 2002: 193) into three aspects of alienation: powerlessness, meaninglessness and social estrangement. Inevitably, the concept of 'culture' and how it affects people's sense of self, values and way of living has gained more and more significance within the discourse of culture and psychotherapy in recent decades (D'Ardenne and Mahtani, 1999; Lago, 2006a, 2006b; Pedersen, 1987; Pope-Davis and Coleman, 1997). Such a discourse is vividly demonstrated by West and McLeod, when they present a view of the post-modern reality of our era as that of living within a 'cultural landscape' where:

> There are some places or territories within this landscape that are safe and familiar, where we feel 'at home'. There are other landscapes that are unknown, frightening and dangerous. There is a horizon, beyond which other landscapes wait to be discovered. Some people are travellers across this landscape, others are interpreters, translators or guides across the border lands. (West and McLeod, 2003: 85)

We suggest that this description, although true, does not comprise the whole picture. There are people in the landscape that lose the comfortable feeling of 'at-homeness', even in the territories that used to be familiar to them and with those figures with whom they used to feel intimate. Even when back 'at home', such persons do not always feel the degree of comfort and familiarity normally associated with home. This very realization that 'home is really not home' is at the core of the experience of re-entry to the culture of origin and is 'a reverse cultural shock', as described vividly by Storti (2003).

Pittu Laungani was one of the living examples of those who have 'travelled across the landscapes and ventured over the horizon' within the psychology, and later, psychotherapy professions, moving from the Eastern territory of India, with all its distinctive cultural characteristics into the Western UK culture, with its own set of norms and attitudes. He seemed to have bridged a kind of connection, a union of the two that inevitably must have involved very challenging and difficult questions and dynamics. This 'union' would have had to happen at both a personal and professional level. And yet, we should be cautious using the word 'union' here since when describing his encounter with England as his host culture, he vividly mentions that 'I was bewildered by the English' (Laungani, 2002: 387) and

> at a personal level, I was opposed to the idea of learning to become like them... I had no desire to become a metaphorical English clone... For me, it would have meant a serious cultural compromise, an assault on my own notions of my 'self' and my 'identity', which I had developed, rightly or wrongly, over the years during the course of living in India. And, more importantly, such a compromise would have meant a sad loss of my own moral integrity. (Laungani, 2002: 388)

This personal stance taken by Laungani is supported in the literature by Berry (1997) who found that those who adapt a bicultural identity generally show a better psychological adaptation than those who assimilate to the new culture, separate from the new culture or identify neither with the new culture nor their former culture. (Arnett, 2002). Further, in an interview with William West, Pittu Laungani notes, 'I found it terribly difficult to get to know them (the English). I found it difficult to distinguish between levity and seriousness, between jest and truth, praise and censure, affection and rejection. I could not befriend them. They seemed 'insular', 'unapproachable' and 'self contained' (West, 2004: 431). He goes on to note that: 'Living in a foreign country, I soon realised, was like fighting a lone battle on several fronts: the weather, the climate, the preserved and processed food, the strange customs and conventions, the patterns of day-to-day life and, of course, the people' Pittu Laungani (2002a: 387). Also, after staying long enough in the British culture, he came to realize that:

> ...in order to relate to the English and thus get on in a reasonable but superficial manner with them, it would be I who would be expected to make all the adjustments. Not they. In other words, I would have to learn to become assimilated into their culture. (Laungani, 2002a: 388)

Talking about such adjustments, Bochner (1982) originally articulated four potential coping strategies that could be chosen by a person living in a new culture. These are (as slightly modified and cited in Laungani, 2004a: 49–50): First, the person may hastily reject the values of the adopted culture on intuitive, experiential or even irrational grounds. The hiatus created by rejecting the dominant values of the host culture is filled by extolling the virtues of their own culture.

Second, such people may choose to denigrate and reject their own culture. In so doing, they may turn away from their own parents and despise their ancestral country of origin, looking upon it and its people as being non-progressive, backward, superstitious, repressive and even primitive.

Third, they may vacillate between two cultural norms, unable to work out the means by which these two may be reconciled. Painfully aware that they belong neither to the host cultural group, nor to their own cultural group, such people may feel marginalized. This may result in a state of perpetual conflict and uncertainty concerning their own ethnic identities, potentially leading to a sense of 'identity confusion' and consequently to an 'identity crisis' (Lago, 2008).

Finally, they may genuinely attempt to integrate into the new culture by acquiring a set of compatible and complementary value systems from their indigenous and from their adopted culture, which would lend meaning and significance to their lives. In other words, they may acquire the rationality and the wisdom to appreciate the positive values of both cultures, and bring about a *mentally* and *spiritually* healthy integration of their identities.

It might even be possible to achieve the state implied by Terence's 'Heauton Timorumenos' in 163 BC where he states 'I am a (hu)-man, I count nothing human foreign to me'. Given the flow of worldwide migration throughout history, there is considerable evidence to suggest that, of course, people have the capacity to transcend their cultures, to live successfully elsewhere. However, it is clear that not all migrants achieve full bicultural competence, and for many, a long-term, (indeed trans-generational) sense of 'not-at-homeness' and alienation may be experienced in the new culture. This also led some to view such an experience as a mental health condition as described below.

## 'UPROOTING DISORDER'?

Though the term 'culture shock' has entered into common parlance in recent decades, two theorists, Zwingmann and Gunn coined the term 'uprooting disorder' in 1983. In their view, the social, emotional and psychological challenges experienced in the process of changing cultures were sufficient to cause (psychiatric) psychological disease. The term, 'uprooting disorder' was thus suggested as a general diagnostic category to apply to those who suffered from mental ill health as a consequence of moving to a new culture. Stimulated by this model and developed further through our reflections we have begun to theoretically develop the following hypotheses.

If a person experiences a difficult (traumatizing, abusive and neglected) upbringing, particularly in their early years, then this difficult early experience might be re-stimulated by the transitional demands of moving to a new culture later in their lives. New, demanding or troubling experiences in the new cultural milieu could further exacerbate this re-stimulation of the earlier distress experienced in childhood and, the implications of these experiences could be further dramatized if the troubled person cannot now easily return to their culture of origin, perhaps because of political, educational, relational and vocational limitations. The sequence of events might also deeply unsettle the person's own sense of 'at-homeness'; that is, it becomes difficult to know where one feels 'at home'. As Lynne Eaker has noted: 'change is one of the greatest stress factors of our time' (Lago and Shipton, 1994). We now explore some possible factors related to moving towards resolution potential.

## CULTURE AND RESILIENCE

Gunnestad has explored the concept of (psychological) resilience and its formation in children. Combining the work of different theorists, Gunnestad hypothesizes three different protective factors that support personal resilience. He lists them as (Gunnestad, 2006: 2):

*Network factors—external support*
*Abilities and skills—internal support*
*Meaning, values and faith—existential support*

Importantly, in relation to this chapter, all three of the above factors are intrinsic to culture. It affects the way we form relationships, and the meanings we assign to them; it determines which skills and activities are appreciated and finally, it provides the existential context of meanings and values in which we are steeped.

For people who move to a new culture, their capacity for resilience in the face of new challenges will depend, to some extent, on their capacity to carry this quality over from their cultural origins and to sustain it within the new cultural milieu. Inevitably, different cultures have different mechanisms for the inculcation of resilience factors in childhood. We can see, here, how critical and important it is, then, for therapists who are consulted by those clients from other cultural origins, to be comfortable, competent, confident and principled practitioners. (See the later section on 'The working together principle' for an expanded articulation of this point.) If the therapist proves not able, not culturally sensitive or not principled, the presenting vulnerability of the client may be further weakened and their resilience pushed to very low levels of coping as a consequence of therapy, a terrible outcome indeed. Gunnestad also cites the work of Stutman et al. (2002) who claim that people who master the rules and norms of their new culture without abandoning their own cultural and linguistic origins and values seem more resilient than those who just keep their own culture and cannot either adjust to the new one or become completely acculturated within it. (This is in accordance with the work of Bochner, (1982) cited above.) Biculturalism also requires, in Gunnestad's conceptualizations, 'safe and good relationships in both cultures' (Gunnestad, 2006: 15). Here again we are alerted to the crucial importance of the potential effect of the therapist assisting a client in transition between cultures. If this therapeutic relationship proves not to be 'good' for any reason, the client's progress towards successful achievement of bicultural competence is further hindered and damaged.

## VALUES CHANGE

Obviously, there are a number of subtle changes potentially occurring in the value system of an individual due to migration from one culture to another, since such individuals are inevitably subjected to two, if not more cultural influences that affect their identity, (for an example referring to India and England, see Laungani, 1999). By values, we refer to the currently held normative expectations underlying individual and social conduct (Laungani, 1995).

With reference to the therapeutic relationship, the questions that arise here are:

- To what extent can there be a sharing of common values between therapist and client, and
- In what ways, if there are any, might client and therapist transcend the cultural boundaries in counselling and psychotherapy?

Laungani discusses the contrast between Western and Eastern values underpinning therapy and concludes by answering the above questions with 'a cautious yes' that depends on a number of factors that have, as a common thread, a kind of 'working together principle' (Laungani, 2004b: 206). Our different experiences lead us to conclude, cautiously, that this mutual effort and commitment, (between therapist and client) to working together through all the challenges occurring in that journey of cultural adjustment and identity integration is of paramount importance in such therapeutic work.

## 'THE WORKING TOGETHER PRINCIPLE': THE VALUE OF THERAPEUTIC RELATIONSHIP

It is a well known finding that metastudies of the success outcomes of counselling/psychotherapy consistently point to the quality of relationship between the therapist and the client, as experienced by the client, as the second highest factor, accounting for 30 per cent of therapeutic success (Lambert, 1992; Lambert et al., 1986). This is acknowledged by Spinelli (2007) who talks of the research-based 'pivotal significance of the relationship and its importance in therapeutic relations'.

The primary factor in successful therapeutic outcome is known as 'client extra therapeutic variables', accounting for some 40 per cent of success outcome (these being factors unique to the client and his/her environment). Disappointingly for many therapists wedded to their theoretical positions, theory only accounts for approximately 15 per cent of the therapeutic success outcome! This is evident from the following finding: '*Outcome research is consistent in its assertion that effective change is related to generic factors rather than the intervention of a particular modality*' (BACP, 2007: 48)'. Known as the 'dodo bird effect' (Stubbs and Bozarth, 1994), the article by Stiles et al. (2006) has yet again demonstrated the equivalence of successful therapeutic outcomes across a spectrum of different theoretical approaches (despite non equivalent theories and techniques) and the above statement (in italics) reflects these findings.

Given the vital importance of relationship as an underpinning principle of psychotherapeutic endeavour, many writers have attempted to explore the implications of and barriers to therapeutic relationship formation in 'cross-cultural' therapy (D'Ardenne and Mahtani, 1999; Lago, 2006a; Moodley et al., 2004; Pedersen, 1987). With potentially such different views, understandings and experiences of the world, the culturally different client and therapist dyad face the considerable challenges of working with one another, with achieving a satisfactory level of communication and mutual understanding and with forming a sufficiently trustworthy relationship that facilitates the client's exploration of previously painful experiences.

Various research initiatives have attempted to highlight the different conducive elements within the cross-cultural therapeutic relationship. These include:

- Thompson and Jenal (1994), in their research on white therapist/black client relationships found that 'race-avoidant' therapists had shorter and less successful therapeutic relationships than those therapists who were not only able to openly acknowledge the differences between themselves and their clients, but also be comfortable with them.
- In a further corroborative piece of research conducted in the USA, it was discovered that therapy proved more successful when the therapist and the client were able to discuss openly the client's ethnic identity (Carter, 1995).
- Extensive research is provided by Carter (1995) to show that the levels of development of identity awareness within therapists can be critical to the outcome of the therapy process—where therapists are at the same stage

or at least one stage of development ahead of their client, then it is more likely that there will be a more successful outcome to the therapy. As Carter has noted, it is not your ethnicity per se that matters (in therapy) but your psychological resolution to it that is critical.

- Some modest research in the early 1990s pointed to possible effectiveness for therapist–client matching but this work has been substantially surpassed by the recognition that what is of most importance is that the counsellor is 'culturally sensitive' to the client. These findings are supported by evidence gathered by Dutch psychologists at Utrecht University (Knipscheer and Kleber, 2004). Various definitions of what constitutes 'cultural sensitivity' are elusive though several authors, (D'Ardenne and Mahtani, 1999; Lago, 2007; Lago, 2010; Ridley, 1995; Sue et al., 1992) elucidate desirable key elements of knowledge, skills and attitudes.

It seems reasonable to hypothesize from the above section on therapeutic relationship that the cross-cultural therapist needs to be a sound practitioner with the capacity to communicate creatively and effectively within the boundaries of good therapeutic practice. He/she needs to be committed to understanding their cross-cultural therapeutic relationships. Additionally, we surmise that there is greater likelihood of good therapeutic outcome when therapists are comfortable and aware of who they are, as persons within themselves and as subjects located within culture and society (Lago and Haugh, 2006c).

## CONCLUSION

We suggest that we might learn from the legacy of Pittu Laungani's work, as we, ourselves, learnt from him directly. Coming back to the tortoise's shell, we are reminded of his wish to maintain his 'birthright', within his host 'home', when he says in his last book:

> At a personal level, I might add that although I have lived in England for more years of my life than I have in India, there is within me an 'Indian-ness', which I can no more discard than a tortoise its shell—nor would I like to! My refusal to transform myself into a compliant English 'clone' often gets me into hot waters. But I would rather the defiance than the surrender. For surrender would mean the loss of my 'birthright' and with it my moral integrity. (Laungani, 2007: 49)

Laungani was an outstanding example of bicultural competence, a state that he managed to embody and maintain with rigour and integrity, without consciously tilting the balance in either direction of his persona, but safeguarding instead an authenticity of identity.

# REFERENCES

Adler, P. (1987). Culture shock and the cross-cultural learning experience. In L. F. Luce and E. S. Smith (Eds). *Towards internationalism* (pp. 24–35). Cambridge: Newbury.

Arnett, J. J. (2002). The psychology of globalization. *American Psychologist, 57*(10), 774–783.

Berry, J. W. (1997). Immigration, acculturation and adaptation. *International Journal of Applied Psychology, 46*(1), 5–34.

Bochner, S. (Ed.). (1982). *Cultures in contact: Studies in cross-cultural interaction.* Oxford: Pergamon.

British Association for Counselling and Psychotherapy (BACP). (2007). The future of counselling and psychotherapy: Responding to the government agenda, *Therapy Today, 18*(1), 47–48.

Carter, R. (1995). *The influence of race and racial identity in psychotherapy: Towards a racially inclusive model.* Westport, CT: Greenwood.

Christodoulidi, F. (2006). Interview with Pittu Laungani. London. Unpublished (October).

D'Ardenne, P. and Mahtani, A. (1999). *Transcultural counselling in action.* London: Sage Publications.

Furnham, A. and Bochner, S. (1986). *Culture shock: Psychological reactions to unfamiliar environments.* London: Methuen.

Gunnestad, A. (2006). Resilience in a cross-cultural perspective: How resilience is generated in different cultures. *Journal of Intercultural Communication, 11*. Retrieved 20 June 2007 from http://www.immi.se/Intercultural/nr11/gunnestad.htm

Hofstede, G. (1980). *Cultures consequences: International differences in work related values.* Beverley Hills, CA: Sage Publications.

Kim, Y. Y. (1988). *Communication and cross-cultural adaptation.* Clevedon: Multilingual Matters.

Knipscheer, J. and Kleber, R. (2004). Research cited in *Counselling and Psychotherapy Journal, 15*(6), 17. Rugby: British Association for Counselling and Psychotherapy.

Koser, K. (2007). *International migration: A very short introduction.* Oxford: Oxford University Press.

Lago, C. (2005). Personal interview with Pittu Laungani. Unpublished.

———. (2006a). *Race, culture and counselling: The ongoing challenge.* Maidenhead: Open University/McGraw-Hill.

———. (2006b). Pittu Laungani in conversation with William West: personal reflections, (some) considered thoughts and emotional impacts. *British Journal for Guidance and Counselling, 34*(3), 391–401.

———. (2007). Counselling across difference and diversity. In M. Cooper, M. O'Hara, G. Proctor and G. Wyatt, (Eds), *Handbook of Person Centred Counselling and Psychotherapy* (pp. 251–265). Basingstoke: Palgrave-MacMillan.

———. (2010). On developing our empathic capacities to work inter-culturally and inter-ethnically: attempting a map for personal and professional development. *Psychotherapy and Politics International, 8*(1), 73–85.

Lago, C. and Haugh, S. (2006c). White counsellor racial identity: The unacknowledged, unknown, unaware aspect of self in relationship. In G. Proctor, M. Cooper, P. Sanders and B. Malcolm (Eds), *The politicisation of the Person Centred Approach: An agenda for social change* (pp. 198–214). Ross-on-Wye, UK: PCCS Books.

Lago, C. and Shipton, G. (1994). *Personal tutoring in action: A handbook for staff involved in working with and supporting students.* Sheffield: Sheffield University Counselling Service.

Lago, C. O. (2008). Sozio-Kulturelle Identitat und Rolle in der Psychotherapie. In M. Tuczai, G. Stumm, D. Kimbacher and N. Nemeskeri (Eds), *Personzentrierte psychotherapie: grundlagen, ansatxe, anwendungen* (pp. 205–223). Wien: Krammer.

Lambert, M. (1992). Psychotherapy outcome research. In J. C. Norcross and M. R. Goldfried (Eds), *Handbook of psychotherapy integration* (pp. 94–129). New York: Basic Books.

Lambert, M. J., Shapiro, D. A. and Bergin, A. E. (1986). The effectiveness of psychotherapy. In S. L. Garfield and A.E. Bergin (Eds), *Handbook of psychotherapy and behaviour change* (pp. 157–211). New York: John Wiley.

Laungani, P. (1995). Stress in Eastern and Western cultures. In J. Brebner, E. Greenglass, P. Laungani and A. O'Roark (Eds), *Stress and Emotion* (pp. 265–280). Washington, DC: Taylor and Francis.

———. (1999). Culture and identity: Implications for counselling. In S. Palmer and P. Laungani (Eds), *Counselling in a multicultural society* (pp. 35–70). London: Sage Publications.

———. (2002a). Cross-cultural psychology: A handmaiden to mainstream Western psychology. *Counselling Psychology Quarterly, 15*(4), 385–397.

———. (2002b). The counselling interview: First impressions. *Counselling Psychology Quarterly, 15*(1), 107–113.

———. (2004a). *Asian perspectives in counselling and psychotherapy.* London: Brunner-Routledge.

———. (2004b). Counselling and therapy in a multi-cultural setting. *Counselling Psychology Quarterly, 17*(2), 195–207.

———. (2007). *Understanding cross-cultural psychology: Eastern and Western perspectives.* New Delhi: Sage Publications.

Leong and Chou. (2002). Counselling International Students and Sojourners. In P. Pedersen et al. (Eds), *Counselling Across Cultures*, 185–208. Thousand Oaks, CA: Sage Publications.

Madison, G. (2006). Existential migration: Conceptualising out of the experiential depths of choosing to leave 'home'. *Existential Analysis, 17*(2), 238–260.

Moodley, R., Lago, C. and Talahite, A. (Eds). (2004). *Carl Rogers counsels a black client: Race and culture in person-centred counselling.* Ross-on-Wye, UK: PCCS Books.

Palmer, S. (2007). Obituary: Pittu Laungani: Eastern psychologist at odds with western counselling methods. *Guardian Unlimited.* Retrieved 26 June, 2007, from http://www.guardian.co.uk/obituaries/story/0,,2111306,00.html

Palmer S. and Laungani, P. (Eds). (1999). *Counselling in a multicultural society.* London: Sage Publications.

Pedersen, P. (Ed.). (1987). *Handbook of cross-cultural counselling and therapy.* Preager: New York.

Pope-Davis, D. B. and Coleman, H. L. K., (Eds). (1997). *Multicultural counselling competencies.* Thousand Oaks, CA: Sage Publications.

Ridley, C. (1995). *Overcoming unintentional racism in counselling and therapy: A practitioners guide to intentional intervention.* Thousand Oaks, CA: Sage Publications.

Schram, J. L. and Lauver, P. J. (1988). Alienation in international students. *Journal of College Student Development, 29*, 146–150.

Spinelli, E. (2007). The therapeutic relationship: A view from existential psychotherapy. *Therapy Today, 18*(1), 11–14.

Stiles, W., Barkham, M., Twigg, E., Mellor-Clark, J. and Cooper, M. (2006). Effectiveness of cognitive-behavioural, person-centred and psychodynamic therapies as practiced in U.K. N.H.S. settings. *Psychological Medicine, 36*(4), 555–566.

Storti, C. (2003). *The art of crossing cultures.* Maine: Intercultural Press.

———. (2003). *The art of coming home.* Boston: Intercultural Press.

Stubbs, J. P. and Bozarth, J. D. (1994). The dodo bird revisited: A qualitative study of psychotherapy efficacy research. *Journal of Applied and Preventive Psychology, 3*(2), 109–120.

Stutman, S., Baruch, R., Grotberg, E. and Rathore, Z. (2002). *Resilience in Latino youth.* Working paper, Institute for Mental Health Initiatives. Washington DC: The George Washington University.

Sue, D. W., Arrendo, P. and McDavis, R. J. (1992). Multicultural counselling competencies and standards: A call to the profession. *Journal of Counselling and Development, 70*(2), 477–486.

Thompson, C. E. and Jenal, S. T. (1994). Interracial and intraracial quasi-counselling interactions when counselors avoid discussing race. *Journal of Counselling Psychology, 41*(4), 484–491.

West, W. (2004). Pittu Laungani in conversation with William West. *British Journal of Guidance and Counselling, 32*(3), 419–435.

West, W. and McLeod, J. (2003). Cultural landscapes in counselling and psychotherapy: Introduction to the Theme Section. *Counselling and Psychotherapy Research, 3*(2), 83–85.

Zwingmann, C. A. and Gunn, D. G. (1983). *Uprooting and health: Psycho-social problems of students from abroad.* Geneva: World Health Organization, Division of Mental Health.

# 18

# Transcending East/West Boundaries: Pittu Laungani and Cross-cultural Counselling

*Maya Hammer and Waseem Alladin*

## INTRODUCTION

**During** his career as a Senior Research Fellow at Manchester University, Pittu Laungani published extensively in the area of cross-cultural psychology.[1] While many of his eloquent and insightful papers discussed the differences between Eastern[2] and Western[3] cultural values (Laungani, 2002a, 2004b), and the subsequent impact on psychological research and practice (Laungani, 2002b, 2004c), a frequent theme was his use of his own personal experiences (Laungani, 2003), which he shared freely and wrote about sensitively in the hope that it would benefit not only professionals but the public at large. Pittu Laungani (2002a) explained that when he moved from India to England as a young man, he faced an unexpected culture shock. He relayed difficulty in understanding British humour and found himself perplexed by interactions and relationships that were reserved, detached and unemotional. Through his transition from growing up as a child in India to living and working in England, Pittu Laungani came to understand significant differences between Eastern and Western cultures.

Drawing on Pittu Laungani's personal experience as well as his prolific body of work on cross-cultural counselling, we can explore issues that arise at the intersection between East and West in therapeutic encounters. This chapter will examine Pittu Laungani's perspective on such cultural differences and how they are played out in the context of counselling an Eastern client in the West. A review of

Pittu Laungani's recommendations for strengthening clinical practice and research in order to provide successful therapy across cultures will follow. But first, we begin with an overview of Pittu Laungani's perspective on the differences between counselling and psychotherapy in the East and the West.

## COUNSELLING AND PSYCHOTHERAPY IN THE EAST AND WEST

The cultural differences that Pittu Laungani experienced when he moved from India to England reflect differences in Eastern and Western cultural values, for example, collectivism versus individualism. This section will briefly highlight his views on cultural differences with respect to values and the nature of the therapeutic relationship. For a more in-depth review of differences between Eastern and Western cultures and how they impact therapy, see Laungani (2004a).

According to Pittu Laungani (2004a, 2004b), in the West, individualism, materialism and secularism permeate the healing relationship between counsellor and therapist, resulting in transactions that are horizontal or non-hierarchical, and generally secular. Clients are viewed as equal in ability to the therapist and are expected and encouraged to solve their own problems. Therapists enact the role of a neutral facilitator or 'sounding board' for clients to examine and address their issues (Laungani, 2004b). Further, it is common in the West to subscribe to a secular notion of free will. Therefore, therapists support clients to pursue or determine their fate according to the choices they make, bereft of divine intervention (Laungani, 2004b).

In comparison, Pittu Laungani (2004a, 2004b) indicated that Eastern values are embedded in collectivism and spirituality. Typically, healing relationships in the East are hierarchical and directive versus the egalitarian, non-directive therapeutic relationships common in the West (Laungani, 2004b, 2004c). In India, for example, healers and practitioners are understood to be imbued with wisdom that they impart to those who seek their services. This type of hierarchical relationship is known in the East as the guru–disciple (teacher–student) approach to healing and learning (Hoch, 1974; Kakar, 1982; Roland, 1988 cited in Laungani, 2004b). Within this hierarchical relationship, the healer or the therapist's role is like a teacher and/or spiritual guide (Laungani, 2004b), a guru who sheds lights on problems, or at least provides suggestions for overcoming problems. The healing relationship is expected to be directive in that the therapist will provide advice or solutions to problems.

Another aspect inherent to therapeutic relationships in the East is the infusion of faith and religion (Laungani, 2004b, 2004c). In Eastern culture, spirituality and religion are infused into all aspects of life. It is common for clients to follow religious precepts, be they Hindu, Muslim or Sikh, to name some of the religions practiced in India. In India, there is a strong belief in fate, for example, known as the will of Allah or the workings of the law of Karma (Laungani, 2002a; 2004b). Such spiritual values are embedded in the process of healing, as both client and therapist believe that life is ordained and predetermined or bound by fate (Laungani, 2004b). Whereas a therapeutic relationship in the West is generally egalitarian, non-hierarchical and secular in nature, a therapeutic relationship in the East is typically hierarchical, directive and suffused with spirituality (Laungani, 2004b).

Values of secularism and individualism that permeate the egalitarian, non-directive and secular nature of therapy in the West lie in stark contrast to Eastern values of spiritualism and collectivism that lead to more directive and hierarchical therapeutic relationships often bound by religious precepts (Laungani, 2004b). Therefore, Pittu Laungani suggested that a Western therapist may be unable to help a client from the East (Laungani, 2004b). Western-European psychotherapy is based on cultural and religious values, and European philosophy (Bhugra, 1996; Fernando, 2003; Sue et al., 1992), which may not resonate with individuals rooted in Eastern values and philosophy. The scholarship on multicultural counselling both accepts cultural differences while promulgating the notion that culturally sensitive therapists can successfully work with clients of varying ethnic backgrounds (Day-Vines et al., 2007; Sue and Sue, 1999; Vontress et al., 1999). The next section will explore Pittu Laungani's perspective on the potential success of cross-cultural counselling.

## COUNSELLING AN EASTERN CLIENT IN THE WEST

In the paper Counselling and therapy in a multi-cultural setting (Laungani, 2004b), Pittu Laungani depicted Eastern and Western world views in the context of psychotherapy, which were discussed previously. The following vignette is a hypothetical case of a Muslim client from India who sought counselling from a Western therapist. It illustrates Pittu Laungani's scepticism with regards to the effectiveness of Western therapy for Eastern clients:

*Client:* Well, Doctor *Sahib*, what should I do? (*He wrings his hands in a gesture of despair and looks imploringly at the therapist.*)

*Therapist:* (*With a mask of neutrality over his expressionless face*) What do you think *you* should do?

*Client:* (*Rather peeved, even angry*) Every time I am asking you a question, you are throwing the question back at me!

*Therapist:* Oh, am I?

*Client:* (*Exasperated*) You have done it again! Look Doctor *Sahib*. You are the expert. I have come to you for help. If I knew how to help myself, surely I would not come to see you.

*Therapist:* (*Not in the least bit put out*) Mr Ahmed, it is really for you to decide what you should do. I cannot decide for you.

*Client:* (*Acutely disturbed and even bewildered*) I understand. But I am not asking you to *decide* for me, Doctor. I am asking your opinion. I have come to you for help. I don't understand why you should not help me. You should be guiding me. Helping me. Showing me the way. I am like a Bedouin, lost in the sand dunes of Arabia. But you don't want to help me to decide what I should do.

*Therapist:* (*Defensively*) That is not quite true.

*Client:* When I go to see my GP, he tells me what I should do, what medicines I should take, how long for, and so on—and then leaves it to me to decide whether I will take them or not. But you don't even tell me what I *should* do! (*Looks at the therapist*) If you were a brain surgeon, would you be asking me to perform my own operation?

*Therapist:* (*In spite of himself*) No, of course not!

*Client:* What's the difference? So if you were a brain surgeon you would perform brain surgery on me. You are a surgeon of the mind and yet you will not perform psychosurgery—which you can!

*Therapist:* (*Reluctantly gets drawn into an argument*) It is not my role to tell you what you should do, or even what you ought to do. My role, as I see it, is to interpret, or throw some light on your problems, to help you to see your problems.

*Client:* I am not asking you to tell me what my problems are. I *know* what my problems are! I am asking for advice, *how to overcome my problems.*

*Therapist:* (*Remains silent*)

*Client:* 'You know what I think, doctor. (*Pointing his index finger to his forehead*) It is fate. It is Allah's will. It is my *kismet*, my '*taqdeer*'. What was to happen has happened. Who can fight against one's fate, against what is written! (*Here, he quotes the well-known couplet from the Persian poet Omar Khayyam*: 'The moving finger writes; and, having writ, moves on: nor all thy piety nor wit shall lure it back to cancel half a line, nor all thy tears wash out a word of it.')

*Therapist:* (*Totally at a loss as he hears the poem, which his client has recited in Persian: sits in embarrassed silence, unable to decide what he should say.*) (Laungani, 2004b: 199–200).

This vignette demonstrated how Eastern and Western expectations of therapy are seemingly incompatible, resulting in more of an argument than a therapeutic discussion. As stated:

> Even without any specific knowledge as to the nature of the problem, one can see that there is a gulf between the client and the therapist. Both of them are locked into their own private cultural worlds. They are either unable or unwilling to step out of them.
>
> Even the manner in which they relate to each other reveals their unique cultural biases. This is not an unusual therapeutic situation: and one can see that there is a genuine clash of cultural values between the therapist and the client. (Laungani, 2004b: 200)

The cultural clash that Pittu Laungani described can be examined with respect to different expectations of the therapeutic relationship. The client expected a vertical or hierarchical relationship with his therapist, which he demonstrated by demanding guidance and help from the therapist in order to address his problem: 'Well, Dr *Sahib*, what should I do?', and 'You are the expert. I have come to you for help' (Laungani, 2004b: 199). The Western therapist, on the other hand, rooted in an egalitarian understanding of the therapeutic relationship, proceeded to work in a fashion that was non-hierarchical. He stated: 'What do you think *you* should do?', and '…it is really for you to decide what you should do. I cannot decide for you' (Laungani, 2004b: 199). The therapist's neutral deflection of the client's search for guidance left the client confused and frustrated, he exclaimed: 'Every time I am asking you a question you are throwing the question back at me!' (Laungani, 2004b: 199). The client did not comprehend the therapist's neutral, distant stance which was adopted so that the client could uncover solutions to his own problem. The client interpreted the therapist's demeanour as insensitive when he stated: 'You should be guiding me. Helping me. Showing me the way' (Laungani, 2004b: 199). The distant, yet equal-footed approach contrasted the client's desire for a more didactic therapeutic relationship common to healing relationships in the East.

Near the end of the vignette, the client pronounced an understanding of his predicament by way of divine guidance. He indicated: 'It is fate. It is Allah's will…Who can fight against one's fate…' (Laungani, 2004b: 200). The client found solace from the notion that his current predicament was meant to occur, in concordance with his fate. This reflects the manner in which spirituality is embodied in the East, with a strong belief in a higher order or fate.[4] The Western therapist, rooted in a world view that values secularism and free will, was rendered speechless by virtue of his ignorance with regards to Eastern faith and wisdom. Moreover, the therapist was either unable or unwilling to engage in the meaning and metaphor of the Persian poem recited by the client (Laungani, 2004b).

Pittu Laungani (2004b) proposed that words and metaphors are the medium for communication in a therapy session. This hypothetical therapeutic encounter was, therefore, unsuccessful because the Eastern client and the Western therapist misunderstood the meaning of each other's words. They applied contrasting interpretations to each other's method of communication based on their respective cultural values that manifest in differing relationships as described previously.

Pittu Laungani (2004b) explained that in this encounter, the client and the therapist were faced with a '...*cultural crossroads*, with no meeting ground in sight. They appear to have reached an impasse. For not only have they encountered linguistic, spiritual, and religious difficulties but have displayed serious cross-cultural differences that impede progress' (Laungani, 2004b: 200). The therapeutic impasse, according to Pittu Laungani, occurred because of the distinct and discrepant cultural contexts in which the client and therapist were embedded. In light of the value differences with respect to the nature of the therapeutic relationship as well as spiritual beliefs, Pittu Laungani proposed that the white Western therapist appeared ill-equipped to provide meaningful support to the Indian client.[5] Further, this hypothetical case reflects current experiences of Eastern clients seeking counselling and psychotherapy in the West. Researchers observed that South Asian[6] clients in the West experience premature termination or poor outcomes of therapy (Duran, 1990; Juthani, 2001; Kumar et al., 2005; Moodley, 1999).

Nevertheless, in spite of Pittu Laungani's depiction of the therapeutic impasse with the Western therapist and the Eastern client, his optimism and hope rendered a curiosity as to whether such an impasse could be overcome. Pittu Laungani (2004b) posed the question: 'Is there a way by which one might transcend the cultural boundaries in counselling and psychotherapy?' (Laungani, 2004b: 206). Pittu Laungani cautiously responded to this question, a reflection of hope tempered by realism. He suggested ways in which therapists in the East and the West could work together to surpass cultural boundaries within counselling and psychotherapy contexts. The following will elaborate on Pittu Laungani's first two suggestions, which advised practitioners in the East and the West to collaborate in an exchange of cultural knowledge and develop training courses to implement cultural knowledge in counselling and therapy.

## TRANSCENDING CULTURAL BOUNDARIES IN COUNSELLING AND PSYCHOTHERAPY

Pittu Laungani (2004b) probed beyond cultural differences in search for ways in which such differences could be surpassed within the context of counselling and psychotherapy. He devised recommendations for practitioners in the East and the West to learn from and value their respective cultures. His first recommendation stated: 'The East and the West would need to meet as joint and equal partners and work together to promote a clearer understanding of differences and similarities in the value systems of Eastern and Western cultures' (Laungani, 2004b: 206).

The supposition is that therapy cannot be successful across cultures without a common ground of understanding between the client and the therapist (Laungani, 2004b). This was evident in the hypothetical case of the Indian client and the Western therapist discussed previously, and in practice Eastern clients in the West report ineffective treatment and poor outcomes (Duran, 1990; Juthani, 2001; Kumar et al., 2005; Moodley, 1999). Therefore, an understanding and acceptance of cultural value systems could create a foundation for a meeting ground between the East and the West in counselling and therapy contexts.

For therapists who wish to understand cultural value systems there should be no problem. However, for reaching a level of acceptance of cultural value systems requires more than good intentions. The multicultural literature, for example, talks about race and the development of racial identity (Fernando, 2003; Sue, 2003). The issue of racism needs tackling and including in international counselling and therapy contexts. Another important point is that a bi-polar characterization of a 'typical' Eastern client and a Western (trained) therapist can be seen as being stereotypical. For example, Sue (1978) and Sue and Sue (1999) proposed a general theory which places clients and therapists on two dimensions—on locus of control and locus of responsibility—which has profound implications for what he called 'the elimination of cultural oppression in counselling'. These are issues Laungani did not include or address and we comment on their importance in our conclusion.

Nevertheless, Laungani's recommendation for equal partnerships to disseminate cultural values could lay the foundation for a meeting ground between the East and the West. Revisiting the case of the Indian client and the Western therapist, if the therapist had an awareness of Eastern cultural values, including the hierarchical world view, belief in fate and the will of Allah, he could have modified his role to meet the client's expectations. For instance, the therapist could address the fact that in the West, therapeutic relationships are generally non-hierarchical and non-directive. He could adopt a more directive approach with the client, or suggest the client contact a religious leader or traditional healer from his community from whom he could receive advice (Moodley and West, 2005). In addition, the therapist could support the client's belief in the will of Allah and expression through poetry (Inayat, 2005). Both client and therapist would need to be open and accepting of each other's cultural backgrounds and value systems as valid ways of being in the world and doing things in the world, in contrast to the tendency to regard things Western as automatically superior and things Eastern as necessarily inferior. This would enable them to understand each other, and hopefully result in a meaningful therapeutic relationship.

Subsequent to the recommendation for mutual education and understanding across Eastern and Western cultures, Laungani recommended the development of training programmes to address multiculturalism. He wrote: 'There is a paramount need to design intensive, meaningful and relevant training courses, which would serve the mutual interests of therapists both from the West and the East when dealing with multicultural issues' (Laungani, 2004b: 206).

In the West, specifically in countries such as England, Canada and the United States, there is a growing need for multicultural counselling in response not just to its ethnic minority communities but in recognition that not everybody who is 'British', Canadian or North American, for example, perceives and relates to the modal (White) British, (White) Canadian or (White) North American way of life. Training for Western-trained therapists should include learning about cultural values and challenges facing new immigrants with respect to living in a foreign country.

In addition, Laungani (2002b) promoted the acceptance of indigenous forms of healing when seeing clients rooted in traditional systems of health. It is common for South Asian mental health clients to seek traditional healing, such as herbs or religious healers, alongside conventional treatment (Dein and Sembhi, 2001; Hilton et al., 2001; Moodley and West, 2005). Moodley (1999) described the case of an Indian client who consulted a *vaidya* (Ayurvedic Physician[7]) while attending psychotherapy in England. This type of collaboration between Eastern healers and Western-trained psychologists has been recommended by several researchers in order to enable the provision of culturally sensitive care among South Asian clients in the West (Hodge, 2004; Kumar et al., 2005; Laungani, 2005; Sandhu, 2004; Van Hoecke, 2006). Thus, Western-trained counsellors and therapists would benefit from training courses, as suggested by Laungani, to enable them to work successfully with clients from the East.

In the East, specifically in India, however, training courses would need to address concerns pertaining to cultural issues that have emerged within the current state of social change and a growing economy. Arulmani (2007) pointed out that, although there are many traditional forms of psychology in India (for example, from Vedic and Buddhist scriptures), some of them may be outdated. He cited the case of a rural family in South India whose daughter moved to Bangalore to study and subsequently work in the Information Technology sector. The family sought therapy as they were devastated when their daughter disconnected herself from them and relinquished traditions from the village (Arulmani, 2007). This case example demonstrates contemporary issues prevalent in India, including rural–urban migration, traditional versus modern proclivities and gender issues. Arulmani (2007) suggested that the challenge for psychologists in India is to draw from traditional forms of Indian psychology while addressing modern concerns. Further, Arulmani (2007) proposed that psychology programmes in India move beyond Western psychology in order to render psychology relevant to the Indian context, a viewpoint shared by Laungani (2002b), and the well-known Indian psychologist Durganand Sinha (1993). Therefore, the development of training courses in India would need to equip counsellors and therapists in the East to address issues related to contemporary issues such as modernization and migration.

It appears that Pittu Laungani may not always have been aware of some of the more specialized or non-mainstream views in counselling and clinical psychology [Sue (2003), who in the American context, talks about 'overcoming our racism' and about 'white privilege' and why equal opportunities legislation only masks the issues], some of which could have added an even greater impact to some of the profound issues he was raising. Further, as one of us (Alladin, 1989) has pointed out, it is racism and the embedded notions of white supremacy, in transcultural counselling and psychotherapy that is the problem and not culture per se. This is why, for example, Eastern psychological views and theories have often been ignored, undervalued or even regarded as inferior to Western (American dominated) psychology.

Nevertheless, Pittu Laungani's recommendations for training programmes to address multicultural issues in the West is particularly relevant in order to prevent traumatic loss of identity and loss of self among Eastern immigrants. In the East, knowledge and training would promote the development of meaningful and relevant psychological services. These recommendations for cultural knowledge exchange and training courses emerged from Pittu Laungani's personal experience with culture shock and the risk of losing his identity, as well as his desire to promote mental health and healing across the Eastern-Western divide. Whether or not these recommendations will bridge the chasm of cultural differences will depend on the dedication, tenacity and compassion among practitioners in both cultures.

## CONCLUSION

Pittu Laungani's discerning and forward-thinking papers examined the cultural differences between the East and the West that emerge during counselling and psychotherapy. In addition, Pittu Laungani offered suggestions for counsellors and psychotherapists to address these cultural differences and perhaps transcend them.

While Pittu Laungani's work was on the vanguard of cross-cultural psychology, it was limited by his focus on Indian clients and therapists. Obviously, he was not seeking to offer views on a universal psychology (see Marsella (1998) for a proposal for a global psychology, and Marsella and Pedersen (2004) for a proposal internationalizing psychology) but could speak from personal and professional experiences. Nevertheless, it seems to us that his insights could be applied to other cultural groups too.

Pittu Laungani's critique of Western psychology was bold and astute. His numerous papers were not only eloquent and poetic, but will continue to stimulate and help promote culturally competent psychological research and practice. To paraphrase the title of Hans Eysenck's book, Pittu Laungani was seen, and saw himself, as a bit of a rebel with a cause. The cause being the passionate search for a more robust approach to thinking about therapy and doing therapy, and caring about the unity of both Eastern and Western perspectives. He relished a good argument.

But what about any limitations to his own work? Were his critiques of Western psychology and psychiatry too forceful, too passionate? We think not. However, it is unfortunate that Pittu Laungani did not directly address racism in his transcultural writings. This, of course, is not peculiar to him but quite characteristic of academic psychologists trained in an earlier era which did not consider it proper to even study, let alone address, the socio-political aspects of psychology itself. Further, it seems that Pittu Laungani (who highly valued aspects of English culture and philosophy) did not encounter direct racism experiences himself, having successfully bridged the divide between his Indian background and his British life. Perhaps his own marriage to his devoted white British wife, Ann Laungani, is a testimony that he was able to not only bridge the divide between cultures but also integrate it into his own personal life.

Pittu Laungani, while making a major contribution to the field, warned that just because an Eastern client adopts the outward trappings of the West, for example, such as wearing a suit or even speaking with an English accent, it should not be assumed that the person has necessarily assimilated or integrated into the wider mainstream society or embraced the values of Western civilization. We get the impression from Pittu Laungani's writings that he did not think it was an easy matter for someone (Eastern or Western) to adopt a new identity and wipe out or shed their cultural origins like how a snake may shed its skin and leave it all behind. However, it is evident that Pittu Laungani was able to temper scepticism with optimism in order to recommend cultural knowledge exchange for practitioners in the East and the West. This reflected his desire to promote healing and transformation through counselling and psychotherapy.

## NOTES

1. It should be noted that Laungani was not trained as a clinical or counselling psychologist nor as a psychotherapist (though he did engage in discourse and debate with counselling and clinical psychologists and psychotherapists). This has both advantages and disadvantages in that he adopted a fresh perspective as he was not socialized into the corpus of clinical or counselling psychology and therefore was not influenced or indoctrinated into a particular way of thinking

about therapy or doing therapy. He could freely express his views without worrying about what the establishment view might be and he was always forthright with his views, sometimes to the point of even possibly offending his listeners with his bluntness. Sometimes the 'truth' can be bitter and it may not be very palatable. But most people who knew him felt both his passion and his compassion. But, lest the reader unfamiliar with Laungani's works get the wrong impression, he read widely and often combined psychology, philosophy and poetry in a fascinating manner and challenged opposing views to devastating effect. Few people, for example, are aware that he was an accomplished poet and playwright, having written a number of witty yet serious-minded plays to which he added a psychological theme and a contemporary perspective. These include: *The Strange Affliction of Hamlet, Prince of Denmark*, *Pillars of Society: A Play in Three Acts* and *Hell is Other People*, which were adopted by psychological societies in the United Kingdom, Australia and Canada.

2. For the purposes of this paper, the East is defined as India and Eastern people, culture, philosophy or scholarship that emerged from India, as Laungani's point of reference was from the Indian subcontinent.
3. The West is defined as England, with a broad definition of Western as people, culture, philosophy or scholarship from England as well as Western Europe and North America. This definition is keeping in mind Laungani's experience living in England.
4. It is important that for the purposes of discussion we are going along with the broad generalizations that Laungani has made to illustrate important principles and to contrast with fundamental differences. It is also important to note that we are not suggesting that people with Eastern thinking do not recognize the part played by effort in the outcomes of life or the need to take practical action oneself. Thus, Muslims are familiar with the exhortation: 'Have faith in Allah but tie your camels!' and recognize that 'God helps those who help themselves.' However, the notion of a pre-ordained life or fate implies that in spite of personal efforts, unexpected outcomes are to be understood as part of the grand design. Thus, there is no personal distress with this acceptance and no loss to self esteem. Thus, personal effort alone is not a necessary or sufficient explanation for a particular outcome. Who has not encountered a fortunate happening without any effort on our part which we attribute to good fortune/luck, for example, being in the right place at the right time? Equally, we can all think of instances when someone has received something which appears underserved or unearned, that is the person did not seem to have put in the effort required for such a reward since achievement implies personal effort.
5. However, Western trained multicultural therapists who adopt, say the paradigm of existential psychotherapy and phenomenology would have been able to reflect the client's concerns more adequately and sensitively (Day-Vines et al., 2007; Leong, 1996; Leong and Lee, 2006; Vontress and Jackson, 2004; Vontress et al., 1999). Nevertheless, we would argue that a Western-trained, client-centred or a cognitive-behavioural therapist would have the difficulties that Laungani focused his attention on.
6. South Asian is defined as a person from India, Sri Lanka, Pakistan or Bangladesh (or East Africa via one of these countries).
7. Ayurveda is the traditional system of health in India. It encompasses preventive and curative medicine that addresses the body, mind, spirit and consciousness (Tirtha, 1998).

## REFERENCES

Alladin, W. J. (1989). Counselling women and ethnic minorities: Problems and prospects. *Counselling Psychology Quarterly, 2*(2), 101–104. [Editorial to Special Issue: Counselling women and ethnic minorities].

Arulmani, G. (2007). Counselling psychology in India: At the confluence of two traditions. *Applied Psychology: An International Review, 56*(1), 69–82.

Bhugra, D. (Ed.) (1996). *Psychiatry and religion: Context, consensus and controversies.* London: Routledge.

Day-Vines, N. L. Wood, S. M., Grothaus, T., Craigen, L., Holman, A. and Dotson-Blake, K. (2007). Broaching the subjects of race, ethnicity, and culture during the counselling process. *Journal of Counselling and Development, 85*(4), 401–409.

Dein, S. and Sembhi, S. (2001). The use of traditional healing in South Asian psychiatric patients in the U.K.: Interactions between professional and folk psychiatries. *Transcultural Psychiatry, 38*(2), 243–257.

Duran, E. (1990). *Transforming the soul wound.* Delhi, India: Arya Offset Press.

Fernando, S. (2003). *Cultural diversity, mental health and psychiatry: The struggle against racism.* Hove, Essex: Brunner-Routledge.

Hilton, B. A., Grewal, S., Popatia, N., Bottorff, J. L., Johnson, J. L., Clarke, H., Venables, L. J., Bilkhu, S. and Sumel, P. (2001). The Desi ways: Traditional health practices of South Asian women in Canada. *Health Care for Women International, 22*(6), 553–567.

Hoch, E. M. (1974). Pir, fakir, and psychotherapist. *The Human Context, 6,* 668–676.

Hodge, D. R. (2004). Working with Hindu clients in a spiritually sensitive manner. *Social Work, 49*(1), 27–38.

Inayat, Q. (2005). Islam, divinity, and spiritual healing. In R. Moodley and W. West (Eds), *Integrating traditional healing practices into counselling and psychotherapy* (pp. 159–169). Thousand Oaks, California: Sage Publications.

Juthani, N. V. (2001). Psychiatric treatment of Hindus. *International Review of Psychiatry, 13*(2), 125–130.

Kakar, S. (1982). *Shamans, mystics and doctors.* London: Unwin Paperbacks.

Kumar M., Bhugra D. and Singh J. (2005). South Asian (Indian) Traditional healing. In R. Moodley and W. West (Eds), *Integrating traditional healing practices into counselling and psychotherapy* (pp. 113–121). Thousand Oaks, California: Sage Publications.

Laungani, P. (2002a). Cross-cultural psychology: A handmaiden to mainstream Western psychology. *Counselling Psychology Quarterly, 15*(4), 385–397.

———. (2002b). Mindless psychiatry and dubious ethics. *Counselling Psychology Quarterly, 15*(1), 23–33.

———. (2003). Therapeutic strategies for coping with a life-threatening illness: A personal testament. *Illness, Crisis, & Loss, 11*(2), 162–182.

———. (2004a). *Asian perspectives in counselling and psychotherapy.* London: Routlege.

———. (2004b). Counselling and therapy in a multi-cultural setting. *Counselling Psychology Quarterly, 17*(2), 195–207.

———. (2004c). Some unresolved issues in philosophy and psychology: Their implications for therapy. *Counselling Psychology Quarterly, 7*(1), 107–123.

———. (2005). Hindu spirituality and healing practices. In R. Moodley and W. West (Eds), *Integrating traditional healing practices into counselling and psychotherapy* (pp. 139–147). Thousand Oaks, California: Sage Publications.

Leong, F. T. L. (1996). Toward an integrative model for cross-cultural counselling and psychotherapy. *Applied and Preventive Psychology, 5*(4), 189–209.

Leong, F. T. L. and Lee, S. Z. (2006). A cultural accommodation model for cross-cultural psychotherapy: Illustrated with the case of Asian Americans. *Psychotherapy, Research, Practice, Training, 45*(4), 410–423.

Marsella, A. J. (1998). Toward a global psychology: Meeting the needs of a changing world. *American Psychologist, 53*(12), 1282–1291.

Marsella, A. J. and Pedersen, P. (2004). Internationalizing the curriculum in counselling psychology. *Counselling Psychology Quarterly, 17*(4), 413–424.

Moodley, R. (1999). Challenges and transformations: Counselling in a multicultural context. *International Journal for the Advancement of Counselling, 21*(2), 139–152.

Moodley, R. and West, W. (Eds) (2005). *Integrating traditional healing practices into counselling and psychotherapy*. Thousand Oaks, California: Sage Publications.

Roland, A. (1988). *In search of self in India and Japan.* Princeton, NJ: Princeton University Press.

Sandhu, J. S. (2004). The Sikh model of the person, suffering, and healing: Implications for counselors. *International Journal for the Advancement of Counselling, 26*(1), 33–46.

Sinha, D. (1993). Indigenization of Psychology in India and its relevance. In U. Kim and J. W. Berry (Eds), *Indigenous psychologies: Research and experience in cultural context* (pp. 30–43). Newbury Park, CA: Sage Publications.

Sue, D. W. (1978). Eliminating cultural oppression in counselling: Toward a general theory. *Journal of Counselling Psychology, 25*(5), 419–428.

———. (2003). *Overcoming our racism: The journey to liberation.* San Francisco: Jossey-Bass.

Sue, D. W. and Sue, D. (1999). *Counselling the culturally different: Theory and practice.* New York: Wiley.

Sue, D. W., Arredondo P. and McDavis, R. J. (1992). Multicultural competencies and standards: A call to the profession. *Journal of Multicultural Counselling and Development, 20*(1), 64–88.

Tirtha, S. S. (1998). *The Ayurvedic encyclopedia.* Bayville, New York: Ayurvedic Holistic Centre Press.

Van Hoecke, G. (2006). Paradigms in Indian psychotherapy: Applicability in a Western approach. *Mental Health, Religion & Culture, 9*(2), 119–125.

Vontress, C. E. and Jackson, M. L. (2004). Reactions to the multicultural counselling competencies. *Journal of Mental Health Counselling, 26*(1), 74–80.

Vontress, C. E., Johnson, J. A. and Epp, L. R. (1999). *Cross-cultural counselling: A case book.* Alexandria, VA: American Counselling Association.

# 19

# Pittu Laungani, Multicultural Humanism and Eclectic Psychotherapy

*Sandra E.S. Neil*

## INTRODUCTION

**Pittu Laungani** has been well known for his profound and erudite observations concerning multicultural aspects of human and societal behaviours. His many works serve as a permanent record of his scholarship, wisdom and insight. I had the privilege of reviewing several of his final works, like 'Counselling the dead' (Laungani, 2007), and his extensive work with John Morgan, on *Death and bereavement around the world* (Morgan and Laungani, 2002, 2003, 2004, 2005).

Laungani was a firm believer in the essential good in humankind and was extremely reluctant to resort to pathological explanations for human behaviours. He was cooperative with and respectful of the scientific and medical models, but retained a strong existential calm in the face of a surge in cognitive and behaviourist approaches in psychology. He believed these approaches to be less valuable because of their essential reductionism. He quotes Voltaire, '…doctors put drugs which they know little in bodies in which they know less, to cure disease in which they know nothing at all…' and he quotes Shakespeare's Romeo and Juliet, '… He jests at scars that never felt a wound'. In his work on health and illness, he refers to the preceding works of such philosophers as Socrates, Plato, Galileo, Newton, Luther, Da Vinci, Beethoven, Nietzsche, Freud, Tolstoy, Dostoyevsky, Proust, Lincoln, Darwin, Hemingway, Picasso, F. Scott, Fitzgerald, Primo Levy, James Joyce, Orwell, William Blake, Stephen Hawking and Gandhi. Pittu Laungani poses the problem that many of the persons mentioned would have been, or were, diagnosed with physical, organic or mental disorders. In 'Counselling the dead!' (2007), Laungani explored the meanings of health, the meanings of illness and the intercultural relationships between health, happiness and illness. He also discusses the cross-cultural model of health, happiness and illness. Within this paradigm, Laungani described happiness in Western society as an individualistic perspective, which emphasizes 'self confidence', related to one's ability 'to express and assert oneself'. He compares this to the Eastern concepts of happiness, which revolve around religious beliefs, familial and communal factors. Pittu Laungani's brilliance of mind understood both the individuality and individualism of the Western society and the collectivism of Eastern society (Laungani, 2006).

Ultimately as a humanist, Laungani accepted Western concepts of humanism as valid. He tentatively accepted the five postulates of Humanistic Psychology given by James Bugental (1964). Bugental declared that human beings cannot be reduced to components; human beings have in them a uniquely human context; human consciousness includes an awareness of oneself in the context of other people; human beings have choices and responsibilities and human beings are intentional, they seek meaning, value and creativity. But in accordance with his continual cross-cultural perspective, he maintained the caveat that these concepts had the best fit in individualistic perspective of Western philosophy, which emphasizes such concepts as 'self-confidence', one's ability 'to express and assert oneself' and 'freedom to choose'. He contrasted these to Eastern concepts of health and happiness, which he asserted were collective and societal based on such constructs as religious beliefs, fate, familial loyalties and communal dynamics.

The brilliance of Pittu Laungani's approach was that he was able to deal with both the individuality requisite for Western-style humanism, and the collectivism vital in Eastern philosophies. He compared, contrasted and integrated these seemingly disparate concepts throughout his distinguished career as demonstrated by the breadth and vastness of his research. As a principal British interpreter and integrator of European and Eastern philosophical approaches to psychotherapy, Laungani expressed a hope that psychotherapists would use humanistic and existential approaches to focus on meaning, rather than just technique. He agreed (Laungani, personal communication, 2003) with Rollo May, who stated that 'Adjustment is not a goal if it precludes self realization based on imperfect values such as integrity, courage and love. Drawing from the humanities, therapy should speak to the higher aspirations of the human race—to values that make life worth living' (May, 1987: 212).

In this chapter, I will discuss how Laungani's work is embedded in meanings. I will also link his work to the ideas offered by Virginia Satir (1967, 1972, 1988), whose pioneering clinical approaches to humanistic psychology has had so many levels of meaning.

## THE MULTICULTURAL FAMILY CHESSBOARD AND PITTU LAUNGANI'S ECLECTIC APPROACH

Eclectic psychology essentially exists to explain human issues, such as the self, self-actualization, health, hope, love, creativity, nature, existence, individuality and meaning—in short, the understanding of what it means to be human. Humanistic psychology tends to look beyond the medical model of psychology in order to open up a non-pathologizing view of the person (Aanstoos et al., 2000). This usually implies that the therapist downplays the pathological aspects of a person's life in favour of the healthy aspects. A key ingredient in this approach is the meeting between the therapist and the client and the possibilities for dialogue. One sees this all the time in the way Laungani worked with his patients. The aim of much humanistic therapy is to help the client approach a stronger and healthier sense of self, also called self-actualization (Clay, 2002). All this is part of Humanistic Psychology's motivation to be a science of human experience, focusing on the actual lived experience of persons (Aanstoos et al., 2000). Working with individuals and groups of many cultures, the psychologist must maintain a high level of cultural awareness and relativity in order to be effective. This is most obvious in clinical work.

Satir's basic thesis was that one learns in the family particular behaviours and beliefs and methods of coping with the self and with each other. She views the family as an essential topic of research. Pittu Laungani also saw the family and group culture as the site for knowledge production. Each family, over generations, passes on morals, rules and attitudes that are absorbed consciously and unconsciously. Character is developed in the process of learning to survive and to cope with the realities of one's particular family. It is a powerful psychodynamic process aimed at recapturing and revisiting key events, experiences and learning from one's family history. It provides the opportunity to update the past in the present and to reduce the negative impacts some experiences had on us.

Working with people in a therapeutic, or indeed an educational or occupational, setting means that one learns many things about the cultures concerned. It is incumbent that one becomes and remains aware of cultural differences and similarities as Laungani emphasizes, especially in terms of social continuity, which depends upon the continuance of the norms and values of that society (Satir, 1967, 1972, 1987, 1988).

Living in a tolerant, even enthusiastically, multicultural society such as that in Australia, one knows that one cannot touch another person without being touched in return. The cultural norms have adapted to the addition of each culture with a common theme running through that is identifiably Australian. Therefore, I believe that we as therapists must become cognizant of each one of the ethnic and transcultural groups to be able to practise authentically, since each one of those cultures from which our clients come from rub off on us as well. Pittu Laungani has maintained the ongoing importance of multicultural bridges. Partly as a result of our discussions with Pittu Laungani, Robert Silverberg and I developed the multicultural family chessboard (Neil and Silverberg, 1995) which explores family systems. This approach adapted Virginia Satir's notion of sculpting families to a more limited environment, where movement of family members is impractical or undesirable. This derivative family sculpture allows us to represent members of the family by chess pieces and to position the family members in two dimensions to indicate intimacy. In a second task, it allows us to indicate the optative, objective and the subjective positions between family members. All relations and positions are recorded, including parents, siblings, step-siblings and non-residential members of the family. It is another vehicle for creating differentiation, integration and awareness for and of change in the family. It allows one or all members of the family to be symbolically represented in a less threatening, but equally rich and complex three-dimensional 'chess board and pieces' interaction. The language that a person uses is his/her own, and the chess pieces are labelled and named explicitly to fit with the perceptions of that person, and make the rules of the family explicit. Family bonds and triangulations, the boundaries of each family, the affection and power roles, gender and occupational issues are identified and often can be transformed using a brief, intensive and process-oriented method. The method can be used to look at turning points and times of change, which are inevitable, and most important in understanding the development of the family's status quo. It has been pointed out by Minuchin and Fishman (1981) and other family therapists that, times of change are opportunities for growth and improved functioning. Often turning points are seen differently by different members of the family. We look to unblocking resistances to change. 'The family chess board' helps show each member reasons how and why patterns of constructive or destructive behaviours occur. The method lends itself in helping to eradicate the influence of the past on the future.

This is in agreement with Pittu Laungani's concepts of Western cultures appearing to adhere to the rationalist, Darwinian philosophies, while inwardly yearning for spiritual, communal and social harmony (Laungani, 2006). He argued that 'West and East are separated not only by oceans but, also by vast stretches of religious, cultural and philosophical, landscapes'. Laungani felt that Westerners have discarded faith in preference to secular rationality, and that the resurgence of religious teachings, the concerted opposition of Darwinian theory, the implementation of creationist policies in many States of America would suggest that God and religion have not been completely abandoned. His writing leaves us with a doubt that people from Eastern cultures, in hedging their bets have arrived at a compromise. Faith plays a major role in their daily lives and reason allows them to understand, engage and share in all the scientific, technological and economic developments around the world (Laungani, 2006).

## CONCLUSION

Pittu Laungani was a writer, psychologist and philosopher cognizant of the importance of context (cultural, multicultural, place, time and space). He has a great understanding of the therapeutic method: the psychoanalytic, cognitive and interpersonal world of patients coloured necessarily by the kairos (καιρός)—the exact right moment—and the chronos (χρόνος)—the life and times—of the persons, the relationships they are in and the contexts of their cultural lives. Pittu Laungani's therapeutic understanding and philosophy, his life laden with meaning, gave new recognitions, choices and freedoms (to and from). He juxtaposed Western philosophies based on analysis and phenomenology with Eastern philosophical traditions favouring determinism and fate. He agreed with my views (Neil and Neil, 2001; Neil and Silverberg, 1995) as a clinical psychologist that the ultimate goals of therapy are: to heal the wounds, feed the hungers and empower the self of the patient, giving them a new freedom to comment in their lives.

## REFERENCES

Aanstoos, C., Serlin, I. and Greening, T. (2000). History of Division 32 (Humanistic Psychology) of the American Psychological Association. In D. Dewsbury (Ed.), *Unification through division: Histories of the divisions of the American Psychological Association,* (Vol. V). Washington, DC: American Psychological Association.

Bugental, J. F. T. (1964). The third force in Psychology. *Journal of Humanistic Psychology, 4*(1), 19–25.

Clay, R. A. (2002). A renaissance for humanistic psychology. The field explores new niches while building on its past. *American Psychological Association Monitor, 33*(8).

Ford, F. R., Doyle, R., Marie, M. and Skelton, J. M. (1994). Theory and interpretation of mapping of rules (MOR). Personal Communication, c/- 13 Marchant Court, Kensington, CA, USA.

Laungani, P. (2006). *Understanding cross-cultural psychology: Eastern and Western perspectives.* London: Sage Publications.

———. (2007). Counselling the dead! *Counselling Psychology Quarterly, 20*(1), 81–95.

May, R. (1987). Therapy in our day. In J. K. Zeig (Ed.), *The evolution of psychotherapy.* New York: Brunner-Mazel.

Minuchin, S. and Fishman, H. C. (1981). *Family therapy techniques.* Cambridge, MA: Harvard University Press.

Morgan, J. D. and Laungani, P. (Eds) (2002). *Death and bereavement around the world, Vol.1: Major religious traditions.* Amityville NY: Baywood.

———. (2003). *Death and bereavement around the world, Vol. 2: Death and bereavement in the Americas.* Amityville NY: Baywood.

———. (2004). *Death and bereavement around the world, Vol. 3: Death and bereavement in Europe.* Amityville NY: Baywood.

———. (2005). *Death and bereavement around the world, Vol. 4: Death and bereavement in Asia, Australia and New Zealand.* Amityville, NY: Baywood.

Neil, S. E. and Neil, S. E. (2001). *Family reconstruction: A journey through three continents and four generations.* Melbourne, Australia: Satir Centre of Australia.

Neil, S. E. and Silverberg, R. L. (1995). *The multicultural family chessboard: Sound moves for a sounder family.* Melbourne, Australia: Satir Centre of Australia.

Satir, V. (1967). *Conjoint family therapy: A guide to theory and technique.* Palo Alto, CA: Science & Behaviour Books.

———. (1972). *Peoplemaking.* Palo Alto, CA: Science & Behaviour Books.

———. (1987). Going behind the obvious: The psychotherapeutic journey. In J. K. Zeig (Ed.), *The evolution of psychotherapy.* New York, NY: Brunner-Mazel.

———. (1988). *The new peoplemaking.* Palo Alto, CA: Science & Behaviour Books.

# 20

# Religious Rites and Rituals in Death and Bereavement: An Indian Experience

*Pittu Laungani*

## INTRODUCTION

**The** theme of death is the centrepiece of Anantha Murthy's (1976) remarkable book *Samskara*. It is set in a small village in South India. The village is dominated and, for all practical purposes, run by a group of orthodox high-caste Brahmin priests, who practice and perform all the rites and rituals in their day-to-day lives in accordance with ancient Vedic teachings. The non-Brahmins who live in the village are dependent on the Brahmins for the performance of all the rites and rituals, the prayers and the sacrifices related to births, marriages and deaths, and for all the ceremonies that need to be performed on festive occasions, of which there are many during the course of the year. The villagers are also in fear of the Brahmins and defer to them in all respects. The Brahmins live within their own enclave, the non-Brahmins in their own. The low-caste Hindus, who are referred to as Sudras (untouchables), live apart. There is very little communication between the Brahmins and the rest of the people in the village, and hardly any between the Brahmins and the Sudras. Each person, regardless of his or her caste and occupation, understands and accepts his or her position within the caste hierarchy, as dictated by ancient Vedic traditions. Peace reigns.

The peace and equanimity of the village is shattered when one of the high-caste Brahmins dies in the home of a sex worker with whom he had formed a continuing relationship. The sex worker, it turns out, comes from the lowest caste, a Sudra, an untouchable. His sudden death throws the entire village into a state of turmoil. The Brahmin, while he had been alive, had brought shame and grief upon his family members and upon the elders of the whole village. He had left his wife and had started to live with Chandri, the low-caste sex worker. He had taken his wife's jewellery and had given it to the sex worker. In so doing he had renounced his own high-caste Brahmin origins. He had started to eat meat and drink alcohol. He had formed social relations with Muslims and other members of the lowest caste, visited their homes and eaten with them. In forming a sexual relationship with a person from the Sudra caste, he had lost his own high-caste status, and had forfeited his right to be called a Brahmin. He himself was in danger of being seen as an untouchable.

His sudden death creates a variety of problems for his wife, his family members, all the other high-caste Hindus in the village, and in particular for the high priest whose duty it is to carry out the necessary funeral rites. There are several questions that disturb the entire village. Who will perform the funeral rites? How will they be performed? Will the deceased be given a Brahminic funeral?

Ancient Hindu customs, enshrined in the Vedas, make it clear that all the funeral rites are to be performed by the deceased's family members, from the laying out of the corpse, the construction of the bier, the transportation to the crematorium, to the final cremation. Only the family members and the members of one's sub-community are allowed to perform the last funeral rites. No outsiders are ever allowed to perform the last rites. To allow an outsider to touch a corpse would bring the family into a state of spiritual pollution. It is of course the sacred duty of the high priest to perform the last rites. Never having encountered such a situation before, the high priest is in a state of acute distress.

He broods. No satisfactory solution presents itself. What is he to do?

1. The body of the deceased lies in the house of the untouchable. For a high-caste Hindu Brahmin to enter the home of an untouchable would result in the Brahmin becoming spiritually polluted.
2. The corpse too cannot be left in the house of the sex worker, unattended. The Vedic texts make it clear that funerals need to be performed within 24 hours of death. The longer the corpse remains in the house of the sex worker, the greater the shame and the ignominy that will fall upon the family members and upon the entire village.
3. How will the deceased be accorded the full funeral rites of a Brahmin, considering that as a result of his moral transgressions he has forfeited his right to be regarded as a Brahmin?
4. Not to accord the deceased the full Brahmin funeral rites would undermine the high status of the family within the community. The Brahmins will become the laughing stock of the village.
5. The high priest, upon whose shoulders rests this gigantic decision, does not know what to do or how to act.

6. Upon consulting the ancient scriptures and texts, the high priest can find no precedents that would guide his actions.
7. He then speaks to other priests from neighbouring villages, but is still unable to come up with a solution.
8. In the meantime the corpse remains in the house of the sex worker, rotting in the heat.
9. The high priest feels that he has failed the villagers, and despite his learning and erudition, has been unable to resolve the crises.

There are other interesting details such as how the body was handled, who was in charge of the funeral, how the funeral rites were performed, who performed them and the consequences of these actions on the villagers and on the high priest in particular. Suffice it to say that the caste-related moral transgressions of the deceased brought untold misery and sorrow upon all the family members. They also led to devastating consequences for the entire village and for the high priest, who was ultimately destroyed by this event.

But our concern is with understanding the rites and rituals related to death among high-caste Hindus, the hierarchical structure of the caste system, notions of pollution and purification which play a major role in the daily lives of orthodox Hindus, and their beliefs concerning death and afterlife.

This event, despite its rarity, is of immense magnitude when seen within the context of orthodox Hindu society. The tragedy which befell the family members of the deceased and the high priest of the village fits into a neat cultural pattern which can be understood by most members of that culture. But to outsiders, unacquainted with Hindu culture, the above event would appear alien and even bewildering.

When I first discussed this particular episode with some of my European and American friends and colleagues, their initial response was one of incredulity. They claimed that there was nothing extraordinary about the event for it to be labelled traumatic. They saw it as a 'storm in a tea-cup'. To them the deceased's sexual relationship with the sex worker was a private affair—it was of no concern whatever to others, with the exception of his wife.

To perceive the above event as a storm in a teacup or as a private affair is in keeping with the philosophy of individualism, which is one of the dominant features of Western society. Individualism, as Triandis (1994) points out, is concerned primarily with giving priority to one's personal goals over the goals of one's group, and where personal choice takes precedence over group considerations. Given their personal adherence to an individualistic philosophy, they failed to understand that the entire structure of Hindu society is centred round caste interdependence and communal norms. They had little awareness of the power that the community wields and is able to exercise over its deviant members.

Consequently, they saw the Brahmin's sexual liaison with the sex worker as a private affair and failed to understand why the sexual liaison, combined with other factors, brought about such unimaginable distress and harm to the other Hindus in the village. Nor could they comprehend why the high priest, unable to find an acceptable solution to the crisis, was totally traumatized and destroyed by the event.

They wondered why the funeral arrangements could not have been passed on to undertakers: such an arrangement to them seemed feasible and offered a neat solution to an otherwise insoluble problem.

Once again, a Western solution was being offered to a culturally unique problem. Sadly, there was no understanding (or perhaps no knowledge) on their part that Hindus, for a variety of religious, philosophical and cultural reasons, do not have undertakers. A variety of other plausible explanations and seemingly 'rational' solutions were also proposed, but none of them seemed conceivable, let alone acceptable, from the context of Hindu culture.

Let us now consider some of the major concepts in Hinduism, which will enable us to understand the cultural issues underlying the story.

## THE CASTE SYSTEM

Indian (Hindu) society, not unlike other Eastern societies, is a family-based and community-oriented society (Basham, 1966; Flood, 1996; Kakar, 1981; Koller, 1982; Klostermaier, 1998; Lannoy, 1976; Lipner, 1994; Laungani, 1997; Laungani, 1998; Mandelbaum, 1972; Sharma, 2000; Zaehner, 1966a). Although in many respects it is similar to most other Eastern societies, its unique distinguishing feature lies in its caste system. No other Eastern society has a social structure analogous to the Indian caste system. The earliest reference to the caste system is to be found in the *Rig Veda*, thus suggesting that the caste system represents a divine, sacred and natural order of things (Zaehner, 1966a; Klostermaier, 1998; Sharma, 2000).

Lannoy (1976) describes the caste system as a form of institutionalized inequality, a social instrument to assimilation, an archaic form of trade unionism, and an extension of the joint family system. None of these descriptions quite captures the essence of what the caste system stands for. The four castes in their hierarchical order are as follows:

1. Brahmins: the learned, the educated elite, the guardians of the Vedas, the priests
2. Kshatriyas: the noble warriors, defenders of the realm
3. Vaishyas: the traders, businessmen, farmers, moneylenders
4. Sudras: their main function is to serve the needs of the upper three castes.

Members of the upper three castes are known as 'twice born' because their male members have undergone an initiation, a rite of passage, which then transforms them into high-caste Hindus. The ceremony, which marks their 'second birth', is the rite of the sacred thread ceremony, after the completion of which they are allowed to read and learn from the Vedas and participate in all religious ceremonies.

Sudras are not permitted such an initiation rite. They fall into two categories: touchables and untouchables. The touchable Sudras engage in occupations that are considered by the upper three castes to be demeaning and to a certain degree polluting: barber, masseur, cleaner, water carrier, etc. Untouchable Sudras, on the other hand, are obliged to engage in occupations which deal with human and animal waste and refuse, viz., slaughter of animals, working in tanneries, abattoirs, crematorium attendants, road sweepers, refuse collectors. Even among the untouchable Sudras there are gradations, and a crematorium attendant is considered to be the lowliest of the lowly within the caste hierarchy. Although the pattern of caste related occupations is beginning to undergo a transformation in the urban areas of India, there is little evidence of such changes in the rural areas of the country, which are inhabited by over 70 per cent of the Indian population. For a high-caste Hindu to come into any form of physical contact with an untouchable leads the Hindu to become spiritually polluted. The polluted person would then be expected to perform a series of ritualistic measures to attain a state of purity. In many Indian villages, the untouchables are expected to live a great distance away from the homes of the high-caste Hindus so that their presence may not 'pollute' the three high-caste Hindus.

Untouchability has been banned in India to help eradicate the poisonous social disease. In recent years there has been a mass movement, an awakening of consciousness among untouchables, who given the fact that they constitute 15 to 17 per cent of the total Indian population are aware of their power as potential vote winners. They have abandoned the old derogatory term Sudra and now refer to themselves as Dalits, the oppressed ones. To grasp the full impact of the caste system on the daily lives of Hindus, it is necessary to understand the fundamental characteristics of the caste system. Let us examine them briefly. The three fundamental characteristics are:

1. Hierarchy
2. Pollution and purification
3. Specialization

## Hierarchical Nature of Castes

Membership into a given caste is through birth only. One is born into a given caste, destined to stay in it until death. It is virtually impossible to move from one caste into another, particularly from the lower caste into the higher. It is, however, possible to slide downwards from a higher caste into a lower caste. Each caste is divided into sub-castes, which also operate on a hierarchical model. Each sub-caste is graded, ranging from the lowest to the highest. Gradations of castes are organized around degrees of purity and pollution and in accordance with marriage customs.

Another factor that determines the hierarchical status of a sub-caste is concerned with who may receive food and water from whom. As Lannoy (1976) points out, '[food and] water is believed to be especially pollution prone, therefore rules are carefully observed and constitute one of the clearest means by which the society represents its status gradations' (p. 150).

## Pollution and Purification

Pollution and purification play an extremely important role in understanding the day-to-day secular and religious behaviours of Hindus. The elimination of dirt in order to impose a sense of order and control over one's environment is a universal human characteristic. Although Indians pay lip service to the idea of eliminating dirt, they are less concerned with hygiene and more with sacred contagion and pollution. Thus, the concepts pollution and purification are best understood within a spiritual context and not in terms of hygiene and biology (Chaudhuri, 1979; Filippi, 1996; Fuller, 1992). The status of a person in India is to an extent determined by the degree of contact with the polluting agent. Proximity to a polluting agent may constitute a permanent pollution. This would mean that certain occupations are permanently polluting—as was mentioned above in relation to the untouchables. Such a form of pollution is collective—the entire family remains polluted. It is also hereditary. In many villages in India the untouchables are often forced to live away from the high-caste Hindus, since their very presence is believed to have a polluting effect on others. In certain instances the high-caste Hindus prevent the untouchables from drawing water from the well, claiming that it is for the exclusive use of the high-caste Hindus. It is clear that the enactment of law does not guarantee its enforcement. There are three major ways in which pollution can be categorized. Pollution may be (*a*) mild and temporary, (*b*) severe and temporary, and (*c*) severe and permanent.

### *Mild and Temporary Pollution*

This is an everyday affair. One is in a state of impurity or pollution upon waking up in the morning, prior to performing one's morning ablutions, when one has eaten food touched by others, when one has not prayed. Pollution occurs during menstruation, after a sexual act, after one has had a haircut, pared one's nails, and in the performance of any activity which is considered to be impure. Such mild states of pollution can be overcome by appropriate actions, such as baths, prayers, wearing dean washed clothes, and engaging in appropriate cleansing and purification rituals.

### *Severe and Temporary Pollution*

This comes about when a high-caste Hindu comes into physical and/or social contact with persons of the lowest caste, the Sudras, or when a high-caste Hindu eats meat (particularly beef). No high-caste Hindu is expected to offer or accept cooked food from a low-caste Hindu. To do so would lead to the high-caste Hindu becoming polluted. Nor is it appropriate for a low-caste Hindu to receive cooked food from a high-caste Hindu. This feature applies not just to inter-caste encounters, but within-caste encounters as well. A person of higher grading within a given sub-caste may neither offer nor receive cooked food from a person of lower grading from the same sub-caste. A Brahmin engaged in temple duties will not accept hospitality from a Brahmin involved in funeral rites. The latter are regarded as being ritually inferior and even polluting to the former. The privileges of superiority are fiercely protected. To overcome this form of pollution it is necessary for the polluted individual to perform a series of appropriate propitiation rites, rituals and religious ceremonies under the guidance of their family priest.

### *Severe and Permanent Pollution*

As noted above, some forms of pollution are collective, hereditary and therefore permanent. Permanent pollution may also occur when a Hindu belonging to the highest caste (Brahmin) marries a person from the lowest caste, thereby breaking the principle of endogamy that has always been regarded as one of the cementing factors that has held the caste system together. The person in such a state of pollution may be ostracized by his family members and maybe forced to become an outcaste. Since pollution and purification is an everyday affair, Hindus in general have learnt to avoid them, or undertake appropriate ritualistic cleansing exercises when avoidance becomes impossible.

Let us now examine the manner in which pollution manifests itself in death and bereavement. When death occurs in a family it leads to severe pollution. The presence of a corpse in the house pollutes the house. The corpse too is in a state of pollution. All members in the house are also polluted. Anyone entering the house becomes polluted. The Brahmin priest who performs the last funeral rites is also polluted. The mourners who accompany the deceased to the crematorium become polluted. Entering the crematorium leads to being polluted. An inappropriate and/or an insincere performance of the cremation rites and rituals of cremation can lead to severe pollution among the family members of the deceased. According to ancient Vedic customs, all the rites related to the preparation of the corpse and the arrangements for the funeral are performed by the family members, although in so doing they themselves enter into a state of pollution. However, such impurity, although serious, is temporary and is considered to be far less serious than the entry of a Sudra into their home (Flood, 1996; Lannoy, 1976; Pandey, 1969).

## Special Skills

In early Vedic times, castes were held together by three prime factors: (*a*) endogamy, (*b*) commensality, and (*c*) specialization.

### *Endogamy*

Endogamy—marrying within one's own caste and sub-caste—was seen as a desired course of action in India. Such a form of marriage was considered to be sacred. The Brahmins argued that an endogamous marriage enabled the parties involved in matrimony to retain the ritual purity of their caste and avoid any form of inter-caste contamination. It was an ideal form of marriage because it ensured the perpetuation of the caste system. However, endogamous marriages came to be questioned.

It is notable that over the centuries the principle of endogamy has not been completely swept aside. It continues to retain its stronghold over Hindus all over India, particularly in the rural areas of the country. Marriages are still arranged and organized by the parents of prospective spouses. Although the 'style' of arranged marriages has undergone a modest change within Indian society, particularly among the affluent members of society in the urban sectors of the country, arranged marriages are still to be norm.

### *Commensality*

Commensality, as we know, is concerned with hospitality—extending and receiving hospitality. Commensality carries a special spiritual meaning within Hindu culture. Since there were strict taboos of ritual purity associated with offering and receiving food, great care had to be taken in terms of who one offered food to and whom one received food from. One could not, willy-nilly, invite people home, nor accept invitations from others. One could offer food and in return receive it only from those who belonged to one's own caste and sub-caste. To offer food to outsiders resulted in breaking the taboos of ritual purity. One could of course offer food (cooked or uncooked) to mendicants, the poor and the needy—but there were strict rules governing the precise manner in which food could be offered. One also had to be extremely careful in deciding the kind of food that one offered or was offered. As Lannoy (1976) points out, among Hindus '...the most important quality of food is the degree to which it is pollution free' (Ibid.: 150). There were distinctions too between cooked food and uncooked food, and between the relative purity of cooked foods. Uncooked food was said to be less pollution prone than cooked food. Thus, one could receive uncooked food from a lower caste, but not cooked food. Again, the kind of food one offered or received was related to the degree of purity of the food. In addition to food, water was believed to be especially pollution prone. To avoid any form of spiritual contamination, orthodox Hindus always carried with them urns and jugs of water whenever they undertook any long journeys. The practice of carrying water is still prevalent among many sections of Hindu society. To a large extent, although such practices have become a thing of the past, they have not vanished entirely. One might still notice such practices being rigidly adhered to among the very orthodox Brahmins in certain parts of India.

### *Specialization*

Each village was expected to be a self-contained and a self-sustaining unit, which could call upon the services of people with specialist skills and expertize to meet the needs of the village community. A vocational caste group expected its members to stick to its hereditary calling. But this was not always possible. As Char (1997) points out, 'often enough, the vocation of the caste failed to provide full employment to its members' (Ibid.: 22). Gradually, as a result of increased opportunities for diversification, more and more sub-castes based on new vocational alignments were formed. Even among the main castes there have been instances of Brahmins entering the army, tending cattle, trading, hunting and even snake charming. Evidence suggests that soldiers too came from all castes and sub-castes (Char, 1997).

While it is true that many vocations in India are still caste based and continue to follow a hereditary pattern, the structure of the caste system, insofar as its vocational base is concerned, is undergoing a metamorphosis. The purity of caste-based vocations has turned out to be a myth. It is not uncommon to see uneducated Brahmins working as cooks and waiters in restaurants, and in many other humble occupations.

We have seen that the meticulous and precise performance of rites and rituals is seen as being desirable for Hindus. It binds and preserves the caste system, which in turn provides a sense of continuity and belonging. Rites and rituals legitimize social order and uphold social institutions. Rituals also enable Hindus to earn merit, which leads to their own spiritual development. Their importance cannot be overstated. Despite the fact that over the centuries many ancient rituals have lost their functional value, and are interpreted in different ways by Hindus in different regions, they have not been abandoned. The question that arises is this: why do Hindus cling to the performance of rituals with such tenacity? In what ways do ritualistic actions lead to one's spiritual development? For a tentative answer to this question, let us briefly turn to the law of karma.

## THE LAW OF KARMA

The law of karma, in its simplest form, states that all human actions lead to consequences. Right actions produce good consequences and wrong actions produce bad consequences. The law of karma is not concerned with consequences in general, but with consequences that affect the individual—the doer of the action. Second, the law of karma applies specifically to the moral sphere. It is therefore not concerned with the general relation between actions and their consequences but 'rather with the moral quality of the actions and their consequences' (Reichenbach, 1990: 1). Hiriyana (1949) explains that the events of our lives are determined by their antecedent causes. Since all actions lead to consequences, which are related to the nature and the type of actions, absolute justice falls to our lot in the sense that good actions lead to happiness and bad actions to unhappiness. The doctrine of karma explains not only pain, suffering and misfortune, but also pleasure, happiness and good fortune. Each of us receives the results of our own actions and not another's. Third, the law of karma asserts that the doer not only deserves the consequences of his or her actions, but is unable to avoid experiencing them (Prasad, 1989). It should be made clear that the actions of the doer may have occurred in his or her present life or in his or her past life. Similarly the consequences of the doer's actions may occur during the person's present life or in his or her future life. It is impossible to avoid the consequences of one's actions.

The law of karma stands out as one of the unique features of Hinduism. Although there is no basis for establishing its empirical validity, Hindus in general have an unswerving belief in the workings of the law of karma. It has shaped the Indian view of life over centuries. One might even go to the extent of saying that the Hindu psyche is built around the notion of karma (O'Flaherty, 1976; O'Flaherty, 1980; Reichenbach, 1990; Sharma 2000; Sinari 1984; Zaehner, 1966b; ). The influence of the law of karma manifests itself at every stage in a Hindu's life: at birth, in childhood, during adolescence and adulthood, in marriage, in illness and health, in good fortune and misfortune, in death and bereavement, and after death.

The deterministic belief that one's present life is shaped by one's actions in one's past life (or lives) allows them to explain and accept a variety of misfortunes (and good fortunes) which befall them through the course of their journey through life. It engenders within their psyche a spirit of passive, if not resigned acceptance of misfortunes, ranging from sudden deaths within the family, glaring inequalities of caste and status, disease and illness, poverty and destitution, to exploitation and prejudice. The main disadvantage of determinism—and there are many—lies in the fact that it often leads to a state of existential, and in certain instances, moral resignation, compounded by a profound sense of inertia. One takes no proactive measures; one merely accepts the vicissitudes of life without qualm. It was fated that such and such should happen becomes the commonly accepted rationalization. But the belief in the cycle of birth and rebirth has its positive side too. It creates an aspiration of hope. They 'know' that they need to act in a manner which would be considered to be meritorious. In so doing they would reap the rewards of their actions in their present life or in their future life. Many Hindus are also guided by the belief that in performing acts of piety, they are likely to be born into a 'better' family and into a higher caste in their next birth.

A Westerner, at this point, might be tempted to ask an important question. If human existence, according to Hindu philosophy, consists of unending cycles of birth and rebirth, is there any purpose to human existence? Is there any purpose to remaining bonded to an unending cycle of births, deaths and rebirths? The answer is simple. In Hindu philosophy, the external world is seen as being illusory. It is maya (Zimmer [1969] (1989)). Since the empirical world, the world of the senses, is constantly changing, it is seen as an inconstant, illusory world.

The ultimate purpose of human existence is to transcend one's illusory physical existence, renounce the world of material aspirations, attain a heightened state of spiritual awareness, and finally liberate oneself from the bondage of the cycle of birth and rebirth, through devotion or the acquisition of knowledge (wisdom) or right moral actions, thereby attaining moksha (Radhakrishnan, [1929] (1989)). It is then that one's soul (*atman*) merges with the ultimate brahman. Any activity that is likely to promote such a state is to be encouraged.

## CONCLUSION

The episode described at the start of the paper now begins to make sense. The high-caste Hindu Brahmin committed a variety of transgressions: he ate beef, which is taboo among orthodox Hindus, he had sex with a sex worker who was a woman of the lowest caste. He brought himself and his family into disrepute by his actions. Moreover, by dying in a sex worker's hut he created insoluble problems for his family members, the villagers, and for the high priest.

He himself had forfeited the rights to an appropriate Hindu Brahmin funeral. For the deceased's family members to enter the house of the sex worker would have resulted in their own spiritual pollution. They could not bring the body to their own home, for that would have resulted in even greater pollution, which would then entail severe austerities and sacrifices to wipe off the spiritual pollution. The high priest left the village in search of counsel from other high priests in other villages. In the meantime the sex worker and her friends took the matter into their own hands and performed the final funeral rites. They burnt down the hut with the corpse in it.

## REFERENCES

Basham, A. L. (1966). *The wonder that was India.* Calcutta: Rupa & Co.

Char, S. V. (1997). *Hinduism and Islam in India: Caste, religion, and society from antiquity to early modern times.* Princeton: Markus Wiener Publishers.

Chaudhuri, N. (1979). *Hinduism.* Oxford: Oxford University Press.

Filippi, S. G. (1996). *Mrtyu: Concept of death in Indian traditions. Reconstructing Indian histroy & culture. No. II.* New Delhi: D.K. Printworld Ltd.

Flood, G. (1996). *An introduction to Hinduism.* Cambridge: Cambridge University Press.

Fuller, C. J. (1992). *The camphor flame. Popular Hinduism and society in India.* Princeton: Princeton University Press.

Hiriyana, M. (1949). *The essentials of Indian philosophy.* London: George Allen & Unwin.

Kakar, S. (1981). *The inner world—Psychoanalytic study of children and society in India.* Delhi: Oxford University Press.

Klostermaier, K. K. (1998). *A short introduction to Hinduism.* Oxford: One World Publications.

Koller, J. M. (1982). *The Indian way: Persepectives.* London: Collier-Macmillan.

Lannoy, R. (1976). *The speaking tree.* Oxford: Oxford University Press.

Laungani, P. (1997). Death in a Hindu family. In C. M. Parkes, P. Laungani and B. Young (Eds), *Death and bereavement across cultures.* London: Routledge.

———. (1998). Cultural influences on identity and behaviour. In Y. T. Lee, C. R. McCauley and J. G. Draguns (Eds), *Personality and person perception across cultures.* Mahwah, NJ: Lawrence Erlbaum Associates.

Lipner, J. (1994). Hindus: Their religious beliefs and practices. London: Routledge.

Mandelbaum, D. G. (1972). *Society in India, Vol. 2.* Berkeley, CA: University of California Press.

Murthy, A. (1976). *Samskara.* New York: Oxford University Press.

O'Flaherty, W. D. (1976). *The origins of evil in Hindu mythology.* Berkeley, CA: University of California Press.

———. (1980). *Karma and rebirth in classical India.* Berkeley, CA: University of California Press.

Pandey, R. (1969). *Hindu samskaras: Socio-religious study of the Hindu sacraments.* Delhi: Motilal Banarasidass Publishers.

Prasad, R. (1989). *Karma causation and retributive morality: Conceptual essays in ethics and metaethics.* Indian Council of Philosophical Research. New Delhi: Munshiram Manoharlal Publishers.

Radhakrishnan, S. [1929] (1989). *Indian philosophy.* Vol. 2. Centenary Edition. Delhi: Oxford University Press.

Reichenbach, B. R. (1990). *The law of karma: A philosophical study.* Honolulu: University of Hawaii Press.
Sharma, A. (2000). *Classical Hindu thought: An introduction.* New Delhi: Oxford University Press.
Sinari, R. A. (1984). *The structure of Indian thought.* Delhi: Oxford University Press.
Triandis, H. C. (1994). *Culture and social behaviour.* New York: McGraw Hill.
Zaehner, R. C. (1966a). *Hinduism.* New York: Oxford University Press.
———. (1966b). *Hindu Scriptures.* JM Dent & Sons.
Zimmer, H. [1969] (1989). *Philosophies of India.* Bollinger Series XXVI. Princeton: Princeton University Press.

# PART FIVE

# Personal Reflections of Friends and Colleagues

# Antoinette D. Thomas

**Pittu** and I were 'old-timers' of the International Council of Psychologists who served on its Board. Participants in conferences, we became close friends in few years. We exchanged over 250 e-mails with authored attachments in less than two years. Our friendship included his loving wife Ann, my husband and daughter. It was so refreshing to be close to a happy couple. Ann was completely in charge of Pittu's health-related issues. In his dedication of his last book, he gave her due credit, 'I owe these 17 years of my life to your love and ceaseless efforts', beyond medical expectations.

I had the pleasure and honour to introduce Pittu Laungani in his Award-given two-days conference held by Toronto University for his life-time achievement in Cross-Cultural Counselling Psychology, in Toronto, Canada, 2005. I was pleasantly surprised to be asked to edit his Keynote address, 17 chapters and a short story.

His readers know that his fascinating style is sprinkled with genuine humour. He referred to my fast e-mailed responses as being 'like lightening'. On his gift-book he wrote, 'I hope it gives you some pleasure and lots of useless information'. His modesty was exemplified in attributing his beautiful handwriting, to 'the Jesuits' who taught him to write. Pittu had a fantastic memory for what he read all his life. It seems that his heroes are present in his thoughts and dreams. English writers particularly Shakespeare, ancient and contemporary philosophers, such as Plato and Popper are well and alive in most of his writings.

Pittu was a gifted poet. During his four-year editing of the ICP Newsletter, he wrote some of his editorial columns in poetry.

## CULTURE BENEFITS COUNSELLING MORE THAN PSYCHIATRY AND PSYCHOLOGY

Pittu put psychotherapy to the test, throwing doubt on its capacity to meet clients' needs, to pave the road for the unique contribution of culture. As early as 1984, his chapter 'Do psychotherapists meet clients' perceived needs?' in Hariman's bold book, *Does psychotherapy really help people?* (Laungani, 1984). As he questioned therapeutic validity, he got his readers to compare and choose between client-centred or culture-centred counselling (Laungani, 1999d) in his co-edited book, *Counselling in a multicultural society* (Palmer and Laungani, 1999a). And, 'The advantages of culture-centred counselling over client-centred counselling' in Morgan's *Meeting the needs of our clients creativity: The impact of art and culture on care giving* (Laungani, 2000a). Pittu generally raised more problems and questions than finding solutions. However, he came forth with his opinion in a journal article, 'Replacing client-centred counselling with cultural-centered counselling' (Laungani, 1997d). He used sets of contrasts between 'pillars of societies' in East and West. Eastern clients cannot accept Western's 'free will' and 'individualism' included in client-centred therapy, which holds them responsible for their success and failure as well as 'equality' with the therapist. 'Determinism' and 'communalism' or fate and submission to hierarchical authorities and the expectation of 'cure' provided by the therapist, are what they know. However, in his last book, *Understanding cross-cultural psychology* (2006b: 208–209), Pittu concluded that 'faith [Eastern] and reason [Western] together are the two sides of the coin of life...the synthesis is the dilemma that faces the world'. He attacked some psychiatric practices and ethics in 'Mindless psychiatry and dubious ethics' (Laungani, 2002h), which serious psychiatrists would agree with.

## CULTURAL COMPARISONS IN PERSONALITY, STRESS AND LEARNING

Laungani contributed the chapter 'Cultural influences on identity and behavior: India and Britain' in Lee, McCauley and Draguns' *Through the looking glass: Personality in culture* (Laungani, 1999a). He wrote a related chapter, 'Cultural influences on the development of identity: India and England' in Mohans' *Personality across cultures* (Laungani, 2000b). In a previous journal article he wrote, 'National differences in personality: India and England' (Laungani, 1985).

He co-edited with Spielberger, Sarason, Brebner, Greenglass and O'Roark *Stress and Emotion*, volumes 15 (Spielberger et al., 1995) and 16 (Spielberger et al., 1996). A contributed chapter was, 'Stress in Eastern and Western cultures' (Laungani, 1995). A related chapter was included in a subsequent volume, 'The experience and management of stress in a life-threatening illness' in Spielberger and Sarason's *Stress and emotion* (Laungani, 2005c).

'Cross-cultural investigations of stress: Conceptual and methodological considerations' (Laungani, 1996b) and 'Stress, trauma and coping strategies: Cross-cultural variations (Laungani, 2002e), appeared in journals.

He compared stress as experienced by people in the two cultures he was well familiar with, 'Stress in India and England' in Pestonjee, Pareek and Agarwal's *Studies in Stress and its Management* (Laungani, 1999b). A modified version, 'The influence of culture on stress: India and England' appeared in Adler and Gielen's *Cross-cultural topics in psychology* (Laungani, 2001a).

'Stress, culture and personality', in Cooper's *Handbook of stress medicine and health* (Laungani, 2005a), presented a link between the two topics, personality and stress.

Concerning cultural comparisons in learning, we find, 'Learning in children: Eastern and Western perspectives' in Bain, Janzen, Peterson, Stewin and Yu's *Psychology and education in the 21st Century: Proceedings of the 54th annual convention of the International Council of Psychologists* (Laungani, 1997c). Pittu contributed, 'Culture, cognition and trauma: Cross-cultural evaluations' in Schumaker and Ward's *Cultural cognition and psychopathology* (Laungani, 2001b).

## COUNSELLING IN DIFFERENT CULTURES

Pittu co-edited with Palmer yet another book, *Counselling in a Multicultural Society* (Palmer and Laungani, 1999a). Included was his chapter, 'Culture and identity: Implications for counselling' (Laungani, 1999c). He also co-authored with him two chapters: the Introduction (Palmer and Laungani, 1999b) and Conclusion (Palmer and Laungani, 1999c). Palmer issued another book *Multicultural counselling,* in which Pittu contributed his chapter, 'Mental illness across cultures: Eastern and Western perspectives' (Laungani, 2002d).

We see the term 'research' for the first time in his article, 'Research in cross-cultural settings: Ethical considerations' in Miao's *Cross-cultural encounter: Proceedings of the 53rd Annual Convention of the International Council of Psychologists* (Laungani, 1996a). A new related book was *Asian Perspectives in Counselling and Psychotherapy* (Laungani, 2004a).

Related journal articles included, 'The counselling interview: First impressions' (Laungani, 2002f), 'Cross-cultural psychology: A handmaiden to mainstream Western psychology' (Laungani, 2002g), 'Sexual abuse in an Asian family' (Laungani, 2003d), 'Counselling and therapy in a multicultural setting' (Laungani, 2004b), 'Some unresolved issues in philosophy and psychology: Their implications for therapy' (Laungani, 2004c) and 'Cast, class and culture: A case study' (Laungani, 2005b).

## THERAPEUTIC TECHNIQUES IN SERIOUS PHYSICAL ILLNESS

Based on personal thrive from paralysis, polymyositis and pulmonary fibrosis, Laungani stretches a strong arm to the terminally ill. He simply refused to be paralyzed. His extensive publications in the past 17 years support the notion of 'mind-over-matter' as a means of survival. Oxygen intake became his closest companion. He wrote a book, *It shouldn't happen to a patient* (Laungani, 1992) about his experience and how he managed to regain a relatively healthy condition. A condensed article followed on, 'Therapeutic strategies for coping with a life-threatening illness: A personal testament' (Laungani, 2003c). He provided eight rules along with relevant logic and suggested practices. The rules are: 'Focus only on what you can do', 'Your illness is unique only to you not to doctors', 'Accept pain as part of human condition', 'Get passionately absorbed in an activity', 'Find humour in each situation', 'Accept consequences of your actions and avoid what you cannot control', 'Reality is to guide hopes' and 'Accept human mortality'. The book and article offer guidelines to the medical staff in hospitals and clinics.

Pittu chose a funny bilingual title for his chapter that dealt with coping with a serious illness 'Vive le life' in Fenton's *Living with Myositis* (Laungani, 2003b). As a strong advocate of the influence of culture and spiritual beliefs that extend to all aspects of one's life, including health and illness, he wrote 'Hindu spirituality and healing practices' in Moodley and West's *Spirituality, religion, and cultural healing* (Laungani, 2005d).

## DEATH AND BEREAVEMENT

In the past decade, Laungani co-edited two widely distributed books: (*a*) *Death and bereavement across cultures* (Laungani et al., 1997a) with Parkes and (*b*) four volumes of *Death and bereavement around the world* between 2002 and 2006 (Morgan and Laungani, 2002, 2003, 2004, 2005) with the late John Morgan. The four prints of *Death and bereavement around the world* sold over 10,000 copies. His included chapters reflected his cultural expertize of his country of origin, India. For example: 'Death in a Hindu family' (Laungani, 1997b), 'Hindu spirituality in life, death and bereavement' (Laungani, 2002a) and 'Cultural considerations in Hindu funerals in India and England' (Laungani, 2003a). He co-authored with Parkes and Young, 'A conceptual framework: Historical and cultural themes' (Laungani et al., 1997b), 'Culture and religion' (Laungani et al., 1997c) and 'Conclusions: Implications for practice and policy' (Parkes et al., 1997d).

He wrote on 'Patterns of Bereavement in Indian and English society' in Morgan's *Readings in thanatology* (Laungani, 1997a). The importance of holding a funeral for family and friends as well as the infiltrating Western cultural variations appeared in 'Why have a funeral? Hindu funerals in England: Past, present and future' (Laungani, 2000c) in Morgan's *Meeting the needs of our clients creatively: The impact of art and culture on care giving* and 'Anglicization of Hindu funerals in England: Its impact on ancient cultural practices' (Laungani, 2002b). He explained 'The Hindu caste system' in Howarth and Leaman's *The encyclopedia of death and dying* (Laungani, 2002c).

Laungani wrote a chapter on 'Death, the final end or a new beginning? Cross-cultural evaluations' (Laungani, 2000d) in Comunian and Gielen's *International Perspectives on Human Development*.

Related journal articles included, 'Death and bereavement in India and England: A comparative analysis' (Laungani, 1996c) and 'Religious rites and rituals in death and bereavement: An Indian experience' (Laungani, 2006a). His co-authored chapter with Roach 'Counselling, death and bereavement (Laungani and Roach, 1997), linked these three concepts. Pittu also wrote on the tragic death of Princess Diana in British national journals.

Death was a common topic, which he talked and wrote about in personal correspondence. A few months before he departed from this world to a better one, he wrote, 'Life keeps ticking away...I can now honestly say that the end is coming... there is nothing I can do about the downward trend...winter is beginning to freeze my heart' (Personal communication, 7 June and 23 November 2006).

Pittu may exaggerate to make a point. It may seem that 'East is better than West and India represents the East'. Yet, he was well aware of the relative mutual infiltration of Eastern and Western cultures in all countries. His own life was an example of strong loyalty to his country of origin and his adaptation to what he found honourable and healthy from the West. In spite of his high regard to Indian life-styles, he was objective in criticizing certain practices, such as entering a room without knocking on the door.

I often smile when Pittu 'ignored' our disagreements. It reflects his high intelligence and tact. We discussed trivial points, such as characters' names. I will always cherish his generous, undeserved complements, a mere projection of his own characteristics, 'In you, I have found the most kind and caring friend'. Pittu was a true gentleman in all his behaviours and a real genius.

## REFERENCES

Laungani, P. (1984). Do psychotherapists meet clients' perceived needs? In J. Hariman (Ed.), *Does psychotherapy really help people?* (pp. 132–143). Springfield, IL: Charles C. Thomas.

Laungani, P. (1985). National differences in personality: India and England. *Personality and Individual Differences, 6*(2), 217–221.

———. (1992). *It shouldn't happen to a patient.* London: Whiting & Birch.

———. (1995). Stress in Eastern and Western cultures. In C. D. Spielberger, I. G. Sarason, J. M. Brebner, E. Greenglass, P. Laungani and M. A. O'Roark, (Eds), *Stress and Emotion, Vol. 15* (pp. 265–280). Washington, DC: Taylor & Francis.

———. (1996a). Research in cross-cultural settings: Ethical considerations. In E. Miao (Ed.), *Cross-cultural encounter: Proceedings of the 53rd annual convention of the International Council of Psychologists* (pp. 107–136). Taipei: General Innovation Service.

———. (1996b). Cross-cultural investigations of stress: Conceptual and methodological considerations. *International Journal of Stress Management, 3*(1), 25–35.

———. (1996c). Death and bereavement in India and England: A comparative analysis. *Mortality, 1*(2), 191–212.

———. (1997a). Patterns of bereavement in Indian and English society. In J. A. Morgan and J. D. Morgan (Eds), *Readings in thanatology* (pp. 67–76). Amityville, NY: Baywood.

———. (1997b). Death in a Hindu family. In C. M. Parkes, P. Laungani and B. Young (Eds), *Death and bereavement across cultures* (pp. 52–72). London: Routledge.

———. (1997c). Learning in children: Eastern and Western perspectives. In B. Bain, H. Janzen, J. Paterson, L. Stewin and A. Yu (Eds), *Psychology and education in the 21st Century: Proceedings of the 54th annual convention of the International Council of Psychologists* (pp. 185–195). Edmonton, AB: IC Press.

———. (1997d). Replacing client-centered counselling with cultural-centered counselling. *Counselling Psychology Quarterly, 10*(4), 343–351.

———. (1999a). Cultural influences on identity and behavior: India and Britain. In Y-T Lee, C. R. McCauley and J. Draguns (Eds), *Through the looking glass: Personality in culture* (pp. 191–212). Mahwah, NJ: Lawrence Erlbaum Associates.

———. (1999b). Stress in India and England. In D. M. Pestonjee, U. Pareek and R. Agarwal (Eds), *Studies in stress and its management* (pp. 219–226). New Delhi: Oxford/India Book House.

———. (1999c). Culture and identity: Implications for counselling. In S. Palmer and P. Laungani (Eds), *Counselling in a multicultural society* (pp. 35–70). London: Sage Publications.

———. (1999d). Client-centered or culture-centered counselling? In S. Palmer and P. Laungani (Eds), *Counselling in a multicultural society* (pp. 133–151). London: Sage Publications.

———. (2000a). The advantages of culture-centered counselling over client-centered counselling. In J. Morgan (Ed.), *Meeting the needs of our clients creatively: The impact of art and culture on care giving* (pp. 37–48). Amityville, NY: Baywood.

———. (2000b). Cultural influences on the development of identity: India and England. In J. Mohan (Ed.), *Personality across cultures* (pp. 284–312). Delhi: Oxford University Press.

———. (2000c). Why have a funeral? Hindu funerals in England: Past, present and future. In J. Morgan (Ed.), *Meeting the needs of our clients creatively: The impact of art and culture on care giving* (pp. 231–242). Amityville, NY: Baywood.

———. (2000d). Death: The final end or a new beginning? Cross-cultural evaluations. In A. L. Comunian and U. Gielen (Eds), *International perspectives on human development* (pp. 637–662). Zagreb: Pabst.

———. (2001a). The influence of culture on stress: India and England. In L. L. Adler and U. Gielen (Eds), *Cross-cultural topics in psychology (2nd ed.)* (pp. 149–170). Westport, CT: Prager.

———. (2001b). Culture, cognition and trauma: Cross-cultural evaluations. In J. F. Schumaker and T. Ward (Eds), *Cultural cognition and psychopathology* (pp. 119–144). Westport, CT: Prager.

———. (2002a). Hindu spirituality in life, death and bereavement. In J. Morgan and P. Laungani (Eds), *Death and bereavement around the world, Vol. 1* (pp. 9–38). Amityville, NY: Baywood.

———. (2002b). Anglicization of Hindu funerals in England: Its impact on ancient cultural practices. *The Proceedings of the International Council of Psychologists, 56th Annual Convention,* Melbourne, Australia.

Laungani, P. (2002c). The Hindu caste system. In G. Howarth and O. Leaman (Eds), *The encyclopedia of death and dying* (pp. 78–80). London: Routledge.

———. (2002d). Mental illness across cultures: Eastern and Western perspectives. In S. Palmer (Ed.), *Multicultural counselling* (pp. 129–156). London: Sage Publications.

———. (2002e). Stress, trauma and coping strategies: Cross-cultural variations. *International Journal of Global Tension, 31*(2), 127–154.

———. (2002f). The counselling interview: First impressions. *Counselling Psychology Quarterly, 15*(1), 107–113.

———. (2002g). Cross-cultural psychology: A handmaiden to mainstream Western psychology. *Counselling Psychology Quarterly, 15*(4), 385–397.

———. (2002h). Mindless psychiatry and dubious ethics. *Counselling Psychology Quarterly, 15*(1), 23–33.

———. (2003a). Cultural considerations in Hindu funerals in India and England. In J. Morgan and P. Laungani (Eds), *Death and bereavement around the world, Vol. 4* (pp. 39–64), *Vol. 2*. Amityville, NY: Baywood.

———. (2003b). Vive le life! In J. Fenton (Ed.), *Living with Myositis.* London: Thoughtful.

———. (2003c). Therapeutic strategies for coping with a life-threatening illness: A personal testament. *Illness, Crisis & Loss, 11*(2), 162–182.

———. (2003d). Sexual abuse in an Asian family. *Counselling Psychology Quarterly, 16*(4), 385–401.

———. (2004a). *Asian Perspectives in Counselling and Psychotherapy.* London: Routledge.

———. (2004b). Counselling and therapy in a multicultural setting. *Counselling Psychology Quarterly, 17*(2), 195–207.

———. (2004c). Some unresolved issues in philosophy and psychology: Their implications for therapy. *Counselling Psychology Quarterly, 7*(1), 107–123.

———. (2005a). Stress, culture and personality. In C. Cooper (Ed.), *Handbook of stress medicine and health* (pp. 209–227). Boca Raton, FL: CRC Press, LLC.

———. (2005b). Cast, class and culture: A case study. *Counselling Psychology Quarterly, 18*(1), 61–71.

———. (2005c). The experience and management of stress in a life-threatening illness. In C. D. Spielberger and I. Sarason, (Eds), *Stress and emotion, 17* (pp. 3–30). Washington, DC: Taylor & Francis.

———. (2005d). Hindu spirituality and healing practices. In R. Moodley and W. West (Eds), *Spirituality, religion, and cultural healing* (pp. 138–147). Thousand Oaks, CA: Sage Publications.

———. (2006a). Religious rites and rituals in death and bereavement: An Indian experience. *International Journal of Health Promotion and Education, 44*(1), 7–13.

———. (2006b). *Understanding cross-cultural psychology.* London: Sage Publications.

Laungani, P. and Roach, F. (1997). Counselling, death and bereavement. In S. Palmer (Ed.), *Handbook of counselling* (pp. 362–381). London: Sage Publications.

Laungani, P., Parkes, C. M. and Young, B. (Eds) (1997a). *Death and bereavement across cultures.* London: Routledge.

———. (1997b). A conceptual framework: Historical and cultural themes. In C. M. Parkes, P. Laungani and B. Young (Eds), *Death and bereavement across cultures* (pp. 3–9). London: Routledge.

———. (1997c). Culture and religion. In C. M. Parkes, P. Laungani and B. Young (Eds), *Death and bereavement across cultures* (pp. 10–26). London: Routledge.

Morgan, J. D. and Laungani, P. (Eds) (2002). *Death and bereavement around the world. Vol. 1. Major religious traditions.* Amytiville, NY: Baywood.

———. (Eds) (2003). *Death and bereavement around the world, Vol. 2, Death and bereavement in the Americas.* Amytiville, NY: Baywood.

———. (Eds) (2004). *Death and bereavement around the world. Vol. 3, Death and bereavement in the Americas.* Amytiville, NY: Baywood.

———. (Eds) (2005). *Death and bereavement around the world. Vol. 4. Death and bereavement in the Americas.* Amytiville, NY: Baywood.

Palmer, S. and Laungani, P. (Eds) (1999a). *Counselling in a multicultural society.* London: Sage Publications.

———. (1999b). Introduction. In S. Palmer and P. Laungani (Eds), *Counselling in a multicultural society* (pp. 1–5). London: Sage Publications.

———. (1999c). Conclusion. In S. Palmer and P. Laungani (Eds), *Counselling in a multicultural society* (pp. Afterword on page 203). London: Sage Publications.

Parkes, C., Laungani, P. and Young, B. (1997d). Conclusions: Implications for practice and policy. In C. M. Parkes, P. Laungani and B. Young (Eds), *Death and bereavement across cultures* (pp. 218–232). London: Routledge.

Spielberger, Charles D. et al. (Eds). (1995). *Stress and emotion, Vol. 15.* Washington, DC: Taylor & Francis.

———. (Eds). (1996). *Stress and emotion, Vol. 16.* Washington, DC: Taylor & Francis.

# Ann R. Laungani

## IN THE BEGINNING

I have to go back to when I first met Pittu in 1977 when he was a Senior Lecturer at South Bank University in London as he made such a memorable first impression on me. He seemed to be a person who was gentle and caring but always expected his students to reach the highest standards in their work. I realized that he was a dynamic person with great presence about him. I soon learnt that he always sought challenges in his life, and he wanted others around him to work towards goals to reach their fullest potential in life.

## EARLY LIFE IN UK

Pittu left India in 1966 to develop his career in psychology in UK, having obtained his first degree in Psychology and the Masters degree at the University of Bombay. He lived initially in London and then moved to Hertfordshire with his Indian partner, who was also a psychologist. After she died he moved back to London. Pittu completed his Ph.D. in 1983 on Cross-Cultural Personality and Conformity in England and India. After this, he started working on psychological issues related to health, social care and bereavement. My links with community health care services encouraged him to move into these areas, which he married up with his doctoral research on Eastern and Western concepts of life. He became involved with child abuse, accident prevention, disability, post-natal depression and other public health issues. Once he became interested in a project, he moved rapidly with his ideas to explore a topic and work out his own interpretation of the current available research and literature in that area. The major area of his research and writing was based on a cross-cultural psychological perspective. His living between two cultures—India and UK for more than 40 years of his life—fuelled this.

Pittu and I were married in 1985. We enjoyed a busy, exciting and hectic four years living in London before he suddenly became ill and developed a life-threatening illness.

## ILLNESS YEARS—FROM THE ACUTE ONSET TO CHRONIC ILLNESS

It was after one of our summer trips to Mumbai that he became ill. We had taken a trip not only to stay with his family but also to undertake research on child health in a major poverty-stricken area in the suburb of Dharavi in Mumbai.

Pittu spent time interviewing families and sampling first hand the life, which the people lived in such a polluted, crowded and stressful environment. On our return Pittu developed joint pain, weakness and swallowing difficulties. Despite seeing doctors, gradually his condition became more serious until he was admitted to a London hospital and taken to the Intensive Care Unit immediately. This was the start of the uncertain times with peaks and troughs in Pittu's health, which kept us constantly anxious. Never again were we able to take anything for granted or feel that we could plan future events without worry as to whether they would actually take place. There were frequent hospital admissions and attendances, creating a dependence on the availability of specialized services.

### The Acute Illness

When Pittu became acutely ill, we were both plunged into an existence centred totally on the hospital ward, doctors, tests, therapists, ward rounds, anxious telephone calls—a life far removed from a 'normal one'. The time it took for the doctors to diagnosis and then initiate the best treatment seemed interminable, with deterioration setting in everyday. When eventually the diagnosis of Polymyositis was made, it was somewhat of a relief as it wasn't cancer or renal failure, which Pittu had feared. However, the treatment was far from effective and the doctors felt that there would be very limited recovery from the illness. Pittu himself was very discouraged by the devastating effects of his illness, the pain, the loss of mobility and the dependence on others. He felt angry with the doctors' pessimistic outlook for a recovery to live once again a 'normal life'. He wrote that 'to learn to cope with pain (if not conquer it) one needs from a practical point of view, a role model and that the role model could be anybody whom one admires and would wish, under such circumstances, to emulate'. The choice of the role model was based on admiration for a great American hero—John Wayne and his portrayal in a film in which he walked into the operating theatre instead of being wheeled on a trolley and walked out again without succumbing to being helpless in any way. Pittu learnt to 'accept pain as part of the human condition', he said that whenever he was 'plagued by pain, sleeplessness, breathing difficulties and other ills' he would ask himself 'What would John Wayne do in my situation? "He'd grin and bear it"'.

After the acute episode of illness subsided, 'the initial flush of excitement at being able to take a few steps soon gave way to a feeling of morbid depression'.

Finding an all-consuming goal was to be the saviour, there was an unexpected offer from Pittu's publisher to write a book about his experiences in hospital. Life, unexpectedly, took on a new turn and he was galvanized into action. This led to his belief to 'find an activity in which you can get passionately absorbed' and action on this premise helped him in moving forward in his recovery.

## Dynamics of Day-to-Day Living

As Pittu's illness became chronic and debilitating, we adjusted our lifestyle and relationship to cope with the anxiety about survival and management of day-to-day living in as risk free a manner as possible. The serious illness affected his life in different ways, which were both positive and negative. On the positive side, in his observations of his experiences he was able to see 'the funny side of situations which would normally be considered grave or sombre' and that 'fun, pleasure and laughter can be squeezed out of most situations'. It was 'humour' that occupied his mind the most. Although 'humour' can be elusive in desperate times and there were times when the illness, which had its exacerbations and remissions, came back with a cruel vengeance and caused extreme distress and anxiety for both of us.

Inevitably with the increasing severity of Pittu's symptoms, our relationship changed. Increasing debility brought about an increasingly dependent mode of behaviour in Pittu in relation to practical matters at home, with a withdrawal from activities outside the home. There was a barely concealed resentment about the need for physical dependence. As the 'healthy' partner, I was aware that at times I could be obsessively controlling in my behaviour—as a manifestation of anxiety, to ensure the best for my 'sick' partner. I felt that we became self absorbed with our own agendas and unaware of the personality changes which we were undergoing, as we were so caught up with concentrating on the difficulties of living and surviving. We were unable to be in the least bit objective about our life and future, which was unbearable to think about, as it was so uncertain. In retrospect, I see this as facing up to loss, loss of a lifestyle and ability to do what one wants to in life without undue impedance and loss of a future.

## Strategies for Living with a Chronic Illness

Pittu wrote about the therapeutic strategies he used and others might use to cope with a chronic illness. In his strategies, he proposed rules and corollaries to rules with which to combat a life-threatening illness.

The belief in a 'role model' was important to him. He believed that 'pain was an integral part of the human condition' and that we had 'to learn to accept it'. He felt that 'wisdom lay in accepting it and transcending it where possible'.

'Finding an activity in which you can get passionately absorbed' was a well-used rule and the corollary that the activity should fit the person in that 'it should be challenging to them and within their natural inclinations, talent and physical capabilities' is appropriate to achieve any development of well-being in life. He believed that 'Humour was important as an antidote to depression and 'makes life worth living' and that you should 'train yourself to see the funny side in any situation'.

The illness seriously affected his active life, which inevitably made him go through periods of depression and anxiety; these he deflected as far as he could by adhering to his 'rules'—humour, creativity, writing, an intensive work programme and meaningful communications with his friends, students and colleagues.

He was not a religious man; he did not have a personal guru. He depended on his own resources to manage the vicissitudes of life. He felt this to be the right path to take, which he did with great vigour and often chagrin. Pittu was hard on himself and on others at times; he expected people to make the best of their talents and cope with adversity in a challenging way as he did.

He found seeing friends and inviting them to the house to be one of the most comforting activities, and our house was always open to whoever wanted to visit. He also enjoyed going out to restaurants in London but this always meant very accessible ones where he could be dropped outside the door.

Different beliefs about illness and health can cause conflict. As the illness progressed, Pittu saw the need to live carefully by taking rest and focussing on eating—never a thing he enjoyed latterly—a healthy nutritious diet and following a programme of regular exercise daily using a treadmill within his limitations. Nutrition can influence health outcomes and I worked consistently with Pittu to optimize his health and reduce the ill-effects of his illness.

Relaxation involved watching cricket test matches passionately and unflinchingly to the end—he had been an excellent cricketer. Reading literature was essential, both serious—Shakespeare, Dostoyevsky, Greek mythology and philosophy, classical Indian writers—and also thrillers of which he was a keen fan and critic. Plays and films, particularly Westerns, were also important to him that he felt were the ultimate in terms of truth and clarity about morals and tales of extreme courage and endurance.

Many people found that he was a source of wisdom and knowledge, which came from his ability to synthesize what he gained from reading across such a wide range of topics. The links he made between literature, philosophy and psychology, gave an illuminating touch to his writing. Psychology scholars worldwide shared his research and writing interests and appreciated his ability to be both analytical and to make ideas accessible to the general reader. He was self-deprecating as well as articulate and learned. The steely resolve to continue working under almost any circumstances caused by his illness continued until his last months, and his charm and 'grave' humour at times were well-remembered.

A friend greeted him once by saying 'you should be dead', he was able to share in this joke without offence or fear by saying 'yes the doctors keep saying that, but here I am still fighting fiercely' a characteristic quality he maintained throughout his life. Humour was something that he valued highly and he resorted to it when a situation became increasingly dire. He managed his ill health shrewdly near the end of his life to optimize his opportunities for work. There were times however when he miscalculated the effects of continuous work on his health and made over-ambitious plans, which sadly at times had to be curtailed.

One of Pittu's aims was to leave something behind, to be remembered for his ideas and work, which was a dominant force in his life. As a person he was brave and determined, there was a sparkle to his conversation and original thought as well as a disarming habit of asking people very direct questions about themselves. By breaking the rules and getting through to people, he could often clearly interpret their motivations, thoughts and actions. Although latterly he preferred to spend his day writing in solitude, he was in fact extremely gregarious and enjoyed having visitors to the house and giving time to his students and the clients who needed his help. He would always listen to people's problems, becoming involved in them by seeking to offer support in reaching solutions. Sometimes he seemed to be hypercritical and demanding but this in itself was often to act as a spur to enable people to gain some insight into their lives and make changes. He was never malevolent and always cared deeply for the welfare of his friends, family and students.

## LIFE ACHIEVEMENT AWARD

When Pittu heard that he had been nominated for the Life Achievement Award from the University of Toronto for his work in psychology, he was initially disbelieving that such an honour should be given to him, as he never felt that he was an exceptionally talented or eminent person and certainly did not promote himself as an eminent person in his field. He was absolutely delighted with being invited to Toronto and found the whole experience moving and fulfilling and was very happy to be recognized for his work. To travel to Toronto put a strain on both of us, as Pittu had to use oxygen almost continuously, which meant that arrangements had to be made with the airlines for oxygen during the flight, and then with the local services to meet him before disembarking to provide him with a portable oxygen supply. However we, he managed it all without any mishaps. He came home with a two-fold sense of achievement from the award and the successful, enjoyable journey and the wonderful friends he made in Toronto.

I was fortunate enough to meet Pittu and marry him. I was aware that life was not going to be peaceful and I would be letting myself in for a challenging life, and it turned out to be an intensely taxing time in terms of physical and mental energy. In the beginning life was like walking on a tightrope with everything; work, research, meeting friends, playing sport, visiting his family, travel, going to theatres and concerts, all taking place at a fast pace.

He was totally focussed on his goals and had a very dominant character. The illness influenced his personality and lifestyle in many ways. He often said to himself that he would never have achieved as much writing, thinking, reflecting and research if he had not become ill; this was some compensation for his illness at times. With good health there would have been more emphasis on 'fun', with holidays, socializing and sports. As a wife and as a carer, the dual role demanded more frequent and closer day-to-day contact and interdependence than might be usual in a marriage. Pittu was always appreciative of my efforts even though he was tired of being encouraged to eat when he wasn't hungry and take increasingly large amounts of medications everyday.

Living with such an inspirational person meant that life was never mundane or dull; he set challenges for many aspects of our lives, which we both worked to meet. He was loyal, supportive and loving as a husband despite the disappointment and despair he felt in the later stages of his illness. There were days when he felt he achieved little and the influence of his early education from the Jesuits drove him to believe that self-worth only came with the work ethic and self-denial.

## REFLECTIONS ON THE LAST YEAR OF HIS LIFE

Death, dying and bereavement were topics, which Pittu had contemplated and written about for many years since he lost his previously robust health. He believed that 'it is necessary to come to terms with one's mortality and that "acknowledgment of one's mortality" acts as a liberating influence in one's life'.

He contributed to a series on death and bereavement with Jack Morgan from the University of Western Ontario, a pioneer in the death awareness movement. Pittu took over the editing of *Death and Bereavement,* Vol. 5, after Jack's death. He was very saddened by Jack's ill health and subsequent death; he had been a very supportive friend to Pittu and his demise came at a time when Pittu's health was very precarious. Any death is a reminder of one's own mortality, and despite his rational belief in coming to terms with one's mortality, he did have emotions about the thought of dying.

In the last year of his life and even before this, he lamented over his failing health, which caused him weakness, breathlessness, difficulty with walking and an increasing restriction to his life activities, such as going out alone, having holidays, attending meetings and conferences and taking any risks. It was a blessing that he lived to complete *Understanding cross cultural psychology* published in January 2007, which he was very pleased and relieved about. He seemed to have a very definite feeling that his life was running out and that he had little fight left in him to finally complete the editing of the remaining volume of *Death and bereavement.*

In the summer of 2006, he learnt that he had developed Aortic Stenosis—a narrowing of the heart valve, which seemed to be causing him increasing breathlessness. This was discouraging as he was aware that surgical treatment was the main option available, and he was not a candidate for surgery. He was unable to enjoy the summer holidays that year, as walking was more difficult and he became tired very quickly after any physical activity. In his daily diary, he wrote of the impending arrival of the 'grim reaper' whom he had eluded and I had determinedly fought off for years. He told a close friend in October that he doubted if he would see him again after the winter. We both had concerns about his health over the winter months, which turned out to be an accurate premonition and acceptance of his deteriorating condition. The Christmas holiday period was a distressing one as despite relatively unchanged lung function tests at a specialist hospital in London, he gradually began to feel weaker, more breathless and more discouraged. This was compounded by sleeping difficulties, all a vicious circle of failing health, causing more fatigue and malaise. In January 2007, he developed a cough and extreme breathlessness, which led to his hospitalization and further emerging complications. The immunosuppressive medications and advanced state of his pulmonary fibrosis meant that had no reserve to cope with any infections or cardiac problems. Despite the specialized medical and nursing care he received, his condition deteriorated, he required palliative care and eventually died on 28 February 2007.

I can only say how much I miss him and remember him as the most important and influential person in my life for all the years we spent together.

Although Pittu did not believe in any one religion or God, he was not an atheist and was a deeply reflective person. He felt that for a long time the 'grim reaper' was seeking him out and he was resisting his power, but that this could not continue for too long.

Pittu will live in the hearts of many; his spirit will be there for us.

## REFERENCE

Laungani P. (2003). Therapeutic strategies for coping with a life-threatening illness: A personal testament in Sage: Center for Death Education and Bioethics. *Illness Crisis and Loss, 11*(2), 172–175.

# Stephen Palmer

**As** I start writing this eulogy, today, 28 February 2008, it is my 53rd birthday. On days such as these it is an occasion when I reflect on my life, the relationships with my family, friends and colleagues and note my personal challenges and achievements. My hopes for the future are becoming more time-bound as I acknowledge my mortality. This whole reflection process takes a little longer each year as I have more to remember and I have become a little more forgetful. It also can be more painful as slowly, very slowly, more people that I am close to have died.

I had the privilege and honour to speak at the funeral of my friend, colleague and mentor, Pittu Laungani. Today I am particularly reflective as it is a year to the very day, since my colleague, friend and mentor, Pittu Laungani, has died. We started the day with a champagne toast to me and then to Pittu. I am now sitting in my study where I have written and edited many of my books in Porthleven, Cornwall. Down here I live above the beach and today the sea and sky are grey with a slight tinge of green. I can see and hear the surf. Now is a good time to give a personal reflection on my relationship with Pittu and his contribution to the fields of psychology and health.

In 1991, I was asked to Chair a conference on *Stress and the Health Services* at the Royal Society of Medicine in London on behalf of the Society of Public Health. I like events to run smoothly so when I was told that one of the speakers could not attend the conference, I offered to step in and give a paper on how health professionals largely create their own levels of stress, and not as widely believed, the United Kingdom's National Health Service (Palmer, 1991). However, as it was going to be a rather challenging paper to give in that the conference delegates may object to my rather cognitive approach to stress and stress management I asked for a volunteer to chair my session. A stranger sitting in the front row, Pittu Laungani, came to the rescue and chaired my session.

Somewhat surprisingly my paper was well received. Later Pittu gave a paper on stress across cultures (Laungani, 1991). He showed the audience fascinating photos of potential stressors in India. He told us that we may whine on about travelling to London on British Rail but at least we don't have to hold on to the outside of the rush hour trains. His photos illustrated the travelling problems, the poverty and poor housing in his own country. His paper and those photos became indelibly imprinted in my mind. Who are we in the West to moan about stress was the message I took from that conference. It was an excellent paper and I had now met Pittu.

In 1994, the International Stress Management Association (UK) held a stress conference at the University of York. It was an enjoyable event. Once again, a number of speakers did not make the event so I gave a few extra impromptu papers instead (Palmer, 1994a, 1994b). I attended Pittu's presentation and afterwards we agreed to travel back together by train. It was a long journey and we talked about stress and other health-related issues, in particular the cross-cultural aspects of stress. In passing, Pittu mentioned that I should consider taking a Ph.D. In addition, we discussed his own poor health and his recent book, *It Shouldn't Happen to Patient* (Laungani, 1992).

Opposite to us was a passenger who had overheard our conversation. He was rather grey in complexion. When there was a pause in our conversation the passenger said he realized we were health professionals and he then proceeded to tell us that even though he was only in his late 40s, he had prostate cancer which had reached his bones and was inoperable. A year or so earlier he had become aware of a dull pain in his back but he was very busy at work and just ignored it. His consultant told him that he did not have long to live. Pittu and I discussed life and death with him. It's strange how a crowded and noisy train carriage can go so quiet in these situations. Pittu took a matter of fact, yet very caring approach. We all parted company at the station and Pittu and I agreed to have regular PSA tests. For years later, Pittu and I often recalled this experience. Discussing impending death with a total stranger became second nature to Pittu, as he had previously spent many hours thinking and writing about death and bereavement, perhaps reflecting his relationship with his own serious illness.

Pittu was a Reader of Psychology at South Bank University, London. He actively encouraged me to do a Ph.D. and subsequently became my Ph.D. advisor. He was supportive, always challenging, always pushing forward the deadlines for the chapters. In fact, one of the most challenging aspects was when he believed that the university should invite an international stress expert to be my external examiner, Professor Charles Spielberger from the Center for Research in Behavioral Medicine and Health Psychology, University of South Florida. The most challenging aspect was to bring forward the Ph.D. viva by almost a year to coincide when Professor Spielberger was next visiting the UK. This did mean I would get it over and done with earlier rather than later but did also mean I gave up a few of my external posts so I could focus on the important task.

Pittu took his relationships with his doctorate candidates seriously. Their success was important. Pittu invited me out for a meal at the Royal Society of Medicine. Over dinner, we went through a mock Ph.D. viva. This was such a useful exercise being asked challenging questions relating to my work. He helped me to consider answers to the trickier questions. This experience has had a lasting impact upon how I have supervised my own doctorate students, actively encouraging them to think of the most difficult questions they could be asked and talking them through them at a mock viva. The real viva went well and it was a great pleasure meeting Charles too.

In 1999, our co-edited book on counselling in a Multicultural Society was published by SAGE (Palmer and Laungani, 1999). However, Pittu's pro-fessional influence went far beyond cultural psychology, psychotherapy and stress management. In 2000 Pittu became President of the Institute of Health Promotion and Education (IHPE). I remember his enthusiasm for conferences. He was responsible for arranging an excellent joint IHPE and St Catherine's Hospice. A memorable event. In 2001, he received the Annual International Journal of Health Promotion and Education Award in recognition of two outstanding Articles Titled: *Hindu Funerals in India; Hindu Deaths in Britain.* But stress was always an interest. In 2003 and 2004 (Laungani and Palmer, 2003, 2004), we co-edited two special issues on stress for the *International Journal of Health Promotion & Education.* By now he was the Associate Editor of the journal.

As his health gradually worsened, paradoxically the number of his publications increased. I recall our last conversation. He was ill in hospital and we talked on the phone. He wanted us to write an article in response to *The God Delusion* by Richard Dawkins. He had strong views about the Dawkin's new book. Pittu always cherished a good debate.

We never wrote that response together, as Pittu died not long later. However, remarkably in January 2009, we did publish a book together on *Death and bereavement* (Morgan et al., 2009). He had been editing this book with his old friend and colleague Jack Morgan. Sadly Jack had died prior to Pittu's death. This book was their unfinished work. So to complete their work, their fifth and final book in the series on Death and Bereavement, I took over the editorship on their behalf.

I said goodbye to Pittu at the funeral. Editing a book with a deceased friend and colleague was a difficult process, literally picking up the pieces. So the process of saying goodbye continued. It's taken almost a year to finish this farewell which I first started to write on the 1st anniversary of his death and coincidentally my birthday. Pittu's professional work reached many people, and will continue to influence a range of professions, yet it was the person that reached me.

## REFERENCES

Laungani, P. (1991). *Stress across cultures: A theoretical analysis.* Paper presented at the Conference of the Society of Public Health on Stress and the Health Services held at the Royal Society of Medicine, London.

Laungani, P. (1992). *It shouldn't happen to patient.* London: Whiting & Birch Ltd.

Laungani, P. and Palmer, S. (2003). Special Symposium Issue: Stress—Part 1. *International Journal of Health Promotion & Education, 41*(4).

———. (2004). Special Symposium Issue: Stress—Part 2. *International Journal of Health Promotion & Education, 42*(1).

Morgan, J. D., Laungani, P. and Palmer, S. (2009). *Death and bereavement around the world. Volume 5: Reflective essays.* Amityville, NY: Baywood.

Palmar, S. (1991). *The people-orientated professional: A cognitive perspective.* Paper presented at 'Stress and the NHS' conference run by the Society of Public Health and published in the conference proceedings.

———. (1994a). *Stress management interventions in the workplace: A practitioner's experience.* Paper presented at the annual conference of the International Stress Management Association (UK) at York University. Published in the conference proceedings.

———. (1994b). *A multimodal approach to stress management.* Paper presented at the annual conference of the International Stress Management Association (UK) at York University. Published in the conference proceedings.

Palmer, S. and Laungani, P. (1999). *Counselling in a multicultural society.* London: Sage Publications.

# Waseem Alladin

**The** first time I heard of Pittu Laungani was in 1992 when he became a contributing author to a special issue of *Counselling Psychology Quarterly* named *Transcultural Psychology: Theory, Research and Practice,* which was guest edited by Vaman Lokare, a British clinical psychologist originally from India. I remember scanning his paper and musing that it was interesting but I confess he did not grab my attention until more recently. For some reason, I cannot place my first acquaintance with Pittu but recall a handwritten letter I received from him, and we made subsequent telephone contact. He asked me in Hindi if I spoke Hindi (that much I understood!) and I said that I understood only a few words but sadly could not speak it. I sensed his disappointment because I think he would have felt a stronger connection and ease in communicating if we shared the same language, the same mother tongue. I was not an active cricket fan either. I did not then know his age, and his telephone voice struck me as youthful and energetic. Neither did I then know about the exact nature of his illness. I was curious to meet the man behind the voice and put a face to the Hindu name.

Several years later the opportunity arose at an international conference where I presented a paper and noticed that he too was presenting and also chairing the symposium. Shortly after, I got an invitation from him and Stephen Palmer to author a chapter on multicultural psychology for a book they were editing. Owing to circumstances, I could not deliver the chapter to the deadline and I apologized to Pittu and pleaded with him to omit my contribution, since I was thoroughly embarrassed as this was out-of-character for me. Pittu had a charming way of persuasion. He impressed upon me that my chapter was essential to the book and offered me a further extension, and nearer the new deadline I rang him again and apologized , fearing that I could not meet it and again asked him to forget about my contribution. Perhaps I caught him on a bad day but in a firm voice he threatened to 'personally strangle' me if I failed to deliver the chapter! Pittu surely knew how to get to the heart of the matter, or should I say how to go for the jugular! I confess to being taken aback but as we continued the conversation, there was clearly something really endearing about him. Needless to say, the chapter was delivered in record time. This chapter not only served as a text for the generations of clinical and counselling psychologists that I trained, but the 'ripples' created by that piece of work still contributed to invitations resulting in my going to different parts of the world even 10 years later! For example, last year, I was invited by the United Nations to present my work at the UNESCO HQ in Paris at an International Conference. This opportunity awakened in me the urgent need for all of us to participate in human rights education.

Since Pittu's health did not allow him to travel to an international conference in Toronto, I was given the honour of reading his scholarly paper and also playing the role of Bhagvan Rajneesh in The Strange Affliction of Prince Hamlet, a play written by Pittu. It was a moving and unique experience for me, and several members of the audience later congratulated me on holding my own against Freud and Rogers and for sounding like the authentic guru! I was tempted then as I am tempted now to give up my day job. Drama, psychodrama and the theatre have always fascinated me but I never had the courage to perform before an audience let alone an international audience but was inspired and greatly amused by Pittu's play.

## OPENING HIS HEART AND HEARTH TO ONE AND ALL

So what is it about Pittu that endeared him to so many people who got to know him? I am not the best person to give a definitive answer to this question but it seems to me that Pittu was a real friend who cared to share his views, open his life to others, welcomed everyone to his home and helped to build up everyone who appreciated his care and attention whatever their position. Pittu spoke from his heart and said what he truly believed in. This refreshing intellectual honesty was no respecter of persons and never afraid of controversy. He had a flair of 'going native' when he spoke or wrote about a topic and inspired me to reflect on what I had mistakenly taken for granted as given or obvious in the field of cross-cultural psychology. Pittu also showed that the interpersonal was often tinged with the political. He had subtle and disarming ways of making profound points in the apparently simplest of interactions. Consider what he had to say about the parochial tendency in the Western world to call the shots in unwittingly (or otherwise) setting the standards for the rest of the world:

> Let me end my talk with a quote from a personal experience. When I was single and lived in a flat in central London, I had appointed a sort of major-domo, whose job it was to look after my flat, clean it...and so on. One day, out of the blue, Bernie paid me what he thought was a supreme compliment:
>
> 'You know, Dr Laungani, you are almost a true Brit! Almost one of us.'
>
> I was aware that he was paying me a genuine compliment. However, the fact that in his compliment lay the implicit cultural assumption that Britain was the gold standard and wanting to be British was the standard to which all non-British automatically aspired, turned it into a back-handed compliment.
>
> I smiled and said: '*Vive la difference*'. (Laungani, 1999: 351)

Most people regard Rogerian client-centred counselling as a humanistic liberating approach but you have to study Pittu's critique (Laungani, 1999) to recognize how culture denying it can be, for Asian peoples. When I met him at his office, I noticed several bound Ph.D.s taking pride of place on his bookshelf. At international conferences I noticed how much some of his former students loved him for the mentoring he must have given them, the time he shared and sacrificed and even when he once stood by a 'prodigal son' who had taken several years to complete the write up of a Ph.D. that others feared would never see the light of day. He had another gift, helping connect people and increase their networking opportunities.

## IT WAS PASSION, PASSION AND PASSION THAT KEPT PITTU'S WORLD GOING

Pittu's prodigious output often put some of us, who are in better health than him, to shame. What kept Pittu going? For those who do not know, Pittu often needed to have regular oxygen which had become a permanent feature of his life. He often said that his writings helped him to carry on and was convinced that without them he would have lost the will to live. But there were additional passions in his life. He was blessed with a passion for cricket and would often stay up late into the early hours to watch it live. Finally, his other great passion which he rarely talked about was the longstanding love he shared with his life partner and wife, Ann. He regarded his wife, Ann as his guardian angel. He often told me he didn't know how he would have survived this long without her support and love. He confessed to having a temper (yes, Pittu was very human!) and that she deserved a medal for putting up with him. This leads me to his self-deprecating humour which suggests to me that Pittu was shy in accepting compliments. When I shared some positive experiences of Pittu to the audience that had gathered to celebrate the publication of yet one more of his books, with a twinkle in his eye, he thanked me for 'telling all those lies about me'!

## PERCHANCE TO DREAM...THE FUTURE'S NOT OURS TO SEE, WHAT WILL BE, WILL BE

At a book promotion event, I was honoured by Pittu's invitation to me to be one of the speakers. I was surprised and touched to notice that Pittu had acknowledged me (among others) in the preface to his book, when I had merely commented on some of the chapters that he had written. It was around that time that I had a dream about Pittu. I feared that the time of his death was closing in but did not feel it appropriate to disclose this personal intuition. However, I shared a humorous aside by relating that in my dream Pittu had not only reached the other side of life but even there he was smartly attired and alighting with aplomb from what seemed like a golden Rolls Royce (Pittu always had good taste in cars!) about to make yet another presentation in a great building reminiscent of the Royal Albert Hall in London. For me it reflected his tireless quest to share his views and his passion to reach others and communicate that we are all different, and our uniqueness must not be stamped out by cloning a modal personality in the globalization that is overtaking us (see Alladin, 2009). This is one part of the legacy, I am sure, Pittu would want us to carry forward. Speaking of precognition, the last word belongs to Pittu as the narration below confirms.

## SEEK NOT TO FIND OUT FOR WHOM THE BELL TOLLS...

When Pittu proposed that he was sending me a manuscript entitled 'Counselling the dead!', I thought he was making a tongue-in-cheek remark. How could we possibly counsel the dead? Surely, he was not talking about some disembodied spirit in need of counselling! In my usual friendly but cautious non-committal manner, I invited him to send in the manuscript and if it passed my editorial scrutiny for relevance, I would send it out for review. As Pittu himself states at the beginning of his paper,

> The title of this paper is absurd and indisputably self-contradictory. It would make anyone wonder if I were a shaman, a miracle worker who had power to resuscitate the dead—or had I gone 'soft' in my head!...As you delve into the paper it will soon become clear what I mean by counselling the dead. (Laungani, 2007: 81)

In that paper, Pittu describes the life of a *Sanyasi*: one who has permanently renounced the world of material aspirations, which also meant parting permanently from one's kith and kin to attain *moksha* that is, liberating one's self from the cosmic cycle of birth and rebirth and which involved the symbolic acceptance of one's own death and the performance of a symbolic funeral ceremony.

> I had focussed all my attention on our discussions on dying and death rather than on his [the *Sanyasi's*] own impending death. Death, he had said was not a stranger to him. It held out no terrors. He has a few close brushes with Lord Yama,[1] the Hindu God of Death in the past....

'Whether he comes in as an executioner, whether he comes charging in like a bull in a china-shop, whether he slays me when I am asleep, or whether he creeps in stealthily like a ghost in the night, I shall be prepared—for who can deny Lord Yama's insatiable appetite for death!'

'But aren't you frightened?' I asked.

'Since it is impossible to avoid Lord Yama, there is no reason to be frightened. I have come to realise that the willing acceptance of one's death is the most liberating experience in one's life! For then one has nothing to fear.' So saying, he hobbled away from me to the courtyard of the temple that had become his home.

I could not help wondering if it were I who had tried to counsel him or it was he, who had counselled me. (Laungani, 2007: 94)[2]

## NOTES

1. The fuller name of Lord Yama is Lord Yama DharmaRaja the latter part roughly translates as King of Charitable Duty since death is liberation from bondage of the earth life and release for the soul and something to be welcomed since Hindus believe death cannot be hastened or delayed even one iota of a second.
2. Ironically this last paper of Pittu's in *Counselling Psychology Quarterly* was published in March 2007, a few days after his death.

## REFERENCES

Alladin, W.J. (2009). Dawkins' delusions: A Buddhist, Hindu and Islamic critique of the God delusion [in preparation].

———. (1999). Models of counselling and psychotherapy for a multiethnic society. In S. Palmer and P. Laungani (Eds) Counselling and psychotherapy in a multicultural society. London: Sage Publications.

Collard, P. (2005). An interview with Dr. Pittu Laungani. *Counselling Psychology Quarterly, 18*(1), 7–18.

Laungani, P. (1999). Replacing client-centred counselling with culture-centred counselling. *Counselling Psychology Quarterly, 10*(4), 343–351.

———. (2007). Counselling the dead! *Counselling Psychology Quarterly, 20*(1), 81–95.

# Uwe P. Gielen

**Some** 15 years ago, I received a letter from an Indian psychologist residing in England who was then unknown to me. The letter stated, 'I found your name in the *Membership Directory* of the International Council of Psychologists...and I noticed that you are involved in cross-cultural psychology and have written about the Tibetan culture of Ladakh [India]'. And so began my friendship with that mysterious letter writer, Pittu Laungani.

Over the years, we met periodically at conferences that were taking place all around the world or—on occasions—in London or New York. We had much to discuss: our respective experiences in India, the vicissitudes of immigration and the ensuing experience of living simultaneously inside and outside one's adopted culture, the international state of cross-cultural psychology, the ups and downs of the International Council of Psychologists together with the people involved in it, Pittu's clever plays, his protracted illness, the deplorable state of English cooking, similarities and differences between Tibetan Buddhism and Hinduism, the arts and showmanship of indigenous healing in India and elsewhere, various plans to publish together, and so much more. In time, I also began to understand his difficult struggle with his progressive disease and how the spectre of death hanging over him during his later years influenced his writing. I began to see how much he relied in this difficult struggle on the emotional support of his admirable wife, Ann. I also learned that he had contracted his life-threatening disease by studying child health in one of Bombay's [Mumbai's] enormous slums.

## HIS SOCIO-CULTURAL BACKGROUND

Pittu Laungani's early years were shaped by growing up in a well-to-do extended family in Bombay during the dying days of the British Raj and the tumultuous birth of modern India. Surrounded by both his Indian peers and the surely sons of India's White *Sahibs*, he attended a Jesuit school and became early on a bicultural person immersed in both English as well as Indian culture and literature. He began to feel that England was his home even while still living in India. Yet, in other ways he forever remained an Indian and as such, would later think of himself as somewhat of an outsider to English society. Although I did not understand it then, his letter to me constituted one of his attempts to reach beyond the intellectual–professional–personal boundaries established by his English colleagues, many of whom did not seem to share his cross-cultural interests or appreciation of India's culture (West, 2004). He perceived in their indifference the long shadow of British colonialism.

## HIS CONTRIBUTIONS TO INTERNATIONAL PSYCHOLOGY

Pittu was well known among international psychologists and multicultural counsellors. In the early 1990s, he became involved in the International Council of Psychologists (ICP) whose newsletter, *International Psychologist,* he edited for four years. Several of his witty yet serious-minded plays, including *The Strange Affliction of Hamlet, Prince of Denmark* and *Pillars of Society: A Play in Three Acts,* received their initial (sight read) performances at ICP conferences in Australia and Canada where his vivid personality made a strong impression. Over the years, he received many academic honours, including a Lifetime Achievement Award in Cross-Cultural Counselling and Multicultural Psychology from the Ontario Institute for Studies in Education, University of Toronto.

He made extensive contributions to cross-cultural psychology in a broad variety of areas such as counselling, stress, health psychology, death and bereavement and child-rearing. Possessed of a lively imagination and given his broad education, philosophical interests and linguistic skills, it is not a surprise that he expressed himself through plays as well as through scientific writings.

Pittu excelled in portraying the human condition in vivid case studies, as well as writing about Hindu funeral customs and beliefs related to death, karma, the transmigration of souls and the afterlife, family life in extended Indian families, the culture-specific nature of stress, intercultural counselling sessions with clients from different parts of the world, and so much more (Laungani, 1997, 1999).

## STUDYING DEATH AND BEREAVEMENT IN INDIA: TWO DIVERGENT CULTURAL TRADITIONS

As a student of both (modern) Western and (traditional) Indian philosophies and psychologies, Pittu vividly underlined that the two cultural traditions are in certain ways irreconcilable, and that these contradictions lead to different attitudes towards death. He wrote,

> In contrast to the philosophies of the West, Indian philosophy is not concerned with exploring and describing the visible world,...due to the strong Hindu belief that the world is illusory and subject to change and decay. Therefore nothing is to be gained by studying and exploring this changing, transient, illusory world. The object therefore is to transcend the illusory world, and concentrate on understanding...the Self...wherein lies 'ultimate reality' or Ultimate Truth. (Laungani, 1999: 86–87)

Yet, that same Indian-born Pittu wrote his dissertation under the tutelage of the arch-empiricist Hans Jürgen Eysenck, and he liked to quote with relish the positivist philosopher of science, Karl Raimund Popper, who claimed that from a scientific point of view it is useless to advance unverifiable hypotheses.

Pittu discussed with great empathy the funeral customs and meanings of death for believing Hindus, yet he did so from an empirical point of view. For the Hindus, the purpose of funeral customs is to help the changeless, eternal, divine-like Self (*atman*) gain release from the body's imprisonment so that it may (re)unite with Ultimate Reality of which it has nevertheless always been a part. Yet Pittu's psychologically informed analysis of Hindu funeral customs also stresses that the 'beliefs and practices of Indians concerning death serve functional and cathartic purposes not only for the bereaved family but also for the community as a whole' (Laungani, 1999: 85).

## CONCLUSION

Here, then, is what I especially admire about Pittu's scientific work: like only a few others he was able to integrate vivid, detailed and often moving culturally informed descriptions and analyses of the inner meanings of human actions with more objective, conceptually driven and functionally conceived explanations of behaviour as seen in socio-cultural context. In the language of modern cross-cultural psychology, he was able to combine the subjectivist, emotionally receptive, EMIC approach advocating cultural uniqueness with the more objective, emotionally cooler, ETIC approach focused on cross-cultural comparison and scientific understanding. As an emic psychologist he insisted that cultural meaning systems must be understood from within but as an etic scientist he also emphasized that cross-cultural comparisons need to be guided by scientific frameworks that to some degree stand outside time, space and cultural subjectivity. While the playwright, Pittu Laungani, contributed specificity, emotional drama and an easy sympathy with his 'subjects' to the scientific enterprise, he—as a faithful student of Eysenck and Popper—never forgot that science must ultimately rely on empirical observation rather than culturally or personally inspired metaphysics. And behind all of that stood Pittu as a counselling psychologist whose rich multicultural experience enabled him to unearth the complexities of human suffering that so often are encapsulated in thick layers of socio-cultural meaning systems (Laungani, 2008).

## REFERENCES

Laungani, P. (1997). Death in a Hindu family. In C. M. Parkes, P. Laungani and B. Young (Eds), *Death and bereavement across cultures* (pp. 52–72). London, UK.: Routledge.

———. (1999). Death among Hindus in India and England. In U. P. Gielen and P. Laungani (Eds), Special Issue: International Perspectives on Death and Bereavement. *International Journal of Group Tensions, 28*(1–2), 85–114.

———. (2008). A clash of cultures: A case study. In U. P. Gielen, J. G. Draguns and J. M. Fish (Eds), *Principles of multicultural counselling and therapy* (pp. 255–294). New York: Routledge.

West, W. (2004). Pittu Laungani in conversation with William West. *British Journal of Guidance and Counselling, 32*(4), 419–435.

# Richard de Zoysa

I first got to know Pittu through a shared passion for cricket. We were both Junior Lecturers in what was then the Polytechnic of the South Bank in London, although engaged in different academic disciplines. Pittu worked in a sort of cave-like dwelling as it had no external window although it was amply furnished with books and a coffee making machine. I would pop in to see him most mornings before lectures began and we would mull over common concerns and interests while drinking coffee. Anyway to get back to the cricket, we eventually set up a team of sorts which was truly one of all talents, without pretension to any particular skill, but a shared love of the game. Pittu opened the bowling with me and was no mean batsman either. I think, from memory, we won perhaps one game every year, not that it mattered, although it did ground our friendship, which has lasted since the 1970s.

Pittu left India on a journey which was to take many unexpected turns over his eventful life. A number of intellectual passions influenced his thinking. From literature, the expressive beauty of the prose and poetry of T. S. Eliot, Shakespeare and the Indian classics informed his writing and gave elegance to his expression; from philosophy, the clarity of thought associated in particular with Bertrand Russell (Russell, 1967) made a profound and lasting impact. Russell in the Prologue to his autobiography wrote: 'three passions simple but overwhelmingly strong, have governed my life: the longing for love, the search for knowledge, and unbearable pity for the suffering of mankind' (Russell, 1967: 13). I think Pittu could claim much affinity with those sentiments. For in Ann he found the love of his life and companion through his later troubled years of ill health. In terms of knowledge, his work was influenced by two immense epistemological streams. The first was the Socratic method of dialectical inquiry trying to pierce out the truth through confronting argument. Pittu believed, along with Socrates, that: 'an unexamined life is a life not worth living'—thus reason, reflection and contemplation were a template to his life. However, knowledge was founded not on a search for an absolute unyielding truth. On the contrary his thinking was Popperian in that any hypothesis or theory was true only insofar as it could withstand intellectual scrutiny and that it was inherently testable, open to refutation at any time. In this respect, his unique immersion in Western rationality and Eastern faith gave him that necessary distance to see the strengths and flaws in both systems and were to feed his immense contribution to the growing discipline of cross-cultural psychology.

Pittu's educational upbringing in Mumbai combined a formal Jesuitical schooling with a traditional Hindu upbringing; so his early formative years were formed in a sort of cultural tapestry and he capitalized on it later. On arriving in England, he was later to gain his doctorate at London University under Professor Hans Eysenck. This led him initially into counselling and psychotherapy both of which, he felt, relied too much on an unquestioned rationality without sufficiently understanding both oneself and the other's beliefs, and how other people constructed their own world views. Admittedly, as he knew all too well, this was an immensely difficult task when different cultures and moralities were involved. As he once wrote: 'Faith without reason is blind and reason without faith is dangerous' (Laungani, 2007). He never despaired of the human condition and did much to enlighten our understanding through his academic and also practical work in hospitals and personal counselling.

In 1989, Pittu was struck with a mystery virus—later diagnosed as polymyositis with pulmonary fibrosis. Few doctors thought his chance of a long or productive life was possible—little did they know! Typically, he wrote up his experience in his first book defining how to cope with illness and survive as a patient so that a wider audience could learn from his example. This was later shared through his membership of the RCP (Royal College of Physicians) Patient/Carer Network. Indeed, his constant battle with ill-health led to a series of books on death and bereavement, which have now become almost the standard reference points on these issues.

His supreme good fortune was that a few years earlier he had met and fallen in love with Ann. They were happily married for 21 years, and it was Ann who was instrumental in introducing Pittu to the possibilities of working within a health environment leading to his research in child care, child abuse and postnatal depression, both here and in India. It was because of Ann's loving care, as Pittu readily acknowledged on many occasions, that he owed his life and ability to work so creatively. They lived a very full life, entertaining regally with numerous parties and dinner engagements at their home, and travelling extensively to India, Canada, the USA and Europe, as Pittu was constantly in demand to deliver papers at conferences.

Pittu's written output increased exponentially, and oddly, perhaps even perversely, his illness acted as a spur to further effort. To date he has had a hand in editing, contributing to or writing 16 books. And always his scholarship was eminently readable and accessible, succinct and elegant in construction combining not just psychology, philosophy, epistemology and literature, but also laced with a deadpan humour to make more effective his argument. He had a play performed—a parody of Hamlet—in which he subjected the Freudians to his wit and insight—as you can imagine 'to be or not to be' offered countless psychological possibilities. Additionally, he wrote a couple of longish novels which combined a strong narrative with analytical touches and may perhaps be published in the future. A student once remarked to me in somewhat accusatory tones that Pittu made his subject appear simple, not realizing perhaps that his skill in delivering a lecture was to make the difficult explicable and digestible through analysis and metaphor, and where necessary destroying pervasive stereotyping.

After a struggle with illness lasting nearly 17 years—going back to the days when the overthrow of eastern European communism was then headline news—I felt he would somehow be indestructible, but sadly this was not to be. He was a man of huge talent who had taken the courageous decision when young to come and live in England and forge a career. A few years ago, he was given the immense academic honour of a lifetime achievement award from the University of Toronto and was due to be honoured later this year in the land of his birth, India.

He was to my wife and I a very dear and close friend. He was loyal and generous, unstinting in his hospitality, intellectual but without any pretension, funny, often a bit mad and occasionally imperious, always a great company, unstinting with his time and ever curious as to what makes us tick. He loved Ann and owed her everything. She kept him going when he was down and frustrated by his medical limitations, managing his life in ways that enabled him to continue making his own unique intellectual contribution. I will greatly miss him as yet another light has gone out, and hope he found his own karma in his own way in a life of great fulfilment. We mourn his death while celebrating his life.

## REFERENCES

Laungani, P. (2007). Counselling the dead. *Counselling Psychology Quarterly, 20*(1), 81–95.

Russell, B. (1967). *The autobiography of Bertrand Russell.* London: George Allen & Unwin Ltd.

# Nicolò Pipitone

**Dr Laungani** has gone through a serious illness, myositis or inflammatory muscle disease, which is both devastating at onset and taxing over time. Myositis causes significant muscle weakness, thus affecting the capacity to perform many activities of daily living that healthy people take for granted. However, it does not invariably leave marks on the body that signal the presence of an underlying disease. Therefore, myositis patients may look healthy even though they are physically impaired. Lung disease, which occurs in one-third of patients with myositis, can further reduce the capacity to function normally and is a leading cause of death. Finally, medications, though undoubtedly ameliorating disease manifestations and prognosis, are fraught with side effects that may have, too, a substantial impact on the quality of life.

I first met Dr Laungani when he attended the muscle clinic at King's College Hospital (London, UK) in 2000. The session, which should have taken no more than half an hour including interview and clinical assessment, lasted in fact over two hours as the conversation gradually shifted from myositis to philosophy, psychology and science. For me, it was a more than welcome opportunity to discuss a whole range of subjects of interest with someone who was both deeply knowledgeable and experienced about them. I guess, for Dr Laungani to come across an unconventional physician that seemed to be at ease in the realms of philosophy just as much as in the nitty-gritty of medical practice, must have come as a surprise. We met as physician and patient; we parted as friends.

Over the next years, until I stayed in London (till 2003), Dr Laungani and I met on various occasions, at parties or simply for lunch in a restaurant or at his home in North London, where he lived with his wife, Ann. Most of the times, our conversations would kick off with the usual questions about each other's activities, but they would soon move on to deeper subjects. Dr Laungani displayed a remarkably lively, almost mercurial, curiosity about any issue that he was not familiar with, while in turn I would listen fascinated to him when he talked about his work, which he pursued with enthusiastic devotion. Although most of the times I was on the receiving end, I felt we both enjoyed our conversations as we shared the same attitude towards culture, which we regarded as a wonderful tool to both illuminate and enrich life. I have also had on several occasions the privilege of having a sneak preview of the drafts and galley-proofs of Dr Laungani's papers, which he used to e-mail me as attachments before submitting them for publication. In all instances, he would ask me if I had any comments or suggestions regarding his writings; sometimes I was able to provide him with some feedback that occasionally was incorporated in the final manuscript. In a way, even when we e-mailed each other, it was as though we were having a conversation, not just conveying pieces of information.

Inevitably, diseases were one of the favourite subjects that came up in our conversations. Though I always asked about his well-being, I never tried to press Dr Laungani on this point as I felt he had the right to say just as much as he wished to. On some occasions, Dr Laungani asked my opinion regarding his disease and the treatment he was receiving; on other occasions, he talked to me about how his condition had impacted his life and work. To me, it was quite clear from the start what a huge change such a disabling illness had brought about but, at the same time, I found initially difficult to fully grasp all the implications that had ensued. As a physician, I was of course aware of the main lines of research going on in health-related quality of life, including myositis, which was (and still is) one of my areas of special interest. However, medical research—right or wrong—often deals with large numbers, statistics and 'bulk', while each patient has a unique response to his or her disease. On the other hand, in clinical practice, owing both to time constraints and to inadequate training in this field, physicians have little opportunity to fully appreciate the impact of a disease on a patient. It took thus some effort on my side to develop an adequate understanding of what a disabling disease such as myositis can actually do to a patient.

Initially, Dr Laungani's disease had manifested as sudden-onset muscle weakness that rapidly deteriorated to the point of causing severe disability and even becoming life-threatening. However, since myositis is a rare disease, it usually takes a while before it is diagnosed, which means that patients are left floundering for some time in a limbo of uncertainty about their condition, while specific treatment is delayed. Dr Laungani has recounted his early, dismaying experiences with his disease in his book *It shouldn't happen to a patient* (Laungani, 1992). This book is a lucid account of what a patient with a serious, rare illness often goes through: the shock of realizing of being ill, often without initially knowing what is going on, the difficulty of communicating with the physicians, who are busy struggling to arrive at a correct diagnosis, and the subsequent reaction to illness.

Dr Laungani—in spite of all odds and of the rather dismal prognosis—not only survived his illness, but also managed to recover to a satisfactory extent his muscle strength, not least thanks to a programme of vigorous physical exercises to which he adhered with unrelenting determination. Unfortunately, while the muscle disease responded well to the medical treatment, he developed a serious complication of myositis, interstitial lung disease. This condition is characterized by inflammation and scarring in the lungs and carries still a rather poor prognosis as it leads in a substantial number of cases to respiratory failure and ultimately death. Clinically, patients with this complication are usually short of breath to a varying extent and are often troubled by a persistent dry cough. These symptoms can considerably interfere with the usual activities of daily living, while the awareness of the poor prognosis lingers in the back of the minds of the patients or sometimes even haunts them.

Dr Laungani never attempted to belittle or deny the devastating consequences that myositis had had on his life; at the same time, he took up right from the start the challenge posed by his condition with extreme determination and courage. He exercised as much as he could, kept regularly his clinical appointments, and took scrupulously his medications. He tried as much as possible to lead an active social life, even though he had to set his own pace. Sometimes he would go through a rough patch and call off mundane events, but these setbacks never really deterred him from trying to pursue a normal life. On the other hand, the illness acted as a powerful catalyst that syphoned a substantial amount of his activities and interests from his social life to his work. This shift of focus was not simply the result of decreased physical fitness, but represented on a deeper level a productive reaction to the illness. Countless writers have testified the importance of creativity in reacting to diseases and, broadly speaking, to events that adversely affect life. Creativity is fundamentally rooted in the need to probe and come to terms with the new aspects of life that illnesses bring to the fore, as well as in the need to move from a passive state (etymologically, 'patient' means 'passive sufferer') to an active response. Dr Laungani used to joke by saying that, if he had not fallen ill, he would have probably played golf instead of writing papers. In fact, as the publications of the last years of his life demonstrate, he proved a very prolific and versatile writer, who could thrash out a whole range of psychological (in particular cross-cultural) issues by drawing on Hume and Kuhn, Plato and Kant. The latest essay I received from him dealt with religion and the meaning of life, as if he was becoming more acutely conscious of the limited lifespan that was granted to him (Laungani, 2007). It was a beautiful paper, in which Dr Laungani argued for the need to give recognition to human values, such as religious beliefs and hope instead of unduly overemphasizing rational thinking. He describes the profound impact that Dr Iyer, a Brahmin whom he met at his father's funerals, made on him. Dr Laungani recalls how, as they sat near the smouldering funeral pyre, Dr Iyer mused on faith and reason: 'Faith and reason...need to go together. Reason without faith can be potentially dangerous. And faith without reason can be blind. They are the two sides of the coin of life. There is great power in faith, just as there is in reason. Reason may solve problems but faith can move mountains. Can you imagine the old, the weak, the frail and the infirm, waking up in the early hours of the morning in the bitter, piercing cold...and plunging into the icy waters of the Ganges to offer their prayers to the Gods? I cannot imagine a person guided by rationality would wish to undertake such arduous austerities.'

Overall, the concept that life cannot be unduly straitjacketed to fit reductionist theories runs like a red thread through Dr Laungani's work. I believe that his disease, if anything, further contributed to broaden his views on life by putting him directly in touch with the hardships of being ill.

It is well conceivable that Dr Laungani's expertise as a psychologist may have proved instrumental in helping him analyze and describe with technical precision his reactions to illness. At the same time, one cannot help feeling that without his keen, strong determination not to let his disease get him down, his experience would not have been so valuable as it has been. I have often experienced as a physician that patients who take up the challenge posed by their condition can emerge from the battle with a strengthened ego, a broader vision of reality and a deeper sense of human values. I feel that all this applies to Dr Laungani. On the other hand, one should not underestimate the burden that a chronic, disabling disorder places on the patient's shoulders. In fact, many patients with chronic disorders would acknowledge the valuable lesson that they have learned from their disease; but they would also like, understandably, to go 'back to normal' at some point. Dr Laungani was not an exception on this score. He would never complain about this health, but the eagerness with which he pursued his work was to me a clear sign of the inner tension that he maintained in order not to fall prey to depression or despair. One day I asked him whether he did not find taxing to have to constantly bear the heavy burden of a chronic disease. He was, as usual, very open. He said that on awakening in the morning he would feel full of energy and eager to get his work done; but that at bedtime—when the tension of the day relaxes—he would feel tired of his life, and wished to die.

I am not able to pass a remotely qualified judgement on the value of Dr Laungani's scientific papers. To me, they have been both a very pleasant reading and a great food for thought. I could lay claim to a more qualified judgement on Dr Laungani's opinions pertaining to the medical profession; but my own experiences as a physician, patient and relative or friend of patients has taught me how different the perspectives are from the different vantage points. On the whole, I am more lenient than Dr Laungani in judging my fellow colleagues, not out of caste solidarity, but because I am aware of the strain and of the difficulties that doctors go through in their everyday work. As physicians, we often put on a mask to shield ourselves—although, admittedly, it is only too easy to go too far and end up becoming blinded to the real needs of the patients that we are supposed to address. For us physicians, and also for all those who deal with patients, Dr Laungani's testimony is a powerful reminder that patients need to get recognition as human beings, and that fighting against the disease without relying on, and boosting, the patients' own resources, means losing half of the battle.

## REFERENCES

Laungani, P. 1992. *It shouldn't happen to a patient*. Whiting & Birch : London, UK.

———. (2007). Counselling the dead. *Counselling Psychology Quarterly, 20*(1), 81–85.

# About the Editors and Contributors

## THE EDITORS

**Roy Moodley**, Ph.D. is Associate Professor in Counselling Psychology at the Ontario Institute for Studies in Education at the University of Toronto. His research and publication interests include traditional and cultural healing; multicultural and diversity counselling; race, culture and ethnicity in psychotherapy; and masculinities. Roy co-edited *Transforming Managers: Gendering Change in the Public Sector* (1999); *Carl Rogers Counsels a Black Client: Race and Culture in Person-Centred Counselling* (2004); *Integrating Traditional Healing Practices into Counselling and Psychotherapy* (2005); and *Race, Culture and Psychotherapy: Critical Perspectives in Multicultural Practice* (2006).

**Aanchal Rai**, MA is a psychotherapist working in Toronto with several years of ex-perience of providing counselling and therapy to clients suffering from a range of psychological difficulties. Her research and publication interests include multicultural and diversity counselling and South Asian traditional forms healing. Her publications include *Bridging the Gap: Western Counselling and South Asian Mental Health Needs* (2009), *Role of South Asian Traditional Healers in Counselling* (M.A. Thesis, University of Toronto, 2008) and *Pilot Study of a Personalized Feedback Intervention for Problem Gamblers* (2009), co-edited *Within and Beyond Borders: Critical Multicultural Counselling in Practice* (2009).

**Waseem Alladin**, Psy.D. is the Editor in Chief of *Counselling Psychology Quarterly*, an international journal of theory, research practice. He is the Clinical Director of the Centre for Work Stress Management/Centre for Cognitive Neuro-psychology Therapy and Head of Psychology department, Autism Care, UK. He is a consultant chartered clinical and counselling psychologist and a forensic clinical neuropsychologist. He has published in the fields of transcultural and clinical psychology and chronic pain. He presented an ethnobiopsychosocial model for counselling and psychotherapy at the 2008 UNESCO Paris Conference.

## THE CONTRIBUTORS

**Fevronia Christodoulidi**, MA, MSc is a qualified counsellor from Greece. She is currently a doctoral candidate at the University of Manchester, UK, researching counsellors and psychotherapists' experiences of moving between cultures and managing cross-cultural transitions.

**Juris G. Draguns**, Ph.D. is Professor Emeritus of Psychology at Penn State University.

**Uwe P. Gielen**, Ph.D. is Professor of Psychology and Executive Director of the Institute for International and Cross-Cultural Psychology at St. Francis College, New York. He has served as president of the International Council of Psychologists and the Society for Cross-Cultural Research and edited/co-edited/co-authored 18 volumes in international psychology.

**Maya Hammer**, MA completed a master's degree in Counselling Psychology from the Ontario Institute from Studies in Education of the University of Toronto.

**Colin Lago**, MA was Director of the Counselling Service at the University of Sheffield, UK from 1987–2003. He now works as an independent counsellor, trainer, supervisor and consultant. He is a Fellow of the British Association for Counselling and Psychotherapy, an accredited counsellor and trainer and UKRC registered practitioner. Deeply committed to transcultural concerns within psychotherapy, he has published articles, videos and books on the subject.

**Ann R. Laungani**, MA spent many years working in London in nursing, health visiting, nurse teaching and management in the UK NHS. She has been involved in patient/career involvement activities at the Royal College of Physicians and the Royal Brompton and Harefield NHS Trust and is now moving on from her health experience to counselling and doing an MSc in Counselling and Psychotherapy at Roehampton University, London, UK.

**Ruth M. Lijtmaer**, Ph.D. is a Senior Supervisor, Training Analyst and Faculty at the Center for Psychoanalysis and Psychotherapy of New Jersey at Fairleigh Dickinson University, NJ, and in private practice in Ridgewood, NJ.

**Amrita Narayanan**, Ph.D. is a Psychologist in practice at a State Hospital in California and a longtime student and teacher of yoga.

**Sandra E.S. Neil**, Ph.D. is a Clinical Psychologist and Family Psychologist, Fellow of the Australian Psychological Society, and Australian National Representative of the International Academy of Family Psychology, and a Past President of the International Council of Psychology. She has been the author of numerous books and papers, and chairs forums throughout the world on Peace, International Relations and Human Rights. In May 2008 she spoke at the United Nations in New York, USA for the UN's Committee on the Family, on 'Fathering: A Job for Real Men and in Some Measure Women'.

**Stephen Palmer**, Ph.D. is Founder Director of the Centre for Stress Management, and Director of the Coaching Psychology Unit at City University, London, UK. He is a Chartered Psychologist and Fellow of the British Association for Counselling and Psychotherapy. He has written/edited 35 books on a range of topics.

**Nicolò Pipitone**, MD is Consultant Rheumatologist at the Rheumatology Unit and Vasculitis Center of the Arcispedale S.M. Nuova of Reggio Emilia, Italy. He is member of the American College of Rheumatology and of the British Society for Rheumatology and has published over 60 papers in peer-reviewed journals.

**Alan Roland**, Ph.D. is a practicing psychoanalyst in New York City, a Training Analyst and a member of the Faculty and Board of Directors Psychological Association for Psychoanalysis. He has worked extensively with Indians and Indian Americans, and has authored two books based on this experience.

**Sabar Rustomjee**, Ph.D. is Honorary Senior Lecturer at Monash University, Melbourne, Australia. She is a clinical member of the American Group Psychotherapy Association and Group Analytic Society London. She is currently working in Individual and Group Psychotherapy in Melbourne, Australia.

**Lana Stermac**, Ph.D. is Professor in the Counselling Psychology Programme at the University of Toronto and a senior adjunct member of the Women's College Hospital Research Institute.

**Antoinette D. Thomas,** Ph.D. is Past-President of the International Council of Psychologists. She is a Canadian and Egyptian culturist, clinical and counselling psychologist.

**William West**, Ph.D. is a Reader in Counselling Studies at University of Manchester. He is chair of the Culture and Psychotherapy section of the Society for Psychotherapy Research (International) and is a Fellow and practitioner member of BACP. He is well known for his research and writing on spirituality, culture, traditional healing, supervision and qualitative methodologies.

**Richard de Zoysa**, Ph.D. was Senior Lecturer in Politics at London South Bank University and an honorary research fellow. He has published numerous academic articles and reviews, lecturing widely in both Europe and the USA, while contributing to radio and television discussion.

# Index